I0127064

The Principle of Non-Discrimination in International Law

The Principle of Non-Discrimination in International Law

Curtis F.J. Doebbler

CDP

CDPublishing

Principle of Non-Discrimination
in International Law
Curtis F.J. Doebbler

Published and Distributed by
CD Publishing
Washington, DC, USA - Mumbai, India - Nablus, Palestine
Tashkent, Uzbekistan - Pristina, Kosova
Fax: +1-206-984-4734
Email: sales@cdpublishing.org
Website: http://cdpublishing.org

© CD Publishing 2007

All Rights Reserved

This book is designed to provide accurate and authoritative information with
respect to the subject matter covered. It is sold with the understanding that the
publisher and author are not engaged in rendering legal or other professional
services. If legal advice or other expert assistance is required, the services of a
competent legal representative or attorney should be sought. While every
attempt has been made to provide accurate information, the author or
publisher cannot be held accountable for errors or omissions.

This book is in copyright. Subject to lawful exception and to provisions of relevant
collective licensing agreements no part of this book may be reproduced, stored in a
retrieval system, or transmitted by any means, electronic, mechanical, photocopying,
recording or otherwise, without written permission from the author.

ISBN: 978-0-9743570-4-1 (pbk)
Stock number: NDIL0015 (ebook)

Printed in the United States of America and Europe.
Printed on acid free paper.

Generic Cataloguing Data:
Doebbler, Curtis, F.J. 1961-
    xix/449 pp, 12.7 cm X 17.78 cm
    The Principle of Non-Discrimination in International Law /
by C.F.J. Doebbler
    Includes table of cases, selected further readings, and index.
    Library of Congress Classification: KZ3410.D6 2007
    Dewey Decimal Classification: 341.62–dc22
    Keywords: 1. international law, 2. international human rights law, 3. discrimination,
    4. international relations, 5. politics, I. Title

Summary Table of Contents

Full Table of Contents

GROUNDS FOR PROHIBITED DISCRIMINATION

Table of Contents

Non-Discrimination in International Law

OTHER INSTRUMENTS

Table of Contents

CASES

Acknowledgements

Many people have contributed to this book. These include almost two decades of clients, students and librarians who have made my practice of international human rights law possible.

My special appreciation to my students at the International Summer University at the University of Bitola in Macedonia, whose careful reading of the book and critical comments helped improve the text.

Of special mention are the librarians in the social science and law reading rooms of the United Nations Library in Geneva, Switzerland; the staff at An-Najah National University in Nablus, Palestine; and my students Donna, James, and Natalie who assisted with research for this book.

Dr. Gerald Doebbler, my father, who has faithfully read numerous of my manuscripts and has been my most faithful critic and 'editor' has once again greatly assisted with comments on early drafts.

Finally, this project would not have been possible without the assistance of Robert Kaplan and everyone else at CD Publishing.

Of course, any errors that remain and the opinions expressed herein are the responsibility of the author.

CFJD
Revised August 2007

Preface

This book is intended as an introductory book or a sourcebook for studying the principle of non-discrimination in international law.

Students, practitioners, and others seeking to understand the principle of non-discrimination in international law will also find that the text provides simple explanations of the principle of non-discrimination as expressed in treaties and interpreted by international human rights mechanisms.

The excerpts from treaties, cases, and other instruments that accompany the text provide the reader a complete set of tools for applying the law. For a better understanding of the treaties and the human rights mechanisms interpreting them see Doebbler, C.F.J., *International Human Rights Law: Cases and Materials* (CD Publishing and Tashkent State Institute of Law, 2004).

This book does not serve as a replacement for legal advice or as a guide to the more complex legal situations. It does provide an overview of the basic parameters of the law and citations to where more information can be found.

CFJD
Revised August 2007

Abbreviations

ACHPR	African Charter of Human and Peoples' Rights
ACommHPR	African Commission of Human and Peoples' Rights
ACHR	American Convention on Human Rights
ADRDM	American Declaration of the Rights and Duties of Man
All ER	All England Law Reports
Appl.	Application
CEDAW	Convention for the Elimination of Discrimination against Women or the Committee for the Elimination of Discrimination against Women
CETS	Council of Europe Treaty Series
CERD	Convention for the Elimination of All Forms of Racial Discrimination or the Committee for the Elimination of All Forms of Racial Discrimination
CESCR	Committee on Economic, Social, and Cultural Rights (created by ECOSOC to monitor ICESCR)
CETS	Consolidated European Treaty Series
CHR of the CIS	Convention on Human Rights of the Commonwealth of Independent States
CMWR	Committee on the Protection of the Rights of All Migrant Workers and Members of their Families
Comm.	Communication
CRC	Convention on the Rights of the Child
CSCE	Conference for Security and Cooperation in Europe
Doc.	Document
e.g.	*Example given*
ECHR	European Convention for the Protection of Human Rights and Fundamental Freedoms
ECJ	European Court of Justice

ECommHR	European Commission on Human Rights
ECR	*European Court Reports* (ECJ)
ECOSOC	UN Economic and Social Council
ECtHR	European Court of Human Rights
EHRR	*European Human Rights Reports*
etc.	*Et cetera*
ETS	*European Treaty Series*
EU	European Union
GA	General Assembly (UN)
GAOR	General Assembly Official Record
HRC	Human Rights Council (before 2006 the Commissions on Human Rights)
IACommHR	Inter-American Commission on Human Rights
IACtHR	Inter-American Court of Human Rights
ICCPR	International Covenant of Civil and Political Rights
ICESCR	International Covenant of Economic, Social and Cultural Rights
ICMWR	International Convention on the Protection of the Rights of All Migrant Workers and Members of their Families
Id.	*Idem*
ILC	International Law Commission
ILO	International Labour Organization
individ.	Individual
No.	Number
p.	Page
para(s).	Paragraph(s)
PCIJ	Permanent Court of International Justice
OAU	Organization of African Unity (now the African Union)

Abbreviations

OJEC	*Official Journal of the European Communities*
OSCE	Organization for Security and Cooperation in Europe
Res.	Resolution
Sess.	Session
Supp	Supplement
UN	United Nations
UNESCO	United Nations Education, Social and Cultural Organization
UN HRC	UN Human Rights Committee (ICCPR)
UNTS	*United Nations Treaty Series*
US	United States of America
US	*United States Supreme Court Reports*
WHO	World Health Organization

Table of Cases

(Excerpted cases found at page numbers in **bold**.)

Table of Cases

Table of Cases

THE NORMS, INSTITUTIONS AND PRINCIPLES

INTRODUCTION TO THE INTERNATIONAL LAW OF NON-DISCRIMINATION

The principle of non-discrimination is fundamental to international law. It means, essentially, that all individuals must have their human rights equally respected. It is found in almost every international human rights instrument in one form or another. It unites all human rights by ensuring that they apply to all persons with no unwarranted exceptions. It does not prohibit all forms of discrimination, but it does put the burden on the state to justify any type of discrimination against individuals who are members of a certain (usually, minority) group.

The principle of non-discrimination is found, among other places, in articles 1 and 8 of the Charter of the United Nations; article 2(1) and 26 of the ICCPR; article 2(2) of the ICESCR; article 14 and Protocol 13 of the ECHR; article 1 of the ACHR; article 2 of the ACHPR; article 20(2) of the CHR of the CIS; article 3 of the RC in relation to refugees; article 2 of the CRC in relation to children; and article 1 of the ICMW in relation to migrant workers and their families.

There are also treaties that are entirely devoted to prohibiting certain types of discrimination. For example, the CERD prohibits racial discrimination and the CEDAW prohibits discrimination against women.

Introduction

There are also provisions in non-binding international instruments of a general nature that prohibit discrimination, such as article 2 of the UDHR and article II of the ADRDM. And finally, there are instruments of a specific nature, such as the Declaration on the Elimination of All Forms of Intolerance and of Discrimination Based on Religion or Belief, which are intended to combat specific forms of discrimination.[1]

In some human rights treaties the principle of non-discrimination expressed in relation to the human rights in the specific treaty. For example, article 2(1) of the ICCPR states that a government must protect individuals under its jurisdiction from discrimination in the enjoyment of their human rights.

Sometimes, however, the principle of non-discrimination is expressed in general terms. Article 26 of the same ICCPR, for example, refers in very general language to all persons being "equal before the law" and having the "equal protection of the law."[2] The UN HRC has interpreted article 26 to include a prohibition of "any distinction, exclusion, restriction or preference which is based on any grounds such as race, colour, sex, language, religion, political or other opinion, national or social origin, property, birth or other status, and which has the purpose or effect of nullifying or impairing the recognition, enjoyment or exercise by all persons, on an equal footing, of all rights and freedoms,"[3] even those not protected in the ICCPR.[4] The Committee noted that while other prohibitions of discrimination apply to specific rights or sometimes only to those rights protected in a particular treaty, "[a]rticle 26 does not specify such limitations."[5] Article 26 therefore "prohibits discrimination in law or in fact in any field regulated and protected by public authorities."[6]

Moreover, this general principle prohibiting discrimination has been called "a basic and general principle relating to the protection of human

---

[1] UN GA Res. No. 36/55, 36 UN GAOR Supp. (No. 51) at 171, UN Doc. A/36/684 (1981).
[2] Art. 26 of the ICCPR. See the annex of Treaties for the text of this article.
[3] United Nations Human Rights Committee, General Comment 18 on Non-Discrimination, adopted at the 37th Sess. (1989), UN Doc. HRI/GEN/1/Rev.6 at 146 (2003) at para. 1.
[4] See, for example, Broeks v. Netherlands (in Case Annex).
[5] See supra, note 3, at para. 12.
[6] Id.

rights"[7] and even a *jus cogens* rule of law, a principle of law from which there can be no derogation,[8] by highly qualified legal scholars. The International Court of Justice (ICJ), the principle judicial organ of the UN, has opined that the prohibition of racial discrimination, one form of discrimination, is so basic that it constitutes an *erga omnes* obligation, a legal obligation which all states have an interest in ensuring.[9]

Non-Discrimination

The principle of non-discrimination requires states to ensure that all individuals are equal before the law, have equal protection of the law, and are treated equally by society in general. While this does not mean absolute equality, it does require that a general degree of equality be provided to all individuals.

The principle of non-discrimination is stated in numerous human rights treaties as the individual human right to treatment without any distinction, exclusion, restriction or preference related to particular group characteristics.[10] It forms the basis of all the human rights protections accorded to individuals. It emphasizes that individuals have human rights because they are human beings and for no other reason.

The principle is usually expressed in terms of particular grounds on which discrimination is prohibited. For example, all the leading human rights treaties prohibit discrimination on the grounds of race, sex (gender), language, and religion. Other grounds like political opinion, national origin, colour, social origin, property, and birth are often, but not always prohibited. And discrimination on other grounds, such as economic status or ethnic group is only rarely prohibited in international instruments.

Furthermore, not all types of discrimination or differentiation are prohibited. Some types of discrimination or differentiation may have a "reasonable and objective justification."[11] However, if a *prime facie* claim of discrimination has been raised then the burden of proof shifts to the state to

---

[7] McKean, W., *Equality and Discrimination under International Law* 271-277 (Clarendon Press: Oxford, 1983).

[8] Brownlie, I., *Principles of Public International Law* 596-598 (3rd ed., 1979). *See* UN HRC General Comment No. 18 in the annex of Other Instruments.

[9] *Barcelona Traction case (Barcelona Traction, Light and Power Co. Case, (Belgium v. Spain), ICJ Reports* 3, 32, at para 175 (1970).

[10] Art. 1 of the CERD.

[11] *Case relating to certain aspects of the laws on the use of languages in education in Belgium v. Belgium (Belgian Linguistics Case)*, Ser. A, No. 6 (23 July 1968) at para. 10.

justify its actions as being proportional to achieving a legitimate goal of state policy.

The principle of non-discrimination is closely associated with the principle of equality.

Equality

Equality—often discussed as the "principle of equality"—is the goal of the principle of non-discrimination. It refers to a broad right of every individual to be treated generally the same way and given the same opportunities in society.

The Inter-American Court of Human Rights (IACtHR) has recognized the fundamental character of the principle of equality holding that

> [t]he notion of equality springs directly from the oneness of the human family and is linked to the essential dignity of the individual. That principle cannot be reconciled with the notion that a given group has the right to privileged treatment because of its perceived superiority. It is equally irreconcilable with that notion [of equality] to characterize a group as inferior and treat it with hostility or otherwise subject it to discrimination in the enjoyment of rights which are accorded to others not so classified. It is impermissible to subject human beings to differences in treatment that are inconsistent with their unique and congenerous character.[12]

At the same time, the Inter-American Court cautioned, that it is important to remember that "[i]nternational law does not ... require the state to guarantee absolute equality."[13] Judge Tanaka writing a dissenting opinion for the International Court of Justice also acknowledged that "[t]he principle of equality before the law does not mean the absolute equality, namely the equal treatment of men without regard to individual, concrete circumstances, but it means relative equality, namely the principle to treat equally what are equal and unequally what are unequal."[14]

Having provided these very basic definitions of equality, one must exercise caution when delving into the details because there are many

---

[12] *Proposed Amendments to the Naturalization Provisions of the Constitution of Costa Rica,* IACtHR Advisory Opinion No. OC-4/84, Ser. A) No. 4 (19 January 1984).at para. 55 (see Cases annex for excerpts from this Advisory Opinion).

[13] *Id.*

[14] Opinion of Judge Tanaka in *South West Africa Case* (second phase), *ICJ Reports* (18 July 1966) at p. 313.

different views on what equality means and especially on what type of equality the state is required to provide to individuals under its jurisdiction.

Equality in its most extreme form might oblige the state to provide a generally equal quality of life to all persons for whom it is responsible. During the 20th century, many socialist or communist countries had this type of *formal* equality as a goal.[15] In the western-capitalist sense equality often refers to *equality of opportunity*. This means that the state must provide every individual an equal chance to participate in society. The equal chance, however, may not have to take into account disadvantages that particular individuals suffer historically or because of their particular vulnerability.

Neither of these forms has been achieved in an absolute sense. Instead most states strive for equality by providing equality of opportunities and assisting those with special vulnerabilities. Problems then arise when historical differences in power, wealth, social status, etc., prevent the achievement of either 'formal equality' or 'equality of opportunity'. To overcome such obstacles to achieving equality, special forms of action— including positive discrimination or affirmative action may be necessary.

This book will not help you decide whether formal equality or equality of opportunity is a better social policy, but it will help you to think about which form of equality (or combination of forms) best guarantees internationally protected human rights. It is the protection of human rights for all that is the basic goal of the non-discrimination in international law. In this book, therefore, our focus will be on equality as defined by the prohibition of certain types of discrimination in human rights treaties.

Types of Discrimination

Discrimination of any kind is prohibited if it does not have a legal justification. This is particularly true of the types of discrimination that are covered in more detail later in this book, namely discrimination based on race, gender, nationality, culture, disability, age, and social status. Other forms of discrimination may also be prohibited.

---

[15] Formal equality is sometimes interpreted to mean equal treatment for similarly situated persons or the form of a rule, *see, for example*, Bartlett, K.T., and Harris, A., *Gender and Law: Theory, Doctrine, Commentary*, 101 and 261 (1998), or, otherwise stated, "if two people are being treated, or are to be treated, differently, there should be some relevant difference between them," Lucas, J.R., "Against Equality," 40 *Philosophy* 296 (1965).

Introduction

Another way of categorizing different types of discrimination is *direct* and *indirect* discrimination. **Direct discrimination** occurs when individuals or groups of individuals who are similarly situated are treated differently. An example of direct discrimination is apartheid in South Africa in the latter part of the 20th century. This practice overtly discriminated against blacks living in South Africa. Much of the discrimination was even based on laws that made it *legal* to discriminate. These laws, however, violated international law and were thus themselves illegal.

In comparison, **indirect discrimination** occurs when a law or a government action has an unjustified disproportionate impact on a certain group of individuals. In this case the law is not *prima facie* a violation of international law, but one of its unintended effects is to cause discrimination. For example, a law that allows anyone to compete for public television licenses may have the consequence of being discriminatory because it excludes ethnic, racial or other minorities from acquiring television licenses because they lack the resources or the experience to win the competition. In this case it is relevant that object of the discrimination is a 'public good'—a right created by the state, the right to a broadcasting license, and that the discrimination can be shown to have lasted for some time. If these two aspects of the claim can be proven then discrimination may be found to exist and the state will have an obligation to end it, to compensate the victims, and to take steps to ensure it is not repeated.

This book does not differentiate between direct and indirect discrimination as both may be forms of prohibited discrimination and the difference in classification is often only one related to the burden of proof. In other words, if the impact of discrimination is direct, the burden proof for the alleged victim may be easier to satisfy, while if the impact of discrimination is indirect the burden of proof may require the examination of statistics, the statements or affidavits of witnesses to past practices, or inferences based on an examination of similar cases.

Sometimes non-discrimination is described in terms of types of actions. The British NGO Interights in their publication entitled *Non-Discrimination in International Law: A Handbook for Practitioners* discusses harassment and victimization as types of discrimination. Harassment consists of "of leering, embarrassing jokes or remarks, unwelcome comments about appearance, dress or person's characteristics, hostile action intended to isolate the victim, unjustifiable criticism, unwanted physical contact, demand for sexual favours and physical assaults" by someone in a position of authority or having a

- 6 -

professional relationship with the victim.[16] Victimization "describes any adverse measure taken by an organisation (including employers and public authorities) or an individual in retaliation for efforts to enforce legal principles, including those of equality and nondiscrimination."[17] It is important to understand that while both types of acts may constitute discrimination, they are only two of many types of acts that may constitute discrimination. While these categories of acts are undoubtedly relevant to the principle of non-discrimination, it is important to evaluate all acts within their specific context to determine if they constitute prohibited discrimination.

Another distinction between types of discrimination is sometimes made between *domestic* and *international* discrimination. This distinction is based on the belief that international law is not always applicable to the domestic activities of states. In so far as a rule of international law exists that prohibits discrimination, this view is flawed. A basic principle of international law is that a state's domestic law can never be a justification for a violation of international law.[18]

As we examine the principle of non-discrimination in international law in this book, we always use international law as our standard of evaluation. Domestic law must always be in conformity with international law or it may create state responsibility for an internationally wrongful act—a violation of international law.

This does not mean that domestic law is unimportant. Indeed, international law often requires recourse to domestic legal forums before one can apply to international human rights mechanisms (the requirement of the exhaustion of domestic remedies). Nor does it mean that domestic law does not protect individuals from discrimination. In fact, most human rights including the prohibition of discrimination are protected first and foremost at the domestic level. This book, however, is concerned with the legal rules that apply at the international level and which are a common denominator for all states. These legal rules provide for the principle of non-discrimination in international law.

---

[16] Interights, *Non-Discrimination in International Law: A Handbook for Practitioners* 92 (2006).
[17] *Id.* at 94.
[18] *See* Art. 27 of the Vienna Convention on the Law of Treaties, 1155 *UNTS* 331, entered into force 27 January 1980 (which likely reflects a rule of customary international law).

Finally, it is important to note that a state may sometimes have a legal justification for differentiating between individuals even on prohibited grounds. We will review the possible legal justifications in more detail in the section on state responsibility.

Reading Cases and Texts on Non-Discrimination

When reading the instruments and cases on non-discrimination that have been annexed to this book, to help you evaluate these tools of the law, ask the following questions.

VICTIM:

1. What is the right that is being exercised and how is it protected?

Some treaties protect all rights created by a state and others only rights enumerated in the treaty. Sometimes these two types of provisions are referred to as 'free-standing' (discrimination in the exercise of any right created by the state is prohibited) and 'dependent' (discrimination in the exercise of rights stated in the specific treaty is prohibited).

2. What is the ground for the distinction in exercise of the right?

This is the basis of the protected group to which the victim belongs. For example, race, religion, sex/gender, etc. These grounds can usually be found in the specific treaty. They may however consist of an 'open-ended' provision such as "other status" or they may be 'specified'. The latter are seen particularly in treaties intended to prevent a certain from of discrimination such as discrimination based on race (CERD).

3. Is the interference with the right based on state action/omission?

It is always necessary to find an act attributable to a state to be able to apply international law concerning non-discrimination. Sometimes the interference might be the failure of the state to act (an omission), even to prevent private actors from harming the victim.

* * *

Once the victim has successfully answered the above
questions with adequate proof, than the burden of proof shifts
to the state to answer the following questions convincingly.

* * *

STATE:

4. Did the state act to achieve a legitimate aim?

> Once a victim has provided *prima facie* evidence of affirmative answers to the first three questions the burden of proof shifts to the state to provide a reason for its action—to show a legitimate aim. This burden can usually be satisfied by thoughtful 'framing' of the state's reason for having acted or failed to act.

5. Was the impact of the state's action on the victim proportionate to the legitimate aim?

> This is the basis upon which most cases are decided. The state must not only show that it had a legitimate aim, but also that the effect of its action or inaction on the victim was not disproportional to achieving the aim. It should be noted that although the burden of proof is on the state, human rights bodies often allow the state a 'margin of appreciation' in determining the action they should take.

Asking these five questions as you read the cases annexed to this book or consider how the treaty provisions which are also annexed apply to practical situations will help you to understand and apply the law.

There is, however, no shortcut for reading many cases, treaty provisions, and the provisions of other instruments. Similarly, ensuing the principle of non-discrimination that is required by international law, may require many different types of action which will depend on your observation and consideration of the societies in which discrimination occurs and your own creative thinking.

This book will help you to understand how law can protect individuals from discrimination in cases before human rights bodies as well as how it can assist in other types of activities because it establishes individual rights that have been widely agreed upon by states.

STATE RESPONSIBILITY FOR NON-DISCRIMINATION

What distinguishes international law from philosophical and moral principles is its legally binding nature. Like all areas of international law, the legal principle of non-discrimination is based on state responsibility. This means that the primary responsibility for ensuring that the law is respected is a responsibility of states. International law establishes some basic rules—'general principles of state responsibility'— that tell us how a state becomes responsible for its internationally wrongful acts.

General Principles of State Responsibility

State responsibility refers to the responsible of a state for its actions under international law. We speak of state responsibility or a state being responsible for a violation of international law when (1) there is an act attributable to a state and (2) that act violates an international legal obligation of that state.

The rules governing this general international responsibility of states are expressed in the International Law Commission's Draft Articles on the Responsibility of States for Internationally Wrongful Acts (ILC Articles) which stress in article 2 that "[e]very internationally wrongful act of a State entails the international responsibility of that State."[19] The ILC Articles also state that there "is an internationally wrongful act of a State when conduct consisting of an action or omission ... (a) Is attributable to the State under international law; and (b) Constitutes a breach of an international obligation of the State."[20]

Whether or not an act or omission is attributable to a state is sometimes very easy to determine, but it may also be a very complex question of proof. An act or omission causing discrimination may be clearly attributable to state when the state itself is acting in a discriminatory manner or failing to act to stop discrimination it is aware is present (an omission). If an act is carried out by a state's public officials or a state's soldiers or police then the act will almost always be attributable to that state. The question is more complicated when an act is carried out by private persons or another state's officials on behalf of the state. Then the control that the state whose responsibility is in question, has over the private or foreign actors is important in determining that state's responsibility.

The question of attribution becomes more complex when a private actor is carrying our discrimination within a state. In such cases, the state will often have an obligation to take action to prevent the discriminatory actions of a private actor. The obligation of the state is then a positive one, requiring that it intervene with action to end, prevent, or redress discrimination by non-state actors.

The international obligations of states are found in treaties and customary international law. Most obligations to end and to prevent discrimination can today be found in treaties. This is because most states have now ratified the main human rights treaties containing obligations of non-discrimination. Even the few states that have not ratified these treaties are bound by customary international law—the practice and *opinio juris* of states—that also prohibits most forms of discrimination. When examining obligations in treaties it is necessary to understand if a state has made any reservations or declarations at the time of ratifying the treaty that limit its obligations.

---

[19] United Nations' International Law Commission, Draft Articles on the Responsibility of States for Internationally Wrongful Acts, *Report of the ILC on the Work of its Fifty-third Session*, UN GAOR, 56th Sess, Supp No 10, p 43, UN Doc A/56/10 (2001) (ILC Articles). *Also see Legal Consequences for States of the Continued Presence of South Africa in Namibia (South West Africa) Notwithstanding Security Council Resolution 276*, ICJ Advisory Opinion, *ICJ Reports.16* (21 June 1971).
[20] *Id.*, ILC Articles, at art. 2.

When a state fails to abide by its international obligations through acts or omissions attributable to the state it is said to be responsible or that state responsibility accrues. In such cases, the state must stop the discriminatory action and compensate the victims of the violation. The obligation to bring to an end a violation of international law is the first and foremost obligation of the state under international law.

States may also have other obligations that arise as a consequence of their illegal action. For example, in certain circumstances, the state may have an obligation "to provide for and implement provisional or interim measures to avoid continuing violations and to endeavour to repair at the earliest possible opportunity any harm that may have been caused by such violations."[21]

The obligations of state are often divided into negative and positive obligations. Both are legal obligations that a state is required to respect. Both are obligations of result requiring states to take action to prevent or end discrimination. Both are found in various international human rights instruments.

Negative Obligations

Negative obligations refer to those international legal obligations that require a state not to do a particular action. A state may not discriminate against any individual in a manner that is prohibited by international law. This is the most common form of international legal obligation. It was the legal obligation that Rhodesia and South Africa violated by maintaining their policies of apartheid. In both cases, the state took affirmative actions to maintain a situation in which the state was ensuring the discrimination of individuals based on their race.

Today most situations of discrimination do not involve states acting or failing to act in ways that overtly violate the prohibition of non-discrimination. Instead cases of discrimination usually involve a state's failure to act sufficiently to prevent discrimination by private actors or to redress discrimination that has been ongoing, even if not directly caused by the state.

And example of a negative obligation is the obligation not to promulgate legislation that discriminates against a certain category of individuals. Article 26 of the ICCPR, for example, prohibits states from adopting legislation that

---

[21] UN Human Rights Committee, General Comment 31 on the Nature of the General Legal Obligation on States Parties to the Covenant, UN Doc. CCPR/C/21/Rev.1/Add.13 (2004) at para. 19.

discriminates against individuals "on any ground such as race, color, sex, language, religion, political or other opinion, national or social origin, property, birth or other status." When states promulgate discriminatory legislation they violate international law even if the legislation is not applied in practice.[22]

A state's negative obligations extend to its policies and practices as well. For example, a state may not have a policy or practice of refusing equal compensation to women who do the same work as men, even if there are no provisions of law governing the matter.

Positive Obligations and Affirmative Action

Positive obligations are those international legal obligations that require a state to do something to prevent, redress, or end discrimination. A state must take action to ensure that its officials do not discriminate against minorities. A state's failure to act to ensure this right for minorities violates international law even if the state is not itself denying a human right. For example, in circumstances where a company refuses to produce records needed to provide the innocence of a criminal defendant, the state would have to either compel the production of a company's records or drop the charges against the individual concerned. If the state does not take action, for example, because the defendant is a member of a minority group, then its omission may lead to it being found responsible for discrimination in the enjoyment of the right to a fair trial.

Positive action also includes affirmative action (sometimes described as 'positive discrimination'). This is action taken to redress a history of discrimination in a manner that is limited in time and breath.

Ironically, while the principle of affirmative action was originally recognized in the domestic courts of the United States of America, it is today under attack by these same courts.[23] Internationally, however, it has become embedded in international human rights instruments and the interpretations given to these instruments.

---

[22]*Toonen v. Australia*, UN HRC Comm. No. 488 (1992) in UN Doc CCPR/C/50/D/488/1992 (1994).

[23] The attacks against affirmative action in the US Supreme Court have been indirect. For example, in 1997 the Court declined to take a case challenging a law in the state of California that abolished all affirmative action programmes in the state. *Also see Grutter v. Bollinger*, 539 US 306 (2003) and *Gratz v. Bollinger*, 539 US 244 (2003).

The UN HRC, for example, has interpreted states obligations under the ICCPR to include requiring a state to "take affirmative action in order to diminish or eliminate conditions which cause or help to perpetuate discrimination prohibited by the Covenant."[24] The CERD also allows states to take affirmative action to redress the effects of past discrimination. In most cases, affirmative action has been found to be a right rather than an obligation of a state. This is due to the fact that states enjoy a wide degree of discretion in determining what action to take to end or redress human rights violations.

The CEDAW, however, does appear to impose more demanding obligations of affirmative action on states in articles 4 and 5.[25] While article 4 states that affirmative action is allowed, article 5 makes it clear that state parties "shall take all appropriate measures" to redress discrimination. Read together these two articles appear to require states to take affirmative action in some cases.

The ECJ has also accepted that affirmative action meant to redress an historical imbalance by favoring women in employment is not prohibited by EU Directives calling for the equal treatment of men and women.[26]

The Consequences of State Responsibility

As already indicated above, the primary obligation arising as a result of state responsibility is the obligation to end a violation of international law. This is not the only obligation that may arise. The international law of state responsibility also provides that when a state fails to prevent or end discrimination or even when it does end an act of discrimination, but individuals have already suffered, the state is responsible for restoring the *status quo* existing prior to the violation or as if the violation had not existed; reasonably compensating the victims of the violation; and taking steps to ensure that the violation does not occur in the future.

While it is hard to force a state—particularly if one is a private individual—to undertake these actions, there may be legal, quasi-legal or political mechanisms that can be addressed to clearly determine that violation has taken place. While we will discuss some of the legal and quasi-legal forums below in more detail, it is important not to underestimate the

---

[24] UN Human Rights Committee, General Comment 18 at para. 10 (this General Comment is reproduced in the Annex of instruments in this book).

[25] *See* Treaties Annex for the text of these articles.

[26] *Marschall v. Land Nordrhein-Westfalen*, ECJ Case No. C-409/95, [1997] *All ER (EC)* 865.

value of the political forums, although they will not be discussed in much detail in this book.[27] This is true because the international community's condemnation of certain forms of discrimination can be so great that states that commit such types of discrimination can be put under substantial international pressure to end their actions.

Another important consequence of a state acting or allowing action that violates the principle of non-discrimination is that the illegal actions of the state may not be recognized and treated as legal by any other state. This consequence is an accepted part of customary international law that was adopted with approval by the ILC Articles on State Responsibility.[28]

Justifications

States may on occasion be able to justify acts of discrimination. The ILC Articles list a number of justifications upon which states may rely to avoid state responsibility for a violation of international law.

These include duress and necessity—acting to protect others—, occurrences that are *force majeure*—prevent a state from respecting its international obligations—or the consent of the victim. The burden of pleading a justification lies on the state.

One of areas where justifications often play a role is when a state acts in a discriminatory manner that give an advantage to the member of a group that has suffered discrimination in the past: affirmative action or positive discrimination. If the state can show that there has been a history of discrimination and that its actions are limited to and effective for redressing this historical imbalance then the state actions may be allowed, even though they otherwise would constitute discrimination. In such cases a state will have a justification that prevents it from being found responsible for a violation of international law.

---

[27] *See, generally, for example,* Access to Justiuce (edited by Mathilda Piehl), *Equal at Work—Easy Access Guide for Practitioners,* available freely at www.accesstojustice.se (2007).

[28] *See, supra* note 19, art. 41.

- 16 -

ENFORCING NON-DISCRIINATION

MECHANISMS FOR ENFORCING NON-DISCRIMINATION

Non-discrimination is a legal right. This is evident from the decisions and views expressed by both judicial and quasi-judicial international human rights mechanisms and the instruments they apply. Below are short descriptions of these mechanisms and how they have dealt with the principle of non-discrimination.

United Nations Mechanisms

The United Nations mechanisms dealing with the non-discrimination includes both general human rights mechanisms and mechanisms that concentrate on specific forms of discrimination.

General international human rights mechanisms include mechanisms with broad authority like the Committee on Human Rights (UN HRC) created by the International Covenant of Civil and Political Rights (ICCPR)[29] and the Committee on Economic, Social, and Cultural Rights (CESCR) created by Economic and Social Council of the United Nations to oversee

---

[29] 999 *UNTS* 171, entered into force 23 March 1976.

the International Covenant of Economic, Social, and Cultural Rights (ICESCR). 30

There are also international human rights mechanisms that concentrate on specific forms of discrimination. They include the Committee on Racial Discrimination or CERD,[31] which focuses on racial discrimination, and the Committee on the Elimination of Discrimination against Women or CEDAW, which focuses on discrimination against women.[32]

The UN HRC can consider complaints from any of the more than 100 states that have accepted its (first) Optional Protocol.[33] It also examines periodic reports from any of the more than 150 states that have ratified the ICCPR. And it also adopts General Comments, two of which have dealt with the principle of non-discrimination in the ICCPR.[34]

It has frequently considered claims that the states have applied the rights in the ICCPR in a discriminatory manner in violations of article 26. In interpreting the prohibition of discrimination it has found that it applies to any rights that the state has granted its citizens and others under its jurisdiction. Thus while the right to social security is not a right in the ICCPR the UN HRC has held that the prohibition of discrimination in article 26 of the ICCPR also applies to ensure both men and women equal access to social security benefits.[35] It has also found that the words "other status" allow the UN HRC to determine what additional types of discrimination are prohibited.[36]

The CESCR does not currently accept individual communications, although this might change once an additional protocol to the ICESCR is adopted. The CESCR does, however, deal with periodic reports by the more than 150 states party to the ICESCR and has frequently considered situations for which it has evidence that sates are not applying social and economic rights in a non-discriminatory manner. Usually these concerns arise from a state's exclusion of certain minorities from social benefits such as education, health care, or social security.

---

[30] 993 *UNTS* 3, entered into force 3 January 1976.

[31] 660 *UNTS* 195, entered into force 4 January 1969.

[32] UN GA Res. 34/180, 34 UN GAOR Supp. (No. 46) at 193, UN Doc. A/34/46, entered into force 3 September 1981.

[33] 999 *UNTS* 302, entered into force 23 March 1976.

[34] The two General Comments of the UN HRC dealing with discrimination are numbers 18 and 23. *See* Comment 18 in Other Instruments Annex.

[35] *See Broeks v. Netherlands* (in Case Annex).

[36] *Gueye v. France*, UN HRC Comm. No. 196/1983.

In both the ICCPR and the ICESCR article 3 prohibits discrimination based on gender or sex. The protections from discrimination in the ICESCR, however, only apply to the human rights in that treaty.[37]

The CERD monitors the Convention on the Elimination of All Forms of Racial Discrimination (also known by the acronym 'CERD'). This is the first convention devoted primarily to eliminating discrimination of a specific type. It prohibits discrimination based on race, colour, descent, nationality, or ethnic origin.[38] The Committee reviews periodic reports by the more than 170 states (almost all states in the international community) who are party to the treaty. It may also accept individual complaints concerning state parties that have made a declaration under article 14 of the CERD, thereby accepting this procedure. About 50 states have done so to date. One of the most significant contributions of the CERD to eliminating racial discrimination has been the determination that states have a legal obligation to take action against private as well as state actors.[39]

The Convention on the Elimination of All Forms Discrimination against Women (CEDAW) prohibits discrimination against women in large part by restating rights that women have with special mention of women's right to enjoy these rights as women. The list of rights in the CEDAW is not exhaustive.[40] This treaty is supervised by the Committee for the Elimination of Discrimination against Woman (also known by the acronym 'CEDAW'). Unlike the CERD, the CEDAW did not originally foresee a mechanism for receiving individual complaints, although it did make recommendations and review states' periodic reports. In 2000 a protocol to the CEDAW was adopted allowing for individual complaints. While the CEDAW is ratified by almost 180 countries, the protocol has less than 100 state parties.

The Convention on the Rights of the Child (CRC), 41 the most widely ratified human rights treaty in the world, also has a Committee on the Rights of the Child (also known by the acronym 'CRC') that can make recommendations and that considers the periodic reports of states party to the CRC. The CRC does not accept individual communications. The treaty

---

[37] Art. 2(2) of the ICESCR. Also note that article 2(3) of the ICESCR expressly allows a state to make some distinctions between nationals and non-nationals in the enjoyment of economic and social rights.

[38] Art. 1(1) of the CERD.

[39] *Yilmaz-Dogan v. Netherlands*, CERD Comm. No. 1 (1984).

[40] Art. 1(1) of the CEDAW.

[41] UN GA Res. 44/25, Annex, 44 UN GAOR Supp. (No. 49) at 167, UN Doc. A/44/49 (1989), entered into force 2 September 1990.

does prohibit discrimination against children in the enjoyment of any of the rights stated in the CRC[42] and applies to all children under the jurisdiction of a state party, without exception.

The International Convention on the Protection of the Rights of All Migrant Workers and Members of Their Families (ICMWR) also has a Committee on the Protection of the Rights of All Migrant Workers and Members of Their Families (CMWR) that can provide recommendations, review periodic reports, and decide individual communications involving those states that have accepted the communications procedure.[43]

In addition to these treaty bodies the new formed 47-state member Human Rights Council (created from the old Human Rights Commission) may deal with cases involving discrimination. It may do so through the discussions of Special Rapporteurs' or experts' reports and through a process known as the 1503 Procedure (named after ECOSOC Resolution 1503 creating the procedure). A new Universal Periodic Review (UPR) procedure will also consider question of discrimination. The later procedure can be used to deal with serious and widespread violations of human rights. Both the old and the new procedures are discursive in nature, but one should not under-estimate the effect of criticism by other states may have in changing the policies of a state. The end of apartheid in South Africa, for example, was as much a result of international pressure as it was of the brave struggle of the South African people led by Nelson Mandela.

In addition to these bodies there are bodies in specialized agencies that deal with problems of discrimination. The International Labour Organization (ILO) and the United Nations Education, Social and Cultural Organization (UNESCO) both have bodies that can decide if rights in their respective fields of interest are being applied without discrimination. ILO treaty number 111, for example, prohibits discrimination based on race, colour, or sex in relation to employment rights[44] and the UNESCO Convention against Discrimination in Education similarly prohibits discrimination in access to education.[45] The World Health Organization (WHO) has also been active in promulgating instruments protecting AIDS/HIV sufferers from discrimination.

---

[42] Art. 2(1) of the CRC.

[43] *See* art. 77 of the ICMWR. *Also see* art. 76 allowing inter-state complaints.

[44] Art 1(1)(b) of this treaty also allows states to *add additional grounds for* which discrimination is prohibited. For the text of this treaty see the Treaties annex.

[45] For the text of this treaty see the Treaties annex.

European Mechanisms

There are numerous human rights mechanisms that deal with cases of discrimination in the European context. The main regional international organizations promulgating the norms that established these human rights mechanisms are the Council of Europe (CoE), the European Union (EU), and the Organization for Security and Cooperation in Europe (OSCE). The following is a broad overview of these organizations and their main mechanisms for dealing with issues of discrimination.

Council of Europe: European Court of Human Rights and the High Commissioner for Human Rights

The CoE consists of 47 states spanning from the British Isles to the furthest edge of Russia.[46] Every state member must become a party to the European Convention on Human Rights (ECHR) that contains a provision prohibiting discrimination in the enjoyment of the human rights in the ECHR (art. 14) and more broadly (Protocol 12).

The European Court of Human Rights (ECtHR) has a judge representing each member state of the CoE (47 as of 2007) and holds sessions in both regular chambers and as a grand chamber. It applies the ECHR with legally-binding effect. This may include the issuing of interim measures. The jurisprudence of the ECtHR is some of the most advanced international human rights jurisprudence existing today. The relatively rapid development of a *corpus* of well-reasoned jurisprudence has made the ECtHR an example for other human rights mechanisms.

The European High Commissioner for Human Rights is elected by the Council of Europe's Parliamentary Assembly. The mandate of the High Commissioner is essentially one of good offices—actions—through which he can promote respect for human rights in member states. Non-discrimination has been one of the areas in which he acts. The High Commissioner has visited several Council of Europe countries and then followed-up these visits with a letter to the governments concerned. For example, after his visit to Slovakia the High Commissioner expressed concern for the plight of the Roma and issued recommendations for combating xenophobia and hate speech.

---

[46] Currently there are two state applications are pending: Montenegro and Belarus.

Council of Europe: Other Mechanisms

Other organs of the Council of Europe that may contribute to ending or preventing discrimination include the Committee of Ministers, the Parliamentary Assembly, the Congress of Local and Regional Authorities, and the Council Secretariat, headed by a Secretary General who is elected by the Parliamentary Assembly. The Secretariat employs almost two thousand individuals drawn proportionately from the different member states.

Many of the activities of these bodies are informal. They include activities such as the dissemination of information in the form of guidelines, recommendations, records of best-practices, etc.[47] They also regularly hold meetings, conferences, or workshops on non-discrimination related topics.

Most of these bodies also some form of decision making authority that they may use to promulgate norms or recommendations concerning non-discrimination.

European Union

The prohibition of discrimination in the European Union (EU) is based of a unique regime of law emanating from the EU treaties and legislative decisions.[48] This *juris corpus* applies only to citizens of EU states and thereby creates an exclusive or privileged protection from certain types of discrimination within the EU. When states ratify the EC Treaty[49] or the new EU Treaty[50] they undertake to the give provisions of EU law direct effect in their domestic legislation and courts.

---

[47]*See, for example,* Commission to the Council, the European Parliament, the European Economic and Social Committee and the Committee of the Regions, *Communication* entitled "Non-Discrimination and Equal Opportunities for All: A Framework Strategy," EU Doc. No. COM(2005)224, (not published in the *Official Journal of the European Union*) (1 June 2005).

[48] For EU legislation see http://europa.eu.

[49] This refers to the consolidated EC Treaty which can be found at http://europa.eu. This is treaty that was formed by the consolidation of the original three treaties creating the European Economic Communities and the subsequent revisions to these treaties.

[50] This is a new treaty that has been adopted to enlarge the responsibility of the European Union from an economic community to a union that can influence foreign and political affair more generally. This treaty is also found at http://europa.eu.

In the EC Treaty[51] articles 2, 3(2), 13 and 141 contained the principle of non-discrimination, usually in relation to gender. Article 141 of the EC Treaty, for example, provides for the principle of equal pay for equal work or male and female workers. In the consolidated EU Treaty from 2002,[52] article 6 refers to fundamental rights. These provisions are given effect in EU and thus national law by EU Directives and Regulations.[53] Article 13 of the EC Treaty gives the EU Council the right to "take appropriate action to combat discrimination." And article 6 of the EU Treaty only protects individuals against discrimination by reference to the ECHR and general principles of international human rights law.

To implement the treaty provisions, particularly using the powers provided in article 13, the EU Council has adopted a Racial Equality Directive[54] and an Framework Directive[55] that require states to prohibit discrimination on the grounds of race, ethnic origin, religion or belief, age, disability, and sexual orientation. In relation to prohibition of discrimination based on sex/gender in article 141 of the EC Treaty, the EU Council has also adopted a Revised Equal Treatment Directive that introduces definitions of direct and indirect discrimination.[56]

The judicial body of the EU is the European Court of Justice (ECJ). Its jurisdiction is limited to the subject matter of the EU treaties (freedom of movement of goods and services) and the directives mentioned above. The ECJ has affirmatively determined that international protected human rights form part of EU law.[57] Moreover, the jurisprudence of the ECJ is significant

---

[51] Consolidated Version of the Treaty Establishing the European Community, originally signed on 25 March 1957, but amended several times.

[52] Consolidated Version of the Treaty on European Union, Official Journal of the European Communities, No. C 325/7, adopted 24 December 2002.

[53] Regulations must be directly implemented in national legislation, although the EU Council may only adopt regulations in a few core areas of concern. Directives must be compiled with in 'effect', thus allowing states more discretion in deciding what actions to take to implement them. Recommendations, opinions, plans, reports and other such instruments are not legally binding.

[54] See Council Directive 2000/43 in the Other Instruments annex.

[55] See Council Directive 2000/78 in the Other Instruments annex.

[56] Council Directive 2002/73/EC of the European Parliament and of the Council of 23 September 2002, OJEC L 269 of 5 October 2002.

[57] *Internazionale Handelgesellschaft mbH v. Einfuhr- und Vorratsstelle fur Getreide und Futtermittel*, ECJ Case No. 11/70 ECR 1125 (1970).

in the field of non-discrimination in relation to the exercise of the rights protected under EC/EU law.[58]

The EU has also adopted a (not-yet-legally-binding) Charter of Fundamental Rights that contains a prohibition of discrimination in December 2000. The ECJ can receive cases brought by individual and states both after domestic remedies have been exhausted and during domestic proceedings when a procedure for referring points of European Union law can be utilized.

The EU's activities in the field of non-discrimination law also extend to education, monitoring, and dissemination. For example, the European Commission's Directorate-General for Employment, Social Affairs and Equal Opportunities also adopts an annual report chronicling the state of equality and non-discrimination in the Europe Union.

Several examples of the jurisprudence of the ECJ and examples of the legislation of the EU are included among the materials annexed to this book.

Organization for Security and Cooperation in Europe

The OSCE (originally called the CSCE or Conference for Security and Cooperation in Europe) began as a forum for discussion about issues that affect matters of European security in the broadest sense. The principle of non-discrimination and the concern of combating intolerance and discrimination have been among the issues discussed.

The principle of non-discrimination is enshrined in the Helsinki Final Act (1975), the Charter of Paris for a New Europe (1990), the Charter for European Security (1999), and several ministerial decisions.[59] Non-discrimination has also been the focus of several OSCE Conferences[60] and

---

[58] Some ECJ Cases are included in the Cases annex, such as *Kalliope and Hansestadt Hamburg, European Commission and Italy*, and *Margret Boyle, et al. and EOC*.

[59] *See, for example*, Decision No. 10/05 on Tolerance and Non-Discrimination: Promoting Mutual Respect and Understanding, adopted at the 13th Ministerial Council Meeting in Ljubljana, Slovenia (2005); Decision No. 12/04 on tolerance and non-discrimination, adopted at the 12th Ministerial Council Meeting, Sofia, Bulgaria (2004); Decision No. 4/03 on tolerance and non-discrimination, adopted at the 11th Ministerial Council Meeting in Maastricht, the Netherlands (2003).

[60] *See, for example*, High-Level Conference on Combating Discrimination and Promoting Mutual Respect and Understanding, held on 7 and 8 June 2007 in Bucharest, Romania in accordance with OSCE Ministerial Council Decision 13/06 of 5 December 2006).

the OSCE's work on minorities. The OSCE clearly views combating discrimination as a priority for security in Europe.

The OSCE's Chairman-in-Office's Personal Representative on Combating Racism, Xenophobia and Discrimination; the OSCE High Commissioner for Minorities; the OSCE Representative on Freedom of the Media; and the OSCE Office for Democratic Institutions and Human Rights based in Warsaw, Poland, all contribute to ensuring awareness about discrimination in Europe.

These mechanisms collect and distribute information and statistics on cases of discrimination; promote tolerance through trainings and the dissemination of best practices and provide technical assistance to states to help them put in place legislation for combating discrimination. They do not make legally binding or even quasi-judicial determination in individual cases.

African Mechanisms

To date the main African human rights body has been the African Commission on Human and Peoples' Rights (ACHPR). 61 This may change soon as African states adopted a Protocol to the African Charter on Human and Peoples' Rights (also referred to as the 'ACHPR') that creates an African Court of Human and Peoples' Rights (ACtHR), which has the potential to become one of the most progressive protectors of human rights in the world because of the breath of the rights protected under the ACHPR.

The African Union also has a Committee on the Rights and Welfare of the African Child and has organized several meeting at the level of ministers of human rights and/or justice to look at human rights issues including non-discrimination.

Inter-American Mechanisms

The Inter-American human rights system consists primarily of the Inter-American Commission on Human Rights (IACommHR, based in Washington, DC, USA) and the Inter-American Court of Human Rights (IACtHR, based in Costa Rica) both under the auspices of the Organization of American States (OAS) headquartered in Washington, DC, USA. The IACtHR applies the American Convention on Human Rights (ACHR) to states parties that have accepted its jurisdiction. The IACommHR also applies the ACHR to states that have accepted it jurisdiction under this treaty

---

[61] OAU Doc. CAB/LEG/67/3 rev. 5, entered into force 21 October 1986.

and the American Declaration on the Rights and Duties of Man (ADRDM) to all other state members of the OAS.

Both the IACommHR and the IACtHR have dealt with the principle of non-discrimination in cases brought before them by individuals.

Arab Mechanisms

Presently, there is no Arab commission or court of human rights and the Arab Charter of Human Rights has not yet entered into force.

This does not mean that human rights—including non-discrimination—are not a concern of the Arab world. In fact both within Arab and Muslim non-governmental and governmental institutions issues of discrimination have been of major concern. Much attention has been given to combating Islamophobia by the Organization of Islamic States (OIC) and the protection of Bedouin and other minorities from discrimination has been often highlighted by NGOs in international forums.

Asian Mechanisms

Like the Arab world, Asia does not have developed human rights mechanisms. Nevertheless, declarations have been adopted under the auspices of the Asian and South East Asian Nations (ASEAN) broadly condemning discrimination.

Other Mechanisms

The international mechanisms mentioned above are not the only one's that exist for combating discrimination. There are many specialized governmental and non-governmental mechanisms that also work to eliminate discrimination in particular areas of concern. The contribution of these specialized bodies should not be underestimated, but they are too numerous to cover in this book.

Suffice it to note that almost every UN organ or specialized agency, every regional organization, thousands of private organizations, and many individuals are working regularly to try to end the scourge of discrimination.

TAKING ACTION AGAINST DISCRIMNATION

There are many activities that contribute to ending discrimination. At an individual level we can all try to be more tolerant. Private entities can implement policies of non-discrimination as many businesses have done. There are even guidelines for action to end or prevent some types of discrimination in the private sector.[62] At the state level there are laws and government action to implement these laws. When laws are not respected or government action fails to prohibit discrimination, then recourse may be had to domestic courts. When a petitioner still believes he or she is suffering discrimination for a reason that is prohibited under international law, then, and only then (after domestic remedies have been exhausted) can recourse be had to international human rights mechanisms. This section deals with the actions that may be taken before international human rights mechanisms. It is important to reiterate that these mechanisms can only be accessed once domestic remedies are exhausted.

---

[62] *See, for example*, The M^{ac}bride Principles (promulgated by Mr. Sean McManus, the President of Irish National Caucus, and adopted December 1997).

Types of Action

The types of action that may be taken to draw attention to discriminatory practices are varied. They may consist of political activities before political bodies, public activities to pressure political bodies, or individual petitions to judicial or quasi-judicial human rights mechanism such as those described above.

International human rights bodies allow a variety of different forms of actions for challenging the acts or polices of a state that appear to constitute discrimination. For example an individual who believes that he or she has been subjected to discrimination by a state can provide information to a human rights mechanism like the UN's CERD. This information may then be used when the CERD considers the periodic reports of the state. 63 This procedure is called the reporting procedure or state reports procedure. It is a procedure created by a treaty, or by the decision of an international human rights mechanism in the case of the new 'universal periodic review (UPR) procedure' that is being considered by the UN Human Rights Council.

Where a state has not agreed to submit to the jurisdiction of a human rights mechanism, the reporting procedure may be the best means of raising claims of discrimination before an international forum.

The information one provides to a human rights body can also be used when these bodies produce general comments, recommendations, or guidelines.

Some human rights bodies, such as the UN HRC, CERD, CEDAW, and the CMWR, also receive individual complaints about discrimination under their respective treaties. Other bodies, such as the Committee on Communications of the Human Rights Council, are able to consider general complaints alleging, with accompanying evidence, discrimination of a "serious and widespread" nature. Still other bodies, primarily regional bodies, can accept individual cases and make binding legal decisions on them. Below some of international human rights bodies are shown and whether they accept individual complaints or merely receive information for consideration of states' reports.

---

[63] The UN Human Rights Council is in the process of forming a Universal Periodic Review Process to replace the reporting process under the eight different human rights treaty regimes, including the ICCPR, CERD, and CEDAW. The Human Rights Council, however, continues to consider issues of discrimination in this process.

Human Rights Bodies/Types of Actions Permitted

UN HRC (treaty body)	State reports & individual complaints
CERD (treaty body)	State reports & individual complaints
CEDAW (treaty body)	State reports & individual complaints
CMWR (treaty body)	State reports & individual complaints
CESCR (treaty body)	State reports
CRC(treaty body)	State reports
Special Mechanisms (HR Council)	individual complaints
1503 Procedure (HR Council)	individual complaints (widespread)
ECtHR	individual complaints
IACommHR	individual complaints
AFCHR	individual complaints

Note that even where an international human rights body accepts individual petitions, it may still only take general action. For example, neither individual communications to the Special Mechanisms of the Human Rights Council nor communications under the 1503 Procedure result in legally binding decisions. Instead these bodies rely on persuasion to encourage states to respect the law.

General Issues Concerning of Litigation

As indicated above there are often international human rights mechanisms available to challenge discriminatory treatment. If an individual petition procedure is not available then there will usually be at least a reporting procedure or a political forum. In both cases individuals and NGOs can be instrumental in bringing evidence of discrimination into public view so that action can be taken.

Sometimes, however, quiet diplomacy, at least initially, might be the best manner to deal with discrimination, especially if the government of the country concerned is sensitive to international pressure. In such cases, resort may still be had to domestic legal procedures and, eventually, international legal procedures when reconciliatory tactics fail.

To utilize an individual communication procedure or to file a case an individual must provide one of the bodies mentioned above with information indicating that prohibited discrimination is taking place. The human rights mechanism will then review the information. If it thinks the information indicates a violation of the prohibition of discrimination that falls within its mandate it will first consider whether the claim is admissible (has met all the formal requirements including having exhausted domestic remedies). After a communication or petition has been declared admissible, the human rights mechanism will then consider the merits of the claim.

In most of these processes the claim or petition is referred to as a "communication." Sometimes the general term Petition is used. In the case of courts, we often speak about 'filing a case'. The comments below, apply to all of these forms of actions, regardless of their names.

Requirements of a Communication

A communication must not only be submitted after domestic remedies have been exhausted or they are proven to be unavailable, but it must also satisfy other requirements. The information must include: (1) the details of the violation (with as much evidence as possible); (2) the details of the person committing the violation; (3) the details of the person whose rights have been violated; (4) the contacts for the victims legal representative, if any; (5) the provisions of the treaty that has been violated; (6) when the violation occurred; (7) details indicating that domestic remedies have been exhausted or are not available, and (8) the relief sought.

The communication itself must be written in clear and civil (not disparaging) language and the state against whom it is made must be a party to the treaty that that the communications claims was violated. One is also well advised to check the reservations declarations that a state has made.

A communication must also be made within a reasonable time after the violation has occurred and after domestic remedies have been exhausted. Sometimes this is specifically stated, but even when it is not this time period is usually determined to be approximately six months from the date of the exhaustion of domestic remedies.

Some mechanisms also require that the matter must not have already been brought before, resolved by, or currently before, another international human rights body. If it is the second body it is brought before may decline to deal with the matter.

Only when all these formalities have been met will a communication be considered on its merits.

Proving Discrimination

The international human rights mechanisms described above will usually find discrimination to be present if the petitioner has made out a *prima facie* case that she or he is be treated in a different way for a prohibited reasons <u>and</u> that this treatment is to his or her detriment <u>and</u> the government has no justification.

It is rarely, necessary to prove that the state intended the discriminatory treatment if the effects of state action or an omission by a state can be shown to have caused discrimination. In this sense liability for discrimination is absolute and requires no element of intention.

Despite the absence of a need to prove intention, proving discrimination is still an arduous task. It often involves obtaining relevant statistics, affidavits, and any other evidence that might create an inference that discrimination is taking place.

It is imperative that a victim or potential victim be advised to secure and preserve evidence at as early a stage as possible.

Justifications for Discrimination

While some forms of discrimination may be absolutely prohibited, this does not mean that even these forms of discrimination are never justified. A state may, for example, discriminate on the basis of race or gender if its actions are intended to redress a situation of past discrimination. Many states provide extra credits to minority groups members or the members of under-privileged groups to allow their members to catch up to others who have a history of benefits that have allowed them to succeed. Such affirmative action is allowed, as long as it can be justified as a reasonable means of redressing past discrimination.

Preparing a Case

It is essential to acquire and preserve as much evidence as possible as early as possible when bringing of a case concerning discrimination to an international body. This requires foresight and often the involvement of an international lawyer during the domestic litigation.

The collection and preservation of evidence cannot be stressed enough. Even the most competent lawyer is at a significant disadvantage when valuable evidence has not been collected or properly preserved. This often requires taking affidavits, collecting and analyzing statistics, examining legislative histories, acquiring expert reports or statements, and comparing the situations of different groups of people through a variety of means.

At the same time as the facts are being established one must research the law. While the fundamental legal points may not be very difficult, applying the law to a particular circumstance often requires a degree of expertise. This expertise comes not only from reading volumes of treaties, cases, and interpretations in General Comments and the writing of highly qualified publicists, but also through creative thinking about these sources of the law. Thus while the legal aspect of preparing a case undoubtedly starts with the review of legal texts, it does not end their. Especially, where the principles of non-discrimination is being applied to unusual facts, to new types of discrimination, or where the evidence is unusual, it is important for the lawyer to be able to think creatively about the existing law (*lex lata*) and be able to extend it to the law applicable to his or her case.

GROUNDS FOR PROHIBITED
DISCRIMINATION

RACE

No single type of discrimination has received so much attention as has racial discrimination. This is perhaps because racial discrimination became a serious problem due to the widespread practice of slavery by which primarily black Africans were treated as chattels by white slave owners in the wealthier European and North American countries. Understanding the legal prohibition of slavery is necessary for understanding the prohibition of race and other related forms of discrimination.

The Legal Prohibition of Slavery

The existence of slavery dates back many centuries. It can be found in ancient societies where persons captured in wartime where forced to work for the party that captured them. Slaves in ancient society were primarily used for labour. They were also considered less valuable than other human beings.

The practice of slavery was historically supported by different religions as well as most monarchs. Gradually religious leaders' rejected slavery as immoral. This led to the wider condemnation of the practice. By the late 1770s several states had begun to denounce slavery. As Great Britain and other European powers outlawed slavery, the slave trade in the United States began to flourish. In addition, new forms of slavery began to appear, such as different forms of economic exploitation. By the end of the 19th century every country in the world had outlawed traditional forms of slavery.

In 1926, the League of Nations (the predecessor to the United Nations) adopted the Slavery Convention to which more than a hundred states are now party.[64]

After the Second World War another slavery treaty was adopted[65] and prohibitions of slavery were included in several human rights instruments, most notably article 8 of the ICCPR. Today slavery is also considered a crime against humanity in article 7(1)(c) of the Statute of the International Court of Justice.[66]

Despite these legal prohibitions, contemporary forms of slavery still exist today. They range from the economic exploitation of whole nations of people by other nations to the trafficking of women and children for forced labour, including prostitution, by criminal groups.

The Legal Definition of Race and the Prohibition of Racial Discrimination

The definition of race and its utility has been frequently debated.[67] Nevertheless, race is often defined by a characteristic related to a common ancestry of a group of people.

Legally, article 1, paragraph 1, of the CERD, defines racial discrimination as

> any distinction, exclusion, restriction or preference based on race, colour, descent, or national or ethnic origin which has the purpose or effect of nullifying or impairing the recognition, enjoyment or exercise, on an equal footing, of human rights and fundamental freedoms in the political, economic, social, cultural or any other field of public life.

This definition was also adopted by the ICJ, the principle judicial body of the United Nations.[68] Since then, the CERD has extended this interpretation to

---

[64] 212 *UNTS* 17, entered into force 7 July 1953. In 1953 a Protocol amending this Convention to expand it to more forms of slavery was adopted and about two-thirds of the states party to the original 1926 treaty also the 1953 Protocol.

[65] Supplementary Convention on the Abolition of Slavery, the Slave Trade, and Institutions and Practices Similar to Slavery, 266 *UNTS* 3, entered into force 30 April 1957.

[66] ICC Statute, 2187 *UNTS* 90, entered into force 1 July 2002.

[67] For an account of this debate see Thompson, W. and Hickey, J., *Society in Focus*, Boston, MA, USA: Pearson Publishing Co. (2005).

include, for example, "descent-based discrimination, such as discrimination on the basis of caste and analogous systems of inherited status..."[69]

Racial discrimination is prohibited by special treaties such as the CERD as well as by general human rights treaties like the ICCPR (art. 2 and 26). Article 20(2) of the ICCPR also requires states to prohibit speech that constitutes racial hatred or incites discrimination.[70] These prohibitions of discrimination apply to all types of social transactions involving or regulated by the state, including, for example, financial transactions[71] and immigration.[72]

Apartheid

One of the most serious forms of racial discrimination is apartheid. This crime against humanity is defined by reference to the treatment of blacks in South Africa in the International Convention on the Suppression and Punishment of the Crime of Apartheid.[73] This treaty makes racial segregation and discrimination an international crime and defines it as actions abusing the human rights of a racial group committed "for the purpose of establishing and maintaining domination by one racial group of persons over any other racial group of persons and systematically oppressing them."[74] Apartheid has been expressly condemned by states as racial discrimination of the most serious type in article 3 of the CERD. Today apartheid still exists by Israel against the Palestinians, according to the UN Special Rapporteur on Palestine.[75]

---

[68] *Legal Consequences for States of the Continued Presence of South Africa in Namibia, supra* note 19.

[69] CERD General Recommendation XXIX (2002).

[70] *See Faurisson v. France,* UN HRC Comm. No. 550/1993.

[71] *See Habassi v. Denmark,* UN CERD Comm. No. 10/1997 [refusing a loan because the applicant was not Danish].

[72] *See East African Asians v. United Kingdom,* ECommHR, App. No. 4403/70 (14 December 1973) [although the Commission could not apply the prohibition of discrimination to the right to enter a country not one's own, it did find that racial discrimination in the enjoyment of this right may constitute inhumane and degrading treatment].

[73] 1015 *UNTS* 243, entered into force 18 July 1976. *Also see* the International Convention against Apartheid in Sports, adopted 10 December 1985, UN GA Res. 40/64, 40 UN GAOR Supp. (No. 51) at 37. UN Doc. A/RES/40164 (1985).

[74] Art 3.

[75] Report of the Special Rapporteur on the situation of human rights in the Palestinian territories occupied since 1967, UN Doc. No. A/HRC/4/17 (29 January 2007) at para. 61.

Racial Discrimination and Other Similar Forms of Intolerance

Racial discrimination is closely linked to discrimination against members of minority groups, persons of colour, persons of particular decent, and persons of a particular ethnic origin. The link to minority rights is particularly important as the protection of minority rights predates modern human rights law. In its Advisory Opinion *Minority Schools in Albania* (*see* Cases annex) the Permanent Court of International Justice stated that the object of minority protections included prohibiting racial discrimination.[76]

Racial discrimination, like other forms of discrimination, may also be linked closely to the violation of other human rights.

The ECtHR has found, for example, that both the right to life and the prohibition of discrimination are violated when a state fails to effectively investigate evidence of racial motivation for a killing.[77] The ECtHR has also frequently linked discrimination to family rights.[78]

The United Nations Human Rights Council is addressing societal intolerance towards persons who are members of minority groups in its followup to the Durban conference.

---

[76] *Minority Schools in Albania*, PCIJ Advisory Opinion No. 64, PCIJ Ser. A/B (1935) at p. 17.

[77] *Nachova v. Bulgaria*, ECtHR Appls. 43577/98 and 43579/98 (28 February 2004).

[78] *See, for example, Abdulaziz, Cabales and Balkandali v. United Kingdom*, ECtHR, Ser. A, No. 94 (28 May 1985).

GENDER

Discrimination based on gender or sex is prohibited in most human rights instruments. Even article 8 of the Charter of the United Nations requires the organization to ensure that men and women can participate equally in the activities of the UN. Like many other areas of society, however, women continue to be treated unequally.[79] More recently, not only discrimination against women, but also against other individuals because of their sexual or gender orientations has drawn increasing attention.

Discrimination based on gender includes both men and women. Thus discrimination against men is also prohibited, for example, in the enjoyment of social and economic rights.[80] Nevertheless, it is discrimination against women on the ground of gender that has given rise to some of the most extensive, most creative, and most well-reasoned jurisprudence in the realm of international human rights law.

Women

The CEDAW prohibits discrimination against women in the enjoyment of a wide range of human rights. Essentially this treaty restates the human rights

---

[79] The United Nations, for example, as of 2007, had still failed to meet the pledge it made at the Beijing Conference on Women to ensure that women are equally represented in the most senior ranks of the UN.

[80] *Wills v. United Kingdom*, ECtHR Appl. No. 36042/97 (11 June 2002).

men and women have with special reference to the prohibition of discrimination against women. Moreover, the CEDAW's statement of rights is not exhaustive.

Most strikingly and uniquely, the CEDAW requires states to take affirmative or positive actions to combat the historical consequences of discrimination. Much of the gains made in ending discrimination against women have been the result of this affirmative action by states.

The prohibition of discrimination against women is found in numerous other human rights instruments. As we have seen article 8 of the Charter of the United Nations expressly requires gender equality in the UN itself. The UN Secretary-General has established a senior post with the responsibility for ensuring women are not discriminated against in the UN system and to encourage more significant representation of women in the UN. Despite this effort women represent less than 40% of the senior UN staff.

The UN HRC has interpreted the prohibition against discrimination based on gender or sex in article 26 of the ICCPR as applying to other individual rights that have been granted by a state or which a state has agreed to grant persons under its jurisdiction.[81] The UN HRC has several times determined that laws that put women at a disadvantage are discriminatory.[82] Although discrimination based on gender may sometimes be justified, such justifications are rare and must withstand a test of strict scrutiny. This test requires that the government prove that its action was not for a discriminatory purpose or for a legitimate aim and was necessary to achieve the legitimate aim.

The IACtHR, when asked to advise the government of Costa Rica on proposed amendments concerning the acquisition of nationality, determined that distinctions based on the marital status of men and women that put women at a disadvantage would violate the prohibition of discrimination based on sex in article 17(4) of the ACHR.[83]

---

[81] *Broeks v. Nederlands*, UN HRC Comm. No. 172 (1984).

[82] *Young v. Australia*, UN HRC Comm. No. 941 (2000); *Avellanal v. Peru*, UN HRC Comm. No. 202 (1986); and *Mauritian Women v. Mauritia*, UN HRC Comm. No. 35 (1978).

[83] *Proposed Amendments to the Naturalization Provisions of the Constitution of Costa Rica*, IACtHR Advisory Opinion No. OC-4/84, Ser. A) No. 4 (19 January 1984).at para. 55 (see Cases annex for excerpts from this Advisory Opinion).

The ECtHR has held that obliging women, but not men, to change their surname when they marry constitutes discrimination based on gender.[84]

In these cases the human rights bodies applied a strict standard of scrutiny that required the government to show it acted in a reasonable and justified way to accomplish a permissible policy goal.[85]

Sexual Orientation

While discrimination based on gender or sex has been traditionally prohibited, the same cannot be said about discrimination based on sexual orientation, which is a relative new ground of prohibited discrimination. The jurisprudence concerning this ground of discrimination is thus less clear.

The UN HRC has found that laws criminalizing sexual relations between consenting adults in private violate the prohibition of discrimination in the ICCPR because sexual orientation is an "other status" mentioned in article 26."[86] The HRC compared the homosexual couple to other (homosexual and heterosexual) couples in find discrimination. The ECJ, on the other hand, has found that the treatment of (female) lesbian employees must be compared to the treatment of homosexual male employees, and not heterosexual men and women, to determine if there was discrimination.[87] This test, of course, makes discrimination based on sexual orientation harder to prove.

The UN HRC has also sometimes interpreted the prohibition of discrimination based on sexual orientation restrictively. For example, it has held that same-sex couples do not have the same right to marry as heterosexual couples under article 23 of the ICCPR, which expressly grants the right to marry to "men and women."[88] The ECtHR, on the other hand,

---

[84] *Unal Tekeli v. Turkey*, ECtHR Appl. No. 29865/96 (2004).

[85] *See, for example, Van Raalte v. the Netherlands*, Appl. No. 20060/92, I *Reports of Judgments and Decisions* 1997 (21 February 1997); *Wessels-Bergervoet v. the Netherlands*, Appl. No. 34462/97, IV *Reports of Judgments and Decisions* 2002 (4 June 2002); and *Willis v. United Kingdom*, Appl. No. 36042/97, *Reports of Judgments and Decisions* 2002 (11 June 2002).

[86] *Toonen v. Australia*, UN HRC Comm. No. 488 (1992). Also see SL *v. Austria*, ECtHR (Grand Chamber) Appl. No. 45330/99 (9 January 2003) and *Young v. Australia*, UN HRC Comm. No. 941 (2000).

[87] *Grant v. South West Trains Ltd.*, I *ECJ* 621 (1998).

[88] *Joslin v. New Zealand*, UN HRC Comm. No. 902 (1999).

has found distinctions between heterosexuals and homosexuals to constitute prohibited discrimination."[89]

Discrimination based on sexual orientation is likely to be an important issue in the years to come as human rights bodies grapple with the views of some states and religions that reject homosexuality and the progress of society that increasingly accepts same-sex relationships.

---

[89] *Sutherland v. United Kingdom*, ECtHR (Grand Chamber) Appl. No. 25186/94 (27 March 2001) and *S.L. v. Austria*, ECtHR (Grand Chamber) Appl. No. 45330/99 (9 January 2003).

NATIONALITY

Nationality is a legal construct over which sovereign states have broad control. The concept of nationality is, however, very often confusing. In some states it refers to all persons who are recognized as 'belonging' to that state as a sovereign entity. In other cases, it is very similar to ethnic or racial identity. For example, former Soviet Union countries frequently list as the nationality of Russian speaking or ethnic Russian nationals "Russian" as well as the nationality of the newly sovereign state. An Uzbek of Russian descent will thus be considered to have Russian nationality, although legally he is only a national of Uzbekistan.

Discrimination on grounds of nationality is often difficult to prove. This is in part because in some areas concerned with distinctions based on nationality, such as immigration, the state enjoys broad discretion. Thus although on their face actions or policies might constitute discrimination, they may not be prohibited. For example, the IACtHR has held that proposed amendments to Costa Rican law that required good Spanish language skills in order to qualify for naturalization—although apparently discriminating against non-Spanish speaking nationalities—was lawfully within the discretion of the state.[90]

At the same time, the 'anti-terrorism' legislation enacted by the United States and its allies—which often uses racial or national profiling—has been found to constitute discrimination based on nationality.[91]

Aliens

Traditionally, aliens have been treated differently than a state's nationals. Sometimes worse, sometimes better. For example, while a state may generally confiscate the property of a national without any particular level of compensation under international law, when a state confiscates the property of an alien it must pay reasonable, fair and prompt compensation.[92]

Article 2 of the ICESCR also allows developing states that cannot afford to provide for the economic and social rights of non-nationals to deny these rights.[93]

Despite a level of allowed distinction, aliens, however, generally enjoy the same rights as nationals of a state.[94] Some rights even have special meaning for aliens. For example, article 12(4) of the ACHPR prohibits states from expelling non-nationals, except in accordance with law, and article 12(5) prohibits mass expulsions.[95]

Migrant and Migrant Workers

With the increased movement of labour across borders migrant workers rights have drawn increased attention in recent years. The essential problem is the exploitation of individuals who are forced to migrant across borders to seek work. As these individuals are often illegally in the country in which they are working, are only temporally there, or do not understand the laws of the country where they are employed, they are often exploited by employers.

---

[90] *Proposed Amendments to the Naturalization Provisions of the Constitution of Costa Rica*, IACtHR Advisory Opinion No. OC-4/84 (19 January 1984).

[91] *A v. Secretary of State for the Home Department*, UK House of Lords, [2005] 2 AC 68 at paras. 58-63.

[92] *See Blazek v. Czech Republic*, UN HRC Comm. No. 857/1999.

[93] Art. 2(3) of the ICESCR (see Treaties annex for the text of this article).

[94] UN HRC General Comment 15 on the Human Rights of Aliens makes it clear that "... in general, the rights set forth in the Covenant apply to everyone, irrespective of reciprocity, and irrespective of his or her nationality and statelessness" (para. 1).

[95] *See UDIH, FIDH and others v. Angola*, ACHPR Comm. No. 159/96 (1996) [holding the mass expulsion of West Africans by Angola to be illegal].

One of the most recent human rights treaties adopted in the United Nations system is the International Convention on the Protection of the Rights of All Migrant Workers and Their Families.[96] This treaty reiterates many human rights migrant workers already have under other general human rights treaties. Article 7 of his treaty makes specific reference to the right to non-discrimination in the enjoyment of these rights.

The rights of migrant workers have also been the concern of the IACtHR. In a lengthy Advisory Opinion responding to request by the Mexican government the IACtHR decided that principle of equality and non-discrimination is of a fundamental character in international law. The Court concluded that discrimination against undocumented migrants in the enjoyment of their basic human rights as protected in the ACHR and ADRDM is prohibited.[97]

The right of European migrant workers within the EU to be free from discrimination in other EU states has also been the subject of many decisions of the ECJ. In this context it is usually a matter of nationality, i.e., when a person is from an EU member state they must be treated the same as the nationals of the EU member state in which they are seeking employment or employed.[98]

---

[96] UN GA Res 45/158, Annex, 45 UN GAOR Suppl (No. 49A) at 262, UN Doc. A/45/49 (1990).

[97] *Legal Status and Rights of Undocumented Migrants*, IACtHR Advisory Opinion OC-18/03 (Ser. A) No. 18 (17 September 2003) (excerpted in the Cases annex).

[98] *See, for example, Margaret Boyle and Others and Equal Opportunities Commission*, ECJ, Opinion No. C-411/96 (27 October 1998) (excerpted in the Cases annex).

LANGUAGE, RELIGION, AND CULTURE

Discrimination on the basis of language, religion or culture are discussed together because these three grounds are often intertwined and because our discussion of each of them in this section is brief because much lengthier works have been done about each of them.[99]

These rights should not be confused with the rights of minorities that are found, for example, in article 27 of the ICCPR. Although these grounds are often important rights enjoyed by minorities,[100] they are types of discrimination that are prohibited in all cases.

Language

One of the most frequent grounds of discrimination based on culture is in relation to language. A state may, for example, instruct its civil servants to use only one particular language. In most cases this will be allowed, but where it

---

[99] Thornberry, P., *International Law and Rights of Minorities* (Oxford, UK: Claredon Press, 1991).
[100] *Diergaardt v. Nambia*, UN HRC Comm. No. 760 (1997).

can be shown that the state is acting to prohibit the use of certain minority languages there may be an issue of discrimination. Although not explicitly mentioned in human rights treaties—with the exception of treaties concerning minority rights[101]—it is widely accepted as being an 'other status' that deserves protection from discrimination.

The African Commission on Human and Peoples' Rights identified the important of language when it held that

> language is an integral part of the structure of culture: it in fact constitutes its pillar and means of expression par excellence. Its usage enriches the individual and enables him to take an active part in the community and its activities. To deprive a man (sic) of such participation amounts to depriving him of his identity.[102]

The UN HRC has found that discrimination based on language, even if not overtly intended, is prohibited.[103] As indicated above, often discrimination on the basis of language has arisen in the context of a minority's right to education in their own language.[104]

Religion

Another essential feature of an individual's identity is his or her religious beliefs. Discrimination based on religion is expressly prohibited in most human rights treaties. In 1993 the UN HRC defined religion as "theistic, non-theistic and atheistic beliefs, as well as the right not to profess any religion or belief." Consequently discrimination on any ground included in this broad definition is prohibited by international law.

The UN HRC has held that a state may not privilege certain religions over others.[105] The ECtHR has determined that religion may not be a ground that may be taken into account when deciding whether or not to grant family rights to individuals.[106]

---

[101] *See, for example,* art. 13 of the Framework Convention for the Protection of National Minorities, *ETS* No. 157, entered into force 1 February 1998, and art. 16 of the Central European Initiative Instrument for the Protection of Minority, adopted 19 November 1994.

[102] *Mauritanienne des Droits de l'Homme v. Mauritania,* AFHPR Comm. No. 210 (1998).

[103] *Diergaardt v. Nambia, supra* note 100.

[104] *Minority Schools in Albania,* PCIJ, Ser. A/B, No. 64, p. 3 and *Cyprus v. Turkey,* ECtHR Appl. No. 25781/94 (10 May 2001).

[105] *Waldman v. Canada,* UN HRC Comm. No. 694 (1996).

[106] *Palau-Martinez v. France,* ECtHR Appl. No. 64927/01 (16 December 2003) and *Hoffmann v. Austria,* ECtHR Appl. No. 12875/87 (23 June 1993).

Cultural Practices

Like language and religion, cultural practices often form an important part of an individual's identity and therefore individuals should be able to enjoy these rights without discrimination. The UNESCO Declaration on Race and Racial Prejudice adopted in 1978 affirmed the importance of culture to the identity of people.

The cases involving discrimination and culture have usually dealt with discrimination in the enjoyment of a cultural right.

For example, in the leading case of *Lovelace v. Canada*, the UN HRC held that Sandra Lovelace had been denied the right to enjoy her Maliseet Indian culture when she was prevented from living in the Maliseet community after divorcing her husband. The HRC found that the interference with her rights under article 27 of the ICCPR (minority rights) were neither reasonable nor objectively justified for the alleged purpose of protecting the Maliseet culture.[107] The right protected in this case was the right to participate in one's culture. It was the enjoyment of this right that was limited because the petitioner did not meet the criteria of belonging to the cultural community of the Maliseet. In reality this right was limited because Sandra Lovelace was a woman—and therefore lost the right to live in the Maliseet community after her divorce.

Nevertheless, there may be cases in which one culture is favored over another. Such discrimination is prohibited unless the state can show that it has an overwhelming interest in making a distinction between cultures.

---

[107] *Lovelace v. Canada*, UN HRC Comm. No. 24 (1977).

DISABILITY

Disability is a vulnerability for which there has been longstanding concern in the international community.[108] Despite this concern, it was not until March 2007 that a treaty was adopted to combat discrimination based on disability.

This treaty is entitled the International Convention on the Protection and Promotion of the Rights and Dignity of Persons with Disabilities ("UN Disability Convention").[109]

In 1999, the regional Inter-American system for the protection of human rights had already adopted a treaty entitled the Inter-American Convention on the Elimination of All Forms of Discrimination against Persons with Disabilities. ("Inter-American Disability Convention").[110] A Committee for the Elimination of All Forms of Discrimination against Persons with

---

[108] *See, for example,* Declaration on the Rights of Mentally Retarded Persons, GA res. 2856 (XXVI), 26 UN GAOR Supp. (No. 29) at 93, UN Doc. A/8429 (1971); Principles for the Protection of Persons with Mental Illnesses and the Improvement of Mental Health Care, GA res. 46/119, 46 UN GAOR Supp. (No. 49) at 189, UN Doc. A/46/49 (1991); and Declaration on the Rights of Disabled Persons, GA res. 3447 (XXX), 30 UN GAOR Supp. (No. 34) at 88, UN Doc. A/10034 (1975).

[109] The Convention on the Rights of Persons with Disabilities was opened for signature at the UN on 30 March 2007. *See* Treaty Annex for text.

[110] OAS Doc. No. AG/RES. 1608 (7 June 1999).

Disabilities is foreseen by this treaty, 111 but only with the authority to review state reports. No individual complaint procedure is foreseen, but there is nothing to stop disabled individuals from claiming their rights before the Inter-American Commission or Court.

Disability Defined

The term 'disabled' has been the subject of significant controversy. This is because it can be defined very broadly. For example, the World Health Organization's *International Classification of Functioning, Disability and Health*[112] defines a disability as any impairment of learning, the physical ability to accomplish general social tasks and demands, communication, mobility, self-care, domestic life, interpersonal interactions and relationships, major life areas, or, community, social, and civic life. International law provides more manageable legal definitions.

The new UN Disability Convention defines a disabled person as any individuals having "long-term physical, mental, intellectual or sensory impairments which in interaction with various barriers may hinder their full and effective participation in society on an equal basis with others."[113]

The Inter-American Disability Convention similarly defines 'disability' as "a physical, mental, or sensory impairment, whether permanent or temporary, that limits the capacity to perform one or more essential activities of daily life, and which can be caused or aggravated by the economic and social environment."[114]

The New UN Convention

The new UN Disability Convention contains general protections against discrimination for all persons suffering from a variety of disabilities (see description above).

The general principles underlying the Convention are stated as (a) respect; (b) non-discrimination; (c) participation in society; (d) respect for difference; (e) equal opportunity; (f) accessibility; (g) equality between men

---

[111] *Id.* at art. VI.

[112] This WHO publication was last significantly revised in May 2001 and can be accessed online at http://www3.who.int/icf/icftemplate.cfm.

[113] Art. 1, para 2 of the UN Disability Convention.

[114] *Supra*, note 110, at art. I.

and women; and (h) respect for the evolving capacities of children with disabilities and their identities.[115]

Although many rights are already protected in other human rights treaties some new ones have been added and others have been specified as being particularly relevant to disabled persons. One of the new rights is the right of disabled persons to be included in their community.[116] This right is important legally because it is one of the articles that appear to require affirmative action by states. In other words, states are required to "take effective and appropriate measures to facilitate full enjoyment by persons with disabilities of this right and their full inclusion and participation in the community."[117]

There are also important provisions on privacy requiring states to specifically "protect the privacy of personal, health and rehabilitation information of persons with disabilities on an equal basis with others."[118]

While the treaty contains provisions for a Committee on the Rights of Persons with Disabilities,[119] only state reports are foreseen by the treaty. There is, however, an Optional Protocol to the UN Disability Convention that has been opened for signature and ratification which, like the first Optional Protocol to the ICCPR, contains the right of individual communications.

---

[115] Art. 3 of the UN Disability Convention.
[116] Art. 19 of the UN Disability Convention.
[117] *Id.*
[118] Art. 22 of the UN Disability Convention.
[119] Artt. 34-39 of the UN Disability Convention.

AGE

An aging population in many counties around the world has made age discrimination an increasingly important concern. It is a serious concern as increasingly cut-throat-capitalist societies renege on their commitments to the welfare of pensioners or retired persons. It is likely that what pensioners do not secure with legal rights may be lost. For this reason issues involving discrimination based on age are likely to become more important in coming years as most populations continue to age.

Age discrimination takes place when someone is disadvantaged because they are considered too old or too young. Children may be the subject of age discrimination when they are not treated with the special care required by international human rights law, for example, in the criminal justice system.[120] More usually, however, age discrimination concerns persons of old age and often matters of employment.

Responding to these concerns the United Nations adopted the Principles of Older Persons in 1991.[121] This was necessary because when many human rights instruments were being drafted between 1965 and 1980 the world's aging population was not a major concern, especially for western states. Now that has changed and particularly western populations are aging.

---

[120] *See, for example*, art. 10(2) (b) of the ICCPR. *Also see* art. 2(1) of the CRC.
[121] UN GA Res. 46/91, UN GAOR, 46th Sess., 74th plen. mtg., Annex 1, UN Doc. A/RES/46/91 (1991).

The ICCPR, for example, does not include a specific prohibition of discrimination based on age, but the words "other status" in articles 2 and 26 of the ICCPR, as in other human rights instruments, have been interpreted as prohibiting age discrimination.[122]

State Discretion

The UN HRC has considered claims of discrimination based on age concluding that "age" is another characteristic for which discrimination is prohibited. It has, however, not yet found discrimination to have occurred. This is in part because of the wide margin of appreciation that has been given to states in considering age. This margin of appreciation allows states to make distinctions based on age for clearly stated reasons—a noticeably less stringent test then for gender, race, or nationality discrimination. For example, states' setting early retirement ages for pilots[123] and denying reductions to pensioners' partners have been found to have been acting in a permissible manner.[124]

Thus while age discrimination constitutes a growing problem, significant discretion (margin of appreciation) has been left to states for determining how they will deal with the problem.

This state discretion or margin of appreciation has been recognized by both the European institutions[125] and the UN HRC.[126] For a petitioner to be successful in proving age discrimination it is necessary not only to show that a distinction is based on age, but also that the distinction is not reasonably justified.

---

[122] *See Love v. Australia*, UN HRC Comm. No. 983 (2001) (although no discrimination was found to be proven in this case).

[123] *Id.*

[124] *Schmitz de Jong v. Nederlands*, UN HRC Comm. No. 855 (1999).

[125] *See* European Union Framework Directive (in the Annex of instruments). This Directive exempts members of the armed forces (art. 3) and age discrimination that is "objectively and reasonably justified" (art. 6).

[126] *See, supra* notes 98-100.

SOCIAL AND POLITICAL STATUS

Social Status is one of the broadest most widespread and most debilitating of all forms of discrimination. It includes discrimination based on, among other types of status, martial status, economic status, and political status.

Family Status

Closely related to gender discrimination is discrimination on the grounds of one's family status. The most common type of discrimination based on family status is that based on martial status. The type of marriage we are concerned with is primarily the legal act that changes one's social status to "married" as compared to the religious ceremony that may or may not have a legal consequence.

A person may be "married" or "single" or "divorced" or "separated" or "living with a partner." A person may also have a relationship with a partner of a different sex, or, in some countries, with a partner of the same sex. The type of relationships that are legally recognized will depend on the local law.

The UN HRC has several times found discrimination based on martial status to be allowed upholding laws that distinguished between married and unmarried couples concerning disability insurance[127] and benefits for as surviving spouse.[128]

There may also be discrimination on the basis of one's biological family status. For example, some countries prevent or make it much more difficult for an illegitimate child to inherit. Similarly, whether a child is cared for by his own parents or a legal guardian may be a ground on which the child is discriminated against. The ECtHR has been less tolerant of such distinctions and has several times found discrimination to exist where the law distinguishes between the visitation rights of unmarried and married parents of biological children.[129] One explanation for these cases would appear to be the special protection that children require, as is evidenced by the CRC.

And finally, whether a woman is pregnant or not may also constitute a ground of discrimination related both to gender discrimination as well as discrimination based on family status.

Political Opinion

Discrimination based on political or other opinion is expressly prohibited in articles 2 and 26 of the ICCPR and in most other universal and regional human rights instruments, but notably not under the laws of the European Union. Proving discrimination based on political opinion is, however, often very difficult.

The UN HRC has held that affirmative action based on redressing past discrimination against members of a certain political group might be warranted even if it constitutes discrimination against persons with particular political views.[130]

---

[127] See *Danning v. Nederlands*, UN HRC Comm. No. 180 (1984).

[128] See *Hoffdman v. Nederlands*, UN HRC. Comm. No. 602 (1994). *Also see Karner v. Austria*, ECtHR Appl. No. 40016/98 (27 July 2003) (finding a violation of article 14 and 8 of the ECHR where the law discriminated against same-sex partners in relation to rights of succession).

[129]*See Sahin v. Germany*, ECtHR Appl. No. 30943/96 (11 October 2001) and *Hoffmann v Germany*, ECtHR Appl. No. 34045 /96 (8 July 2001).

[130] *Stalla Costa v. Uruguay*, UN HRC Comm. No. 198 (1985).

The UN HRC has also held that imposing longer terms of service on conscientious objectors doing alternative service than on soldiers, constitutes prohibited discrimination.[131]

The protection of this right has often been connected to the right to freedom of expression.[132]

Economic Status

Approximately half the people in the world live on less than 2 Euro per day and as a significant consequence of this economic disparity they lose billions of life years each year to preventable diseases, occupational injuries, and inadequate access to health care. Given this picture of disparity in economic status one might expect that some steps would be taken to provide protection for people who are *de facto* suffering from economic discrimination. Instead society general accepts these economic disparities.

Although discrimination on the basis economic status may be among the most serious forms of discrimination, it is not addressed by any of the universally applicable treaties. Instead, it is usually left to be dealt with under specific economic rights that are granted in the ICESCR and the regional instruments such as the European Social Charter. Whether these human rights can be applied so as to effectively overcome a substantial history of economic disparity against person of lower economic means has yet to be seen.

In the regional context, there has been some attention to paid to non-discrimination in instruments such as the ACHR, ACHPR, and ACRWC.[133] Article 1 of the ACHR refers to economic status. Article 2 of the ACHPR and article 3 of the ACRWC protect all individuals and children respectively, from discrimination based on fortune. And, article 2 of the CRC, the most widely ratified human rights treaty in the world, and article 1 of the CRMW, protect children from discrimination from discrimination based on property.[134]

---

[131] *Foin v. France*, UN HRC Comm. No. 666 (1995).

[132] *For example, see, Amnesty International v. Zambia*, ACHPR Comm. No. 212 (1998) (in which the Commission held that two prominent political figures had been discriminated against because of their political opinions when they were deported from their own country).

[133] For the text of each of these provisions consult the Treaties annex.

[134] *Also see* artt. 1 and 2 of the Arab Charter on Human Rights in Treaties annex.

In a related development, on 26 April 2006, the government of the Dominican Republic lodged a communication with the ICJ claiming that one of its diplomats had been denied recognition by the Swiss government because he was allegedly "a business man."[135] Here the claim seems to be that the Swiss state is discriminating against a diplomat because of his economic activities, which the government of the Dominican Republic argues are not prohibited by diplomatic law.

---

[135] *Commonwealth of Dominica v. Switzerland*, Application of the Commonwealth of Dominica, filed with the ICJ on 26 April 2006.

OTHER FORMS OF DISCRIMINATION

Many individuals are protected from discrimination because of their special characteristic of belonging to a special vulnerable group. This is true of the types of discrimination already described as well as of discrimination of other groups such as refugees, displaced persons, and minorities. Protection from certain forms of discrimination is also possible through special regime. For example, European nationals are protected from discrimination based on nationality in any EU state when involved in a variety of economic activities.

Refugees

Refugees are protected from discrimination in most countries around the world by the UN inspired Geneva Refugee Convention from 1951. The treaty provides that refugees' rights will be respected to same degree as the human rights of nationals or as those of all other aliens. This protection is particularly important because the usual protector of an individual's rights when they are abroad is his or her state. In the case of refugees, persecution by their home state is the reason they are abroad.

While not all refugee rights involve discrimination, the rights of refugees to be treated equality with other aliens or even with a state's own nationals raises special issues of non-discrimination.

Displaced Persons

While the estimated ten million refugees around the world enjoy the both specific treaty protections and an inter-governmental body to defend their rights, more than twice as many internally displaced persons (IDPs) around the world have no special treaty to protect them. Instead only a non-binding set of principles have been adopted by the General Assembly.[136] These principles do, however, prohibit states from treating displaced persons less favorably then other citizens and even provide internally displaced person rights of special protection.

It would seem that for the same reasons as refugees, IDPs deserve protection. Perhaps the need of IDPs is even greater as they do not have another state to protect them and they often fall into a gap between the state's limited resources and the state's obligations to its already settled citizens. At the moment, however, there seems to be little will in the international community to create a new treaty protecting IDPs from discrimination. As a result they must rely on the existing prohibitions of discrimination in general human rights treaties.

Indigenous Peoples

The protection of indigenous peoples from discrimination can be found in the ILO Convention concerning Indigenous and Tribal Peoples in Independent Countries (No. 169)[137] and has been an issue of contention in relation to the rights of indigenous peoples that has been before the UNGA or the UN's human rights bodies for many years.

The right to be free from discrimination based on one's membership in an indigenous group of people is very closely related to the right to self-determination that such people enjoy. On the one hand, the state that exercises jurisdiction over a group of indigenous people must ensure that these people are not discriminated against. On the other hand, the failure of

---

[136] Guiding Principles on Internal Displacement, UN Doc. E/CN.4/1998/ 53/Add.2 (11 February 1998).

[137] See Treaties annex for the text of this treaty.

the state to ensure this protection against discrimination is often what provides the basis for the right to self-determination. The situation in South Africa—although commonly viewed as one of race—also concerns the rights of the indigenous black population.

Minorities

The protection of minorities from discrimination is not new. After World War I the victorious states adopted provisions in the Treaty of Versailles (1919) treaty giving minorities procedural rights and encouraging states to adopt bi- and multilateral treaties securing the rights of minorities.

The protections enjoyed by members of minorities in article 27 of the ICCPR are well-known, but they are not clearly protections against discrimination. Instead they are special rights to which members of a minority are entitled, namely the right to use their own language, the right to practice their religion, and the right to participate in practices related to their own culture.

The more recent European Framework Convention for the Protection of National Minorities[138] does provide specific protections against discrimination, but its weak link is that it allows states to determine which people constitute national minorities.[139] Some states have used this provision to declare that they have no minorities within their borders.

Other Protections for Specific Groups

Although it is not technically correct to call persons in this group privileged it is nevertheless a means of setting them apart from those who are protected because of special vulnerability. The privilege of protection against certain forms of discrimination is usually granted by a special treaty regime.

Perhaps the best example of this type of protection is that offered by the EU legal regime which consists of the EU treaties and legislation of EU bodies. Applying the principle of non-discrimination in this context the ECJ has determined that interferences with the free movement of services, goods, and workers may constitute discrimination prohibited by EU law. The three grounds of prohibited discrimination are (1) EU nationality, (2) gender or sex, and (3) producers and consumers in the field of agriculture.[140] It is

---

[138] See excerpt of text in Treaties annex.

[139] CETS No. 157, entered into force 1 February 1998.

[140] Graig, P., and Búrca, de, G., *EC Law: Text, Cases and Materials*, Oxford, UK: Claredon Press (1995) at 357. *Also see* Consolidated Versions of the Treaty on

important to note that these protections do not apply to non-European citizens.

The ECJ has found a general principle of non-discrimination on grounds of nationality—still of course, only applicable to EU citizens—in Article 12 of the EU treaty, but holding that this provision "applies independently only to situations governed by Community law for which the Treaty lays down no specific rules of non-discrimination."[141]

Some of the specific rules of non-discrimination referred to by the Court are the EU Directives.[142]

Another group of persons protected with much less legislation, are Roma. Roma are members of an ethnic group numbering about 15 million worldwide who are believed to originate in the Indian sub-continent or Southern and Eastern Europe,[143] although today they can be found in many parts of the world. While once characterized as nomadic, today most Roma are established members of the permanent community in which they live.

Nevertheless, Roma often suffer discrimination because in he communities in which they live, the majority often consider the Roma to be migrants and not indigenous, despite the fact that the Roma are often settled there for many generations.

The European Parliament has adopted resolutions on Roma[144] and the European Commissioner for Human Rights has produced a report documenting the human rights abuses against Roma in Europe.[145] There are also cases of the European Court of Human Rights finding Roma rights to

---

European Union and of the Treaty Establishing the European Community in the *Official Journal of the European Union*, No. C 321 E/1 (29 December 2006).

[141] *Kaj Lyyski v. Umeå universitet*, ECJ Case No. C-40/05 (11 January 2007) at para. 33. Also *see Oteiza Olazabal*, ECJ Case No. C-100/01, I ECR 10981 (2002) at para. 25; AMOK, ECJ Case No. C-289/02, I ECR 15059 (2003) at para. 25 and *Weigel*, ECJ Case No. C-387/01, I ECR 4981 (2004) at para. 57.

[142] See the Other Instruments annex for examples of these Directives.

[143] Because the Roma rely on oral instead of written history their exact origins are often contested. Moreover, several different linguistic and cultural categories of Roma ethnicity can be found today.

[144] *See, for example*, European Parliament resolution on the situation of the Roma in the European Union, EP Doc. No. P6_TA(2005)0151 adopted on 28 April 2005.

[145] Final Report by Mr. Alvaro Gil-Robles, Commissioner For Human Rights, on The Human Rights Situation of the Roma, Sinti and Travellers in Europe for the Attention of the Committee of Ministers and the Parliamentary Assembly. EC Doc. CommDH(2006)1.

have been violated. For example, in the leading case of *Nachova v. Bulgaria*,[146] the Court found Roma to have been discriminated against when the government failed to take into consideration possible discriminatory motives when investigating the killing of an individual of Roma ethnicity.

---

[146] For excerpts of this case see Cases annex.

EMERGING AREAS OF CONCERN

The international law relating to non-discrimination is constantly changing. This change is predominately driven by the creation of new protections against specific forms of discrimination as well as by efforts to ensure the implementation of the existing legal obligations of states.

New Standards

Although there are already numerous general and some specific prohibitions of non-discrimination under existing international law, the international community continues to create new prohibitions for specific forms of discrimination and to include general prohibitions under new human rights treaties that are meant to protect specific groups of persons.

The international community also continues to adopt non-binding instruments that include aspirations to end new forms of discrimination. Examples of these non-binding instruments are the resolution adopted by the

UN ECOSOC ensuring non-discrimination on genetic grounds[147] and the Principles on Older Persons adopted in 1991 by the UN General Assembly.[148]

Implementation

Racism is one of the forms of discrimination that has long been prohibited. Not only did states agreed to its legal prohibition in the widely-ratified CERD, but at the World Conference against Racism, Racial Discrimination, Xenophobia and Related Intolerances held in South Africa 2002 the international community committed itself to taking enhanced steps to implement the legal prohibition of racial discrimination. To achieve this goal the international community agreed to meet regularly to follow-up on the commitments it had made.

In 2003, the governments that had met in Durban a year earlier formed the Inter-Governmental Working Group on the effective implementation of the Durban Declaration and Programme of Action. This Working Group further created the Working Group of Five Independent Experts on People of African Descent at its first meeting. This later body is to provide guidance for eliminating racial discrimination after consultations with states, other experts, and members of civil society. Both these Working Groups consist of mainly developing countries, and have been virtually boycotted by developed countries. One may thus question whether or not they can successfully accomplish their goals.

Indeed the lack of cooperation of developed states is a major obstacle for dealing with issues such as economic, racial, or nationality discrimination. It will be extremely difficult without the involvement of developed states, who often maintain exploitive relationships with developing states, to overcome these types of discrimination.

* * *

As these efforts and these obstacles indicate, discrimination remains a problem that has not yet been brought under control. As long as these efforts continue the hope remains that the international community can muster the courage and the will to eliminate discrimination on the most serious grounds, such as race, religion and gender. The continued attention that

---

[147] ECOSOC Res. 2004/9 46th plenary meeting (21 July 2004).
[148] UN GA Res. 46/91, UN GAOR, 46th Sess., 74th plen. mtg., Annex 1, UN Doc. A/RES/46/91 (1991).

these and similar efforts bring to the struggle to rid the world of discriminatory practices offers some reason for hope. However, if these efforts do not begin to show concrete results that hope may quickly turn to confrontation. Despite the obstacles we must hope that eradicating discrimination from the world is, as Nelson Mandela once said, one of those things that "always seems impossible until it's done."

TREATIES

Charter of the United Nations

Adopted 26 June 1945, entered into force 24 Oct. 1945.

Article 1

The Purposes of the United Nations are ...

2. To develop friendly relations among nations based on respect for the principle of equal rights and self-determination of peoples, and to take other appropriate measures to strengthen universal peace;

3. To achieve international cooperation in solving international problems of an economic, social, cultural, or humanitarian character, and in promoting and encouraging respect for human rights and for fundamental freedoms for all without distinction as to race, sex, language, or religion...

Article 8

The United Nations shall place no restrictions on the eligibility of men and women to participate in any capacity and under conditions of equality in its principal and subsidiary organs ...

Article 55

With a view to the creation of conditions of stability and well-being which are necessary for peaceful and friendly relations among nations based on respect for the principle of equal rights and self-determination of peoples, the United Nations shall promote:

...

c. universal respect for, and observance of, human rights and fundamental freedoms for all without distinction as to race, sex, language, or religion ...

Article 56

All Members pledge themselves to take joint and separate action in co-operation with the Organization for the achievement of the purposes set forth in Article 55 ...

International Covenant on Civil and Political Rights

999 *UNTS* 14668, entered into force 23 March 1976.

Article 2

1. Each State Party to the present Covenant undertakes to respect and to ensure to all individuals within its territory and subject to its jurisdiction the rights recognized in the present Covenant, without distinction of any kind, such as race, colour, sex, language, religion, political or other opinion, national or social origin, property, birth or other status. ...

Article 26

All persons are equal before the law and are entitled without any discrimination to the equal protection of the law. In this respect, the law shall prohibit any discrimination and guarantee to all persons equal and effective protection against discrimination on any ground such as race, colour, sex, language, religion, political or other opinion, national or social origin, property, birth or other status.

International Covenant on Economic, Social and Cultural Rights

993 *UNTS* 3, entered into force 3 January 1976.

PART II

Article 2

... 2. The States Parties to the present Covenant undertake to guarantee that the rights enunciated in the present Covenant will be exercised without discrimination of any kind as to race, colour, sex, language, religion, political or other opinion, national or social origin, property, birth or other status.

3. Developing countries, with due regard to human rights and their national economy, may determine to what extent they would guarantee the economic rights recognized in the present Covenant to non-nationals.

Article 3

The States Parties to the present Covenant undertake to ensure the equal right of men and women to the enjoyment of all economic, social and cultural rights set forth in the present Covenant.

Article 7

The States Parties to the present Covenant recognize the right of everyone to the enjoyment of just and favourable conditions of work which ensure, in particular:

... (i) Fair wages and equal remuneration for work of equal value without distinction of any kind, in particular women being guaranteed conditions of work not inferior to those enjoyed by men, with equal pay for equal work;

International Convention on the Elimination of All Forms of Racial Discrimination

Adopted 21 Dec. 1965, entered into force 4 January 1969.

PART I

Article 1

1. In this Convention, the term "racial discrimination" shall mean any distinction, exclusion, restriction or preference based on race, colour, descent, or national or ethnic origin which has the purpose or effect of nullifying or impairing the recognition, enjoyment or exercise, on an equal footing, of human rights and fundamental freedoms in the political, economic, social, cultural or any other field of public life.

2. This Convention shall not apply to distinctions, exclusions, restrictions or preferences made by a State Party to this Convention between citizens and non-citizens.

3. Nothing in this Convention may be interpreted as affecting in any way the legal provisions of States Parties concerning nationality, citizenship or naturalization, provided that such provisions do not discriminate against any particular nationality.

4. Special measures taken for the sole purpose of securing adequate advancement of certain racial or ethnic groups or individuals requiring such protection as may be necessary in order to ensure such groups or individuals equal enjoyment or exercise of human rights and fundamental freedoms shall not be deemed racial discrimination, provided, however, that such measures do not, as a consequence, lead to the maintenance of separate rights for different racial groups and that they shall not be continued after the objectives for which they were taken have been achieved.

Article 2

1. States Parties condemn racial discrimination and undertake to pursue by all appropriate means and without delay a policy of eliminating racial discrimination in all its forms and promoting understanding among all races, and, to this end: (a) Each State Party undertakes to engage in no act or practice of racial discrimination against persons, groups of persons or institutions and to en sure that all public authorities and public institutions, national and local, shall act in conformity with this obligation;

(b) Each State Party undertakes not to sponsor, defend or support racial discrimination by any persons or organizations;

(c) Each State Party shall take effective measures to review governmental, national and local policies, and to amend, rescind or nullify any laws and regulations which have the effect of creating or perpetuating racial discrimination wherever it exists;

(d) Each State Party shall prohibit and bring to an end, by all appropriate means, including legislation as required by circumstances, racial discrimination by any persons, group or organization;

(e) Each State Party undertakes to encourage, where appropriate, integrationist multiracial organizations and movements and other means of eliminating barriers between races, and to discourage anything which tends to strengthen racial division.

2. States Parties shall, when the circumstances so warrant, take, in the social, economic, cultural and other fields, special and concrete measures to ensure the adequate development and protection of certain racial groups or individuals belonging to them, for the purpose of guaranteeing them the full and equal enjoyment of human rights and fundamental freedoms. These measures shall in no case en tail as a con sequence the maintenance of unequal or separate rights for different racial groups after the objectives for which they were taken have been achieved.

Article 3

States Parties particularly condemn racial segregation and apartheid and undertake to prevent, prohibit and eradicate all practices of this nature in territories under their jurisdiction.

Article 4

States Parties condemn all propaganda and all organizations which are based on ideas or theories of superiority of one race or group of persons of one colour or ethnic origin, or which attempt to justify or promote racial hatred and discrimination in any form, and undertake to adopt immediate and positive measures designed to eradicate all incitement to, or acts of, such discrimination and, to this end, with due regard to the principles embodied in the Universal Declaration of Human Rights and the rights expressly set forth in article 5 of this Convention, *inter alia*:

(a) Shall declare an offence punishable by law all dissemination of ideas based on racial superiority or hatred, incitement to racial discrimination, as well as all acts of violence or incitement to such acts against any race or group of persons of another colour or ethnic origin, and also the provision of any assistance to racist activities, including the financing thereof;

(b) Shall declare illegal and prohibit organizations, and also organized and all other propaganda activities, which promote and incite racial discrimination, and shall recognize participation in such organizations or activities as an offence punishable by law;

(c) Shall not permit public authorities or public institutions, national or local, to promote or incite racial discrimination.

Article 5

In compliance with the fundamental obligations laid down in article 2 of this Convention, States Parties undertake to prohibit and to eliminate racial discrimination in all its forms and to guarantee the right of everyone, without distinction as to race, colour, or national or ethnic origin, to equality before the law, notably in the enjoyment of the following rights:

(a) The right to equal treatment before the tribunals and all other organs administering justice;

(b) The right to security of person and protection by the State against violence or bodily harm, whether inflicted by government officials or by any individual group or institution;

(c) Political rights, in particular the right to participate in elections-to vote and to stand for election-on the basis of universal and equal suffrage, to take part in the Government as well as in the conduct of public affairs at any level and to have equal access to public service;

(d) Other civil rights, in particular:

(i) The right to freedom of movement and residence within the border of the State;

(ii) The right to leave any country, including one's own, and to return to one's country;

(iii) The right to nationality;

(iv) The right to marriage and choice of spouse;

(v) The right to own property alone as well as in association with others;

(vi) The right to inherit;

(vii) The right to freedom of thought, conscience and religion;

(viii) The right to freedom of opinion and expression;

(ix) The right to freedom of peaceful assembly and association;

(e) Economic, social and cultural rights, in particular:

(i) The rights to work, to free choice of employment, to just and favourable conditions of work, to protection against unemployment, to equal pay for equal work, to just and favourable remuneration;

(ii) The right to form and join trade unions;

(iii) The right to housing;

(iv) The right to public health, medical care, social security and social services;

(v) The right to education and training;

(vi) The right to equal participation in cultural activities;

(f) The right of access to any place or service intended for use by the general public, such as transport hotels, restaurants, cafes, theatres and parks.

Article 6

States Parties shall assure to everyone within their jurisdiction effective protection and remedies, through the competent national tribunals and other State institutions, against any acts of racial discrimination which violate his human rights and fundamental freedoms contrary to this Convention, as well as the right to seek from such tribunals just and adequate reparation or satisfaction for any damage suffered as a result of such discrimination.

Article 7

States Parties undertake to adopt immediate and effective measures, particularly in the fields of teaching, education, culture and information, with a view to combating prejudices which lead to racial discrimination and to promoting understanding, tolerance and friendship among nations and racial or ethnical groups, as well as to propagating the purposes and principles of the Charter of the United Nations, the Universal Declaration of Human Rights, the United Nations Declaration on the Elimination of All Forms of Racial Discrimination, and this Convention.

PART II

Article 8

1. There shall be established a Committee on the Elimination of Racial Discrimination (hereinafter referred to as the Committee) consisting of eighteen experts of high moral standing and acknowledged impartiality elected by States Parties from among their nationals, who shall serve in their personal capacity, consideration being given to equitable geographical

distribution and to the representation of the different forms of civilization as well as of the principal legal systems.

2. The members of the Committee shall be elected by secret ballot from a list of persons nominated by the States Parties. Each State Party may nominate one person from among its own nationals.

3. The initial election shall be held six months after the date of the entered into force of this Convention. At least three months before the date of each election the Secretary-General of the United Nations shall address a letter to the States Parties inviting them to submit their nominations within two months. The Secretary-General shall prepare a list in alphabetical order of all persons thus nominated, indicating the States Parties which have nominated them, and shall submit it to the States Parties.

4. Elections of the members of the Committee shall be held at a meeting of States Parties convened by the Secretary-General at United Nations Headquarters. At that meeting, for which two thirds of the States Parties shall constitute a quorum, the persons elected to the Committee shall be nominees who obtain the largest number of votes and an absolute majority of the votes of the representatives of States Parties present and voting.

5. (a) The members of the Committee shall be elected for a term of four years. However, the terms of nine of the members elected at the first election shall expire at the end of two years; immediately after the first election the names of these nine members shall be chosen by lot by the Chairman of the Committee;

(b) For the filling of casual vacancies, the State Party whose expert has ceased to function as a member of the Committee shall appoint another expert from among its nationals, subject to the approval of the Committee.

6. States Parties shall be responsible for the expenses of the members of the Committee while they are in performance of Committee duties.

Article 9

1. States Parties undertake to submit to the Secretary-General of the United Nations, for consideration by the Committee, a report on the legislative, judicial, administrative or other measures which they have adopted and which give effect to the provisions of this Convention: (a) within one year after the entered into force of the Convention for the State concerned; and

(b) thereafter every two years and whenever the Committee so requests. The Committee may request further information from the States Parties.

2. The Committee shall report annually, through the Secretary General, to the General Assembly of the United Nations on its activities and may make suggestions and general recommendations based on the examination of the reports and information received from the States Parties. Such suggestions and general recommendations shall be reported to the General Assembly together with comments, if any, from States Parties.

Article 10

1. The Committee shall adopt its own rules of procedure.

2. The Committee shall elect its officers for a term of two years.

3. The secretariat of the Committee shall be provided by the Secretary General of the United Nations.

4. The meetings of the Committee shall normally be held at United Nations Headquarters.

Article 11

1. If a State Party considers that another State Party is not giving effect to the provisions of this Convention, it may bring the matter to the attention of the Committee. The Committee shall then transmit the communication to the State Party concerned. Within three months, the receiving State shall submit to the Committee written explanations or statements clarifying the matter and the remedy, if any, that may have been taken by that State.

2. If the matter is not adjusted to the satisfaction of both parties, either by bilateral negotiations or by any other procedure open to them, within six months after the receipt by the receiving State of the initial communication, either State shall have the right to refer the matter again to the Committee by notifying the Committee and also the other State.

3. The Committee shall deal with a matter referred to it in accordance with paragraph 2 of this article after it has ascertained that all available domestic remedies have been invoked and exhausted in the case, in conformity with the generally recognized principles of international law. This shall not be the rule where the application of the remedies is unreasonably prolonged.

4. In any matter referred to it, the Committee may call upon the States Parties concerned to supply any other relevant information.

5. When any matter arising out of this article is being considered by the Committee, the States Parties concerned shall be entitled to send a representative to take part in the proceedings of the Committee, without voting rights, while the matter is under consideration.

Article 12

1. (a) After the Committee has obtained and collated all the information it deems necessary, the Chairman shall appoint an ad hoc Conciliation Commission (hereinafter referred to as the Commission) comprising five persons who may or may not be members of the Committee. The members of the Commission shall be appointed with the unanimous consent of the parties to the dispute, and its good offices shall be made available to the States concerned with a view to an amicable solution of the matter on the basis of respect for this Convention;

(b) If the States parties to the dispute fail to reach agreement within three months on all or part of the composition of the Commission, the members of the Commission not agreed upon by the States parties to the dispute shall be elected by secret ballot by a two-thirds majority vote of the Committee from among its own members.

2. The members of the Commission shall serve in their personal capacity. They shall not be nationals of the States parties to the dispute or of a State not Party to this Convention.

3. The Commission shall elect its own Chairman and adopt its own rules of procedure.

4. The meetings of the Commission shall normally be held at United Nations Headquarters or at any other convenient place as determined by the Commission.

5. The secretariat provided in accordance with article 10, paragraph 3, of this Convention shall also service the Commission whenever a dispute among States Parties brings the Commission into being.

6. The States parties to the dispute shall share equally all the expenses of the members of the Commission in accordance with estimates to be provided by the Secretary-General of the United Nations.

7. The Secretary-General shall be empowered to pay the expenses of the members of the Commission, if necessary, before reimbursement by the States parties to the dispute in accordance with paragraph 6 of this article.

8. The information obtained and collated by the Committee shall be made available to the Commission, and the Commission may call upon the States concerned to supply any other relevant information.

Article 13

1. When the Commission has fully considered the matter, it shall prepare and submit to the Chairman of the Committee a report embodying its findings on all questions of fact relevant to the issue between the parties and containing such recommendations as it may think proper for the amicable solution of the dispute.

2. The Chairman of the Committee shall communicate the report of the Commission to each of the States parties to the dispute. These States shall, within three months, inform the Chairman of the Committee whether or not they accept the recommendations contained in the report of the Commission.

3. After the period provided for in paragraph 2 of this article, the Chairman of the Committee shall communicate the report of the Commission and the declarations of the States Parties concerned to the other States Parties to this Convention.

Article 14

1. A State Party may at any time declare that it recognizes the competence of the Committee to receive and consider communications from individuals or groups of individuals within its jurisdiction claiming to be victims of a violation by that State Party of any of the rights set forth in this Convention. No communication shall be received by the Committee if it concerns a State Party which has not made such a declaration.

2. Any State Party which makes a declaration as provided for in paragraph I of this article may establish or indicate a body within its national legal order which shall be competent to receive and consider petitions from individuals and groups of individuals within its jurisdiction who claim to be victims of a violation of any of the rights set forth in this Convention and who have exhausted other available local remedies.

3. A declaration made in accordance with paragraph 1 of this article and the name of any body established or indicated in accordance with paragraph 2 of this article shall be deposited by the State Party concerned with the Secretary-General of the United Nations, who shall transmit copies thereof to the other States Parties. A declaration may be withdrawn at any time by notification to the Secretary-General, but such a withdrawal shall not affect communications pending before the Committee.

4. A register of petitions shall be kept by the body established or indicated in accordance with paragraph 2 of this article, and certified copies of the register shall be filed annually through appropriate channels with the Secretary-General on the understanding that the contents shall not be publicly disclosed.

5. In the event of failure to obtain satisfaction from the body established or indicated in accordance with paragraph 2 of this article, the petitioner shall have the right to communicate the matter to the Committee within six months.

6. (a) The Committee shall confidentially bring any communication referred to it to the attention of the State Party alleged to be violating any provision of this Convention, but the identity of the individual or groups of individuals concerned shall not be revealed without his or their express consent. The Committee shall not receive anonymous communications;

(b) Within three months, the receiving State shall submit to the Committee written explanations or statements clarifying the matter and the remedy, if any, that may have been taken by that State.

7. (a) The Committee shall consider communications in the light of all information made available to it by the State Party concerned and by the petitioner. The Committee shall not consider any communication from a petitioner unless it has ascertained that the petitioner has exhausted all available domestic remedies. However, this shall not be the rule where the application of the remedies is unreasonably prolonged;

(b) The Committee shall forward its suggestions and recommendations, if any, to the State Party concerned and to the petitioner.

8. The Committee shall include in its annual report a summary of such communications and, where appropriate, a summary of the explanations and statements of the States Parties concerned and of its own suggestions and recommendations.

9. The Committee shall be competent to exercise the functions provided for in this article only when at least ten States Parties to this Convention are bound by declarations in accordance with paragraph I of this article.

Article 15

1. Pending the achievement of the objectives of the Declaration on the Granting of Independence to Colonial Countries and Peoples, contained in General Assembly resolution 1514 (XV) of 14 December 1960, the provisions of this Convention shall in no way limit the right of petition

granted to these peoples by other international instruments or by the United Nations and its specialized agencies.

2. (a) The Committee established under article 8, paragraph 1, of this Convention shall receive copies of the petitions from, and submit expressions of opinion and recommendations on these petitions to, the bodies of the United Nations which deal with matters directly related to the principles and objectives of this Convention in their consideration of petitions from the inhabitants of Trust and Non-Self-Governing Territories and all other territories to which General Assembly resolution 1514 (XV) applies, relating to matters covered by this Convention which are before these bodies;

(b) The Committee shall receive from the competent bodies of the United Nations copies of the reports concerning the legislative, judicial, administrative or other measures directly related to the principles and objectives of this Convention applied by the administering Powers within the Territories mentioned in subparagraph (a) of this paragraph, and shall express opinions and make recommendations to these bodies.

3. The Committee shall include in its report to the General Assembly a summary of the petitions and reports it has received from United Nations bodies, and the expressions of opinion and recommendations of the Committee relating to the said petitions and reports.

4. The Committee shall request from the Secretary-General of the United Nations all information relevant to the objectives of this Convention and available to him regarding the Territories mentioned in paragraph 2 (a) of this article.

Article 16

The provisions of this Convention concerning the settlement of disputes or complaints shall be applied without prejudice to other procedures for settling disputes or complaints in the field of discrimination laid down in the constituent instruments of, or conventions adopted by, the United Nations and its specialized agencies, and shall not prevent the States Parties from having recourse to other procedures for settling a dispute in accordance with general or special international agreements in force between them ...

Convention on the Elimination of All Forms of Discrimination against Women

Adopted and opened for signature, ratification and accession by UN GA Res.
34/180 of 18 December 1979
entered into force 3 September 1981.

PART I

Article 1

For the purposes of the present Convention, the term "discrimination against women" shall mean any distinction, exclusion or restriction made on the basis of sex which has the effect or purpose of impairing or nullifying the recognition, enjoyment or exercise by women, irrespective of their marital status, on a basis of equality of men and women, of human rights and fundamental freedoms in the political, economic, social, cultural, civil or any other field.

Article 2

States Parties condemn discrimination against women in all its forms, agree to pursue by all appropriate means and without delay a policy of eliminating discrimination against women and, to this end, undertake:

(a) To embody the principle of the equality of men and women in their national constitutions or other appropriate legislation if not yet incorporated therein and to ensure, through law and other appropriate means, the practical realization of this principle;

(b) To adopt appropriate legislative and other measures, including sanctions where appropriate, prohibiting all discrimination against women; (c) To establish legal protection of the rights of women on an equal basis with men and to ensure through competent national tribunals and other public institutions the effective protection of women against any act of discrimination;

(d) To refrain from engaging in any act or practice of discrimination against women and to ensure that public authorities and institutions shall act in conformity with this obligation;

(e) To take all appropriate measures to eliminate discrimination against women by any person, organization or enterprise;

(f) To take all appropriate measures, including legislation, to modify or abolish existing laws, regulations, customs and practices which constitute discrimination against women;

(g) To repeal all national penal provisions which constitute discrimination against women.

Article 3

States Parties shall take in all fields, in particular in the political, social, economic and cultural fields, all appropriate measures, including legislation, to en sure the full development and advancement of women , for the purpose of guaranteeing them the exercise and enjoyment of human rights and fundamental freedoms on a basis of equality with men.

Article 4

1. Adoption by States Parties of temporary special measures aimed at accelerating de facto equality between men and women shall not be considered discrimination as defined in the present Convention, but shall in no way entail as a consequence the maintenance of unequal or separate standards; these measures shall be discontinued when the objectives of equality of opportunity and treatment have been achieved.

2. Adoption by States Parties of special measures, including those measures contained in the present Convention, aimed at protecting maternity shall not be considered discriminatory.

Article 5

States Parties shall take all appropriate measures:

(a) To modify the social and cultural patterns of conduct of men and women, with a view to achieving the elimination of prejudices and customary and all other practices which are based on the idea of the inferiority or the superiority of either of the sexes or on stereotyped roles for men and women;

 (b) To ensure that family education includes a proper understanding of maternity as a social function and the recognition of the common responsibility of men and women in the upbringing and development of their children, it being understood that the interest of the children is the primordial consideration in all cases.

Article 6

States Parties shall take all appropriate measures, including legislation, to suppress all forms of traffic in women and exploitation of prostitution of women.

PART II

Article 7

States Parties shall take all appropriate measures to eliminate discrimination against women in the political and public life of the country and, in particular, shall ensure to women, on equal terms with men, the right:

(a) To vote in all elections and public referenda and to be eligible for election to all publicly elected bodies;

(b) To participate in the formulation of government policy and the implementation thereof and to hold public office and perform all public functions at all levels of government;

(c) To participate in non-governmental organizations and associations concerned with the public and political life of the country.

Article 8

States Parties shall take all appropriate measures to ensure to women, on equal terms with men and without any discrimination, the opportunity to represent their Governments at the international level and to participate in the work of international organizations.

Article 9

1. States Parties shall grant women equal rights with men to acquire, change or retain their nationality. They shall ensure in particular that neither marriage to an alien nor change of nationality by the husband during marriage shall automatically change the nationality of the wife, render her stateless or force upon her the nationality of the husband. 2. States Parties shall grant women equal rights with men with respect to the nationality of their children.

PART III

Article 10

States Parties shall take all appropriate measures to eliminate discrimination against women in order to ensure to them equal rights with men in the field of education and in particular to ensure, on a basis of equality of men and women:

(a) The same conditions for career and vocational guidance, for access to studies and for the achievement of diplomas in educational establishments of all categories in rural as well as in urban areas; this equality shall be ensured in pre-school, general, technical, professional and higher technical education, as well as in all types of vocational training;

(b) Access to the same curricula, the same examinations, teaching staff with qualifications of the same standard and school premises and equipment of the same quality;

(c) The elimination of any stereotyped concept of the roles of men and women at all levels and in all forms of education by encouraging coeducation and other types of education which will help to achieve this aim and, in particular, by the revision of textbooks and school programmes and the adaptation of teaching methods;

(d) The same opportunities to benefit from scholarships and other study grants;

(e) The same opportunities for access to programmes of continuing education, including adult and functional literacy programmes, particularly those aimed at reducing, at the earliest possible time, any gap in education existing between men and women;

(f) The reduction of female student drop-out rates and the organization of programmes for girls and women who have left school prematurely;

(g) The same Opportunities to participate actively in sports and physical education;

(h) Access to specific educational information to help to ensure the health and well-being of families, including information and advice on family planning.

Article 11

1. States Parties shall take all appropriate measures to eliminate discrimination against women in the field of employment in order to ensure, on a basis of equality of men and women, the same rights, in particular:

(a) The right to work as an inalienable right of all human beings;

(b) The right to the same employment opportunities, including the application of the same criteria for selection in matters of employment;

(c) The right to free choice of profession and employment, the right to promotion, job security and all benefits and conditions of service and the right to receive vocational training and retraining, including apprenticeships, advanced vocational training and recurrent training;

(d) The right to equal remuneration, including benefits, and to equal treatment in respect of work of equal value, as well as equality of treatment in the evaluation of the quality of work;

(e) The right to social security, particularly in cases of retirement, unemployment, sickness, invalidity and old age and other incapacity to work, as well as the right to paid leave;

(f) The right to protection of health and to safety in working conditions, including the safeguarding of the function of reproduction.

2. In order to prevent discrimination against women on the grounds of marriage or maternity and to ensure their effective right to work, States Parties shall take appropriate measures:

(a) To prohibit, subject to the imposition of sanctions, dismissal on the grounds of pregnancy or of maternity leave and discrimination in dismissals on the basis of marital status;

(b) To introduce maternity leave with pay or with comparable social benefits without loss of former employment, seniority or social allowances;

(c) To encourage the provision of the necessary supporting social services to enable parents to combine family obligations with work responsibilities and participation in public life, in particular through promoting the establishment and development of a network of child-care facilities;

(d) To provide special protection to women during pregnancy in types of work proved to be harmful to them.

3. Protective legislation relating to matters covered in this article shall be reviewed periodically in the light of scientific and technological knowledge and shall be revised, repealed or extended as necessary.

Article 12

1. States Parties shall take all appropriate measures to eliminate discrimination against women in the field of health care in order to ensure, on a basis of equality of men and women, access to health care services, including those related to family planning.

2. Notwithstanding the provisions of paragraph I of this article, States Parties shall ensure to women appropriate services in connection with pregnancy, confinement and the post-natal period, granting free services where necessary, as well as adequate nutrition during pregnancy and lactation.

Article 13

States Parties shall take all appropriate measures to eliminate discrimination against women in other areas of economic and social life in order to ensure, on a basis of equality of men and women, the same rights, in particular:

(a) The right to family benefits;

(b) The right to bank loans, mortgages and other forms of financial credit;

(c) The right to participate in recreational activities, sports and all aspects of cultural life.

Article 14

1. States Parties shall take into account the particular problems faced by rural women and the significant roles which rural women play in the economic survival of their families, including their work in the non-monetized sectors of the economy, and shall take all appropriate measures to ensure the application of the provisions of the present Convention to women in rural areas.

2. States Parties shall take all appropriate measures to eliminate discrimination against women in rural areas in order to ensure, on a basis of equality of men and women, that they participate in and benefit from rural development and, in particular, shall ensure to such women the right:

(a) To participate in the elaboration and implementation of development planning at all levels;

(b) To have access to adequate health care facilities, including information, counselling and services in family planning;

(c) To benefit directly from social security programmes;

(d) To obtain all types of training and education, formal and non-formal, including that relating to functional literacy, as well as, inter alia, the benefit of all community and extension services, in order to increase their technical proficiency;

(e) To organize self-help groups and co-operatives in order to obtain equal access to economic opportunities through employment or self employment;

(f) To participate in all community activities;

(g) To have access to agricultural credit and loans, marketing facilities, appropriate technology and equal treatment in land and agrarian reform as well as in land resettlement schemes;

(h) To enjoy adequate living conditions, particularly in relation to housing, sanitation, electricity and water supply, transport and communications.

PART IV

Article 15

1. States Parties shall accord to women equality with men before the law.

2. States Parties shall accord to women, in civil matters, a legal capacity identical to that of men and the same opportunities to exercise that capacity. In particular, they shall give women equal rights to conclude contracts and to administer property and shall treat them equally in all stages of procedure in courts and tribunals.

3. States Parties agree that all contracts and all other private instruments of any kind with a legal effect which is directed at restricting the legal capacity of women shall be deemed null and void.

4. States Parties shall accord to men and women the same rights with regard to the law relating to the movement of persons and the freedom to choose their residence and domicile.

Article 16

1. States Parties shall take all appropriate measures to eliminate discrimination against women in all matters relating to marriage and family relations and in particular shall ensure, on a basis of equality of men and women:

(a) The same right to enter into marriage;

(b) The same right freely to choose a spouse and to enter into marriage only with their free and full consent;

(c) The same rights and responsibilities during marriage and at its dissolution;

(d) The same rights and responsibilities as parents, irrespective of their marital status, in matters relating to their children; in all cases the interests of the children shall be paramount;

(e) The same rights to decide freely and responsibly on the number and spacing of their children and to have access to the information, education and means to enable them to exercise these rights;

(f) The same rights and responsibilities with regard to guardianship, wardship, trusteeship and adoption of children, or similar institutions where these concepts exist in national legislation; in all cases the interests of the children shall be paramount;

(g) The same personal rights as husband and wife, including the right to choose a family name, a profession and an occupation;

(h) The same rights for both spouses in respect of the ownership, acquisition, management, administration, enjoyment and disposition of property, whether free of charge or for a valuable consideration.

2. The betrothal and the marriage of a child shall have no legal effect, and all necessary action, including legislation, shall be taken to specify a minimum age for marriage and to make the registration of marriages in an official registry compulsory.

PART V

Article 17

1. For the purpose of considering the progress made in the implementation of the present Convention, there shall be established a Committee on the Elimination of Discrimination against Women (hereinafter referred to as the Committee) consisting, at the time of entered into force of the Convention, of eighteen and, after ratification of or accession to the Convention by the thirty-fifth State Party, of twenty-three experts of high moral standing and competence in the field covered by the Convention. The experts shall be elected by States Parties from among their nationals and shall serve in their personal capacity, consideration being given to equitable geographical distribution and to the representation of the different forms of civilization as well as the principal legal systems.

2. The members of the Committee shall be elected by secret ballot from a list of persons nominated by States Parties. Each State Party may nominate one person from among its own nationals.

3. The initial election shall be held six months after the date of the entered into force of the present Convention. At least three months before the date of each election the Secretary-General of the United Nations shall address a letter to the States Parties inviting them to submit their nominations within two months. The Secretary-General shall prepare a list in alphabetical order

of all persons thus nominated, indicating the States Parties which have nominated them, and shall submit it to the States Parties.

4. Elections of the members of the Committee shall be held at a meeting of States Parties convened by the Secretary-General at United Nations Headquarters. At that meeting, for which two thirds of the States Parties shall constitute a quorum, the persons elected to the Committee shall be those nominees who obtain the largest number of votes and an absolute majority of the votes of the representatives of States Parties present and voting.

5. The members of the Committee shall be elected for a term of four years. However, the terms of nine of the members elected at the first election shall expire at the end of two years; immediately after the first election the names of these nine members shall be chosen by lot by the Chairman of the Committee.

6. The election of the five additional members of the Committee shall be held in accordance with the provisions of paragraphs 2, 3 and 4 of this article, following the thirty-fifth ratification or accession. The terms of two of the additional members elected on this occasion shall expire at the end of two years, the names of these two members having been chosen by lot by the Chairman of the Committee.

7. For the filling of casual vacancies, the State Party whose expert has ceased to function as a member of the Committee shall appoint another expert from among its nationals, subject to the approval of the Committee.

8. The members of the Committee shall, with the approval of the General Assembly, receive emoluments from United Nations resources on such terms and conditions as the Assembly may decide, having regard to the importance of the Committee's responsibilities.

9. The Secretary-General of the United Nations shall provide the necessary staff and facilities for the effective performance of the functions of the Committee under the present Convention.

Article 18

1. States Parties undertake to submit to the Secretary-General of the United Nations, for consideration by the Committee, a report on the legislative, judicial, administrative or other measures which they have adopted to give effect to the provisions of the present Convention and on the progress made in this respect:

(a) Within one year after the entered into force for the State concerned;

(b) Thereafter at least every four years and further whenever the Committee so requests.

2. Reports may indicate factors and difficulties affecting the degree of fulfilment of obligations under the present Convention.

Article 19

1. The Committee shall adopt its own rules of procedure. 2. The Committee shall elect its officers for a term of two years.

Article 20

1. The Committee shall normally meet for a period of not more than two weeks annually in order to consider the reports submitted in accordance with article 18 of the present Convention.

2. The meetings of the Committee shall normally be held at United Nations Headquarters or at any other convenient place as determined by the Committee.

Article 21

1. The Committee shall, through the Economic and Social Council, report annually to the General Assembly of the United Nations on its activities and may make suggestions and general recommendations based on the examination of reports and information received from the States Parties. Such suggestions and general recommendations shall be included in the report of the Committee together with comments, if any, from States Parties.

2. The Secretary-General of the United Nations shall transmit the reports of the Committee to the Commission on the Status of Women for its information.

Article 22

The specialized agencies shall be entitled to be represented at the consideration of the implementation of such provisions of the present Convention as fall within the scope of their activities. The Committee may invite the specialized agencies to submit reports on the implementation of the Convention in areas falling within the scope of their activities.

PART VI

Article 23

Nothing in the present Convention shall affect any provisions that are more conducive to the achievement of equality between men and women which may be contained:

(a) In the legislation of a State Party; or

(b) In any other international convention, treaty or agreement in force for that State.

Article 24

States Parties undertake to adopt all necessary measures at the national level aimed at achieving the full realization of the rights recognized in the present Convention...

Convention against Discrimination in Education

Adopted by the General Conference of UNESCO
on 14 December 1960, entered 22 May 1962.

Article 1

1. For the purpose of this Convention, the term "discrimination" includes any distinction, exclusion, limitation or preference which, being based on race, colour, sex, language, religion, political or other opinion, national or social origin, economic condition or birth, has the purpose or effect of nullifying or impairing equality of treatment in education and in particular:

(a) Of depriving any person or group of persons of access to education of any type or at any level;

(b) Of limiting any person or group of persons to education of an inferior standard;

(c) Subject to the provisions of article 2 of this Convention, of establishing or maintaining separate educational systems or institutions for persons or groups of persons; or

(d) Of inflicting on any person or group of persons conditions which are incompatible with the dignity of man.

2. For the purposes of this Convention, the term "education" refers to all types and levels of education, and includes access to education, the standard and quality of education, and the conditions under which it is given.

Article 2

When permitted in a State, the following situations shall not be deemed to constitute discrimination, within the meaning of article 1 of this Convention:

(a) The establishment or maintenance of separate educational systems or institutions for pupils of the two sexes, if these systems or institutions offer equivalent access to education, provide a teaching staff with qualifications of the same standard as well as school premises and equipment of the same quality, and afford the opportunity to take the same or equivalent courses of study;

b) The establishment or maintenance, for religious or linguistic reasons, of separate educational systems or institutions offering an education which is in keeping with the wishes of the pupil's parents or legal guardians, if participation in such systems or attendance at such institutions is optional and if the education provided conforms to such standards as may be laid down or approved by the competent authorities, in particular for education of the same level;

(c) The establishment or maintenance of private educational institutions, if the object of the institutions is not to secure the exclusion of any group but to provide educational facilities in addition to those provided by the public authorities, if the institutions are conducted in accordance with that object, and if the education provided conforms with such standards as may be laid down or approved by the competent authorities, in particular for education of the same level.

Article 3

In order to eliminate and prevent discrimination within the meaning of this Convention, the States Parties thereto undertake:

(a) To abrogate any statutory provisions and any administrative instructions and to discontinue any administrative practices which involve discrimination in education;

(b) To ensure, by legislation where necessary, that there is no discrimination in the admission of pupils to educational institutions;

(c) Not to allow any differences of treatment by the public authorities between nationals, except on the basis of merit or need, in the matter of school fees and the grant of scholarships or other forms of assistance to pupils and necessary permits and facilities for the pursuit of studies in foreign countries;

(d) Not to allow, in any form of assistance granted by the public authorities to educational institutions, any restrictions or preference based solely on the ground that pupils belong to a particular group;

(e) To give foreign nationals resident within their territory the same access to education as that given to their own nationals.

Article 4

The States Parties to this Convention undertake furthermore to formulate, develop and apply a national policy which, by methods appropriate to the circumstances and to national usage, will tend to promote equality of opportunity and of treatment in the matter of education and in particular:

(a) To make primary education free and compulsory; make secondary education in its different forms generally available and accessible to all; make higher education equally accessible to all on the basis of individual capacity;

assure compliance by all with the obligation to attend school prescribed by law;

(b) To ensure that the standards of education are equivalent in all public education institutions of the same level, and that the conditions relating to the quality of education provided are also equivalent;

(c) To encourage and intensify by appropriate methods the education of persons who have not received any primary education or who have not completed the entire primary education course and the continuation of their education on the basis of individual capacity;

(d) To provide training for the teaching profession without discrimination.

Article 5

1. The States Parties to this Convention agree that:
(a) Education shall be directed to the full development of the human personality and to the strengthening of respect for human rights and fundamental freedoms; it shall promote understanding, tolerance and friendship among all nations, racial or religious groups, and shall further the activities of the United Nations for the maintenance of peace;

(b) It is essential to respect the liberty of parents and, where applicable, of legal guardians, firstly to choose for their children institutions other than those maintained by the public authorities but conforming to such minimum educational standards as may be laid down or approved by the competent authorities and, secondly, to ensure in a manner consistent with the procedures followed in the State for the application of its legislation, the religious and moral education of the children in conformity with their own convictions; and no person or group of persons should be compelled to receive religious instruction inconsistent with his or their conviction;

(c) It is essential to recognize the right of members of national minorities to carry on their own educational activities, including the maintenance of schools and, depending on the educational policy of each State, the use or the teaching of their own language, provided however:

(i) That this right is not exercised in a manner which prevents the members of these minorities from understanding the culture and language of the community as a whole and from participating in its activities, or which prejudices national sovereignty;

(ii) That the standard of education is not lower than the general standard laid down or approved by the competent authorities; and

(iii) That attendance at such schools is optional.

2. The States Parties to this Convention undertake to take all necessary measures to ensure the application of the principles enunciated in paragraph 1 of this article.

Article 6

In the application of this Convention, the States Parties to it undertake to pay the greatest attention to any recommendations hereafter adopted by the General Conference of the United Nations Educational, Scientific and Cultural Organization defining the measures to be taken against the different forms of discrimination in education and for the purpose of ensuring equality of opportunity and treatment in education.

Article 7

The States Parties to this Convention shall in their periodic reports submitted to the General Conference of the United Nations Educational, Scientific and Cultural Organization on dates and in a manner to be determined by it, give information on the legislative and administrative provisions which they have adopted and other action which they have taken for the application of this Convention, including that taken for the formulation and the development of the national policy defined in article 4 as well as the results achieved and the obstacles encountered in the application of that policy.

Article 8

Any dispute which may arise between any two or more States Parties to this Convention concerning the interpretation or application of this Convention which is not settled by negotiations shall at the request of the parties to the dispute be referred, failing other means of settling the dispute, to the International Court of Justice for decision.

Article 9

Reservations to this Convention shall not be permitted.

Article 10

This Convention shall not have the effect of diminishing the rights which individuals or groups may enjoy by virtue of agreements concluded between two or more States, where such rights are not contrary to the letter or spirit of this Convention.

Protocol Instituting a Conciliation and Good Offices Commission to be responsible for seeking a settlement of any disputes which may arise between States Parties to the Convention against Discrimination in Education

Adopted by the General Conference of the UNESCO on 10 December 1962, entered into force: 24 October 1968.

Article 1

There shall be established under the auspices of the United Nations Educational, Scientific and Cultural Organization a Conciliation and Good Offices Commission, hereinafter referred to as the Commission, to be responsible for seeking the amicable settlement of disputes between States Parties to the Convention against Discrimination in Education, hereinafter referred to as the Convention, concerning the application or interpretation of the Convention.

Article 2

1. The Commission shall consist of eleven members who shall be persons of high moral standing and acknowledged impartiality and shall be elected by the General Conference of the United Nations Educational, Scientific and Cultural Organization, hereinafter referred to as the General Conference.

2. The members of the Commission shall serve in their personal capacity.

Article 3

1. The members of the Commission shall be elected from a list of persons nominated for the purpose by the States Parties to this Protocol. Each State shall, after consulting its National Commission for UNESCO, nominate not more than four persons. These persons must be nationals of States Parties to this Protocol.

2. At least four months before the date of each election to the Commission, the Director-General of the United Nations Educational, Scientific and Cultural Organization, hereinafter referred to as the Director-General, shall invite the States Parties to the present Protocol to send within two months, their nominations of the persons referred to in paragraph 1 of this article. He shall prepare a list in alphabetical order of the persons thus nominated and shall submit it, at least one month before the election, to the Executive Board of the United Nations Educational, Scientific and Cultural Organization, hereinafter referred to as the Executive Board, and to the States Parties to the Convention. The Executive Board shall transmit the aforementioned list, with such suggestions as it may consider useful, to the General Conference, which shall carry out the election of members of the Commission in

conformity with the procedure it normally follows in elections of two or more persons ...

Article 14
The Commission shall deal with a matter referred to it under article 12 or article 13 of this Protocol only after it has ascertained that all available domestic remedies have been invoked and exhausted in the case, in conformity with the generally recognized principles of international law.

Article 15
Except in cases where new elements have been submitted to it, the Commission shall not consider matters it has already dealt with.

Article 16
In any matter referred to it, the Commission may call upon the States concerned to supply any relevant information.

Article 17
1. Subject to the provisions of article 14, the Commission, after obtaining all the information it thinks necessary, shall ascertain the facts, and make available its good offices to the States concerned with a view to an amicable solution of the matter on the basis of respect for the Convention.

2. The Commission shall in every case, and in no event later than eighteen months after the date of receipt by the Director-General of the notice under article 12, paragraph 2, draw up a report in accordance with the provisions of paragraph 3 below which will be sent to the States concerned and then communicated to the Director-General for publication. When an advisory opinion is requested of the International Court of Justice, in accordance with article 18, the time-limit shall be extended appropriately.

3. If a solution within the terms of paragraph 1 of this article is reached, the Commission shall confine its report to a brief statement of the facts and of the solution reached. If such a solution is not reached, the Commission shall draw up a report on the facts and indicate the recommendations which it made with a view to conciliation. If the report does not represent in whole or in part the unanimous opinion of the members of the Commission, any member of the Commission shall be entitled to attach to it a separate opinion. The written and oral submissions made by the parties to the case in accordance with article 11, paragraph 2 (c), shall be attached to the report.

Article 18

The Commission may recommend to the Executive Board, or to the General Conference if the recommendation is made within two months before the opening of one of its sessions, that the International Court of Justice be requested to give an advisory opinion on any legal question connected with a matter laid before the Commission.

Article 19

The Commission shall submit to the General Conference at each of its regular sessions a report on its activities, which shall be transmitted to the General Conference by the Executive Board.

Article 20

1. The Director-General shall convene the first meeting of the Commission at the Headquarters of the United Nations Educational, Scientific and Cultural Organization within three months after its nomination by the General Conference.

2. Subsequent meetings of the Commission shall be convened when necessary by the Chairman of the Commission to whom, as well as to all other members of the Commission, the Director-General shall transmit all matters referred to the Commission in accordance with the provisions of this Protocol.

3. Notwithstanding paragraph 2 of this article, when at least one third of the members of the Commission consider that the Commission should examine a matter in accordance with the provisions of this Protocol, the Chairman shall on their so requiring convene a meeting of the Commission for that purpose.

Article 25

Any State may, at the time of ratification, acceptance or accession or at any subsequent date, declare, by notification to the Director-General, that it agrees, with respect to any other State assuming the same obligation, to refer to the International Court of Justice, after the drafting of the report provided for in article 17, paragraph 3, any dispute covered by this Protocol on which no amicable solution has been reached in accordance with article 17, paragraph 1.

Article 26

1. Each State Party to this Protocol may denounce it.

2. The denunciation shall be notified by an instrument in writing, deposited with the Director-General.

3. Denunciation of the Convention shall automatically entail denunciation of this Protocol.

4. The denunciation shall take effect twelve months after the receipt of the instrument of denunciation. The State denouncing the Protocol shall, however, remain bound by its provisions in respect of any cases concerning it which have been referred to the Commission before the end of the time-limit stipulated in this paragraph ...

International Convention on the Protection and Promotion of the Rights and Dignity of Persons with Disabilities

UNGA Res. A/61/611 (2006).

Article 1
Purpose

The purpose of the present Convention is to promote, protect and ensure the full and equal enjoyment of all human rights and fundamental freedoms by all persons with disabilities, and to promote respect for their inherent dignity.

Persons with disabilities include those who have long-term physical, mental, intellectual or sensory impairments which in interaction with various barriers may hinder their full and effective participation in society on an equal basis with others.

Article 2
Definitions

For the purposes of the present Convention:

"Communication" includes languages, display of text, Braille, tactile communication, large print, accessible multimedia as well as written, audio, plain-language, human-reader and augmentative and alternative modes, means and formats of communication, including accessible information and communication technology;

"Language" includes spoken and signed languages and other forms of non spoken languages;

"Discrimination on the basis of disability" means any distinction, exclusion or restriction on the basis of disability which has the purpose or effect of impairing or nullifying the recognition, enjoyment or exercise, on an equal basis with others, of all human rights and fundamental freedoms in the political, economic, social, cultural, civil or any other field. It includes all forms of discrimination, including denial of reasonable accommodation;

"Reasonable accommodation" means necessary and appropriate modification and adjustments not imposing a disproportionate or undue burden, where needed in a particular case, to ensure to persons with disabilities the enjoyment or exercise on an equal basis with others of all human rights and fundamental freedoms;

"Universal design" means the design of products, environments, programmes and services to be usable by all people, to the greatest extent possible, without the need for adaptation or specialized design. "Universal design" shall not exclude assistive devices for particular groups of persons with disabilities where this is needed.

Article 3
General principles

The principles of the present Convention shall be:

(a) Respect for inherent dignity, individual autonomy including the freedom to make one's own choices, and independence of persons;

(b) Non-discrimination;

(c) Full and effective participation and inclusion in society;

(d) Respect for difference and acceptance of persons with disabilities as part of human diversity and humanity;

(e) Equality of opportunity;

(f) Accessibility;

(g) Equality between men and women;

(h) Respect for the evolving capacities of children with disabilities and respect for the right of children with disabilities to preserve their identities.

Article 4
General obligations

1. States Parties undertake to ensure and promote the full realization of all human rights and fundamental freedoms for all persons with disabilities without discrimination of any kind on the basis of disability. To this end, States Parties undertake:

(a) To adopt all appropriate legislative, administrative and other measures for the implementation of the rights recognized in the present Convention;

(b) To take all appropriate measures, including legislation, to modify or abolish existing laws, regulations, customs and practices that constitute discrimination against persons with disabilities;

(c) To take into account the protection and promotion of the human rights of persons with disabilities in all policies and programmes;

(d) To refrain from engaging in any act or practice that is inconsistent with the present Convention and to ensure that public authorities and institutions act in conformity with the present Convention;

(e) To take all appropriate measures to eliminate discrimination on the basis of disability by any person, organization or private enterprise;

(f) To undertake or promote research and development of universally designed goods, services, equipment and facilities, as defined in article 2 of the present Convention, which should require the minimum possible adaptation and the least cost to meet the specific needs of a person with disabilities, to promote their availability and use, and to promote universal design in the development of standards and guidelines;

(g) To undertake or promote research and development of, and to promote the availability and use of new technologies, including information and communications technologies, mobility aids, devices and assistive technologies, suitable for persons with disabilities, giving priority to technologies at an affordable cost;

(h) To provide accessible information to persons with disabilities about mobility aids, devices and assistive technologies, including new technologies, as well as other forms of assistance, support services and facilities;

(i) To promote the training of professionals and staff working with persons with disabilities in the rights recognized in this Convention so as to better provide the assistance and services guaranteed by those rights.

2. With regard to economic, social and cultural rights, each State Party undertakes to take measures to the maximum of its available resources and, where needed, within the framework of international cooperation, with a view to achieving progressively the full realization of these rights, without prejudice to those obligations contained in the present Convention that are immediately applicable according to international law.

3. In the development and implementation of legislation and policies to implement the present Convention, and in other decision-making processes concerning issues relating to persons with disabilities, States Parties shall closely consult with and actively involve persons with disabilities, including children with disabilities, through their representative organizations.

4. Nothing in the present Convention shall affect any provisions which are more conducive to the realization of the rights of persons with disabilities and which may be contained in the law of a State Party or international law in force for that State. There shall be no restriction upon or derogation from

any of the human rights and fundamental freedoms recognized or existing in any State Party to the present Convention pursuant to law, conventions, regulation or custom on the pretext that the present Convention does not recognize such rights or freedoms or that it recognizes them to a lesser extent.

5. The provisions of the present Convention shall extend to all parts of federal states without any limitations or exceptions.

Article 5
Equality and non-discrimination

1. States Parties recognize that all persons are equal before and under the law and are entitled without any discrimination to the equal protection and equal benefit of the law.

2. States Parties shall prohibit all discrimination on the basis of disability and guarantee to persons with disabilities equal and effective legal protection against discrimination on all grounds.

3. In order to promote equality and eliminate discrimination, States Parties shall take all appropriate steps to ensure that reasonable accommodation is provided.

4. Specific measures which are necessary to accelerate or achieve de facto equality of persons with disabilities shall not be considered discrimination under the terms of the present Convention.

Article 6
Women with disabilities

1. States Parties recognize that women and girls with disabilities are subject to multiple discrimination, and in this regard shall take measures to ensure the full and equal enjoyment by them of all human rights and fundamental freedoms.

2. States Parties shall take all appropriate measures to ensure the full development, advancement and empowerment of women, for the purpose of guaranteeing them the exercise and enjoyment of the human rights and fundamental freedoms set out in the present Convention.

Article 7
Children with disabilities

1. States Parties shall take all necessary measures to ensure the full enjoyment by children with disabilities of all human rights and fundamental freedoms on an equal basis with other children.

2. In all actions concerning children with disabilities, the best interests of the child shall be a primary consideration.

3. States Parties shall ensure that children with disabilities have the right to express their views freely on all matters affecting them, their views being given due weight in accordance with their age and maturity, on an equal basis with other children, and to be provided with disability and age-appropriate assistance to realize that right.

Article 8
Awareness-raising

1. States Parties undertake to adopt immediate, effective and appropriate measures:

(a) To raise awareness throughout society, including at the family level, regarding persons with disabilities, and to foster respect for the rights and dignity of persons with disabilities;

(b) To combat stereotypes, prejudices and harmful practices relating to persons with disabilities, including those based on sex and age, in all areas of life;

(c) To promote awareness of the capabilities and contributions of persons with disabilities.

2. Measures to this end include:

(a) Initiating and maintaining effective public awareness campaigns designed:

(i) To nurture receptiveness to the rights of persons with disabilities;
(ii) To promote positive perceptions and greater social awareness towards persons with disabilities;

(iii) To promote recognition of the skills, merits and abilities of persons with disabilities, and of their contributions to the workplace and the labour market;

(b) Fostering at all levels of the education system, including in all children from an early age, an attitude of respect for the rights of persons with disabilities;

(c) Encouraging all organs of the media to portray persons with disabilities in a manner consistent with the purpose of the present Convention;

(d) Promoting awareness-training programmes regarding persons with disabilities and the rights of persons with disabilities.

Article 9
Accessibility

1. To enable persons with disabilities to live independently and participate fully in all aspects of life, States Parties shall take appropriate measures to ensure to persons with disabilities access, on an equal basis with others, to the physical environment, to transportation, to information and communications, including information and communications technologies and systems, and to other facilities and services open or provided to the public, both in urban and in rural areas. These measures, which shall include the identification and elimination of obstacles and barriers to accessibility, shall apply to, inter alia:

(a) Buildings, roads, transportation and other indoor and outdoor facilities, including schools, housing, medical facilities and workplaces;

(b) Information, communications and other services, including electronic services and emergency services.

2. States Parties shall also take appropriate measures to:

(a) Develop, promulgate and monitor the implementation of minimum standards and guidelines for the accessibility of facilities and services open or provided to the public;

(b) Ensure that private entities that offer facilities and services which are open or provided to the public take into account all aspects of accessibility for persons with disabilities;

(c) Provide training for stakeholders on accessibility issues facing persons with disabilities;

(d) Provide in buildings and other facilities open to the public signage in Braille and in easy to read and understand forms;

(e) Provide forms of live assistance and intermediaries, including guides, readers and professional sign language interpreters, to facilitate accessibility to buildings and other facilities open to the public;

(f) Promote other appropriate forms of assistance and support to persons with disabilities to ensure their access to information;

(g) Promote access for persons with disabilities to new information and communications technologies and systems, including the Internet;

(h) Promote the design, development, production and distribution of accessible information and communications technologies and systems at an early stage, so that these technologies and systems become accessible at minimum cost.

Article 10
Right to life

States Parties reaffirm that every human being has the inherent right to life and shall take all necessary measures to ensure its effective enjoyment by persons with disabilities on an equal basis with others.

Article 11
Situations of risk and humanitarian emergencies

States Parties shall take, in accordance with their obligations under international law, including international humanitarian law and international human rights law, all necessary measures to ensure the protection and safety of persons with disabilities in situations of risk, including situations of armed conflict, humanitarian emergencies and the occurrence of natural disasters.

Article 12
Equal recognition before the law

1. States Parties reaffirm that persons with disabilities have the right to recognition everywhere as persons before the law.

2. States Parties shall recognize that persons with disabilities enjoy legal capacity on an equal basis with others in all aspects of life.

3. States Parties shall take appropriate measures to provide access by persons with disabilities to the support they may require in exercising their legal capacity.

4. States Parties shall ensure that all measures that relate to the exercise of legal capacity provide for appropriate and effective safeguards to prevent abuse in accordance with international human rights law. Such safeguards shall ensure that measures relating to the exercise of legal capacity respect the rights, will and preferences of the person, are free of conflict of interest and undue influence, are proportional and tailored to the person's circumstances, apply for the shortest time possible and are subject to regular review by a competent, independent and impartial authority or judicial body. The safeguards shall be proportional to the degree to which such measures affect the person's rights and interests.

5. Subject to the provisions of this article, States Parties shall take all appropriate and effective measures to ensure the equal right of persons with

disabilities to own or inherit property, to control their own financial affairs and to have equal access to bank loans, mortgages and other forms of financial credit, and shall ensure that persons with disabilities are not arbitrarily deprived of their property.

Article 13
Access to justice

1. States Parties shall ensure effective access to justice for persons with disabilities on an equal basis with others, including through the provision of procedural and age-appropriate accommodations, in order to facilitate their effective role as direct and indirect participants, including as witnesses, in all legal proceedings, including at investigative and other preliminary stages.

2. In order to help to ensure effective access to justice for persons with disabilities, States Parties shall promote appropriate training for those working in the field of administration of justice, including police and prison staff.

Article 14
Liberty and security of the person

1. States Parties shall ensure that persons with disabilities, on an equal basis with others:
(a) Enjoy the right to liberty and security of person;
(b) Are not deprived of their liberty unlawfully or arbitrarily, and that any deprivation of liberty is in conformity with the law, and that the existence of a disability shall in no case justify a deprivation of liberty.
2. States Parties shall ensure that if persons with disabilities are deprived of their liberty through any process, they are, on an equal basis with others, entitled to guarantees in accordance with international human rights law and shall be treated in compliance with the objectives and principles of this Convention, including by provision of reasonable accommodation.

Article 15
Freedom from torture or cruel, inhuman or degrading treatment or punishment

1. No one shall be subjected to torture or to cruel, inhuman or degrading treatment or punishment. In particular, no one shall be subjected without his or her free consent to medical or scientific experimentation.
2. States Parties shall take all effective legislative, administrative, judicial or other measures to prevent persons with disabilities, on an equal basis with others, from being subjected to torture or cruel, inhuman or degrading treatment or punishment.

Article 16
Freedom from exploitation, violence and abuse

1. States Parties shall take all appropriate legislative, administrative, social, educational and other measures to protect persons with disabilities, both within and outside the home, from all forms of exploitation, violence and abuse, including their gender-based aspects.

2. States Parties shall also take all appropriate measures to prevent all forms of exploitation, violence and abuse by ensuring, inter alia, appropriate forms of gender- and age-sensitive assistance and support for persons with disabilities and their families and caregivers, including through the provision of information and education on how to avoid, recognize and report instances of exploitation, violence and abuse. States Parties shall ensure that protection services are age-, gender- and disability-sensitive.

3. In order to prevent the occurrence of all forms of exploitation, violence and abuse, States Parties shall ensure that all facilities and programmes designed to serve persons with disabilities are effectively monitored by independent authorities.

4. States Parties shall take all appropriate measures to promote the physical, cognitive and psychological recovery, rehabilitation and social reintegration of persons with disabilities who become victims of any form of exploitation, violence or abuse, including through the provision of protection services. Such recovery and reintegration shall take place in an environment that fosters the health, welfare, self-respect, dignity and autonomy of the person and takes into account gender- and age-specific needs.

5. States Parties shall put in place effective legislation and policies, including women- and child-focused legislation and policies, to ensure that instances of exploitation, violence and abuse against persons with disabilities are identified, investigated and, where appropriate, prosecuted.

Article 17
Protecting the integrity of the person

Every person with disabilities has a right to respect for his or her physical and mental integrity on an equal basis with others.

Article 18
Liberty of movement and nationality

1. States Parties shall recognize the rights of persons with disabilities to liberty of movement, to freedom to choose their residence and to a nationality, on

an equal basis with others, including by ensuring that persons with disabilities:

(a) Have the right to acquire and change a nationality and are not deprived of their nationality arbitrarily or on the basis of disability;

(b) Are not deprived, on the basis of disability, of their ability to obtain, possess and utilize documentation of their nationality or other documentation of identification, or to utilize relevant processes such as immigration proceedings, that may be needed to facilitate exercise of the right to liberty of movement;

(c) Are free to leave any country, including their own;

(d) Are not deprived, arbitrarily or on the basis of disability, of the right to enter their own country.

2. Children with disabilities shall be registered immediately after birth and shall have the right from birth to a name, the right to acquire a nationality and, as far as possible, the right to know and be cared for by their parents.

Article 19

Living independently and being included in the community

States Parties to this Convention recognize the equal right of all persons with disabilities to live in the community, with choices equal to others, and shall take effective and appropriate measures to facilitate full enjoyment by persons with disabilities of this right and their full inclusion and participation in the community, including by ensuring that:

(a) Persons with disabilities have the opportunity to choose their place of residence and where and with whom they live on an equal basis with others and are not obliged to live in a particular living arrangement;

(b) Persons with disabilities have access to a range of in-home, residential and other community support services, including personal assistance necessary to support living and inclusion in the community, and to prevent isolation or segregation from the community;

(c) Community services and facilities for the general population are available on an equal basis to persons with disabilities and are responsive to their needs.

Article 20
Personal mobility

States Parties shall take effective measures to ensure personal mobility with the greatest possible independence for persons with disabilities, including by:

(a) Facilitating the personal mobility of persons with disabilities in the manner and at the time of their choice, and at affordable cost;

(b) Facilitating access by persons with disabilities to quality mobility aids, devices, assistive technologies and forms of live assistance and intermediaries, including by making them available at affordable cost;

(c) Providing training in mobility skills to persons with disabilities and to specialist staff working with persons with disabilities;

(d) Encouraging entities that produce mobility aids, devices and assistive technologies to take into account all aspects of mobility for persons with disabilities.

Article 21
Freedom of expression and opinion, and access to information

States Parties shall take all appropriate measures to ensure that persons with disabilities can exercise the right to freedom of expression and opinion, including the freedom to seek, receive and impart information and ideas on an equal basis with others and through all forms of communication of their choice, as defined in article 2 of the present Convention, including by:

(a) Providing information intended for the general public to persons with disabilities in accessible formats and technologies appropriate to different kinds of disabilities in a timely manner and without additional cost;

(b) Accepting and facilitating the use of sign languages, Braille, augmentative and alternative communication, and all other accessible means, modes and formats of communication of their choice by persons with disabilities in official interactions;

(c) Urging private entities that provide services to the general public, including through the Internet, to provide information and services in accessible and usable formats for persons with disabilities;

(d) Encouraging the mass media, including providers of information through the Internet, to make their services accessible to persons with disabilities;

(e) Recognizing and promoting the use of sign languages.

Article 22
Respect for privacy

1. No person with disabilities, regardless of place of residence or living arrangements, shall be subjected to arbitrary or unlawful interference with his or her privacy, family, home or correspondence or other types of communication or to unlawful attacks on his or her honour and reputation. Persons with disabilities have the right to the protection of the law against such interference or attacks.

2. States Parties shall protect the privacy of personal, health and rehabilitation information of persons with disabilities on an equal basis with others.

Article 23
Respect for home and the family

1. States Parties shall take effective and appropriate measures to eliminate discrimination against persons with disabilities in all matters relating to marriage, family, parenthood and relationships, on an equal basis with others, so as to ensure that:

(a) The right of all persons with disabilities who are of marriageable age to marry and to found a family on the basis of free and full consent of the intending spouses is recognized;

(b) The rights of persons with disabilities to decide freely and responsibly on the number and spacing of their children and to have access to age-appropriate information, reproductive and family planning education are recognized, and the means necessary to enable them to exercise these rights are provided;

(c) Persons with disabilities, including children, retain their fertility on an equal basis with others.

2. States Parties shall ensure the rights and responsibilities of persons with disabilities, with regard to guardianship, wardship, trusteeship, adoption of children or similar institutions, where these concepts exist in national legislation; in all cases the best interests of the child shall be paramount. States Parties shall render appropriate assistance to persons with disabilities in the performance of their child-rearing responsibilities.

3. States Parties shall ensure that children with disabilities have equal rights with respect to family life. With a view to realizing these rights, and to prevent concealment, abandonment, neglect and segregation of children with disabilities, States Parties shall undertake to provide early and comprehensive

information, services and support to children with disabilities and their families.

4. States Parties shall ensure that a child shall not be separated from his or her parents against their will, except when competent authorities subject to judicial review determine, in accordance with applicable law and procedures, that such separation is necessary for the best interests of the child. In no case shall a child be separated from parents on the basis of a disability of either the child or one or both of the parents.

5. States Parties shall, where the immediate family is unable to care for a child with disabilities, undertake every effort to provide alternative care within the wider family, and failing that, within the community in a family setting.

Article 24
Education

1. States Parties recognize the right of persons with disabilities to education. With a view to realizing this right without discrimination and on the basis of equal opportunity, States Parties shall ensure an inclusive education system at all levels and life long learning directed to:

(a) The full development of human potential and sense of dignity and self-worth, and the strengthening of respect for human rights, fundamental freedoms and human diversity;

(b) The development by persons with disabilities of their personality, talents and creativity, as well as their mental and physical abilities, to their fullest potential;

(c) Enabling persons with disabilities to participate effectively in a free society.

2. In realizing this right, States Parties shall ensure that:

(a) Persons with disabilities are not excluded from the general education system on the basis of disability, and that children with disabilities are not excluded from free and compulsory primary education, or from secondary education, on the basis of disability;

(b) Persons with disabilities can access an inclusive, quality and free primary education and secondary education on an equal basis with others in the communities in which they live;

(c) Reasonable accommodation of the individual's requirements is provided;

(d) Persons with disabilities receive the support required, within the general education system, to facilitate their effective education;

(e) Effective individualized support measures are provided in environments that maximize academic and social development, consistent with the goal of full inclusion.

3. States Parties shall enable persons with disabilities to learn life and social development skills to facilitate their full and equal participation in education and as members of the community. To this end, States Parties shall take appropriate measures, including:

(a) Facilitating the learning of Braille, alternative script, augmentative and alternative modes, means and formats of communication and orientation and mobility skills, and facilitating peer support and mentoring;

(b) Facilitating the learning of sign language and the promotion of the linguistic identity of the deaf community;

(c) Ensuring that the education of persons, and in particular children, who are blind, deaf or deafblind, is delivered in the most appropriate languages and modes and means of communication for the individual, and in environments which maximize academic and social development.

4. In order to help ensure the realization of this right, States Parties shall take appropriate measures to employ teachers, including teachers with disabilities, who are qualified in sign language and/or Braille, and to train professionals and staff who work at all levels of education. Such training shall incorporate disability awareness and the use of appropriate augmentative and alternative modes, means and formats of communication, educational techniques and materials to support persons with disabilities.

5. States Parties shall ensure that persons with disabilities are able to access general tertiary education, vocational training, adult education and lifelong learning without discrimination and on an equal basis with others. To this end, States Parties shall ensure that reasonable accommodation is provided to persons with disabilities.

Article 25
Health

States Parties recognize that persons with disabilities have the right to the enjoyment of the highest attainable standard of health without discrimination on the basis of disability. States Parties shall take all appropriate measures to ensure access for persons with disabilities to health services that are gender-sensitive, including health-related rehabilitation. In particular, States Parties shall:

(a) Provide persons with disabilities with the same range, quality and standard of free or affordable health care and programmes as provided to other persons, including in the area of sexual and reproductive health and population-based public health programmes;

(b) Provide those health services needed by persons with disabilities specifically because of their disabilities, including early identification and intervention as appropriate, and services designed to minimize and prevent further disabilities, including among children and older persons;

(c) Provide these health services as close as possible to people's own communities, including in rural areas;

(d) Require health professionals to provide care of the same quality to persons with disabilities as to others, including on the basis of free and informed consent by, inter alia, raising awareness of the human rights, dignity, autonomy and needs of persons with disabilities through training and the promulgation of ethical standards for public and private health care;

(e) Prohibit discrimination against persons with disabilities in the provision of health insurance, and life insurance where such insurance is permitted by national law, which shall be provided in a fair and reasonable manner;

(f) Prevent discriminatory denial of health care or health services or food and fluids on the basis of disability.

Article 26
Habilitation and rehabilitation

1. States Parties shall take effective and appropriate measures, including through peer support, to enable persons with disabilities to attain and maintain maximum independence, full physical, mental, social and vocational ability, and full inclusion and participation in all aspects of life. To that end, States Parties shall organize, strengthen and extend comprehensive habilitation and rehabilitation services and programmes, particularly in the areas of health, employment, education and social services, in such a way that these services and programmes:

(a) Begin at the earliest possible stage, and are based on the multidisciplinary assessment of individual needs and strengths;

(b) Support participation and inclusion in the community and all aspects of society, are voluntary, and are available to persons with disabilities as close as possible to their own communities, including in rural areas.

2. States Parties shall promote the development of initial and continuing training for professionals and staff working in habilitation and rehabilitation services.

3. States Parties shall promote the availability, knowledge and use of assistive devices and technologies, designed for persons with disabilities, as they relate to habilitation and rehabilitation.

Article 27
Work and employment

1. States Parties recognize the right of persons with disabilities to work, on an equal basis with others; this includes the right to the opportunity to gain a living by work freely chosen or accepted in a labour market and work environment that is open, inclusive and accessible to persons with disabilities. States Parties shall safeguard and promote the realization of the right to work, including for those who acquire a disability during the course of employment, by taking appropriate steps, including through legislation, to, inter alia:

(a) Prohibit discrimination on the basis of disability with regard to all matters concerning all forms of employment, including conditions of recruitment, hiring and employment, continuance of employment, career advancement and safe and healthy working conditions;

(b) Protect the rights of persons with disabilities, on an equal basis with others, to just and favourable conditions of work, including equal opportunities and equal remuneration for work of equal value, safe and healthy working conditions, including protection from harassment, and the redress of grievances;

(c) Ensure that persons with disabilities are able to exercise their labour and trade union rights on an equal basis with others;

(d) Enable persons with disabilities to have effective access to general technical and vocational guidance programmes, placement services and vocational and continuing training;

(e) Promote employment opportunities and career advancement for persons with disabilities in the labour market, as well as assistance in finding, obtaining, maintaining and returning to employment;

(f) Promote opportunities for self-employment, entrepreneurship, the development of cooperatives and starting one's own business;

(g) Employ persons with disabilities in the public sector;

(h) Promote the employment of persons with disabilities in the private sector through appropriate policies and measures, which may include affirmative action programmes, incentives and other measures;

(i) Ensure that reasonable accommodation is provided to persons with disabilities in the workplace;

(j) Promote the acquisition by persons with disabilities of work experience in the open labour market;

(k) Promote vocational and professional rehabilitation, job retention and return-to-work programmes for persons with disabilities.

2. States Parties shall ensure that persons with disabilities are not held in slavery or in servitude, and are protected, on an equal basis with others, from forced or compulsory labour.

Article 28
Adequate standard of living and social protection

1. States Parties recognize the right of persons with disabilities to an adequate standard of living for themselves and their families, including adequate food, clothing and housing, and to the continuous improvement of living conditions, and shall take appropriate steps to safeguard and promote the realization of this right without discrimination on the basis of disability.

2. States Parties recognize the right of persons with disabilities to social protection and to the enjoyment of that right without discrimination on the basis of disability, and shall take appropriate steps to safeguard and promote the realization of this right, including measures:

(a) To ensure equal access by persons with disabilities to clean water services, and to ensure access to appropriate and affordable services, devices and other assistance for disability-related needs;

(b) To ensure access by persons with disabilities, in particular women and girls with disabilities and older persons with disabilities, to social protection programmes and poverty reduction programmes;

(c) To ensure access by persons with disabilities and their families living in situations of poverty to assistance from the State with disability-related expenses, including adequate training, counselling, financial assistance and respite care;

(d) To ensure access by persons with disabilities to public housing programmes;

(e) To ensure equal access by persons with disabilities to retirement benefits and programmes.

Article 29
Participation in political and public life

States Parties shall guarantee to persons with disabilities political rights and the opportunity to enjoy them on an equal basis with others, and shall undertake to:

(a) Ensure that persons with disabilities can effectively and fully participate in political and public life on an equal basis with others, directly or through freely chosen representatives, including the right and opportunity for persons with disabilities to vote and be elected, inter alia, by:

(i) Ensuring that voting procedures, facilities and materials are appropriate, accessible and easy to understand and use;

(ii) Protecting the right of persons with disabilities to vote by secret ballot in elections and public referendums without intimidation, and to stand for elections, to effectively hold office and perform all public functions at all levels of government, facilitating the use of assistive and new technologies where appropriate;

(iii) Guaranteeing the free expression of the will of persons with disabilities as electors and to this end, where necessary, at their request, allowing assistance in voting by a person of their own choice;

(b) Promote actively an environment in which persons with disabilities can effectively and fully participate in the conduct of public affairs, without discrimination and on an equal basis with others, and encourage their participation in public affairs, including:

(i) Participation in non-governmental organizations and associations concerned with the public and political life of the country, and in the activities and administration of political parties;

(ii) Forming and joining organizations of persons with disabilities to represent persons with disabilities at international, national, regional and local levels.

Article 30
Participation in cultural life, recreation, leisure and sport

1. States Parties recognize the right of persons with disabilities to take part on an equal basis with others in cultural life, and shall take all appropriate measures to ensure that persons with disabilities:

(a) Enjoy access to cultural materials in accessible formats;

(b) Enjoy access to television programmes, films, theatre and other cultural activities, in accessible formats;

(c) Enjoy access to places for cultural performances or services, such as theatres, museums, cinemas, libraries and tourism services, and, as far as possible, enjoy access to monuments and sites of national cultural importance.

2. States Parties shall take appropriate measures to enable persons with disabilities to have the opportunity to develop and utilize their creative, artistic and intellectual potential, not only for their own benefit, but also for the enrichment of society.

3. States Parties shall take all appropriate steps, in accordance with international law, to ensure that laws protecting intellectual property rights do not constitute an unreasonable or discriminatory barrier to access by persons with disabilities to cultural materials.

4. Persons with disabilities shall be entitled, on an equal basis with others, to recognition and support of their specific cultural and linguistic identity, including sign languages and deaf culture.

5. With a view to enabling persons with disabilities to participate on an equal basis with others in recreational, leisure and sporting activities, States Parties shall take appropriate measures:

(a) To encourage and promote the participation, to the fullest extent possible, of persons with disabilities in mainstream sporting activities at all levels;

(b) To ensure that persons with disabilities have an opportunity to organize, develop and participate in disability-specific sporting and recreational activities and, to this end, encourage the provision, on an equal basis with others, of appropriate instruction, training and resources;
(c) To ensure that persons with disabilities have access to sporting, recreational and tourism venues;

(d) To ensure that children with disabilities have equal access with other children to participation in play, recreation and leisure and sporting activities, including those activities in the school system;

(e) To ensure that persons with disabilities have access to services from those involved in the organization of recreational, tourism, leisure and sporting activities.

Article 31
Statistics and data collection

1. States Parties undertake to collect appropriate information, including statistical and research data, to enable them to formulate and implement policies to give effect to the present Convention. The process of collecting and maintaining this information shall:

(a) Comply with legally established safeguards, including legislation on data protection, to ensure confidentiality and respect for the privacy of persons with disabilities;

(b) Comply with internationally accepted norms to protect human rights and fundamental freedoms and ethical principles in the collection and use of statistics.

2. The information collected in accordance with this article shall be disaggregated, as appropriate, and used to help assess the implementation of States Parties' obligations under the present Convention and to identify and address the barriers faced by persons with disabilities in exercising their rights.

3. States Parties shall assume responsibility for the dissemination of these statistics and ensure their accessibility to persons with disabilities and others.

Article 32
International cooperation

1. States Parties recognize the importance of international cooperation and its promotion, in support of national efforts for the realization of the purpose and objectives of the present Convention, and will undertake appropriate and effective measures in this regard, between and among States and, as appropriate, in partnership with relevant international and regional organizations and civil society, in particular organizations of persons with disabilities. Such measures could include, inter alia:

(a) Ensuring that international cooperation, including international development programmes, is inclusive of and accessible to persons with disabilities;

(b) Facilitating and supporting capacity-building, including through the exchange and sharing of information, experiences, training programmes and best practices;

(c) Facilitating cooperation in research and access to scientific and technical knowledge;

(d) Providing, as appropriate, technical and economic assistance, including by facilitating access to and sharing of accessible and assistive technologies, and through the transfer of technologies.

2. The provisions of this article are without prejudice to the obligations of each State Party to fulfil its obligations under the present Convention.

Article 33
National implementation and monitoring

1. States Parties, in accordance with their system of organization, shall designate one or more focal points within government for matters relating to the implementation of the present Convention, and shall give due consideration to the establishment or designation of a coordination mechanism within government to facilitate related action in different sectors and at different levels.

2. States Parties shall, in accordance with their legal and administrative systems, maintain, strengthen, designate or establish within the State Party, a framework, including one or more independent mechanisms, as appropriate, to promote, protect and monitor implementation of the present Convention. When designating or establishing such a mechanism, States Parties shall take into account the principles relating to the status and functioning of national institutions for protection and promotion of human rights.

3. Civil society, in particular persons with disabilities and their representative organizations, shall be involved and participate fully in the monitoring process.

Article 34
Committee on the Rights of Persons with Disabilities

1. There shall be established a Committee on the Rights of Persons with Disabilities (hereafter referred to as "the Committee"), which shall carry out the functions hereinafter provided.

2. The Committee shall consist, at the time of entered into force of the present Convention, of twelve experts. After an additional sixty ratifications or accessions to the Convention, the membership of the Committee shall increase by six members, attaining a maximum number of eighteen members.

3. The members of the Committee shall serve in their personal capacity and shall be of high moral standing and recognized competence and experience in the field covered by the present Convention. When nominating their candidates, States Parties are invited to give due consideration to the provision set out in article 4.3 of the present Convention.

4. The members of the Committee shall be elected by States Parties, consideration being given to equitable geographical distribution, representation of the different forms of civilization and of the principal legal systems, balanced gender representation and participation of experts with disabilities.

5. The members of the Committee shall be elected by secret ballot from a list of persons nominated by the States Parties from among their nationals at meetings of the Conference of States Parties. At those meetings, for which two thirds of States Parties shall constitute a quorum, the persons elected to the Committee shall be those who obtain the largest number of votes and an absolute majority of the votes of the representatives of States Parties present and voting.

6. The initial election shall be held no later than six months after the date of entered into force of the present Convention. At least four months before the date of each election, the Secretary-General of the United Nations shall address a letter to the States Parties inviting them to submit the nominations within two months. The Secretary-General shall subsequently prepare a list in alphabetical order of all persons thus nominated, indicating the State Parties which have nominated them, and shall submit it to the States Parties to the present Convention.

7. The members of the Committee shall be elected for a term of four years. They shall be eligible for re-election once. However, the term of six of the members elected at the first election shall expire at the end of two years; immediately after the first election, the names of these six members shall be chosen by lot by the chairperson of the meeting referred to in paragraph 5 of this article.

8. The election of the six additional members of the Committee shall be held on the occasion of regular elections, in accordance with the relevant provisions of this article.

9. If a member of the Committee dies or resigns or declares that for any other cause she or he can no longer perform her or his duties, the State Party which nominated the member shall appoint another expert possessing the qualifications and meeting the requirements set out in the relevant provisions of this article, to serve for the remainder of the term.

10. The Committee shall establish its own rules of procedure.

11. The Secretary-General of the United Nations shall provide the necessary staff and facilities for the effective performance of the functions of the Committee under the present Convention, and shall convene its initial meeting.

12. With the approval of the General Assembly, the members of the Committee established under the present Convention shall receive emoluments from United Nations resources on such terms and conditions as the Assembly may decide, having regard to the importance of the Committee's responsibilities.

13. The members of the Committee shall be entitled to the facilities, privileges and immunities of experts on mission for the United Nations as laid down in the relevant sections of the Convention on the Privileges and Immunities of the United Nations.

Article 35
Reports by States Parties

1. Each State Party shall submit to the Committee, through the Secretary-General of the United Nations, a comprehensive report on measures taken to give effect to its obligations under the present Convention and on the progress made in that regard, within two years after the entered into force of the present Convention for the State Party concerned.

2. Thereafter, States Parties shall submit subsequent reports at least every four years and further whenever the Committee so requests.

3. The Committee shall decide any guidelines applicable to the content of the reports.

4. A State Party which has submitted a comprehensive initial report to the Committee need not, in its subsequent reports, repeat information previously provided. When preparing reports to the Committee, States Parties are invited to consider doing so in an open and transparent process and to give due consideration to the provision set out in article 4.3 of the present Convention.

5. Reports may indicate factors and difficulties affecting the degree of fulfilment of obligations under the present Convention.

Article 36
Consideration of reports

1. Each report shall be considered by the Committee, which shall make such suggestions and general recommendations on the report as it may consider appropriate and shall forward these to the State Party concerned. The State Party may respond with any information it chooses to the Committee. The Committee may request further information from States Parties relevant to the implementation of the present Convention.

2. If a State Party is significantly overdue in the submission of a report, the Committee may notify the State Party concerned of the need to examine the implementation of the present Convention in that State Party, on the basis of reliable information available to the Committee, if the relevant report is not submitted within three months following the notification. The Committee shall invite the State Party concerned to participate in such examination. Should the State Party respond by submitting the relevant report, the provisions of paragraph 1 of this article will apply.

3. The Secretary-General of the United Nations shall make available the reports to all States Parties.

4. States Parties shall make their reports widely available to the public in their own countries and facilitate access to the suggestions and general recommendations relating to these reports.

5. The Committee shall transmit, as it may consider appropriate, to the specialized agencies, funds and programmes of the United Nations, and other competent bodies, reports from States Parties in order to address a request or indication of a need for technical advice or assistance contained therein, along with the Committee's observations and recommendations, if any, on these requests or indications.

Article 37
Cooperation between States Parties and the Committee

1. Each State Party shall cooperate with the Committee and assist its members in the fulfilment of their mandate.

2. In its relationship with States Parties, the Committee shall give due consideration to ways and means of enhancing national capacities for the

implementation of the present Convention, including through international cooperation ...

Article 39
Report of the Committee

The Committee shall report every two years to the General Assembly and to the Economic and Social Council on its activities, and may make suggestions and general recommendations based on the examination of reports and information received from the States Parties. Such suggestions and general recommendations shall be included in the report of the Committee together with comments, if any, from States Parties.

Article 40
Conference of States Parties

1. The States Parties shall meet regularly in a Conference of States Parties in order to consider any matter with regard to the implementation of the present Convention.

2. No later than six months after the entered into force of the present Convention, the Conference of the States Parties shall be convened by the Secretary-General of the United Nations. The subsequent meetings shall be convened by the Secretary-General of the United Nations biennially or upon the decision of the Conference of States Parties ...

Article 46
Reservations

1. Reservations incompatible with the object and purpose of the present Convention shall not be permitted.

2. Reservations may be withdrawn at any time.

Optional Protocol to the Convention on the Rights of Persons with Disabilities

UNGA Res. A/61/611 (2006).

The States Parties to the present Protocol have agreed as follows:

Article 1

1. A State Party to the present Protocol ("State Party") recognizes the competence of the Committee on the Rights of Persons with Disabilities ("the Committee") to receive and consider communications from or on behalf of individuals or groups of individuals subject to its jurisdiction who claim to be victims of a violation by that State Party of the provisions of the Convention.

2. No communication shall be received by the Committee if it concerns a State Party to the Convention that is not a party to the present Protocol.

Article 2

The Committee shall consider a communication inadmissible when:

(a) The communication is anonymous;

(b) The communication constitutes an abuse of the right of submission of such communications or is incompatible with the provisions of the Convention;

(c) The same matter has already been examined by the Committee or has been or is being examined under another procedure of international investigation or settlement;

(d) All available domestic remedies have not been exhausted. This shall not be the rule where the application of the remedies is unreasonably prolonged or unlikely to bring effective relief;

(e) It is manifestly ill-founded or not sufficiently substantiated; or when

(f) The facts that are the subject of the communication occurred prior to the entered into force of the present Protocol for the State Party concerned unless those facts continued after that date.

Article 3

Subject to the provisions of article 2 of the present Protocol, the Committee shall bring any communications submitted to it confidentially to the attention of the State Party. Within six months, the receiving State shall submit to the Committee written explanations or statements clarifying the matter and the remedy, if any, that may have been taken by that State.

Article 4

1. At any time after the receipt of a communication and before a determination on the merits has been reached, the Committee may transmit to the State Party concerned for its urgent consideration a request that the State Party take such interim measures as may be necessary to avoid possible irreparable damage to the victim or victims of the alleged violation.

2. Where the Committee exercises its discretion under paragraph 1 of this article, this does not imply a determination on admissibility or on the merits of the communication.

Article 5

The Committee shall hold closed meetings when examining communications under the present Protocol. After examining a communication, the Committee shall forward its suggestions and recommendations, if any, to the State Party concerned and to the petitioner.

Article 6

1. If the Committee receives reliable information indicating grave or systematic violations by a State Party of rights set forth in the Convention, the Committee shall invite that State Party to cooperate in the examination of the information and to this end submit observations with regard to the information concerned.

2. Taking into account any observations that may have been submitted by the State Party concerned as well as any other reliable information available to it, the Committee may designate one or more of its members to conduct an inquiry and to report urgently to the Committee. Where warranted and with the consent of the State Party, the inquiry may include a visit to its territory.

3. After examining the findings of such an inquiry, the Committee shall transmit these findings to the State Party concerned together with any comments and recommendations.

4. The State Party concerned shall, within six months of receiving the findings, comments and recommendations transmitted by the Committee, submit its observations to the Committee.

5. Such an inquiry shall be conducted confidentially and the cooperation of the State Party shall be sought at all stages of the proceedings.

Article 7

1. The Committee may invite the State Party concerned to include in its report under article 35 of the Convention details of any measures taken in response to an inquiry conducted under article 6 of the present Protocol.

2. The Committee may, if necessary, after the end of the period of six months referred to in article 6.4, invite the State Party concerned to inform it of the measures taken in response to such an inquiry.

Article 8

Each State Party may, at the time of signature or ratification of the present Protocol or accession thereto, declare that it does not recognize the competence of the Committee provided for in articles 6 and 7.

Article 9

The Secretary-General of the United Nations shall be the depositary of the present Protocol.

Article 10

The present Protocol shall be open for signature by signatory States and regional integration organizations of the Convention at United Nations Headquarters in New York as of 30 March 2007.

Article 11

The present Protocol shall be subject to ratification by signatory States of this Protocol which have ratified or acceded to the Convention. It shall be subject to formal confirmation by signatory regional integration organizations of this Protocol which have formally confirmed or acceded to the Convention. It shall be open for accession by any State or regional integration organization which has ratified, formally confirmed or acceded to the Convention and which has not signed the Protocol.

Article 12

1. "Regional integration organization" shall mean an organization constituted by sovereign States of a given region, to which its member States have transferred competence in respect of matters governed by the Convention and this Protocol. Such organizations shall declare, in their instruments of formal confirmation or accession, the extent of their competence with respect to matters governed by the Convention and this Protocol. Subsequently, they shall inform the depositary of any substantial modification in the extent of their competence.

2. References to "States Parties" in the present Protocol shall apply to such organizations within the limits of their competence.

3. For the purposes of article 13, paragraph 1, and article 15, paragraph 2, any instrument deposited by a regional integration organization shall not be counted.

4. Regional integration organizations, in matters within their competence, may exercise their right to vote in the meeting of States Parties, with a number of votes equal to the number of their member States that are Parties to this Protocol. Such an organization shall not exercise its right to vote if any of its member States exercises its right, and vice versa.

Article 13

1. Subject to the entered into force of the Convention, the present Protocol shall enter into force on the thirtieth day after the deposit of the tenth instrument of ratification or accession.

2. For each State or regional integration organization ratifying, formally confirming or acceding to the Protocol after the deposit of the tenth such instrument, the Protocol shall enter into force on the thirtieth day after the deposit of its own such instrument.

Article 14

1. Reservations incompatible with the object and purpose of the present Protocol shall not be permitted.

2. Reservations may be withdrawn at any time.

Article 15

1. Any State Party may propose an amendment to the present Protocol and submit it to the Secretary-General of the United Nations. The Secretary-General shall communicate any proposed amendments to States Parties, with a request to be notified whether they favour a meeting of States Parties for the purpose of considering and deciding upon the proposals. In the event that, within four months from the date of such communication, at least one third of the States Parties favour such a meeting, the Secretary-General shall convene the meeting under the auspices of the United Nations. Any amendment adopted by a majority of two thirds of the States Parties present and voting shall be submitted by the Secretary-General to the General Assembly for approval and thereafter to all States Parties for acceptance.

2. An amendment adopted and approved in accordance with paragraph 1 of this article shall enter into force on the thirtieth day after the number of

instruments of acceptance deposited reaches two thirds of the number of States Parties at the date of adoption of the amendment. Thereafter, the amendment shall enter into force for any State Party on the thirtieth day following the deposit of its own instrument of acceptance. An amendment shall be binding only on those States Parties which have accepted it.

Article 16

A State Party may denounce the present Protocol by written notification to the Secretary-General of the United Nations. The denunciation shall become effective one year after the date of receipt of the notification by the Secretary-General.

Article 17

The text of the present Protocol shall be made available in accessible formats.

Article 18

The Arabic, Chinese, English, French, Russian and Spanish texts of the present Protocol shall be equally authentic. In witness thereof the undersigned plenipotentiaries, being duly authorized thereto b by their respective Governments, have signed the present Protocol.

Equal Remuneration Convention (No. 100)

Adopted on 29 June 1951 by the General Conference of the International Labour Organisation at its 34th session, entered into force 23 May 1953.

The General Conference of the International Labour Organisation,

Having been convened at Geneva by the Governing Body of the International Labour Office, and having met in its thirty-fourth session on 6 June 1951, and

Having decided upon the adoption of certain proposals with regard to the principle of equal remuneration for men and women workers for work of equal value, which is the seventh item on the agenda of the session, and

Having determined that these proposals shall take the form of an international Convention,

Adopts this twenty-ninth day of June of the year one thousand nine hundred and fifty-one the following Convention, which may be cited as the Equal Remuneration Convention, 1951:

Article 1

For the purpose of this Convention:

(a) The term "remuneration" includes the ordinary, basic or minimum wage or salary and any additional emoluments whatsoever payable directly or indirectly, whether in cash or in kind, by the employer to the worker and arising out of the worker's employment;

(b) The term "equal remuneration for men and women workers for work of equal value" refers to rates of remuneration established without discrimination based on sex.

Article 2

1. Each Member shall, by means appropriate to the methods in operation for determining rates of remuneration, promote and, in so far as is consistent with such methods, ensure the application to all workers of the principle of equal remuneration for men and women workers for work of equal value.

2. This principle may be applied by means of:

(a) National laws or regulations;

(b) Legally established or recognised machinery for wage determination;

(c) Collective agreements between employers and workers; or

(d) A combination of these various means.

Article 3

1. Where such action will assist in giving effect to the provisions of this Convention, measures shall be taken to promote objective appraisal of jobs on the basis of the work to be performed.

2. The methods to be followed in this appraisal may be decided upon by the authorities responsible for the determination of rates of remuneration, or, where such rates are determined by collective agreements, by the parties thereto.

3. Differential rates between workers, which correspond, without regard to sex, to differences, as determined by such objective appraisal, in the work to be performed, shall not be considered as being contrary to the principle of equal remuneration for men and women workers for work of equal value.

Article 4

Each Member shall co-operate as appropriate with the employers' and workers' organisations concerned for the purpose of giving effect to the provisions of this Convention.

Article 5

The formal ratification of this Convention shall be communicated to the Director-General of the International Labour Office for registration.

Article 6

1. This Convention shall be binding only upon those Members of the International Labour Organisation whose ratifications have been registered with the Director-General.

2. It shall come into force twelve months after the date on which the ratifications of two Members have been registered with the Director-General.

3. Thereafter, this Convention shall come into force for any Member twelve months after the date on which its ratification has been registered.

Article 7

1. Declarations communicated to the Director-General of the International Labour Office in accordance with paragraph 2 of article 35 of the Constitution of the International Labour Organisation shall indicate:

(a) The territories in respect of which the Member concerned undertakes that the provisions of the Convention shall be applied without modification;

(b) The territories in respect of which it undertakes that the provisions of the Convention shall be applied subject to modifications, together with details of the said modifications;

(c) The territories in respect of which the Convention is inapplicable and in such cases the grounds on which it is inapplicable;

(d) The territories in respect of which it reserves its decisions pending further consideration of the position.

2. The undertakings referred to in subparagraphs (a) and (b) of paragraph 1 of this article shall be deemed to be an integral part of the ratification and shall have the force of ratification.

3. Any member may at any time by a subsequent declaration cancel in whole or in part any reservation made in its original declaration by virtue of subparagraphs (b), (c) or (d) of paragraph 1 of this article.

4. Any Member may, at any time at which the Convention is subject to denunciation in accordance with the provisions of article 9, communicate to the Director-General a declaration modifying in any other respect the terms of any former declaration and stating the present position in respect of such territories as it may specify.

Article 8

1. Declarations communicated to the Director-General of the International Labour Office in accordance with paragraphs 4 and 5 of article 35 of the Constitution of the International Labour Organisation shall indicate whether the provisions of the Convention will be applied in the territory concerned without modification or subject to modification; when the declaration indicates that the provisions of the Convention will be applied subject to modification, it shall give details of the said modifications.

2. The Member, Members or international authority concerned may at any time by a subsequent declaration renounce in whole or in part the right to have recourse to any modification indicated in any former declaration.

3. The Member, Members or international authority concerned may, at any time at which this Convention is subject to denunciation in accordance with the provisions of article 9, communicate to the Director-General a declaration modifying in any other respect the terms of any former declaration and stating the present position in respect of the application of the Convention.

Article 9

1. A Member which has ratified this Convention may denounce it after the expiration of ten years from the date on which the Convention first comes into force, by an act communicated to the Director-General of the International Labour Office for registration. Such denunciation shall not take effect until one year after the date on which it is registered.

2. Each Member which has ratified this Convention and which does not, within the year following the expiration of the period of ten years mentioned in the preceding paragraph, exercise the right of denunciation provided for in this article, will be bound for another period of ten years and, thereafter, may denounce this Convention at the expiration of each period of ten years under the terms provided for in this article.

Article 10

1. The Director-General of the International Labour Office shall notify all Members of the International Labour Organisation of the registration of all ratifications, declarations and denunciations communicated to him by the Members of the Organisation.

2. When notifying the Members of the Organisation of the registration of the second ratification communicated to him, the Director-General shall draw the attention of the Members of the Organisation to the date upon which the Convention will come into force.

Article 11

The Director-General of the International Labour Office shall communicate to the Secretary-General of the United Nations for registration in accordance with Article 102 of the Charter of the United Nations full particulars of all ratifications, declarations and acts of denunciation registered by him in accordance with the provisions of the preceding articles.

Article 12

At such times as it may consider necessary, the Governing Body of the International Labour Office shall present to the General Conference a report on the working of this Convention and shall examine the desirability of placing on the agenda of the Conference the question of its revision in whole or in part.

Article 13

1. Should the Conference adopt a new Convention revising this Convention in whole or in part, then, unless the new Convention otherwise provides:

(a) The ratification by a Member of the new revising Convention shall ipso jure involve the immediate denunciation of this Convention, notwithstanding the provisions of article 9 above, if and when the new revising Convention shall have come into force;

(b) As from the date when the new revising Convention comes into force this Convention shall cease to be open to ratification by the Members.

2. This Convention shall in any case remain in force in its actual form and content for those Members which have ratified it but have not ratified the revising Convention.

Discrimination (Employment and Occupation) Convention (No. 111)

Adopted on 25 June 1958 by the General Conference of the ILO entered into force 15 June 1960.

The General Conference of the International Labour Organisation ,

Having been convened at Geneva by the Governing Body of the International Labour Office, and having met in its forty-second session on 4 June 1958, and

Having decided upon the adoption of certain proposals with regard to discrimination in the field of employment and occupation, which is the fourth item on the agenda of the session, and

Having determined that these proposals shall take the form of an international Convention, and

Considering that the Declaration of Philadelphia affirms that all human beings, irrespective of race, creed or sex, have the right to pursue both their material well-being and their spiritual development in conditions of freedom and dignity, of economic security and equal opportunity, and

Considering further that discrimination constitutes a violation of rights enunciated by the Universal Declaration of Human Rights,

Adopts this twenty-fifth day of June of the year one thousand nine hundred and fifty-eight the following Convention, which may be cited as the Discrimination (Employment and Occupation) Convention, 1958:

Article 1

1. For the purpose of this Convention the term "discrimination" includes:

(a) Any distinction, exclusion or preference made on the basis of race, colour, sex, religion, political opinion, national extraction or social origin, which has the effect of nullifying or impairing equality of opportunity or treatment in employment or occupation;

(b) Such other distinction, exclusion or preference which has the effect of nullifying or impairing equality of opportunity or treatment in employment or occupation as may be determined by the Member concerned after consultation with representative employers' and workers' organisations, where such exist, and with other appropriate bodies.

2. Any distinction, exclusion or preference in respect of a particular job based on the inherent requirements thereof shall not be deemed to be discrimination.

3. For the purpose of this Convention the terms "employment" and "occupation" include access to vocational training, access to employment and to particular occupations, and terms and conditions of employment.

Article 2

Each Member for which this Convention is in force undertakes to declare and pursue a national policy designed to promote, by methods appropriate to national conditions and practice, equality of opportunity and treatment in respect of employment and occupation, with a view to eliminating any discrimination in respect thereof.

Article 3

Each Member for which this Convention is in force undertakes, by methods appropriate to national conditions and practice:

(a) To seek the co-operation of employers' and workers' organisations and other appropriate bodies in promoting the acceptance and observance of this policy;

(b) To enact such legislation and to promote such educational programmes as may be calculated to secure the acceptance and observance of the policy;

(c) To repeal any statutory provisions and modify any administrative instructions or practices which are inconsistent with the policy;

(d) To pursue the policy in respect of employment under the direct control of a national authority;

(e) To ensure observance of the policy in activities of vocational guidance, vocational training and placement services under the direction of a national authority;

(f) To indicate in its annual reports on the application of the Convention the action taken in pursuance of the policy and the results secured by such action.

Article 4

Any measures affecting an individual who is justifiably suspected of, or engaged in, activities prejudicial to the security of the State shall not be deemed to be discrimination, provided that the individual concerned shall have the right to appeal to a competent body established in accordance with national practice.

Article 5

1. Special measures of protection or assistance provided in other Conventions or Recommendations adopted by the International Labour Conference shall not be deemed to be discrimination.

2. Any Member may, after consultation with representative employers' and workers' organisations, where such exist, determine that other special measures designed to meet the particular requirements of persons who, for reasons such as sex, age, disablement, family responsibilities or social or cultural status, are generally recognised to require special protection or assistance, shall not be deemed to be discrimination.

Article 6

Each Member which ratifies this Convention undertakes to apply it to non-metropolitan territories in accordance with the provisions of the Constitution of the International Labour Organisation.

Article 7

The formal ratifications of this Convention shall be communicated to the Director-General of the International Labour Office for registration.

Article 8

1. This Convention shall be binding only upon those Members of the International Labour Organisation whose ratifications have been registered with the Director-General.

2. It shall come into force twelve months after the date on which the ratifications of two Members have been registered with the Director General.

3. Thereafter, this Convention shall come into force for any Member twelve months after the date on which its ratification has been registered.

Article 9

1. A Member which has ratified this Convention may denounce it after the expiration of ten years from the date on which the Convention first comes into force, by an act communicated to the Director-General of the International Labour Office for registration. Such denunciation shall not take effect until one year after the date on which it is registered.

2. Each Member which has ratified this Convention and which does not, within the year following the expiration of the period of ten years mentioned in the preceding paragraph, exercise the right of denunciation provided for in this article, will be bound for another period often years and, thereafter, may denounce this Convention at the expiration of each period of ten years under the terms provided for in this article.

Article 10

1. The Director-General of the International Labour Office shall notify all Members of the International Labour Organisation of the registration of all ratifications and denunciations communicated to him by the Members of the Organisation.

2. When notifying the Members of the Organisation of the registration of the second ratification communicated to him, the Director-General shall draw the attention of the Members of the Organisation to the date upon which the Convention will come into force.

Article 11

The Director-General of the International Labour Office shall communicate to the Secretary-General of the United Nations for registration in accordance with Article 102 of the Charter of the United Nations full particulars of all ratifications and acts of denunciation registered by him in accordance with the provisions of the preceding articles.

Article 12

At such times as it may consider necessary the Governing Body of the International Labour Office shall present to the General Conference a report on the working of this Convention and shall examine the desirability of placing on the agenda of the Conference the question of its revision in whole or in part.

Article 13

1. Should the Conference adopt a new Convention revising this Convention in whole or in part, then, unless the new Convention otherwise provides:

(a) The ratification by a Member of the new revising Convention shall ipso jure involve the immediate denunciation of this Convention, notwithstanding the provisions of article 9 above, if and when the new revising Convention shall have come into force;

(b) As from the date when the new revising Convention comes into force this Convention shall cease to be open to ratification by the Members.

2. This Convention shall in any case remain in force in its actual form and content for those Members which have ratified it but have not ratified the revising Convention.

Article 14

The English and French versions of the text of this Convention are equally authoritative.

The foregoing is the authentic text of the Convention duly adopted by the General Conference of the International Labour Organisation during its forty-second session which was held at Geneva and declared closed the twenty-sixth day of June 1958.

In faith whereof we have appended our signatures this fifth day of July 1958.

Convention concerning Vocational Rehabilitation and Employment (Disabled Persons), Convention No. 159

Entered into force 20 June 1985

The General Conference of the International Labour Organisation,

Having been convened at Geneva by the Governing Body of the International Labour Office and having met in its Sixty-ninth Session on 1 June 1983, and

Noting the existing international standards contained in the Vocational Rehabilitation (Disabled) Recommendation, 1955, and the Human Resources Development Recommendation, 1975, and

Noting that since the adoption of the Vocational Rehabilitation (Disabled) Recommendation, 1955, significant developments have occurred in the understanding of rehabilitation needs, the scope and organisation of rehabilitation services, and the law and practice of many Members on the questions covered by that Recommendation, and

Considering that the year 1981 was declared by the United Nations General Assembly the International Year of Disabled Persons, with the theme "full participation and equality" and that a comprehensive World Programme of Action concerning Disabled Persons is to provide effective measures at the international and national levels for the realisation of the goals of "full participation" of disabled persons in social life and development, and of "equality", and

Considering that these developments have made it appropriate to adopt new international standards on the subject which take account, in particular, of the need to ensure equality of opportunity and treatment to all categories of disabled persons, in both rural and urban areas, for employment and integration into the community, and

Having decided upon the adoption of certain proposals with regard to vocational rehabilitation which is the fourth item on the agenda of the session, and

Having determined that these proposals shall take the form of an international Convention,

adopts this twentieth day of June of the year one thousand nine hundred and eighty-three the following Convention, which may be cited as the Vocational Rehabilitation and Employment (Disabled Persons) Convention, 1983:

Treaties

Part I. Definition and scope

Article 1

1. For the purposes of this Convention, the term disabled person means an individual whose prospects of securing, retaining and advancing in suitable employment are substantially reduced as a result of a duly recognised physical or mental impairment.

2. For the purposes of this Convention, each Member shall consider the purpose of vocational rehabilitation as being to enable a disabled person to secure, retain and advance in suitable employment and thereby to further such person's integration or reintegration into society.

3. The provisions of this Convention shall be applied by each Member through measures which are appropriate to national conditions and consistent with national practice.

4. The provisions of this Convention shall apply to all categories of disabled persons.

Part II. Principles of vocational rehabilitation and employment policies for disabled persons

Article 2

Each Member shall, in accordance with national conditions, practice and possibilities, formulate, implement and periodically review a national policy on vocational rehabilitation and employment of disabled persons.

Article 3

The said policy shall aim at ensuring that appropriate vocational rehabilitation measures are made available to all categories of disabled persons, and at promoting employment opportunities for disabled persons in the open labour market.

Article 4

The said policy shall be based on the principle of equal opportunity between disabled workers and workers generally. Equality of opportunity and treatment for disabled men and women workers shall be respected. Special positive measures aimed at effective equality of opportunity and treatment between disabled workers and other workers shall not be regarded as discriminating against other workers.

Article 5

The representative organisations of employers and workers shall be consulted on the implementation of the said policy, including the measures to be taken to promote co-operation and co-ordination between the public and private bodies engaged in vocational rehabilitation activities. The representative organisations of and for disabled persons shall also be consulted.

Part III. Action at the national level for the development of vocational rehabilitation and employment services for disabled persons

Article 6

Each Member shall, by laws or regulations or by any other method consistent with national conditions and practice, take such steps as may be necessary to give effect to Articles 2, 3, 4 and 5 of this Convention.

Article 7

The competent authorities shall take measures with a view to providing and evaluating vocational guidance, vocational training, placement, employment and other related services to enable disabled persons to secure, retain and advance in employment; existing services for workers generally shall, wherever possible and appropriate, be used with necessary adaptations.

Article 8

Measures shall be taken to promote the establishment and development of vocational rehabilitation and employment services for disabled persons in rural areas and remote communities.

Article 9

Each Member shall aim at ensuring the training and availability of rehabilitation counsellors and other suitably qualified staff responsible for the vocational guidance, vocational training, placement and employment of disabled persons.

Convention concerning Indigenous and Tribal Peoples in Independent Countries (No. 169)

72 *ILO Official Bulletin* 59, entered into force 5 Sept. 1991.

The General Conference of the International Labour Organisation,

Having been convened at Geneva by the Governing Body of the International Labour Office ... 7 June 1989 ...,

Noting the international standards contained in the Indigenous and Tribal Populations Convention and Recommendation, 1957, and

Recalling the terms of the Universal Declaration of Human Rights, the International Covenant on Economic, Social and Cultural Rights, the International Covenant on Civil and Political Rights, and the many international instruments on the prevention of discrimination, and

Considering that the developments which have taken place in international law since 1957, as well as developments in the situation of indigenous and tribal peoples in all regions of the world, have made it appropriate to adopt new international standards on the subject with a view to removing the assimilationist orientation of the earlier standards, and

Recognising the aspirations of these peoples to exercise control over their own institutions, ways of life and economic development and to maintain and develop their identities, languages and religions, within the framework of the States in which they live, and

Noting that in many parts of the world these peoples are unable to enjoy their fundamental human rights to the same degree as the rest of the population of the States within which they live, and that their laws, values, customs and perspectives have often been eroded, and

Calling attention to the distinctive contributions of indigenous and tribal peoples to the cultural diversity and social and ecological harmony of humankind and to international co-operation and understanding, and

Noting that the following provisions have been framed with the cooperation of the United Nations, the Food and Agriculture Organization of the United Nations, the United Nations Educational, Scientific and Cultural Organization and the World Health Organization, as well as of the Inter-American Indian Institute, at appropriate levels and in their respective fields and that it is proposed to continue this co-operation in promoting and securing the application of these provisions, and

Having decided upon the adoption of certain proposals with regard to the partial revision of the Indigenous and Tribal Populations Convention, 1957 (No. 107), which is the fourth item on the agenda of the session, and

Having determined that these proposals shall take the form of an international Convention revising the Indigenous and Tribal Populations Convention, 1957,

Adopts this twenty-seventh day of June of the year one thousand nine hundred and eighty-nine the following Convention. which may be cited as the Indigenous and Tribal Peoples Convention, 1989;

PART I. GENERAL POLICY

Article 1

1. This Convention applies to:

(a) Tribal peoples in independent countries whose social, cultural and economic conditions distinguish them from other sections of the national community, and whose status is regulated wholly or partially by their own customs or traditions or by special laws or regulations;

(b) Peoples in independent countries who are regarded as indigenous on account of their descent from the populations which inhabited the country, or a geographical region to which the country belongs, at the time of conquest or colonisation or the establishment of present State boundaries and who, irrespective of their legal status, retain some or all of their own social, economic, cultural and political institutions.

2. Self-identification as indigenous or tribal shall be regarded as a fundamental criterion for determining the groups to which the provisions of this Convention apply.

3. The use of the term "peoples" in this Convention shall not be construed as having any implications as regards the rights which may attach to the term under international law.

Article 2

1. Governments shall have the responsibility for developing, with the participation of the peoples concerned, co-ordinated and systematic action to protect the rights of these peoples and to guarantee respect for their integrity.

2. Such action shall include measures for:

(a) Ensuring that members of these peoples benefit on an equal footing from the rights and opportunities which national laws and regulations grant to other members of the population;

(b) Promoting the full realisation of the social, economic and cultural rights of these peoples with respect for their social and cultural identity, their customs and traditions and their institutions;

(c) Assisting the members of the peoples concerned to eliminate socio-economic gaps that may exist between indigenous and other members of the national community, in a manner compatible with their aspirations and ways of life.

Article 3

1. Indigenous and tribal peoples shall enjoy the full measure of human rights and fundamental freedoms without hindrance or discrimination. The provisions of the Convention shall be applied without discrimination to male and female members of these peoples.

2. No form of force or coercion shall be used in violation of the human rights and fundamental freedoms of the peoples concerned, including the rights contained in this Convention.

Article 4

1. Special measures shall be adopted as appropriate for safeguarding the persons, institutions, property, labour, cultures and environment of the peoples concerned.

2. Such special measures shall not be contrary to the freely-expressed wishes of the peoples concerned.

3. Enjoyment of the general rights of citizenship, without discrimination, shall not be prejudiced in any way by such special measures.

Article 5

In applying the provisions of this Convention:

(a) The social, cultural, religious and spiritual values and practices of these peoples shall be recognised and protected, and due account shall be taken of the nature of the problems which face them both as groups and as individuals;

(b) The integrity of the values, practices and institutions of these peoples shall be respected;

(c) Policies aimed at mitigating the difficulties experienced by these peoples in facing new conditions of life and work shall be adopted, with the participation and co-operation of the peoples affected.

Article 6

1. In applying the provisions of this Convention, Governments shall:

(a) Consult the peoples concerned, through appropriate procedures and in particular through their representative institutions, whenever consideration is being given to legislative or administrative measures which may affect them directly;

(b) Establish means by which these peoples can freely participate, to at least the same extent as other sectors of the population, at all levels of decision-making in elective institutions and administrative and other bodies responsible for policies and programmes which concern them;

(c) Establish means for the full development of these peoples' own institutions and initiatives, and in appropriate cases provide the resources necessary for this purpose.

2. The consultations carried out in application of this Convention shall be undertaken, in good faith and in a form appropriate to the circumstances, with the objective of achieving agreement or consent to the proposed measures.

Article 7

1. The peoples concerned shall have the right to decide their own priorities for the process of development as it affects their lives, beliefs, institutions and spiritual well-being and the lands they occupy or otherwise use, and to exercise control, to the extent possible, over their own economic, social and cultural development. In addition, they shall participate in the formulation, implementation and evaluation of plans and programmes for national and regional development which may affect them directly.

2. The improvement of the conditions of life and work and levels of health and education of the peoples concerned, with their participation and co-operation, shall be a matter of priority in plans for the overall economic development of areas they inhabit. Special projects for development of the areas in question shall also be so designed as to promote such improvement.

3. Governments shall ensure that, whenever appropriate, studies are carried out, in co-operation with the peoples concerned, to assess the social, spiritual, cultural and environmental impact on them of planned development

activities. The results of these studies shall be considered as fundamental criteria for the implementation of these activities.

4. Governments shall take measures, in co-operation with the peoples concerned, to protect and preserve the environment of the territories they inhabit.

Article 8

1. In applying national laws and regulations to the peoples concerned, due regard shall be had to their customs or customary laws.

2. These peoples shall have the right to retain their own customs and institutions, where these are not incompatible with fundamental rights defined by the national legal system and with internationally recognized human rights. Procedures shall be established, whenever necessary, to resolve conflicts which may arise in the application of this principle.

3. The application of paragraphs I and 2 of this Article shall not prevent members of these peoples from exercising the rights granted to all citizens and from assuming the corresponding duties.

Article 9

1. To the extent compatible with the national legal system and internationally recognised human rights, the methods customarily practised by the peoples concerned for dealing with offences committed by their members shall be respected.

2. The customs of these peoples in regard to penal matters shall be taken into consideration by the authorities and courts dealing with such cases.

Article 10

1. In imposing penalties laid down by general law on members of these peoples account shall be taken of their economic, social and cultural characteristics .

2. Preference shall be given to methods of punishment other than confinement in prison.

Article 11

The exaction from members of the peoples concerned of compulsory personal services in any form, whether paid or unpaid, shall be prohibited and punishable by law, except in cases prescribed by law for all citizens.

Article 12

The peoples concerned shall be safeguarded against the abuse of their rights and shall be able to take legal proceedings, either individually or through their representative bodies, for the effective protection of these rights. Measures shall be taken to ensure that members of these peoples can understand and be understood in legal proceedings, where necessary through the provision of interpretation or by other effective means.

PART II. LAND

Article 13

1. In applying the provisions of this Part of the Convention governments shall respect the special importance for the cultures and spiritual values of the peoples concerned of their relationship with the lands or territories, or both as applicable, which they occupy or otherwise use, and in particular the collective aspects of this relationship.

2. The use of the term "lands" in Articles 15 and 16 shall include the concept of territories, which covers the total environment of the areas which the peoples concerned occupy or otherwise use.

Article 14

1. The rights of ownership and possession of the peoples concerned over the lands which they traditionally occupy shall be recognised. In addition, measures shall be taken in appropriate cases to safeguard the right of the peoples concerned to use lands not exclusively occupied by them, but to which they have traditionally had access for their subsistence and traditional activities. Particular attention shall be paid to the situation of nomadic peoples and shifting cultivators in this respect.

2. Governments shall take steps as necessary to identify the lands which the peoples concerned traditionally occupy, and to guarantee effective protection of their rights of ownership and possession.

3. Adequate procedures shall be established within the national legal system to resolve land claims by the peoples concerned.

Article 15

1. The rights of the peoples concerned to the natural resources pertaining to their lands shall be specially safeguarded. These rights include the right of these peoples to participate in the use, management and conservation of these resources.

2. In cases in which the State retains the ownership of mineral or sub-surface resources or rights to other resources pertaining to lands, governments shall establish or maintain procedures through which they shall consult these peoples, with a view to ascertaining whether and to what degree their interests would be prejudiced, before undertaking or permitting any programmes for the exploration or exploitation of such resources pertaining to their lands. The peoples concerned shall wherever possible participate in the benefits of such activities, and shall receive fair compensation for any damages which they may sustain as a result of such activities.

Article 16

1. Subject to the following paragraphs of this Article, the peoples concerned shall not be removed from the lands which they occupy.

2. Where the relocation of these peoples is considered necessary as an exceptional measure, such relocation shall take place only with their free and informed consent. Where their consent cannot be obtained, such relocation shall take place only following appropriate procedures established by national laws and regulations, including public inquiries where appropriate, which provide the opportunity for effective representation of the peoples concerned.

3. Whenever possible, these peoples shall have the right to return to their traditional lands, as soon as the grounds for relocation cease to exist.

4. When such return is not possible, as determined by agreement or, in the absence of such agreement, through appropriate procedures, these peoples shall be provided in all possible cases with lands of quality and legal status at least equal to that of the lands previously occupied by them, suitable to provide for their present needs and future development. Where the peoples concerned express a preference for compensation in money or in kind, they shall be so compensated under appropriate guarantees.

5. Persons thus relocated shall be fully compensated for any resulting loss or injury.

Article 17

1. Procedures established by the peoples concerned for the transmission of land rights among members of these peoples shall be respected.

2. The peoples concerned shall be consulted whenever consideration is being given to their capacity to alienate their lands or otherwise transmit their rights outside their own community.

3. Persons not belonging to these peoples shall be prevented from taking advantage of their customs or of lack of understanding of the laws on the part of their members to secure the ownership, possession or use of land belonging to them.

Article 18

Adequate penalties shall be established by law for unauthorised intrusion upon, or use of, the lands of the peoples concerned, and governments shall take measures to prevent such offences.

Article 19

National agrarian programmes shall secure to the peoples concerned treatment equivalent to that accorded to other sectors of the population with regard to:

(a) The provision of more land for these peoples when they have not the area necessary for providing the essentials of a normal existence, or for any possible increase in their numbers;

(b) The provision of the means required to promote the development of the lands which these peoples already possess.

PART III. RECRUITMENT AND CONDITIONS OF EMPLOYMENT

Article 20

1. Governments shall, within the framework of national laws and regulations, and in co-operation with the peoples concerned, adopt special measures to ensure the effective protection with regard to recruitment and conditions of employment of workers belonging to these peoples, to the extent that they are not effectively protected by laws applicable to workers in general.

2. Governments shall do everything possible to prevent any discrimination between workers belonging to the peoples concerned and other workers, in particular as regards:

(a) Admission to employment, including skilled employment, as well as measures for promotion and advancement;

(b) Equal remuneration for work of equal value;

(c) Medical and social assistance, occupational safety and health, all social security benefits and any other occupationally related benefits, and housing;

(d) The right of association and freedom for all lawful trade union activities, and the right to conclude collective agreements with employers or employers' organisations.

3. The measures taken shall include measures to ensure:

(a) That workers belonging to the peoples concerned, including seasonal, casual and migrant workers in agricultural and other employment, as well as those employed by labour contractors, enjoy the protection afforded by national law and practice to other such workers in the same sectors, and that they are fully informed of their rights under labour legislation and of the means of redress available to them;

(b) That workers belonging to these peoples are not subjected to working conditions hazardous to their health, in particular through exposure to pesticides or other toxic substances;

(c) That workers belonging to these peoples are not subjected to coercive recruitment systems, including bonded labour and other forms of debt servitude;

(d) That workers belonging to these peoples enjoy equal opportunities and equal treatment in employment for men and women, and protection from sexual harassment.

4. Particular attention shall be paid to the establishment of adequate labour inspection services in areas where workers belonging to the peoples concerned undertake wage employment, in order to ensure compliance with the provisions of this Part of this Convention.

PART IV. VOCATIONAL TRAINING, HANDICRAFTS AND RURAL INDUSTRIES

Article 21

Members of the peoples concerned shall enjoy opportunities at least equal to those of other citizens in respect of vocational training measures.

Article 22

1. Measures shall be taken to promote the voluntary participation of members of the peoples concerned in vocational training programmes of general application.

2. Whenever existing programmes of vocational training of general application do not meet the special needs of the peoples concerned,

governments shall, with the participation of these peoples, ensure the provision of special training programmes and facilities.

3. Any special training programmes shall be based on the economic environment, social and cultural conditions and practical needs of the peoples concerned. Any studies made in this connection shall be carried out in co-operation with these peoples, who shall be consulted on the organisation and operation of such programmes. Where feasible, these peoples shall progressively assume responsibility for the organisation and operation of such special training programmes, if they so decide.

Article 23

1. Handicrafts, rural and community-based industries, and subsistence economy and traditional activities of the peoples concerned, such as hunting, fishing, trapping and gathering, shall be recognised as important factors in the maintenance of their cultures and in their economic self-reliance and development. Governments shall, with the participation of these peoples and whenever appropriate, ensure that these activities are strengthened and promoted.

2. Upon the request of the peoples concerned, appropriate technical and financial assistance shall be provided wherever possible, taking into account the traditional technologies and cultural characteristics of these peoples, as well as the importance of sustainable and equitable development.

PART V. SOCIAL SECURITY AND HEALTH

Article 24

Social security schemes shall be extended progressively to cover the peoples concerned, and applied without discrimination against them.

Article 25

1. Governments shall ensure that adequate health services are made available to the peoples concerned, or shall provide them with resources to allow them to design and deliver such services under their own responsibility and control, so that they may enjoy the highest attainable standard of physical and mental health.

2. Health services shall, to the extent possible, be community-based. These services shall be planned and administered in co-operation with the peoples concerned and take into account their economic, geographic, social and cultural conditions as well as their traditional preventive care, healing practices and medicines.

3. The health care system shall give preference to the training and employment of local community health workers, and focus on primary health care while maintaining strong links with other levels of health care services.

4. The provision of such health services shall be co-ordinated with other social, economic and cultural measures in the country.

PART VI. EDUCATION AND MEANS OF COMMUNICATION

Article 26

Measures shall be taken to ensure that members of the peoples concerned have the opportunity to acquire education at all levels on at least an equal footing with the rest of the national community.

Article 27

1. Education programmes and services for the peoples concerned shall be developed and implemented in co-operation with them to address their special needs, and shall incorporate their histories, their knowledge and technologies, their value systems and their further social, economic and cultural aspirations.

2. The competent authority shall ensure the training of members of these peoples and their involvement in the formulation and implementation of education programmes, with a view to the progressive transfer of responsibility for the conduct of these programmes to these peoples as appropriate.

3. In addition, governments shall recognise the right of these peoples to establish their own educational institutions and facilities, provided that such institutions meet minimum standards established by the competent authority in consultation with these peoples. Appropriate resources shall be provided for this purpose.

Article 28

1. Children belonging to the peoples concerned shall, wherever practicable, be taught to read and write in their own indigenous language or in the language most commonly used by the group to which they belong. When this is not practicable, the competent authorities shall undertake consultations with these peoples with a view to the adoption of measures to achieve this objective.

2. Adequate measures shall be taken to ensure that these peoples have the opportunity to attain fluency in the national language or in one of the official languages of the country.

3. Measures shall be taken to preserve and promote the development and practice of the indigenous languages of the peoples concerned.

Article 29

The imparting of general knowledge and skills that will help children belonging to the peoples concerned to participate fully and on an equal footing in their own community and in the national community shall be an aim of education for these peoples.

Article 30

1. Governments shall adopt measures appropriate to the traditions and cultures of the peoples concerned, to make known to them their rights and duties, especially in regard to labour, economic opportunities, education and health matters, social welfare and their rights deriving from this Convention.
2. If necessary, this shall be done by means of written translations and through the use of mass communications in the languages of these peoples.

Article 31

Educational measures shall be taken among all sections of the national community, and particularly among those that are in most direct contact with the peoples concerned, with the object of eliminating prejudices that they may harbour in respect of these peoples. To this end, efforts shall be made to ensure that history textbooks and other educational materials provide a fair, accurate and informative portrayal of the societies and cultures of these peoples.

PART V. CONTACTS AND CO-OPERATION ACROSS BORDERS

Article 32

Governments shall take appropriate measures, including by means of international agreements, to facilitate contacts and co-operation between indigenous and tribal peoples across borders, including activities in the economic, social, cultural, spiritual and environmental fields.

PART VIII. ADMINISTRATION

Article 33

1. The governmental authority responsible for the matters covered in this Convention shall ensure that agencies or other appropriate mechanisms exist to administer the programmes affecting the peoples concerned and shall

ensure that they have the means necessary for the proper fulfilment of the functions assigned to them.

2. These programmes shall include:

(a) The planning, co-ordination, execution and evaluation, in cooperation with the peoples concerned, of the measures provided for in this Convention;

(b) The proposing of legislative and other measures to the competent authorities and supervision of the application of the measures taken, in cooperation with the peoples concerned.

PART IX. GENERAL PROVISIONS

Article 34

The nature and scope of the measures to be taken to give effect to this Convention shall be determined in a flexible manner, having regard to the conditions characteristic of each country.

Article 35

The application of the provisions of this Convention shall not adversely affect rights and benefits of the peoples concerned pursuant to other Conventions and Recommendations, international instruments, treaties, or national laws, awards, custom or agreements.

Convention on the Rights of the Child

1577 *UNTS* 3, entered into force 2 September 1990.

Article 2

1. States Parties shall respect and ensure the rights set forth in the present Convention to each child within their jurisdiction without discrimination of any kind, irrespective of the child's or his or her parent's or legal guardian's race, colour, sex, language, religion, political or other opinion, national, ethnic or social origin, property, disability, birth or other status.

2. States Parties shall take all appropriate measures to ensure that the child is protected against all forms of discrimination or punishment on the basis of the status, activities, expressed opinions, or beliefs of the child's parents, legal guardians, or family members.

Convention relating to the Status of Refugees

189 *UNTS* 150, entered into force 22 April 1954.

Article 3
Non-discrimination

The Contracting States shall apply the provisions of this Convention to refugees without discrimination as to race, religion or country of origin.

International Convention on the Protection of the Rights of All Migrant Workers and Members of Their Families

UN GA Res. 45/158, Annex, 45 UN GAOR Supp. (No. 49A) at 262, UN Doc. A/45/49 (1990), entered into force 1 July 2003.

Article 1

1. The present Convention is applicable, except as otherwise provided hereafter, to all migrant workers and members of their families without distinction of any kind such as sex, race, colour, language, religion or conviction, political or other opinion, national, ethnic or social origin, nationality, age, economic position, property, marital status, birth or other status.

African Charter on Human and Peoples' Rights

Adopted 27 June1981, OAU Doc. CAB/LEG/67/3 rev. 5 (1982), entered into force 21 October 1986.

Article 2

Every individual shall be entitled to the enjoyment of the rights and freedoms recognized and guaranteed in the present Charter without distinction of any kind such as race, ethnic group, color, sex, language, religion, political or any other opinion, national and social origin, fortune, birth or other status.

African Charter on the Rights and Welfare of the Child

OAU Doc. CAB/LEG/24.9/49 (1990),
entered into force 29 November 1999.

Article 3
Non-Discrimination

Every child shall be entitled to the enjoyment of the rights and freedoms recognized and guaranteed in this Charter irrespective of the child's or his/her parents' or legal guardians' race, ethnic group, colour, sex, language, religion, political or other opinion, national and social origin, fortune, birth or other status.

Convention Governing the Specific Aspects of Refugee Problems in Africa

1001 *UNTS* 45, entered into force 20 June 1974.

Article 4
Non-Discrimination

Member States undertake to apply the provisions of this Convention to all refugees without discrimination as to race, religion, nationality, membership of a particular social group or political opinions.

Protocol to the African Charter on Human and Peoples' Rights on the Rights of Women in Africa

OAU Doc. No. CAB/LEG/66.6 (Sept. 13, 2000),
entered into force 25 November 2005.

Article 2
Elimination of Discrimination Against Women

1. States Parties shall combat all forms of discrimination against women through appropriate legislative, institutional and other measures. In this regard they shall:

a) include in their national constitutions and other legislative instruments, if not already done, the principle of equality between women and men and ensure its effective application;

b) enact and effectively implement appropriate legislative or regulatory measures, including those prohibiting and curbing all forms of discrimination particularly those harmful practices which endanger the health and general well-being of women;

c) integrate a gender perspective in their policy decisions, legislation, development plans, programmes and activities and in all other spheres of life;

d) take corrective and positive action in those areas where discrimination against women in law and in fact continues to exist;

e) support the local, national, regional and continental initiatives directed at eradicating all forms of discrimination against women.

2. States Parties shall commit themselves to modify the social and cultural patterns of conduct of women and men through public education, information, education and communication strategies, with a view to achieving the elimination of harmful cultural and traditional practices and all other practices which are based on the idea of the inferiority or the superiority of either of the sexes, or on stereotyped roles for women and men.

European Convention for the Protection of Human Rights and Fundamental Freedoms

ETS No. 5, 213 *UNTS* 222, entered into force 3 September1953.

Article 14
Prohibition of discrimination

The enjoyment of the rights and freedoms set forth in this Convention shall be secured without discrimination on any ground such as sex, race, colour, language, religion, political or other opinion, national or social origin, association with a national minority, property, birth or other status.

Protocol No. 12 to the ECHR

ETS No. 177, entered into force 1 April 2005.

Article 1
General prohibition of discrimination

1. The enjoyment of any right set forth by law shall be secured without discrimination on any ground such as sex, race, colour, language, religion, political or other opinion, national or social origin, association with a national minority, property, birth or other status.

2. No one shall be discriminated against by any public authority on any ground such as those mentioned in paragraph 1.

European Social Charter (revised)

CETS No. 168, entered into force 1 July 1999 (revised).

Article E
Non-discrimination

The enjoyment of the rights set forth in this Charter shall be secured without discrimination on any ground such as race, colour, sex, language, religion, political or other opinion, national extraction or social origin, health, association with a national minority, birth or other status.

Framework Convention for the Protection of National Minorities

CETS No. 157, entered into force 1 February 1998.

Section I

Article 1

The protection of national minorities and of the rights and freedoms of persons belonging to those minorities forms an integral part of the international protection of human rights, and as such falls within the scope of international co-operation.

Article 2

The provisions of this framework Convention shall be applied in good faith, in a spirit of understanding and tolerance and in conformity with the principles of good neighbourliness, friendly relations and co-operation between States.

Article 3

1. Every person belonging to a national minority shall have the right freely to choose to be treated or not to be treated as such and no disadvantage shall result from this choice or from the exercise of the rights which are connected to that choice.

2. Persons belonging to national minorities may exercise the rights and enjoy the freedoms flowing from the principles enshrined in the present framework Convention individually as well as in community with others.

Section II

Article 4

1. The Parties undertake to guarantee to persons belonging to national minorities the right of equality before the law and of equal protection of the law. In this respect, any discrimination based on belonging to a national minority shall be prohibited.

2. The Parties undertake to adopt, where necessary, adequate measures in order to promote, in all areas of economic, social, political and cultural life, full and effective equality between persons belonging to a national minority and those belonging to the majority. In this respect, they shall take due account of the specific conditions of the persons belonging to national minorities.

3. The measures adopted in accordance with paragraph 2 shall not be considered to be an act of discrimination.

Article 5

1. The Parties undertake to promote the conditions necessary for persons belonging to national minorities to maintain and develop their culture, and to preserve the essential elements of their identity, namely their religion, language, traditions and cultural heritage.

2. Without prejudice to measures taken in pursuance of their general integration policy, the Parties shall refrain from policies or practices aimed at assimilation of persons belonging to national minorities against their will and shall protect these persons from any action aimed at such assimilation.

Article 6

1. The Parties shall encourage a spirit of tolerance and intercultural dialogue and take effective measures to promote mutual respect and understanding and co-operation among all persons living on their territory, irrespective of those persons' ethnic, cultural, linguistic or religious identity, in particular in the fields of education, culture and the media.

2. The Parties undertake to take appropriate measures to protect persons who may be subject to threats or acts of discrimination, hostility or violence as a result of their ethnic, cultural, linguistic or religious identity.

Article 7

The Parties shall ensure respect for the right of every person belonging to a national minority to freedom of peaceful assembly, freedom of association, freedom of expression, and freedom of thought, conscience and religion.

Article 8

The Parties undertake to recognise that every person belonging to a national minority has the right to manifest his or her religion or belief and to establish religious institutions, organisations and associations.

Article 9

1. The Parties undertake to recognise that the right to freedom of expression of every person belonging to a national minority includes freedom to hold opinions and to receive and impart information and ideas in the minority language, without interference by public authorities and regardless of frontiers. The Parties shall ensure, within the framework of their legal

systems, that persons belonging to a national minority are not discriminated against in their access to the media.

2. Paragraph 1 shall not prevent Parties from requiring the licensing, without discrimination and based on objective criteria, of sound radio and television broadcasting, or cinema enterprises.

3. The Parties shall not hinder the creation and the use of printed media by persons belonging to national minorities. In the legal framework of sound radio and television broadcasting, they shall ensure, as far as possible, and taking into account the provisions of paragraph 1, that persons belonging to national minorities are granted the possibility of creating and using their own media.

4. In the framework of their legal systems, the Parties shall adopt adequate measures in order to facilitate access to the media for persons belonging to national minorities and in order to promote tolerance and permit cultural pluralism.

Article 10

1. The Parties undertake to recognise that every person belonging to a national minority has the right to use freely and without interference his or her minority language, in private and in public, orally and in writing.

2. In areas inhabited by persons belonging to national minorities traditionally or in substantial numbers, if those persons so request and where such a request corresponds to a real need, the Parties shall endeavour to ensure, as far as possible, the conditions which would make it possible to use the minority language in relations between those persons and the administrative authorities.

3. The Parties undertake to guarantee the right of every person belonging to a national minority to be informed promptly, in a language which he or she understands, of the reasons for his or her arrest, and of the nature and cause of any accusation against him or her, and to defend himself or herself in this language, if necessary with the free assistance of an interpreter.

Article 11

1. The Parties undertake to recognise that every person belonging to a national minority has the right to use his or her surname (patronym) and first names in the minority language and the right to official recognition of them, according to modalities provided for in their legal system.

2. The Parties undertake to recognise that every person belonging to a national minority has the right to display in his or her minority language signs, inscriptions and other information of a private nature visible to the public.

3. In areas traditionally inhabited by substantial numbers of persons belonging to a national minority, the Parties shall endeavour, in the framework of their legal system, including, where appropriate, agreements with other States, and taking into account their specific conditions, to display traditional local names, street names and other topographical indications intended for the public also in the minority language when there is a sufficient demand for such indications.

Article 12

1. The Parties shall, where appropriate, take measures in the fields of education and research to foster knowledge of the culture, history, language and religion of their national minorities and of the majority.

2. In this context the Parties shall inter alia provide adequate opportunities for teacher training and access to textbooks, and facilitate contacts among students and teachers of different communities.

3. The Parties undertake to promote equal opportunities for access to education at all levels for persons belonging to national minorities.

Article 13

1. Within the framework of their education systems, the Parties shall recognise that persons belonging to a national minority have the right to set up and to manage their own private educational and training establishments.

2. The exercise of this right shall not entail any financial obligation for the Parties.

Article 14

1. The Parties undertake to recognise that every person belonging to a national minority has the right to learn his or her minority language.

2. In areas inhabited by persons belonging to national minorities traditionally or in substantial numbers, if there is sufficient demand, the Parties shall endeavour to ensure, as far as possible and within the framework of their education systems, that persons belonging to those minorities have adequate opportunities for being taught the minority language or for receiving instruction in this language.

3. Paragraph 2 of this article shall be implemented without prejudice to the learning of the official language or the teaching in this language.

Article 15

The Parties shall create the conditions necessary for the effective participation of persons belonging to national minorities in cultural, social and economic life and in public affairs, in particular those affecting them.

Article 16

The Parties shall refrain from measures which alter the proportions of the population in areas inhabited by persons belonging to national minorities and are aimed at restricting the rights and freedoms flowing from the principles enshrined in the present framework Convention.

Article 17

1. The Parties undertake not to interfere with the right of persons belonging to national minorities to establish and maintain free and peaceful contacts across frontiers with persons lawfully staying in other States, in particular those with whom they share an ethnic, cultural, linguistic or religious identity, or a common cultural heritage.

2. The Parties undertake not to interfere with the right of persons belonging to national minorities to participate in the activities of non-governmental organisations, both at the national and international levels.

Article 18

1. The Parties shall endeavour to conclude, where necessary, bilateral and multilateral agreements with other States, in particular neighbouring States, in order to ensure the protection of persons belonging to the national minorities concerned.

2. Where relevant, the Parties shall take measures to encourage transfrontier co-operation.

Article 19

The Parties undertake to respect and implement the principles enshrined in the present framework Convention making, where necessary, only those limitations, restrictions or derogations which are provided for in international legal instruments, in particular the Convention for the Protection of Human Rights and Fundamental Freedoms, in so far as they are relevant to the rights and freedoms flowing from the said principles.

Section III

Article 20

In the exercise of the rights and freedoms flowing from the principles enshrined in the present framework Convention, any person belonging to a national minority shall respect the national legislation and the rights of others, in particular those of persons belonging to the majority or to other national minorities.

Article 21

Nothing in the present framework Convention shall be interpreted as implying any right to engage in any activity or perform any act contrary to the fundamental principles of international law and in particular of the sovereign equality, territorial integrity and political independence of States.

Article 22

Nothing in the present framework Convention shall be construed as limiting or derogating from any of the human rights and fundamental freedoms which may be ensured under the laws of any Contracting Party or under any other agreement to which it is a Party.

Article 23

The rights and freedoms flowing from the principles enshrined in the present framework Convention, in so far as they are the subject of a corresponding provision in the Convention for the Protection of Human Rights and Fundamental Freedoms or in the Protocols thereto, shall be understood so as to conform to the latter provisions.

Section IV

Article 24

1. The Committee of Ministers of the Council of Europe shall monitor the implementation of this framework Convention by the Contracting Parties.

2. The Parties which are not members of the Council of Europe shall participate in the implementation mechanism, according to modalities to be determined.

Article 25

1. Within a period of one year following the entered into force of this framework Convention in respect of a Contracting Party, the latter shall transmit to the Secretary General of the Council of Europe full information

on the legislative and other measures taken to give effect to the principles set out in this framework Convention.

2. Thereafter, each Party shall transmit to the Secretary General on a periodical basis and whenever the Committee of Ministers so requests any further information of relevance to the implementation of this framework Convention.

3. The Secretary General shall forward to the Committee of Ministers the information transmitted under the terms of this Article.

Article 26

1. In evaluating the adequacy of the measures taken by the Parties to give effect to the principles set out in this framework Convention the Committee of Ministers shall be assisted by an advisory committee, the members of which shall have recognised expertise in the field of the protection of national minorities.

2. The composition of this advisory committee and its procedure shall be determined by the Committee of Ministers within a period of one year following the entered into force of this framework Convention.

Section V

Article 27

This framework Convention shall be open for signature by the member States of the Council of Europe. Up until the date when the Convention enters into force, it shall also be open for signature by any other State so invited by the Committee of Ministers. It is subject to ratification, acceptance or approval. Instruments of ratification, acceptance or approval shall be deposited with the Secretary General of the Council of Europe.

Article 28

1. This framework Convention shall enter into force on the first day of the month following the expiration of a period of three months after the date on which twelve member States of the Council of Europe have expressed their consent to be bound by the Convention in accordance with the provisions of Article 27.

2. In respect of any member State which subsequently expresses its consent to be bound by it, the framework Convention shall enter into force on the first day of the month following the expiration of a period of three months after the date of the deposit of the instrument of ratification, acceptance or approval.

Treaties

Article 29

1. After the entered into force of this framework Convention and after consulting the Contracting States, the Committee of Ministers of the Council of Europe may invite to accede to the Convention, by a decision taken by the majority provided for in Article 20.d of the Statute of the Council of Europe, any non-member State of the Council of Europe which, invited to sign in accordance with the provisions of Article 27, has not yet done so, and any other non-member State.

2. In respect of any acceding State, the framework Convention shall enter into force on the first day of the month following the expiration of a period of three months after the date of the deposit of the instrument of accession with the Secretary General of the Council of Europe.

Article 30

1. Any State may at the time of signature or when depositing its instrument of ratification, acceptance, approval or accession, specify the territory or territories for whose international relations it is responsible to which this framework Convention shall apply.

2. Any State may at any later date, by a declaration addressed to the Secretary General of the Council of Europe, extend the application of this framework Convention to any other territory specified in the declaration. In respect of such territory the framework Convention shall enter into force on the first day of the month following the expiration of a period of three months after the date of receipt of such declaration by the Secretary General.

3. Any declaration made under the two preceding paragraphs may, in respect of any territory specified in such declaration, be withdrawn by a notification addressed to the Secretary General. The withdrawal shall become effective on the first day of the month following the expiration of a period of three months after the date of receipt of such notification by the Secretary General.

Article 31

1. Any Party may at any time denounce this framework Convention by means of a notification addressed to the Secretary General of the Council of Europe.

2. Such denunciation shall become effective on the first day of the month following the expiration of a period of six months after the date of receipt of the notification by the Secretary General.

Article 32

The Secretary General of the Council of Europe shall notify the member States of the Council, other signatory States and any State which has acceded to this framework Convention, of:

a. any signature;

b. the deposit of any instrument of ratification, acceptance, approval or accession;

c. any date of entered into force of this framework Convention in accordance with Articles 28, 29 and 30;

d. any other act, notification or communication relating to this framework Convention...

Charter of Fundamental Rights of the European Union

EU Doc. No. C 364/14, *OJEC* (18 December 2000).

CHAPTER III

EQUALITY

Article 20
Equality before the law

Everyone is equal before the law.

Article 21
Non-discrimination

1. Any discrimination based on any ground such as sex, race, colour, ethnic or social origin, genetic features, language, religion or belief, political or any other opinion, membership of a national minority, property, birth, disability, age or sexual orientation shall be prohibited.

2. Within the scope of application of the Treaty establishing the European Community and of the Treaty on European Union, and without prejudice to the special provisions of those Treaties, any discrimination on grounds of nationality shall be prohibited.

Article 22
Cultural, religious and linguistic diversity

The Union shall respect cultural, religious and linguistic diversity.

Article 23
Equality between men and women

Equality between men and women must be ensured in all areas, including employment, work and pay.

The principle of equality shall not prevent the maintenance or adoption of measures providing for specific advantages in favour of the under-represented sex.

Article 24
The rights of the child

1. Children shall have the right to such protection and care as is necessary for their well-being. They may express their views freely. Such views shall be

taken into consideration on matters which concern them in accordance with their age and maturity.

2. In all actions relating to children, whether taken by public authorities or private institutions, the child's best interests must be a primary consideration.

3. Every child shall have the right to maintain on a regular basis a personal relationship and direct contact with both his or her parents, unless that is contrary to his or her interests.

Article 25
The rights of the elderly

The Union recognises and respects the rights of the elderly to lead a life of dignity and independence and to participate in social and cultural life.

Article 26
Integration of persons with disabilities

The Union recognises and respects the right of persons with disabilities to benefit from measures designed to ensure their independence, social and occupational integration and participation in the life of the community.

American Convention on Human Rights

OAS *Treaty Series* No. 36, 1144 *UNTS* 123,
entered into force 18 July 1978.

Article 1
Obligation to Respect Rights

1. The States Parties to this Convention undertake to respect the rights and freedoms recognized herein and to ensure to all persons subject to their jurisdiction the free and full exercise of those rights and freedoms, without any discrimination for reasons of race, color, sex, language, religion, political or other opinion, national or social origin, economic status, birth, or any other social condition.

Inter-American Convention on the Elimination of All Forms of Discrimination against Persons with Disabilities

O.A.S. AG/Res. 1608, 7 June 1999,
entered into force 14 September 2001.

Article I

For the purposes of this Convention, the following terms are defined:

1. Disability

The term "disability" means a physical, mental, or sensory impairment, whether permanent or temporary, that limits the capacity to perform one or more essential activities of daily life, and which can be caused or aggravated by the economic and social environment.

2. Discrimination against persons with disabilities

a. The term "discrimination against persons with disabilities" means any distinction, exclusion, or restriction based on a disability, record of disability, condition resulting from a previous disability, or perception of disability, whether present or past, which has the effect or objective of impairing or nullifying the recognition, enjoyment, or exercise by a person with a disability of his or her human rights and fundamental freedoms.

b. A distinction or preference adopted by a state party to promote the social integration or personal development of persons with disabilities does not constitute discrimination provided that the distinction or preference does not in itself limit the right of persons with disabilities to equality and that individuals with disabilities are not forced to accept such distinction or preference. If, under a state's internal law, a person can be declared legally incompetent, when necessary and appropriate for his or her well-being, such declaration does not constitute discrimination.

Article II

The objectives of this Convention are to prevent and eliminate all forms of discrimination against persons with disabilities and to promote their full integration into society.

Article III

To achieve the objectives of this Convention, the states parties undertake:

1. To adopt the legislative, social, educational, labor-related, or any other measures needed to eliminate discrimination against persons with disabilities

and to promote their full integration into society, including, but not limited to:

a. Measures to eliminate discrimination gradually and to promote integration by government authorities and/or private entities in providing or making available goods, services, facilities, programs, and activities such as employment, transportation, communications, housing, recreation, education, sports, law enforcement and administration of justice, and political and administrative activities;

b. Measures to ensure that new buildings, vehicles, and facilities constructed or manufactured within their respective territories facilitate transportation, communications, and access by persons with disabilities;

c. Measures to eliminate, to the extent possible, architectural, transportation, and communication obstacles to facilitate access and use by persons with disabilities; and

d. Measures to ensure that persons responsible for applying this Convention and domestic law in this area are trained to do so.

2. To work on a priority basis in the following areas:

a. Prevention of all forms of preventable disabilities;

b. Early detection and intervention, treatment, rehabilitation, education, job training, and the provision of comprehensive services to ensure the optimal level of independence and quality of life for persons with disabilities; and

c. Increasing of public awareness through educational campaigns aimed at eliminating prejudices, stereotypes, and other attitudes that jeopardize the right of persons to live as equals, thus promoting respect for and coexistence with persons with disabilities;

Article IV

To achieve the objectives of this Convention, the states parties undertake to:

1. Cooperate with one another in helping to prevent and eliminate discrimination against persons with disabilities;

2. Collaborate effectively in:

a. Scientific and technological research related to the prevention of disabilities and to the treatment, rehabilitation, and integration into society of persons with disabilities; and

b. The development of means and resources designed to facilitate or promote the independence, self-sufficiency, and total integration into society of persons with disabilities, under conditions of equality.

Article V

1. To the extent that it is consistent with their respective internal laws, the states parties shall promote participation by representatives of organizations of persons with disabilities, nongovernmental organizations working in this area, or, if such organizations do not exist, persons with disabilities, in the development, execution, and evaluation of measures and policies to implement this Convention.

2. The states parties shall create effective communication channels to disseminate among the public and private organizations working with persons with disabilities the normative and juridical advances that may be achieved in order to eliminate discrimination against persons with disabilities.

Article VI

1. To follow up on the commitments undertaken in this Convention, a Committee for the Elimination of All Forms of Discrimination against Persons with Disabilities, composed of one representative appointed by each state party, shall be established.

2. The committee shall hold its first meeting within the 90 days following the deposit of the 11th instrument of ratification. Said meeting shall be convened by the General Secretariat of the Organization of American States and shall be held at the Organization's headquarters, unless a state party offers to host it.

3. At the first meeting, the states parties undertake to submit a report to the Secretary General of the Organization for transmission to the Committee so that it may be examined and reviewed. Thereafter, reports shall be submitted every four years.

4. The reports prepared under the previous paragraph shall include information on measures adopted by the member states pursuant to this Convention and on any progress made by the states parties in eliminating all forms of discrimination against persons with disabilities. The reports shall indicate any circumstances or difficulties affecting the degree of fulfillment of the obligations arising from this Convention.

5. The Committee shall be the forum for assessment of progress made in the application of the Convention and for the exchange of experience among the states parties. The reports prepared by the committee shall reflect the deliberations; shall include information on any measures adopted by the states parties pursuant to this Convention, on any progress they have made in eliminating all forms of discrimination against persons with disabilities, and on any circumstances or difficulties they have encountered in the implementation of the Convention; and shall include the committee's conclusions, its observations, and its general suggestions for the gradual fulfillment of the Convention.

6. The committee shall draft its rules of procedure and adopt them by a simple majority.

7. The Secretary General shall provide the Committee with the support it requires in order to perform its functions.

Article VII

No provision of this Convention shall be interpreted as restricting, or permitting the restriction by states parties of the enjoyment of the rights of persons with disabilities recognized by customary international law or the international instruments by which a particular state party is bound ...

Arab Charter on Human Rights

Adopted 15 September 1994, not yet entered into force.

Part I

Article 1

(a) All peoples have the right of self-determination and control over their natural wealth and resources and, accordingly, have the right to freely determine the form of their political structure and to freely pursue their economic, social and cultural development.

(b) Racism, zionism, occupation and foreign domination pose a challenge to human dignity and constitute a fundamental obstacle to the realization of the basic rights of peoples. There is a need to condemn and endeavour to eliminate all such practices.

Part II

Article 2

Each State Party to the present Charter undertakes to ensure to all individuals within its territory and subject to its Jurisdiction the right to enjoy all the rights and freedoms recognized herein, without any distinction on grounds of race, colour, sex, language, religion, political opinion, national or social origin, property, birth or other status and without any discrimination between men and women.

OTHER INSTRUMENTS

Universal Declaration of Human Rights

Adopted 10 December 1948 by the UNGA

Article 1

All human beings are born free and equal in dignity and rights. They are endowed with reason and conscience and should act towards one another in a spirit of brotherhood ...

Article 2

Everyone is entitled to all the rights and freedoms set forth in this Declaration, without distinction of any kind, such as race, colour, sex, language, religion, political or other opinion, national or social origin, property, birth or other status. ...

Furthermore, no distinction shall be made on the basis of the political, jurisdictional or international status of the country or territory to which a person belongs, whether it be independent, trust, non-self-governing or under any other limitation of sovereignty. ...

Article 7

All are equal before the law and are entitled without any discrimination to equal protection of the law. All are entitled to equal protection against any discrimination in violation of this Declaration and against any incitement to such discrimination.

Declaration of the World Conference against Racism, Racial Discrimination, Xenophobia and Related Intolerance

UN Doc. A/ CONF.189/12 (2001).

General issues

1. We declare that for the purpose of the present Declaration and Programme of Action, the victims of racism, racial discrimination, xenophobia and related intolerance are individuals or groups of individuals who are or have been negatively affected by, subjected to, or targets of these scourges;

2. We recognize that racism, racial discrimination, xenophobia and related intolerance occur on the grounds of race, colour, descent or national or ethnic origin and that victims can suffer multiple or aggravated forms of discrimination based on other related grounds such as sex, language, religion, political or other opinion, social origin, property, birth or other status;

3. We recognize and affirm that, at the outset of the third millennium, a global fight against racism, racial discrimination, xenophobia and related intolerance and all their abhorrent and evolving forms and manifestations is a matter of priority for the international community, and that this Conference offers a unique and historic opportunity for assessing and identifying all dimensions of those devastating evils of humanity with a view to their total elimination through, inter alia, the initiation of innovative and holistic approaches and the strengthening and enhancement of practical and effective measures at the national, regional and international levels;

4. We express our solidarity with the people of Africa in their continuing struggle against racism, racial discrimination, xenophobia and related intolerance and recognize the sacrifices made by them, as well as their efforts in raising international public awareness of these inhuman tragedies;

5. We also affirm the great importance we attach to the values of solidarity, respect, tolerance and multiculturalism, which constitute the moral ground and inspiration for our worldwide struggle against racism, racial discrimination, xenophobia and related intolerance, inhuman tragedies which have affected people throughout the world, especially in Africa, for too long;

6. We further affirm that all peoples and individuals constitute one human family, rich in diversity. They have contributed to the progress of civilizations and cultures that form the common heritage of humanity. Preservation and

promotion of tolerance, pluralism and respect for diversity can produce more inclusive societies;

7. We declare that all human beings are born free, equal in dignity and rights and have the potential to contribute constructively to the development and well-being of their societies. Any doctrine of racial superiority is scientifically false, morally condemnable, socially unjust and dangerous, and must be rejected along with theories which attempt to determine the existence of separate human races;

8. We recognize that religion, spirituality and belief play a central role in the lives of millions of women and men, and in the way they live and treat other persons. Religion, spirituality and belief may and can contribute to the promotion of the inherent dignity and worth of the human person and to the eradication of racism, racial discrimination, xenophobia and related intolerance;

9. We note with concern that racism, racial discrimination, xenophobia and related intolerance may be aggravated by, inter alia, inequitable distribution of wealth, marginalization and social exclusion;

10. We reaffirm that everyone is entitled to a social and international order in which all human rights can be fully realized for all, without any discrimination;

11. We note that the process of globalization constitutes a powerful and dynamic force which should be harnessed for the benefit, development and prosperity of all countries, without exclusion. We recognize that developing countries face special difficulties in responding to this central challenge. While globalization offers great opportunities, at present its benefits are very unevenly shared, while its costs are unevenly distributed. We thus express our determination to prevent and mitigate the negative effects of globalization. These effects could aggravate, inter alia, poverty, underdevelopment, marginalization, social exclusion, cultural homogenization and economic disparities which may occur along racial lines, within and between States, and have an adverse impact. We further express our determination to maximize the benefits of globalization through, inter alia, the strengthening and enhancement of international cooperation to increase equality of opportunities for trade, economic growth and sustainable development, global communications through the use of new technologies and increased intercultural exchange through the preservation and promotion of cultural diversity, which can contribute to the eradication of racism, racial discrimination, xenophobia and related intolerance. Only through broad and sustained efforts to create a shared future based upon our common

humanity, and all its diversity, can globalization be made fully inclusive and equitable;

12. We recognize that interregional and intraregional migration has increased as a result of globalization, in particular from the South to the North, and stress that policies towards migration should not be based on racism, racial discrimination, xenophobia and related intolerance;

Sources, causes, forms and contemporary manifestations of racism, racial discrimination, xenophobia and related intolerance

13. We acknowledge that slavery and the slave trade, including the transatlantic slave trade, were appalling tragedies in the history of humanity not only because of their abhorrent barbarism but also in terms of their magnitude, organized nature and especially their negation of the essence of the victims, and further acknowledge that slavery and the slave trade are a crime against humanity and should always have been so, especially the transatlantic slave trade and are among the major sources and manifestations of racism, racial discrimination, xenophobia and related intolerance, and that Africans and people of African descent, Asians and people of Asian descent and indigenous peoples were victims of these acts and continue to be victims of their consequences;

14. We recognize that colonialism has led to racism, racial discrimination, xenophobia and related intolerance, and that Africans and people of African descent, and people of Asian descent and indigenous peoples were victims of colonialism and continue to be victims of its consequences. We acknowledge the suffering caused by colonialism and affirm that, wherever and whenever it occurred, it must be condemned and its reoccurrence prevented. We further regret that the effects and persistence of these structures and practices have been among the factors contributing to lasting social and economic inequalities in many parts of the world today;

15. We recognize that apartheid and genocide in terms of international law constitute crimes against humanity and are major sources and manifestations of racism, racial discrimination, xenophobia and related intolerance, and acknowledge the untold evil and suffering caused by these acts and affirm that wherever and whenever they occurred, they must be condemned and their recurrence prevented;

16. We recognize that xenophobia against non-nationals, particularly migrants, refugees and asylum-seekers, constitutes one of the main sources of contemporary racism and that human rights violations against members of

such groups occur widely in the context of discriminatory, xenophobic and racist practices;

17. We note the importance of paying special attention to new manifestations of racism, racial discrimination, xenophobia and related intolerance to which youth and other vulnerable groups might be exposed;

18. We emphasize that poverty, underdevelopment, marginalization, social exclusion and economic disparities are closely associated with racism, racial discrimination, xenophobia and related intolerance, and contribute to the persistence of racist attitudes and practices which in turn generate more poverty;

19. We recognize the negative economic, social and cultural consequences of racism, racial discrimination, xenophobia and related intolerance, which have contributed significantly to the underdevelopment of developing countries and, in particular, of Africa and resolve to free every man, woman and child from the abject and dehumanizing conditions of extreme poverty to which more than one billion of them are currently subjected, to make the right to development a reality for everyone and to free the entire human race from want;

20. We recognize that racism, racial discrimination, xenophobia and related intolerance are among the root causes of armed conflict and very often one of its consequences and recall that non-discrimination is a fundamental principle of international humanitarian law. We underscore the need for all parties to armed conflicts to abide scrupulously by this principle and for States and the international community to remain especially vigilant during periods of armed conflict and continue to combat all forms of racial discrimination;

21. We express our deep concern that socio-economic development is being hampered by widespread internal conflicts which are due, among other causes, to gross violations of human rights, including those arising from racism, racial discrimination, xenophobia and related intolerance, and from lack of democratic, inclusive and participatory governance;

22. We express our concern that in some States political and legal structures or institutions, some of which were inherited and persist today, do not correspond to the multi-ethnic, pluricultural and plurilingual characteristics of the population and, in many cases, constitute an important factor of discrimination in the exclusion of indigenous peoples;

23. We fully recognize the rights of indigenous peoples consistent with the principles of sovereignty and territorial integrity of States, and therefore stress

the need to adopt the appropriate constitutional, administrative, legislative and judicial measures, including those derived from applicable international instruments;

24. We declare that the use of the term "indigenous peoples" in the Declaration and Programme of Action of the World Conference against Racism, Racial Discrimination, Xenophobia and Related Intolerance is in the context of, and without prejudice to the outcome of, ongoing international negotiations on texts that specifically deal with this issue, and cannot be construed as having any implications as to rights under international law;

25. We express our profound repudiation of the racism, racial discrimination, xenophobia and related intolerance that persist in some States in the functioning of the penal systems and in the application of the law, as well as in the actions and attitudes of institutions and individuals responsible for law enforcement, especially where this has contributed to certain groups being over-represented among persons under detention or imprisoned;

26. We affirm the need to put an end to impunity for violations of the human rights and fundamental freedoms of individuals and groups of individuals who are victimized by racism, racial discrimination, xenophobia and related intolerance;

27. We express our concern that, beyond the fact that racism is gaining ground, contemporary forms and manifestations of racism and xenophobia are striving to regain political, moral and even legal recognition in many ways, including through the platforms of some political parties and organizations and the dissemination through modern communication technologies of ideas based on the notion of racial superiority;

28. We recall that persecution against any identifiable group, collectivity or community on racial, national, ethnic or other grounds that are universally recognized as impermissible under international law, as well as the crime of apartheid, constitute serious violations of human rights and, in some cases, qualify as crimes against humanity;

29. We strongly condemn the fact that slavery and slavery-like practices still exist today in parts of the world and urge States to take immediate measures as a matter of priority to end such practices, which constitute flagrant violations of human rights;

30. We affirm the urgent need to prevent, combat and eliminate all forms of trafficking in persons, in particular women and children, and recognize that

victims of trafficking are particularly exposed to racism, racial discrimination, xenophobia and related intolerance;

Victims of racism, racial discrimination, xenophobia and related intolerance

31. We also express our deep concern whenever indicators in the fields of, inter alia, education, employment, health, housing, infant mortality and life expectancy for many peoples show a situation of disadvantage, particularly where the contributing factors include racism, racial discrimination, xenophobia and related intolerance;

32. We recognize the value and diversity of the cultural heritage of Africans and people of African descent and affirm the importance and necessity of ensuring their full integration into social, economic and political life with a view to facilitating their full participation at all levels in the decision-making process;

33. We consider it essential for all countries in the region of the Americas and all other areas of the African Diaspora to recognize the existence of their population of African descent and the cultural, economic, political and scientific contributions made by that population, and recognize the persistence of racism, racial discrimination, xenophobia and related intolerance that specifically affect them, and recognize that, in many countries, their long-standing inequality in terms of access to, inter alia, education, health care and housing has been a profound cause of the socio-economic disparities that affect them;

34. We recognize that people of African descent have for centuries been victims of racism, racial discrimination and enslavement and of the denial by history of many of their rights, and assert that they should be treated with fairness and respect for their dignity and should not suffer discrimination of any kind. Recognition should therefore be given to their rights to culture and their own identity; to participate freely and in equal conditions in political, social, economic and cultural life; to development in the context of their own aspirations and customs; to keep, maintain and foster their own forms of organization, their mode of life, culture, traditions and religious expressions; to maintain and use their own languages; to the protection of their traditional knowledge and their cultural and artistic heritage; to the use, enjoyment and conservation of the natural renewable resources of their habitat and to active participation in the design, implementation and development of educational systems and programmes, including those of a specific and characteristic nature; and where applicable to their ancestrally inhabited land;

35. We recognize that in many parts of the world, Africans and people of African descent face barriers as a result of social biases and discrimination prevailing in public and private institutions and express our commitment to work towards the eradication of all forms of racism, racial discrimination, xenophobia and related intolerance faced by Africans and people of African descent;

36. We recognize that in many parts of the world, Asians and people of Asian descent face barriers as a result of social biases and discrimination prevailing in public and private institutions and express our commitment to work towards the eradication of all forms of racism, racial discrimination, xenophobia and related intolerance faced by Asians and people of Asian descent;

37. We note with appreciation that despite the racism, racial discrimination, xenophobia and related intolerance faced by them for centuries, people of Asian descent have contributed and continue to contribute significantly to the economic, social, political, scientific and cultural life of the countries where they live;

38. We call upon all States to review and, where necessary, revise any immigration policies which are inconsistent with international human rights instruments, with a view to eliminating all discriminatory policies and practices against migrants, including Asians and people of Asian descent;

39. We recognize that the indigenous peoples have been victims of discrimination for centuries and affirm that they are free and equal in dignity and rights and should not suffer any discrimination, particularly on the basis of their indigenous origin and identity, and we stress the continuing need for action to overcome the persistent racism, racial discrimination, xenophobia and related intolerance that affect them;

40. We recognize the value and diversity of the cultures and the heritage of indigenous peoples, whose singular contribution to the development and cultural pluralism of society and full participation in all aspects of society, in particular on issues that are of concern to them, are fundamental for political and social stability, and for the development of the States in which they live;

41. We reiterate our conviction that the full realization by indigenous peoples of their human rights and fundamental freedoms is indispensable for eliminating racism, racial discrimination, xenophobia and related intolerance. We firmly reiterate our determination to promote their full and equal enjoyment of civil, political, economic, social and cultural rights, as

well as the benefits of sustainable development, while fully respecting their distinctive characteristics and their own initiatives;

42. We emphasize that, in order for indigenous peoples freely to express their own identity and exercise their rights, they should be free from all forms of discrimination, which necessarily entails respect for their human rights and fundamental freedoms. Efforts are now being made to secure universal recognition for those rights in the negotiations on the draft declaration on the rights of indigenous peoples, including the following: to call themselves by their own names; to participate freely and on an equal footing in their country's political, economic, social and cultural development; to maintain their own forms of organization, lifestyles, cultures and traditions; to maintain and use their own languages; to maintain their own economic structures in the areas where they live; to take part in the development of their educational systems and programmes; to manage their lands and natural resources, including hunting and fishing rights; and to have access to justice on a basis of equality;

43. We also recognize the special relationship that indigenous peoples have with the land as the basis for their spiritual, physical and cultural existence and encourage States, wherever possible, to ensure that indigenous peoples are able to retain ownership of their lands and of those natural resources to which they are entitled under domestic law;

44. We welcome the decision to create the Permanent Forum on Indigenous Issues within the United Nations system, giving concrete expression to major objectives of the International Decade of the World's Indigenous People and the Vienna Declaration and Programme of Action;

45. We welcome the appointment by the United Nations of the Special Rapporteur on the situation of human rights and fundamental freedoms of indigenous people and express our commitment to cooperate with the Special Rapporteur;

46. We recognize the positive economic, social and cultural contributions made by migrants to both countries of origin and destination;

47. We reaffirm the sovereign right of each State to formulate and apply its own legal framework and policies for migration, and further affirm that these policies should be consistent with applicable human rights instruments, norms and standards, and designed to ensure that they are free of racism, racial discrimination, xenophobia and related intolerance;

48. We note with concern and strongly condemn the manifestations and acts of racism, racial discrimination, xenophobia and related intolerance against

migrants and the stereotypes often applied to them; reaffirm the responsibility of States to protect the human rights of migrants under their jurisdiction and reaffirm the responsibility of States to safeguard and protect migrants against illegal or violent acts, in particular acts of racial discrimination and crimes perpetrated with racist or xenophobic motivation by individuals or groups; and stress the need for their fair, just and equitable treatment in society and in the workplace;

49. We highlight the importance of creating conditions conducive to greater harmony, tolerance and respect between migrants and the rest of society in the countries in which they find themselves, in order to eliminate manifestations of racism and xenophobia against migrants. We underline that family reunification has a positive effect on integration and emphasize the need for States to facilitate family reunion;

50. We are mindful of the situation of vulnerability in which migrants frequently find themselves, owing, inter alia, to their departure from their countries of origin and to the difficulties they encounter because of differences in language, customs and culture, as well as economic and social difficulties and obstacles to the return of migrants who are undocumented or in an irregular situation;

51. We reaffirm the necessity of eliminating racial discrimination against migrants, including migrant workers, in relation to issues such as employment, social services, including education and health, as well as access to justice, and that their treatment must be in accordance with international human rights instruments, free from racism, racial discrimination, xenophobia and related intolerance;

52. We note with concern that, among other factors, racism, racial discrimination, xenophobia and related intolerance contribute to forced displacement and the movement of people from their countries of origin as refugees and asylum-seekers;

53. We recognize with concern that, despite efforts to combat racism, racial discrimination, xenophobia and related intolerance, instances of various forms of racism, racial discrimination, xenophobia and related intolerance against refugees, asylum-seekers and internally displaced persons, among others, continue;

54. We underline the urgency of addressing the root causes of displacement and of finding durable solutions for refugees and displaced persons, in particular voluntary return in safety and dignity to the countries of origin, as

well as resettlement in third countries and local integration, when and where appropriate and feasible;

55. We affirm our commitment to respect and implement humanitarian obligations relating to the protection of refugees, asylum-seekers, returnees and internally displaced persons, and note in this regard the importance of international solidarity, burden-sharing and international cooperation to share responsibility for the protection of refugees, reaffirming that the 1951 Convention relating to the Status of Refugees and its 1967 Protocol remain the foundation of the international refugee regime and recognizing the importance of their full application by States parties;

56. We recognize the presence in many countries of a Mestizo population of mixed ethnic and racial origins and its valuable contribution to the promotion of tolerance and respect in these societies, and we condemn discrimination against them, especially because such discrimination may be denied owing to its subtle nature;

57. We are conscious of the fact that the history of humanity is replete with major atrocities as a result of gross violations of human rights and believe that lessons can be learned through remembering history to avert future tragedies;

58. We recall that the Holocaust must never be forgotten;

59. We recognize with deep concern religious intolerance against certain religious communities, as well as the emergence of hostile acts and violence against such communities because of their religious beliefs and their racial or ethnic origin in various parts of the world which in particular limit their right to freely practise their belief;

60. We also recognize with deep concern the existence in various parts of the world of religious intolerance against religious communities and their members, in particular limitation of their right to practise their beliefs freely, as well as the emergence of increased negative stereotyping, hostile acts and violence against such communities because of their religious beliefs and their ethnic or so-called racial origin;

61. We recognize with deep concern the increase in anti-Semitism and Islamophobia in various parts of the world, as well as the emergence of racial and violent movements based on racism and discriminatory ideas against Jewish, Muslim and Arab communities;

62. We are conscious that humanity's history is replete with terrible wrongs inflicted through lack of respect for the equality of human beings and note

with alarm the increase of such practices in various parts of the world, and we urge people, particularly in conflict situations, to desist from racist incitement, derogatory language and negative stereotyping;

63. We are concerned about the plight of the Palestinian people under foreign occupation. We recognize the inalienable right of the Palestinian people to self-determination and to the establishment of an independent State and we recognize the right to security for all States in the region, including Israel, and call upon all States to support the peace process and bring it to an early conclusion;

64. We call for a just, comprehensive and lasting peace in the region in which all peoples shall co-exist and enjoy equality, justice and internationally recognized human rights, and security;

65. We recognize the right of refugees to return voluntarily to their homes and properties in dignity and safety, and urge all States to facilitate such return;

66. We affirm that the ethnic, cultural, linguistic and religious identity of minorities, where they exist, must be protected and that persons belonging to such minorities should be treated equally and enjoy their human rights and fundamental freedoms without discrimination of any kind;

67. We recognize that members of certain groups with a distinct cultural identity face barriers arising from a complex interplay of ethnic, religious and other factors, as well as their traditions and customs, and call upon States to ensure that measures, policies and programmes aimed at eradicating racism, racial discrimination, xenophobia and related intolerance address the barriers that this interplay of factors creates;

68. We recognize with deep concern the ongoing manifestations of racism, racial discrimination, xenophobia and related intolerance, including violence, against Roma/Gypsies/Sinti/Travellers and recognize the need to develop effective policies and implementation mechanisms for their full achievement of equality;

69. We are convinced that racism, racial discrimination, xenophobia and related intolerance reveal themselves in a differentiated manner for women and girls, and can be among the factors leading to a deterioration in their living conditions, poverty, violence, multiple forms of discrimination, and the limitation or denial of their human rights. We recognize the need to integrate a gender perspective into relevant policies, strategies and programmes of action against racism, racial discrimination, xenophobia and related intolerance in order to address multiple forms of discrimination;

70. We recognize the need to develop a more systematic and consistent approach to evaluating and monitoring racial discrimination against women, as well as the disadvantages, obstacles and difficulties women face in the full exercise and enjoyment of their civil, political, economic, social and cultural rights because of racism, racial discrimination, xenophobia and related intolerance;

71. We deplore attempts to oblige women belonging to certain faiths and religious minorities to forego their cultural and religious identity, or to restrict their legitimate expression, or to discriminate against them with regard to opportunities for education and employment;

72. We note with concern the large number of children and young people, particularly girls, among the victims of racism, racial discrimination, xenophobia and related intolerance and stress the need to incorporate special measures, in accordance with the principle of the best interests of the child and respect for his or her views, in programmes to combat racism, racial discrimination, xenophobia and related intolerance, in order to give priority attention to the rights and the situation of children and young people who are victims of these practices;

73. We recognize that a child belonging to an ethnic, religious or linguistic minority or who is indigenous shall not be denied the right, individually or in community with other members of his or her group, to enjoy his or her own culture, to profess and practise his or her own religion, or to use his or her own language;

74. We recognize that child labour is linked to poverty, lack of development and related socio-economic conditions and could in some cases perpetuate poverty and racial discrimination by disproportionately denying children from affected groups the opportunity to acquire the human capabilities needed in productive life and to benefit from economic growth;

75. We note with deep concern the fact that, in many countries, people infected or affected by HIV/AIDS, as well as those who are presumed to be infected, belong to groups vulnerable to racism, racial discrimination, xenophobia and related intolerance, which has a negative impact and impedes their access to health care and medication;

Measures of prevention, education and protection aimed at the eradication of racism, racial discrimination, xenophobia and related intolerance at the national, regional and international levels

76. We recognize that inequitable political, economic, cultural and social conditions can breed and foster racism, racial discrimination, xenophobia

and related intolerance, which in turn exacerbate the inequity. We believe that genuine equality of opportunity for all, in all spheres, including that for development, is fundamental for the eradication of racism, racial discrimination, xenophobia and related intolerance;

77. We affirm that universal adherence to and full implementation of the International Convention on the Elimination of All Forms of Racial Discrimination are of paramount importance for promoting equality and non-discrimination in the world;

78. We affirm the solemn commitment of all States to promote universal respect for, and observance and protection of, all human rights, economic, social, cultural, civil and political, including the right to development, as a fundamental factor in the prevention and elimination of racism, racial discrimination, xenophobia and related intolerance;

79. We firmly believe that the obstacles to overcoming racial discrimination and achieving racial equality mainly lie in the lack of political will, weak legislation and lack of implementation strategies and concrete action by States, as well as the prevalence of racist attitudes and negative stereotyping;

80. We firmly believe that education, development and the faithful implementation of all international human rights norms and obligations, including enactment of laws and political, social and economic policies, are crucial to combat racism, racial discrimination, xenophobia and related intolerance;

81. We recognize that democracy, transparent, responsible, accountable and participatory governance responsive to the needs and aspirations of the people, and respect for human rights, fundamental freedoms and the rule of law are essential for the effective prevention and elimination of racism, racial discrimination, xenophobia and related intolerance. We reaffirm that any form of impunity for crimes motivated by racist and xenophobic attitudes plays a role in weakening the rule of law and democracy and tends to encourage the recurrence of such acts;

82. We affirm that the Dialogue among Civilizations constitutes a process to attain identification and promotion of common grounds among civilizations, recognition and promotion of the inherent dignity and of the equal rights of all human beings and respect for fundamental principles of justice; in this way, it can dispel notions of cultural superiority based on racism, racial discrimination, xenophobia and related intolerance, and facilitate the building of a reconciled world for the human family;

83. We underline the key role that political leaders and political parties can and ought to play in combating racism, racial discrimination, xenophobia and related intolerance and encourage political parties to take concrete steps to promote solidarity, tolerance and respect;

84. We condemn the persistence and resurgence of neo-Nazism, neo-Fascism and violent nationalist ideologies based on racial or national prejudice, and state that these phenomena can never be justified in any instance or in any circumstances;

85. We condemn political platforms and organizations based on racism, xenophobia or doctrines of racial superiority and related discrimination, as well as legislation and practices based on racism, racial discrimination, xenophobia and related intolerance, as incompatible with democracy and transparent and accountable governance. We reaffirm that racism, racial discrimination, xenophobia and related intolerance condoned by governmental policies violate human rights and may endanger friendly relations among peoples, cooperation among nations and international peace and security;

86. We recall that the dissemination of all ideas based upon racial superiority or hatred shall be declared an offence punishable by law with due regard to the principles embodied in the Universal Declaration of Human Rights and the rights expressly set forth in article 5 of the International Convention on the Elimination of All Forms of Racial Discrimination;

87. We note that article 4, paragraph b, of the International Convention on the Elimination of All Forms of Racial Discrimination places an obligation upon States to be vigilant and to proceed against organizations that disseminate ideas based on racial superiority or hatred, acts of violence or incitement to such acts. These organizations shall be condemned and discouraged;

88. We recognize that the media should represent the diversity of a multicultural society and play a role in fighting racism, racial discrimination, xenophobia and related intolerance. In this regard we draw attention to the power of advertising;

89. We note with regret that certain media, by promoting false images and negative stereotypes of vulnerable individuals or groups of individuals, particularly of migrants and refugees, have contributed to the spread of xenophobic and racist sentiments among the public and in some cases have encouraged violence by racist individuals and groups;

90. We recognize the positive contribution that the exercise of the right to freedom of expression, particularly by the media and new technologies, including the Internet, and full respect for the freedom to seek, receive and impart information can make to the fight against racism, racial discrimination, xenophobia and related intolerance; we reiterate the need to respect the editorial independence and autonomy of the media in this regard;

91. We express deep concern about the use of new information technologies, such as the Internet, for purposes contrary to respect for human values, equality, non-discrimination, respect for others and tolerance, including to propagate racism, racial hatred, xenophobia, racial discrimination and related intolerance, and that, in particular, children and youth having access to this material could be negatively influenced by it;

92. We also recognize the need to promote the use of new information and communication technologies, including the Internet, to contribute to the fight against racism, racial discrimination, xenophobia and related intolerance; new technologies can assist the promotion of tolerance and respect for human dignity, and the principles of equality and non-discrimination;

93. We affirm that all States should recognize the importance of community media that give a voice to victims of racism, racial discrimination, xenophobia and related intolerance;

94. We reaffirm that the stigmatization of people of different origins by acts or omissions of public authorities, institutions, the media, political parties or national or local organizations is not only an act of racial discrimination but can also incite the recurrence of such acts, thereby resulting in the creation of a vicious circle which reinforces racist attitudes and prejudices, and which must be condemned;

95. We recognize that education at all levels and all ages, including within the family, in particular human rights education, is a key to changing attitudes and behaviour based on racism, racial discrimination, xenophobia and related intolerance and to promoting tolerance and respect for diversity in societies; we further affirm that such education is a determining factor in the promotion, dissemination and protection of the democratic values of justice and equity, which are essential to prevent and combat the spread of racism, racial discrimination, xenophobia and related intolerance;

96. We recognize that quality education, the elimination of illiteracy and access to free primary education for all can contribute to more inclusive societies, equity, stable and harmonious relations and friendship among

nations, peoples, groups and individuals, and a culture of peace, fostering mutual understanding, solidarity, social justice and respect for all human rights for all;

97. We underline the links between the right to education and the struggle against racism, racial discrimination, xenophobia and related intolerance and the essential role of education, including human rights education and education which is sensitive to and respects cultural diversity, especially amongst children and young people, in the prevention and eradication of all forms of intolerance and discrimination;

Provision of effective remedies, recourse, redress, and compensatory and other measures at the national, regional and international levels

98. We emphasize the importance and necessity of teaching about the facts and truth of the history of humankind from antiquity to the recent past, as well as of teaching about the facts and truth of the history, causes, nature and consequences of racism, racial discrimination, xenophobia and related intolerance, with a view to achieving a comprehensive and objective cognizance of the tragedies of the past;

99. We acknowledge and profoundly regret the massive human suffering and the tragic plight of millions of men, women and children caused by slavery, the slave trade, the transatlantic slave trade, apartheid, colonialism and genocide, and call upon States concerned to honour the memory of the victims of past tragedies and affirm that, wherever and whenever these occurred, they must be condemned and their recurrence prevented. We regret that these practices and structures, political, socio-economic and cultural, have led to racism, racial discrimination, xenophobia and related intolerance;

100. We acknowledge and profoundly regret the untold suffering and evils inflicted on millions of men, women and children as a result of slavery, the slave trade, the transatlantic slave trade, apartheid, genocide and past tragedies. We further note that some States have taken the initiative to apologize and have paid reparation, where appropriate, for grave and massive violations committed;

101. With a view to closing those dark chapters in history and as a means of reconciliation and healing, we invite the international community and its members to honour the memory of the victims of these tragedies. We further note that some have taken the initiative of regretting or expressing remorse or presenting apologies, and call on all those who have not yet contributed to

restoring the dignity of the victims to find appropriate ways to do so and, to this end, appreciate those countries that have done so;

102. We are aware of the moral obligation on the part of all concerned States and call upon these States to take appropriate and effective measures to halt and reverse the lasting consequences of those practices;

103. We recognize the consequences of past and contemporary forms of racism, racial discrimination, xenophobia and related intolerance as serious challenges to global peace and security, human dignity and the realization of human rights and fundamental freedoms of many people in the world, in particular Africans, people of African descent, people of Asian descent and indigenous peoples;

104. We also strongly reaffirm as a pressing requirement of justice that victims of human rights violations resulting from racism, racial discrimination, xenophobia and related intolerance, especially in the light of their vulnerable situation socially, culturally and economically, should be assured of having access to justice, including legal assistance where appropriate, and effective and appropriate protection and remedies, including the right to seek just and adequate reparation or satisfaction for any damage suffered as a result of such discrimination, as enshrined in numerous international and regional human rights instruments, in particular the Universal Declaration of Human Rights and the International Convention on the Elimination of All Forms of Racial Discrimination;

105. Guided by the principles set out in the Millennium Declaration and the recognition that we have a collective responsibility to uphold the principles of human dignity, equality and equity and to ensure that globalization becomes a positive force for all the world's people, the international community commits itself to working for the beneficial integration of the developing countries into the global economy, resisting their marginalization, determined to achieve accelerated economic growth and sustainable development and to eradicate poverty, inequality and deprivation;

106. We emphasize that remembering the crimes or wrongs of the past, wherever and whenever they occurred, unequivocally condemning its racist tragedies and telling the truth about history are essential elements for international reconciliation and the creation of societies based on justice, equality and solidarity;

Strategies to achieve full and effective equality, including international
cooperation and enhancement of the United Nations and other
international mechanisms in combating racism, racial discrimination,
xenophobia and related intolerance

107. We underscore the need to design, promote and implement at the
national, regional and international levels strategies, programmes and
policies, and adequate legislation, which may include special and positive
measures, for furthering equal social development and the realization of the
civil and political, economic, social and cultural rights of all victims of racism,
racial discrimination, xenophobia and related intolerance, including through
more effective access to the political, judicial and administrative institutions,
as well as the need to promote effective access to justice, as well as to
guarantee that the benefits of development, science and technology
contribute effectively to the improvement of the quality of life for all, without
discrimination;

108. We recognize the necessity for special measures or positive actions for
the victims of racism, racial discrimination, xenophobia and related
intolerance in order to promote their full integration into society. Those
measures for effective action, including social measures, should aim at
correcting the conditions that impair the enjoyment of rights and the
introduction of special measures to encourage equal participation of all racial
and cultural, linguistic and religious groups in all sectors of society and to
bring all onto an equal footing. Those measures should include measures to
achieve appropriate representation in educational institutions, housing,
political parties, parliaments and employment, especially in the judiciary,
police, army and other civil services, which in some cases might involve
electoral reforms, land reforms and campaigns for equal participation;

109. We recall the importance of enhancing international cooperation to
promote (a) the fight against racism, racial discrimination, xenophobia and
related intolerance; (b) the effective implementation by States of
international treaties and instruments that forbid these practices; (c) the goals
of the Charter of the United Nations in this regard; (d) the achievement of
the goals established by the United Nations Conference on Environment and
Development held in Rio de Janeiro in 1992, the World Conference on
Human Rights held in Vienna in 1993, the International Conference on
Population and Development held in Cairo in 1994, the World Summit for
Social Development held in Copenhagen in 1995, the Fourth World
Conference on Women held in Beijing in 1995, the United Nations
Conference on Human Settlements (Habitat II) held in Istanbul in 1996; and
the World Food Summit held in Rome in 1996, making sure that such goals

encompass with equity all the victims of racism, racial discrimination, xenophobia and related intolerance;

110. We recognize the importance of cooperation among States, relevant international and regional organizations, the international financial institutions, non-governmental organizations and individuals in the worldwide fight against racism, racial discrimination, xenophobia and related intolerance, and that success in this fight requires specifically taking into consideration the grievances, opinions and demands of the victims of such discrimination;

111. We reiterate that the international response and policy, including financial assistance, towards refugees and displaced persons in different parts of the world should not be based on discrimination on the grounds of race, colour, descent, or national or ethnic origin of the refugees and displaced persons concerned and, in this context, we urge the international community to provide adequate assistance on an equitable basis to host countries, in particular to host developing countries and countries in transition;

112. We recognize the importance of independent national human rights institutions conforming to the Principles relating to the status of national institutions for the promotion and protection of human rights, annexed to General Assembly resolution 48/134 of 20 December 1993, and other relevant specialized institutions created by law for the promotion and protection of human rights, including ombudsman institutions, in the struggle against racism, racial discrimination, xenophobia and related intolerance, as well as for the promotion of democratic values and the rule of law. We encourage States, as appropriate, to establish such institutions and call upon the authorities and society in general in those countries where they are performing their tasks of promotion, protection and prevention to cooperate to the maximum extent possible with these institutions, while respecting their independence;

113. We recognize the important role relevant regional bodies, including regional associations of national human rights institutions, can play in combating racism, racial discrimination, xenophobia and related intolerance, and the key role they can play in monitoring and raising awareness about intolerance and discrimination at the regional level, and reaffirm support for such bodies where they exist and encourage their establishment;

114. We recognize the paramount role of parliaments in the fight against racism, racial discrimination, xenophobia and related intolerance in adopting appropriate legislation, overseeing its implementation and allocating the requisite financial resources;

115. We stress the importance of involving social partners and other non-governmental organizations in the design and implementation of training and development programmes;

116. We recognize the fundamental role of civil society in the fight against racism, racial discrimination, xenophobia and related intolerance, in particular in assisting States to develop regulations and strategies, in taking measures and action against such forms of discrimination and through follow-up implementation;

117. We also recognize that promoting greater respect and trust among different groups within society must be a shared but differentiated responsibility of government institutions, political leaders, grass-roots organizations and citizens. We underline that civil society plays an important role in promoting the public interest, especially in combating racism, racial discrimination, xenophobia and related intolerance;

118. We welcome the catalytic role that non-governmental organizations play in promoting human rights education and raising awareness about racism, racial discrimination, xenophobia and related intolerance. They can also play an important role in raising awareness of such issues in the relevant bodies of the United Nations, based upon their national, regional or international experiences. Bearing in mind the difficulties they face, we commit ourselves to creating an atmosphere conducive to the effective functioning of human rights non-governmental organizations, in particular anti-racist non-governmental organizations, in combating racism, racial discrimination, xenophobia and related intolerance. We recognize the precarious situation of human rights non-governmental organizations, including anti-racist non-governmental organizations, in many parts of the world and express our commitment to adhere to our international obligations and to lift any unlawful barriers to their effective functioning;

119. We encourage the full participation of non-governmental organizations in the follow-up to the World Conference;

120. We recognize that international and national exchange and dialogue, and the development of a global network among youth, are important and fundamental elements in building intercultural understanding and respect, and will contribute to the elimination of racism, racial discrimination, xenophobia and related intolerance;

121. We underline the usefulness of involving youth in the development of forward-looking national, regional and international strategies and in policies to fight racism, racial discrimination, xenophobia and related intolerance;

122. We affirm that our global drive for the total elimination of racism, racial discrimination, xenophobia and related intolerance is undertaken, and that the recommendations contained in the Programme of Action are made, in a spirit of solidarity and international cooperation and are inspired by the purposes and principles of the Charter of the United Nations and other relevant international instruments. These recommendations are made with due consideration for the past, the present and the future, and with a constructive and forward-looking approach. We recognize that the formulation and implementation of these strategies, policies, programmes and actions, which should be carried out efficiently and promptly, are the responsibility of all States, with the full involvement of civil society at the national, regional and international levels.

Programme of Action of the World Conference Against Racism, Racial Discrimination, Xenophobia and Related Intolerance

UN Doc. A/ CONF.189/12 (2001).

Recognizing the urgent need to translate the objectives of the Declaration into a practical and workable Programme of Action, the World Conference against Racism, Racial Discrimination, Xenophobia and Related Intolerance:

I. Sources, causes, forms and contemporary manifestations of racism, racial discrimination, xenophobia and related intolerance

1. Urges States in their national efforts, and in cooperation with other States, regional and international organizations and financial institutions, to promote the use of public and private investment in consultation with the affected communities in order to eradicate poverty, particularly in those areas in which victims of racism, racial discrimination, xenophobia and related intolerance predominantly live;

2. Urges States to take all necessary and appropriate measures to end enslavement and contemporary forms of slavery-like practices, to initiate constructive dialogue among States and implement measures with a view to correcting the problems and the damage resulting therefrom;

II. Victims of racism, racial discrimination, xenophobia and related intolerance

Victims: General

3. Urges States to work nationally and in cooperation with other States and relevant regional and international organizations and programmes to strengthen national mechanisms to promote and protect the human rights of victims of racism, racial discrimination, xenophobia and related intolerance who are infected, or presumably infected, with pandemic diseases such as HIV/AIDS and to take concrete measures, including preventive action, appropriate access to medication and treatment, programmes of education, training and mass media dissemination, to eliminate violence, stigmatization, discrimination, unemployment and other negative consequences arising from these pandemics;

Africans and people of African descent

4. Urges States to facilitate the participation of people of African descent in all political, economic, social and cultural aspects of society and in the

advancement and economic development of their countries, and to promote a greater knowledge of and respect for their heritage and culture;

5. Requests States, supported by international cooperation as appropriate, to consider positively concentrating additional investments in health-care systems, education, public health, electricity, drinking water and environmental control, as well as other affirmative or positive action initiatives, in communities of primarily African descent;

6. Calls upon the United Nations, international financial and development institutions and other appropriate international mechanisms to develop capacity-building programmes intended for Africans and people of African descent in the Americas and around the world;

7. Requests the Commission on Human Rights to consider establishing a working group or other mechanism of the United Nations to study the problems of racial discrimination faced by people of African descent living in the African Diaspora and make proposals for the elimination of racial discrimination against people of African descent;

8. Urges financial and development institutions and the operational programmes and specialized agencies of the United Nations, in accordance with their regular budgets and the procedures of their governing bodies:

(a) To assign particular priority, and allocate sufficient funding, within their areas of competence and budgets, to improving the situation of Africans and people of African descent, while devoting special attention to the needs of these populations in developing countries, inter alia through the preparation of specific programmes of action;

(b) To carry out special projects, through appropriate channels and in collaboration with Africans and people of African descent, to support their initiatives at the community level and to facilitate the exchange of information and technical know-how between these populations and experts in these areas;

(c) To develop programmes intended for people of African descent allocating additional investments to health systems, education, housing, electricity, drinking water and environmental control measures and promoting equal opportunities in employment, as well as other affirmative or positive action initiatives;

9. Requests States to increase public actions and policies in favour of women and young males of African descent, given that racism affects them more deeply, placing them in a more marginalized and disadvantaged situation;

10. Urges States to ensure access to education and promote access to new technologies that would offer Africans and people of African descent, in particular women and children, adequate resources for education, technological development and long-distance learning in local communities, and further urges States to promote the full and accurate inclusion of the history and contribution of Africans and people of African descent in the education curriculum;

11. Encourages States to identify factors which prevent equal access to, and the equitable presence of, people of African descent at all levels of the public sector, including the public service, and in particular the administration of justice, and to take appropriate measures to remove the obstacles identified and also to encourage the private sector to promote equal access to, and the equitable presence of, people of African descent at all levels within their organizations;

12. Calls upon States to take specific steps to ensure full and effective access to the justice system for all individuals, particularly those of African descent;

13. Urges States, in accordance with international human rights standards and their respective domestic legal framework, to resolve problems of ownership of ancestral lands inhabited for generations by people of African descent and to promote the productive utilization of land and the comprehensive development of these communities, respecting their culture and their specific forms of decision-making;

14. Urges States to recognize the particularly severe problems of religious prejudice and intolerance that many people of African descent experience and to implement policies and measures that are designed to prevent and eliminate all such discrimination on the basis of religion and belief, which, when combined with certain other forms of discrimination, constitutes a form of multiple discrimination;

Indigenous peoples

15. Urges States:

(a) To adopt or continue to apply, in concert with them, constitutional, administrative, legislative, judicial and all necessary measures to promote, protect and ensure the enjoyment by indigenous peoples of their rights, as well as to guarantee them the exercise of their human rights and fundamental freedoms on the basis of equality, non-discrimination and full and free participation in all areas of society, in particular in matters affecting or concerning their interests;

(b) To promote better knowledge of and respect for indigenous cultures and heritage;

(c) and welcomes measures already taken by States in these respects;

16. Urges States to work with indigenous peoples to stimulate their access to economic activities and increase their level of employment, where appropriate, through the establishment, acquisition or expansion by indigenous peoples of enterprises, and the implementation of measures such as training, the provision of technical assistance and credit facilities;

17. Urges States to work with indigenous peoples to establish and implement programmes that provide access to training and services that could benefit the development of their communities;

18. Requests States to adopt public policies and give impetus to programmes on behalf of and in concert with indigenous women and girls, with a view to promoting their civil, political, economic, social and cultural rights; to putting an end to their situation of disadvantage for reasons of gender and ethnicity; to dealing with urgent problems affecting them in regard to education, their physical and mental health, economic life and in the matter of violence against them, including domestic violence; and to eliminating the situation of aggravated discrimination suffered by indigenous women and girls on multiple grounds of racism and gender discrimination;

19. Recommends that States examine, in conformity with relevant international human rights instruments, norms and standards, their Constitutions, laws, legal systems and policies in order to identify and eradicate racism, racial discrimination, xenophobia and related intolerance towards indigenous peoples and individuals, whether implicit, explicit or inherent;

20. Calls upon concerned States to honour and respect their treaties and agreements with indigenous peoples and to accord them due recognition and observance;

21. Calls upon States to give full and appropriate consideration to the recommendations produced by indigenous peoples in their own forums on the World Conference;

22. Requests States:

(a) To develop and, where they already exist, support institutional mechanisms to promote the accomplishment of the objectives and measures relating to indigenous peoples agreed in this Programme of Action;

(b) To promote, in concert with indigenous organizations, local authorities and non-governmental organizations, actions aimed at overcoming racism, racial discrimination, xenophobia and related intolerance against indigenous peoples and to make regular assessments of the progress achieved in this regard;

(c) To promote understanding among society at large of the importance of special measures to overcome disadvantages faced by indigenous peoples;

(d) To consult indigenous representatives in the process of decision-making concerning policies and measures that directly affect them;

23. Calls upon States to recognize the particular challenges faced by indigenous peoples and individuals living in urban environments and urges States to implement effective strategies to combat the racism, racial discrimination, xenophobia and related intolerance they encounter, paying particular attention to opportunities for their continued practice of their traditional, cultural, linguistic and spiritual ways of life;

Migrants

24. Requests all States to combat manifestations of a generalized rejection of migrants and actively to discourage all racist demonstrations and acts that generate xenophobic behaviour and negative sentiments towards, or rejection of, migrants;

25. Invites international and national non-governmental organizations to include monitoring and protection of the human rights of migrants in their programmes and activities and to sensitize Governments and increase public awareness in all States about the need to prevent racist acts and manifestations of discrimination, xenophobia and related intolerance against migrants;

26. Requests States to promote and protect fully and effectively the human rights and fundamental freedoms of all migrants, in conformity with the Universal Declaration of Human Rights and their obligations under international human rights instruments, regardless of the migrants' immigration status;

27. Encourages States to promote education on the human rights of migrants and to engage in information campaigns to ensure that the public receives accurate information regarding migrants and migration issues, including the positive contribution of migrants to the host society and the vulnerability of migrants, particularly those who are in an irregular situation;

28. Calls upon States to facilitate family reunification in an expeditious and effective manner which has a positive effect on integration of migrants, with due regard for the desire of many family members to have an independent status;

29. Urges States to take concrete measures that would eliminate racism, racial discrimination, xenophobia and related intolerance in the workplace against all workers, including migrants, and ensure the full equality of all before the law, including labour law, and further urges States to eliminate barriers, where appropriate, to: participating in vocational training, collective bargaining, employment, contracts and trade union activity; accessing judicial and administrative tribunals dealing with grievances; seeking employment in different parts of their country of residence; and working in safe and healthy conditions;

30. Urges States:

(a) To develop and implement policies and action plans, and to reinforce and implement preventive measures, in order to foster greater harmony and tolerance between migrants and host societies, with the aim of eliminating manifestations of racism, racial discrimination, xenophobia and related intolerance, including acts of violence, perpetrated in many societies by individuals or groups;

(b) To review and revise, where necessary, their immigration laws, policies and practices so that they are free of racial discrimination and compatible with States' obligations under international human rights instruments;

(c) To implement specific measures involving the host community and migrants in order to encourage respect for cultural diversity, to promote the fair treatment of migrants and to develop programmes, where appropriate, that facilitate their integration into social, cultural, political and economic life;

(d) To ensure that migrants, regardless of their immigration status, detained by public authorities are treated with humanity and in a fair manner, and receive effective legal protection and, where appropriate, the assistance of a competent interpreter in accordance with the relevant norms of international law and human rights standards, particularly during interrogation;

(e) To ensure that the police and immigration authorities treat migrants in a dignified and non-discriminatory manner, in accordance with international standards, through, inter alia, organizing specialized training courses for administrators, police officers, immigration officials and other interested groups;

(f) To consider the question of promoting the recognition of the educational, professional and technical credentials of migrants, with a view to maximizing their contribution to their new States of residence;

(g) To take all possible measures to promote the full enjoyment by all migrants of all human rights, including those related to fair wages and equal remuneration for work of equal value without distinction of any kind, and to the right to security in the event of unemployment, sickness, disability, widowhood, old age or other lack of livelihood in circumstances beyond their control, social security, including social insurance, access to education, health care, social services and respect for their cultural identity;

(h) To consider adopting and implementing immigration policies and programmes that would enable immigrants, in particular women and children who are victims of spousal or domestic violence, to free themselves from abusive relationships;

31. Urges States, in the light of the increased proportion of women migrants, to place special focus on gender issues, including gender discrimination, particularly when the multiple barriers faced by migrant women intersect; detailed research should be undertaken not only in respect of human rights violations perpetrated against women migrants, but also on the contribution they make to the economies of their countries of origin and their host countries, and the findings should be included in reports to treaty bodies;

32. Urges States to recognize the same economic opportunities and responsibilities to documented long-term migrants as to other members of society;

33. Recommends that host countries of migrants consider the provision of adequate social services, in particular in the areas of health, education and adequate housing, as a matter of priority, in cooperation with the United Nations agencies, the regional organizations and international financial bodies; also requests that these agencies provide an adequate response to requests for such services;

Refugees

34. Urges States to comply with their obligations under international human rights, refugee and humanitarian law relating to refugees, asylum-seekers and displaced persons, and urges the international community to provide them with protection and assistance in an equitable manner and with due regard

to their needs in different parts of the world, in keeping with principles of international solidarity, burden-sharing and international cooperation, to share responsibilities;

35. Calls upon States to recognize the racism, racial discrimination, xenophobia and related intolerance that refugees may face as they endeavour to engage in the life of the societies of their host countries and encourages States, in accordance with their international obligations and commitments, to develop strategies to address this discrimination and to facilitate the full enjoyment of the human rights of refugees. States parties should ensure that all measures relating to refugees must be in full accordance with the 1951 Convention relating to the Status of Refugees and its 1967 Protocol;

36. Urges States to take effective steps to protect refugee and internally displaced women and girls from violence, to investigate any such violations and to bring those responsible to justice, in collaboration, when appropriate, with the relevant and competent organizations;

Other victims

37. Urges States to take all possible measures to ensure that all persons, without any discrimination, are registered and have access to the necessary documentation reflecting their legal identity to enable them to benefit from available legal procedures, remedies and development opportunities, as well as to reduce the incidence of trafficking;

38. Recognizes that victims of trafficking are particularly exposed to racism, racial discrimination, xenophobia and related intolerance. States shall ensure that all measures taken against trafficking in persons, in particular those that affect the victims of such trafficking, are consistent with internationally recognized principles of non-discrimination, including the prohibition of racial discrimination and the availability of appropriate legal redress;

39. Calls upon States to ensure that Roma/Gypsy/Sinti/Traveller children and youth, especially girls, are given equal access to education and that educational curricula at all levels, including complementary programmes on intercultural education, which might, inter alia, include opportunities for them to learn the official languages in the pre-school period and to recruit Roma/Gypsy/Sinti/Traveller teachers and classroom assistants in order for such children and youth to learn their mother tongue, are sensitive and responsive to their needs;

40. Encourages States to adopt appropriate and concrete policies and measures, to develop implementation mechanisms, where these do not already exist, and to exchange experiences, in cooperation with

representatives of the Roma/Gypsies/Sinti/Travellers, in order to eradicate discrimination against them, enable them to achieve equality and ensure their full enjoyment of all their human rights, as recommended in the case of the Roma by the Committee on the Elimination of Racial Discrimination in its general recommendation XXVII, so that their needs are met;

41. Recommends that the intergovernmental organizations address, as appropriate, in their projects of cooperation with and assistance to various States, the situation of the Roma/Gypsies/Sinti/Travellers and promote their economic, social and cultural advancement;

42. Calls upon States and encourages non-governmental organizations to raise awareness about the racism, racial discrimination, xenophobia and related intolerance experienced by the Roma/Gypsies/Sinti/Travellers, and to promote knowledge and respect for their culture and history;

43. Encourages the media to promote equal access to and participation in the media for the Roma/Gypsies /Sinti/Travellers, as well as to protect them from racist, stereotypical and discriminatory media reporting, and calls upon States to facilitate the media's efforts in this regard;

44. Invites States to design policies aimed at combating racism, racial discrimination, xenophobia and related intolerance that are based on reliable statistical data recognizing the concerns identified in consultation with the Roma/Gypsies/Sinti/Travellers themselves reflecting as accurately as possible their status in society. All such information shall be collected in accordance with provisions on human rights and fundamental freedoms, such as data protection regulations and privacy guarantees, and in consultation with the persons concerned;

45. Encourages States to address the problems of racism, racial discrimination, xenophobia and related intolerance against people of Asian descent and urges States to take all necessary measures to eliminate the barriers that such persons face in participating in economic, social, cultural and political life;

46. Urges States to ensure within their jurisdiction that persons belonging to national or ethnic, religious and linguistic minorities can exercise fully and effectively all human rights and fundamental freedoms without any discrimination and in full equality before the law, and also urges States and the international community to promote and protect the rights of such persons;

47. Urges States to guarantee the rights of persons belonging to national or ethnic, religious and linguistic minorities, individually or in community with

other members of their group, to enjoy their own culture, to profess and practise their own religion, and to use their own language, in private and in public, freely and without interference, and to participate effectively in the cultural, social, economic and political life of the country in which they live, in order to protect them from any form of racism, racial discrimination, xenophobia and related intolerance that they are or may be subjected to;

48. Urges States to recognize the effect that discrimination, marginalization and social exclusion have had and continue to have on many racial groups living in a numerically based minority situation within a State, and to ensure that persons in such groups can exercise, as individual members of such groups, fully and effectively, all human rights and fundamental freedoms without distinction and in full equality before the law, and to take, where applicable, appropriate measures in respect of employment, housing and education with a view to preventing racial discrimination;

49. Urges States to take, where applicable, appropriate measures to prevent racial discrimination against persons belonging to national or ethnic, religious and linguistic minorities in respect of employment, health care, housing, social services and education, and in this context forms of multiple discrimination should be taken into account;

50. Urges States to incorporate a gender perspective in all programmes of action against racism, racial discrimination, xenophobia and related intolerance and to consider the burden of such discrimination which falls particularly on indigenous women, African women, Asian women, women of African descent, women of Asian descent, women migrants and women from other disadvantaged groups, ensuring their access to the resources of production on an equal footing with men, as a means of promoting their participation in the economic and productive development of their communities;

51. Urges States to involve women, especially women victims of racism, racial discrimination, xenophobia and related intolerance, in decision-making at all levels when working towards the eradication of such discrimination, and to develop concrete measures to incorporate race and gender analysis in the implementation of all aspects of the Programme of Action and national plans of action, particularly in the fields of employment programmes and services and resource allocation;

52. Recognizing that poverty shapes economic and social status and establishes obstacles to the effective political participation of women and men in different ways and to different extents, urges States to undertake gender analyses of all economic and social policies and programmes, especially

poverty eradication measures, including those designed and implemented to benefit those individuals or groups of individuals who are victims of racism, racial discrimination, xenophobia and related intolerance;

53. Urges States and encourages all sectors of society to empower women and girls who are victims of racism, racial discrimination, xenophobia and related intolerance, so that they can fully exercise their rights in all spheres of public and private life, and to ensure the full, equal and effective participation of women in decision-making at all levels, in particular in the design, implementation and evaluation of policies and measures which affect their lives;

54. Urges States:

(a) To recognize that sexual violence which has been systematically used as a weapon of war, sometimes with the acquiescence or at the instigation of the State, is a serious violation of international humanitarian law that, in defined circumstances, constitutes a crime against humanity and/or a war crime, and that the intersection of discrimination on grounds of race and gender makes women and girls particularly vulnerable to this type of violence, which is often related to racism, racial discrimination, xenophobia and related intolerance;

(b) To end impunity and prosecute those responsible for crimes against humanity and war crimes, including crimes related to sexual and other gender-based violence against women and girls, as well as to ensure that persons in authority who are responsible for such crimes, including by committing, ordering, soliciting, inducing, aiding in, abetting, assisting or in any other way contributing to their commission or attempted commission, are identified, investigated, prosecuted and punished;

55. Requests States, in collaboration where necessary with international organizations, having the best interests of the child as a primary consideration, to provide protection against racism, racial discrimination, xenophobia and related intolerance against children, especially those in circumstances of particular vulnerability, and to pay special attention to the situation of such children when designing relevant policies, strategies and programmes;

56. Urges States, in accordance with their national law and their obligations under the relevant international instruments, to take all measures to the maximum extent of their available resources to guarantee, without any discrimination, the equal right of all children to the immediate registration of birth, in order to enable them to exercise their human rights and

fundamental freedoms. States shall grant women equal rights with men with respect to nationality;

57. Urges States and international and regional organizations, and encourages non-governmental organizations and the private sector, to address the situation of persons with disabilities who are also subject to racism, racial discrimination, xenophobia and related intolerance; also urges States to take necessary measures to ensure their full enjoyment of all human rights and to facilitate their full integration into all fields of life;

III. Measures of prevention, education and protection aimed at the eradication of racism, racial discrimination, xenophobia and related intolerance at the national, regional and international levels

58. Urges States to adopt and implement, at both the national and international levels, effective measures and policies, in addition to existing anti-discrimination national legislation and relevant international instruments and mechanisms, which encourage all citizens and institutions to take a stand against racism, racial discrimination, xenophobia and related intolerance, and to recognize, respect and maximize the benefits of diversity within and among all nations in working together to build a harmonious and productive future by putting into practice and promoting values and principles such as justice, equality and non-discrimination, democracy, fairness and friendship, tolerance and respect within and between communities and nations, in particular through public information and education programmes to raise awareness and understanding of the benefits of cultural diversity, including programmes where the public authorities work in partnership with international and non-governmental organizations and other sectors of civil society;

59. Urges States to mainstream a gender perspective in the design and development of measures of prevention, education and protection aimed at the eradication of racism, racial discrimination, xenophobia and related intolerance at all levels, to ensure that they effectively target the distinct situations of women and men;

60. Urges States to adopt or strengthen, as appropriate, national programmes for eradicating poverty and reducing social exclusion which take account of the needs and experiences of individuals or groups of individuals who are victims of racism, racial discrimination, xenophobia and related intolerance, and also urges that they expand their efforts to foster bilateral, regional and international cooperation in implementing those programmes;

61. Urges States to work to ensure that their political and legal systems reflect the multicultural diversity within their societies and, where necessary, to improve democratic institutions so that they are more fully participatory and avoid marginalization, exclusion and discrimination against specific sectors of society;

62. Urges States to take all necessary measures to address specifically, through policies and programmes, racism and racially motivated violence against women and girls and to increase cooperation, policy responses and effective implementation of national legislation and of their obligations under relevant international instruments, and other protective and preventive measures aimed at the elimination of all forms of racially motivated discrimination and violence against women and girls;

63. Encourages the business sector, in particular the tourist industry and Internet providers, to develop codes of conduct, with a view to preventing trafficking in persons and protecting the victims of such traffic, especially those in prostitution, against gender-based and racial discrimination and promoting their rights, dignity and security;

64. Urges States to devise, enforce and strengthen effective measures at the national, regional and international levels to prevent, combat and eliminate all forms of trafficking in women and children, in particular girls, through comprehensive anti-trafficking strategies which include legislative measures, prevention campaigns and information exchange. It also urges States to allocate resources, as appropriate, to provide comprehensive programmes designed to provide assistance to, protection for, healing, reintegration into society and rehabilitation of victims. States shall provide or strengthen training for law enforcement, immigration and other relevant officials who deal with victims of trafficking in this regard;

65. Encourages the bodies, agencies and relevant programmes of the United Nations system and States to promote and to make use of the Guiding Principles on Internal Displacement (E/CN.4/1998/53/Add.2), particularly those provisions relating to non-discrimination,

A. National level

1. Legislative, judicial, regulatory, administrative and other measures to prevent and protect against racism, racial discrimination, xenophobia and related intolerance

66. Urges States to establish and implement without delay national policies and action plans to combat racism, racial discrimination, xenophobia and related intolerance, including their gender-based manifestations;

67. Urges States to design or reinforce, promote and implement effective legislative and administrative policies, as well as other preventive measures, against the serious situation experienced by certain groups of workers, including migrant workers, who are victims of racism, racial discrimination, xenophobia and related intolerance. Special attention should be given to protecting people engaged in domestic work and trafficked persons from discrimination and violence, as well as to combating prejudice against them;

68. Urges States to adopt and implement, or strengthen, national legislation and administrative measures that expressly and specifically counter racism and prohibit racial discrimination, xenophobia and related intolerance, whether direct or indirect, in all spheres of public life, in accordance with their obligations under the International Convention on the Elimination of All Forms of Racial Discrimination, ensuring that their reservations are not contrary to the object and purpose of the Convention;

69. Urges States to enact and implement, as appropriate, laws against trafficking in persons, especially women and children, and smuggling of migrants, taking into account practices that endanger human lives or lead to various kinds of servitude and exploitation, such as debt bondage, slavery, sexual exploitation or labour exploitation; also encourages States to create, if they do not already exist, mechanisms to combat such practices and to allocate adequate resources to ensure law enforcement and the protection of the rights of victims, and to reinforce bilateral, regional and international cooperation, including with non-governmental organizations that assist victims, to combat this trafficking in persons and smuggling of migrants;

70. Urges States to take all necessary constitutional, legislative and administrative measures to foster equality among individuals and groups of individuals who are victims of racism, racial discrimination, xenophobia and related intolerance, and to review existing measures with a view to amending or repealing national legislation and administrative provisions that may give rise to such forms of discrimination;

71. Urges States, including their law enforcement agencies, to design and fully implement effective policies and programmes to prevent, detect and ensure accountability for misconduct by police officers and other law enforcement personnel which is motivated by racism, racial discrimination, xenophobia and related intolerance, and to prosecute perpetrators of such misconduct;

72. Urges States to design, implement and enforce effective measures to eliminate the phenomenon popularly known as "racial profiling" and comprising the practice of police and other law enforcement officers relying,

to any degree, on race, colour, descent or national or ethnic origin as the basis for subjecting persons to investigatory activities or for determining whether an individual is engaged in criminal activity;

73. Urges States to take measures to prevent genetic research or its applications from being used to promote racism, racial discrimination, xenophobia and related intolerance, to protect the privacy of personal genetic information and to prevent such information from being used for discriminatory or racist purposes;

74. Urges States and invites non-governmental organizations and the private sector:

(a) To create and implement policies that promote a high-quality and diverse police force free from racism, racial discrimination, xenophobia and related intolerance, and recruit actively all groups, including minorities, into public employment, including the police force and other agencies within the criminal justice system (such as prosecutors);

(b) To work to reduce violence, including violence motivated by racism, racial discrimination, xenophobia and related intolerance, by:

(i) Developing educational materials to teach young people the importance of tolerance and respect;

(ii) Addressing bias before it manifests itself in violent criminal activity;

(iii) Establishing working groups consisting of, among others, local community leaders and national and local law enforcement officials, to improve coordination, community involvement, training, education and data collection, with the aim of preventing such violent criminal activity;

(iv) Ensuring that civil rights laws that prohibit violent criminal activity are strongly enforced;

(v) Enhancing data collection regarding violence motivated by racism, racial discrimination, xenophobia and related intolerance;

(vi) Providing appropriate assistance to victims, and public education to prevent future incidents of violence motivated by racism, racial discrimination, xenophobia and related intolerance;

Ratification of and effective implementation of relevant international and regional legal instruments on human rights and non-discrimination

75. Urges States that have not yet done so to consider ratifying or acceding to the international human rights instruments which combat racism, racial

discrimination, xenophobia and related intolerance, in particular to accede to the International Convention on the Elimination of All Forms of Racial Discrimination as a matter of urgency, with a view to universal ratification by the year 2005, and to consider making the declaration envisaged under article 14, to comply with their reporting obligations, and to publish and act upon the concluding observations of the Committee on the Elimination of Racial Discrimination. It also urges States to withdraw reservations contrary to the object and purpose of that Convention and to consider withdrawing other reservations;

76. Urges States to give due consideration to the observations and recommendations of the Committee on the Elimination of Racial Discrimination. To that effect, States should consider setting up appropriate national monitoring and evaluation mechanisms to ensure that all appropriate steps are taken to follow up on these observations and recommendations;

77. Urges States [to ratify a long list of human rights treaties]...

It further urges States parties to these instruments to implement them fully;

79. Calls upon States to promote and protect the exercise of the rights set out in the Declaration on the Elimination of All Forms of Intolerance and of Discrimination Based on Religion or Belief, proclaimed by the General Assembly in its resolution 36/55 of 25 November 1981, in order to obviate religious discrimination which, when combined with certain other forms of discrimination, constitutes a form of multiple discrimination;

80. Urges States to seek full respect for, and compliance with, the Vienna Convention on Consular Relations of 1963, especially as it relates to the right of foreign nationals, regardless of their legal and immigration status, to communicate with a consular officer of their own State in the case of arrest or detention;

81. Urges all States to prohibit discriminatory treatment based on race, colour, descent or national or ethnic origin against foreigners and migrant workers, inter alia, where appropriate, concerning the granting of work visas and work permits, housing, health care and access to justice;

82. Underlines the importance of combating impunity, including for crimes with a racist or xenophobic motivation, also at the international level, noting that impunity for violations of human rights and international humanitarian law is a serious obstacle to a fair and equitable justice system and, ultimately, reconciliation and stability; it also fully supports the work of the existing international criminal tribunals and ratification of the Rome Statute of the

International Criminal Court, and urges all States to cooperate with these international criminal tribunals;

83. Urges States to make every effort to apply fully the relevant provisions of the International Labour Organization Declaration on Fundamental Principles and Rights at Work of 1998, in order to combat racism, racial discrimination, xenophobia and related intolerance;

Prosecution of perpetrators of racist acts

84. Urges States to adopt effective measures to combat criminal acts motivated by racism, racial discrimination, xenophobia and related intolerance, to take measures so that such motivations are considered an aggravating factor for the purposes of sentencing, to prevent these crimes from going unpunished and to ensure the rule of law;

85. Urges States to undertake investigations to examine possible links between criminal prosecution, police violence and penal sanctions, on the one hand, and racism, racial discrimination, xenophobia and related intolerance, on the other, so as to have evidence for taking the necessary steps for the eradication of any such links and discriminatory practices;

86. Calls upon States to promote measures to deter the emergence of and to counter neo-fascist, violent nationalist ideologies which promote racial hatred and racial discrimination, as well as racist and xenophobic sentiments, including measures to combat the negative influence of such ideologies especially on young people through formal and non-formal education, the media and sport;

87. Urges States parties to adopt legislation implementing the obligations they have assumed to prosecute and punish persons who have committed or ordered to be committed grave breaches of the Geneva Conventions of 12 August 1949 and Additional Protocol I thereto and of other serious violations of the laws and customs of war, in particular in relation to the principle of non-discrimination;

88. Calls upon States to criminalize all forms of trafficking in persons, in particular women and children, and to condemn and penalize traffickers and intermediaries, while ensuring protection and assistance to the victims of trafficking, with full respect for their human rights;

89. Urges States to carry out comprehensive, exhaustive, timely and impartial investigations of all unlawful acts of racism and racial discrimination, to prosecute criminal offences ex officio, as appropriate, or initiate or facilitate all appropriate actions arising from offences of a racist or xenophobic nature,

to ensure that criminal and civil investigations and prosecutions of offences of a racist or xenophobic nature are given high priority and are actively and consistently undertaken, and to ensure the right to equal treatment before the tribunals and all other organs administering justice. In this regard, the World Conference underlines the importance of fostering awareness and providing training to the various agents in the criminal justice system to ensure fair and impartial application of the law. In this respect, it recommends that anti-discrimination monitoring services be established;

Establishment and reinforcement of independent specialized national institutions and mediation

90. Urges States, as appropriate, to establish, strengthen, review and reinforce the effectiveness of independent national human rights institutions, particularly on issues of racism, racial discrimination, xenophobia and related intolerance, in conformity with the Principles relating to the status of national institutions for the promotion and protection of human rights, annexed to General Assembly resolution 48/134 of 20 December 1993, and to provide them with adequate financial resources, competence and capacity for investigation, research, education and public awareness activities to combat these phenomena;

91. Also urges States:

(a) To foster cooperation between these institutions and other national institutions;

(b) To take steps to ensure that those individuals or groups of individuals who are victims of racism, racial discrimination, xenophobia and related intolerance can participate fully in these institutions;

(c) To support these institutions and similar bodies, inter alia through the publication and circulation of existing national laws and jurisprudence, and cooperation with institutions in other countries, so that knowledge can be gained of the manifestations, functions and mechanisms of these practices and the strategies designed to prevent, combat and eradicate them;

2. Policies and practices
Data collection and disaggregation, research and study

92. Urges States to collect, compile, analyse, disseminate and publish reliable statistical data at the national and local levels and undertake all other related measures which are necessary to assess regularly the situation of individuals and groups of individuals who are victims of racism, racial discrimination, xenophobia and related intolerance;

(a) Such statistical data should be disaggregated in accordance with national legislation. Any such information shall, as appropriate, be collected with the explicit consent of the victims, based on their self-identification and in accordance with provisions on human rights and fundamental freedoms, such as data protection regulations and privacy guarantees. This information must not be misused;

(b) The statistical data and information should be collected with the objective of monitoring the situation of marginalized groups, and the development and evaluation of legislation, policies, practices and other measures aimed at preventing and combating racism, racial discrimination, xenophobia and related intolerance, as well as for the purpose of determining whether any measures have an unintentional disparate impact on victims. To that end, it recommends the development of voluntary, consensual and participatory strategies in the process of collecting, designing and using information;

(c) The information should take into account economic and social indicators, including, where appropriate, health and health status, infant and maternal mortality, life expectancy, literacy, education, employment, housing, land ownership, mental and physical health care, water, sanitation, energy and communications services, poverty and average disposable income, in order to elaborate social and economic development policies with a view to closing the existing gaps in social and economic conditions;

93. Invites States, intergovernmental organizations, non-governmental organizations, academic institutions and the private sector to improve concepts and methods of data collection and analysis; to promote research, exchange experiences and successful practices and develop promotional activities in this area; and to develop indicators of progress and participation of individuals and groups of individuals in society subject to racism, racial discrimination, xenophobia and related intolerance;

94. Recognizes that policies and programmes aimed at combating racism, racial discrimination, xenophobia and related intolerance should be based on quantitative and qualitative research, incorporating a gender perspective. Such policies and programmes should take into account priorities identified by individuals and groups of individuals who are victims of, or subject to, racism, racial discrimination, xenophobia and related intolerance;

95. Urges States to establish regular monitoring of acts of racism, racial discrimination, xenophobia and related intolerance in the public and private sectors, including those committed by law enforcement officials;

96. Invites States to promote and conduct studies and adopt an integral, objective and long-term approach to all phases and aspects of migration which will deal effectively with both its causes and manifestations. These studies and approaches should pay special attention to the root causes of migratory flows, such as lack of full enjoyment of human rights and fundamental freedoms, and the effects of economic globalization on migration trends;

97. Recommends that further studies be conducted on how racism, racial discrimination, xenophobia and related intolerance may be reflected in laws, policies, institutions and practices and how this may have contributed to the victimization and exclusion of migrants, especially women and children;

98. Recommends that States include where applicable in their periodic reports to United Nations human rights treaty bodies, in an appropriate form, statistical information relating to individuals, members of groups and communities within their jurisdiction, including statistical data on participation in political life and on their economic, social and cultural situation. All such information shall be collected in accordance with provisions on human rights and fundamental freedoms, such as data protection regulations and privacy guarantees;

Action-oriented policies and action plans, including affirmative action to ensure non-discrimination, in particular as regards access to social services, employment, housing, education, health care, etc.

99. Recognizes that combating racism, racial discrimination, xenophobia and related intolerance is a primary responsibility of States. It therefore encourages States to develop or elaborate national action plans to promote diversity, equality, equity, social justice, equality of opportunity and the participation of all. Through, among other things, affirmative or positive actions and strategies, these plans should aim at creating conditions for all to participate effectively in decision-making and realize civil, cultural, economic, political and social rights in all spheres of life on the basis of non-discrimination. The World Conference encourages States, in developing and elaborating such action plans, to establish, or reinforce, dialogue with non-governmental organizations in order to involve them more closely in designing, implementing and evaluating policies and programmes;

100. Urges States to establish, on the basis of statistical information, national programmes, including affirmative or positive measures, to promote the access of individuals and groups of individuals who are or may be victims of

racial discrimination to basic social services, including primary education, basic health care and adequate housing;

101. Urges States to establish programmes to promote the access without discrimination of individuals or groups of individuals who are victims of racism, racial discrimination, xenophobia and related intolerance to health care, and to promote strong efforts to eliminate disparities, inter alia in the infant and maternal mortality rates, childhood immunizations, HIV/AIDS, heart diseases, cancer and contagious diseases;

102. Urges States to promote residential integration of all members of the society at the planning stage of urban development schemes and other human settlements, as well as while renewing neglected areas of public housing, so as to counter social exclusion and marginalization;

Employment

103. Urges States to promote and support where appropriate the organization and operation of enterprises owned by persons who are victims of racism, racial discrimination, xenophobia and related intolerance by promoting equal access to credit and to training programmes;

104. Urges States and encourages non-governmental organizations and the private sector:

(a) To support the creation of workplaces free of discrimination through a multifaceted strategy that includes civil rights enforcement, public education and communication within the workplace, and to promote and protect the rights of workers who are subject to racism, racial discrimination, xenophobia and related intolerance;

(b) To foster the creation, growth and expansion of businesses dedicated to improving economic and educational conditions in underserved and disadvantaged areas, by increasing access to capital through, inter alia, community development banks, recognizing that new businesses can have a positive, dynamic impact on communities in need, and to work with the private sector to create jobs, help retain existing jobs and stimulate industrial and commercial growth in economically distressed areas;

(c) To improve the prospects of targeted groups facing, inter alia, the greatest obstacles in finding, keeping or regaining work, including skilled employment. Particular attention should be paid to persons subject to multiple discrimination;

105. Urges States to give special attention, when devising and implementing legislation and policies designed to enhance the protection of workers' rights,

to the serious situation of lack of protection, and in some cases exploitation, as in the case of trafficked persons and smuggled migrants, which makes them more vulnerable to ill-treatment such as confinement in the case of domestic workers and also being employed in dangerous and poorly paid jobs;

106. Urges States to avoid the negative effects of discriminatory practices, racism and xenophobia in employment and occupation by promoting the application and observance of international instruments and norms on workers' rights;

107. Calls upon States and encourages representative trade unions and the business sector to advance non-discriminatory practices in the workplace and protect the rights of workers, including, in particular, the victims of racism, racial discrimination, xenophobia and related intolerance;

108. Calls upon States to provide effective access to administrative and legal procedures and other remedial action to victims of racism, racial discrimination, xenophobia and related intolerance in the workplace;

Health, environment

109. Urges States, individually and through international cooperation, to enhance measures to fulfil the right of everyone to the enjoyment of the highest attainable standard of physical and mental health, with a view to eliminating disparities in health status, as indicated in standard health indexes, which might result from racism, racial discrimination, xenophobia and related intolerance;

110. Urges States and encourages non-governmental organizations and the private sector:

(a) To provide effective mechanisms for monitoring and eliminating racism, racial discrimination, xenophobia and related intolerance in the health-care system, such as the development and enforcement of effective anti-discrimination laws;

(b) To take steps to ensure equal access to comprehensive, quality health care affordable for all, including primary health care for medically underserved people, facilitate the training of a health workforce that is both diverse and motivated to work in underserved communities, and work to increase diversity in the health-care profession by recruiting on merit and potential women and men from all groups, representing the diversity of their societies, for health-care careers and by retaining them in the health professions;

(c) To work with health-care professionals, community-based health providers, non-governmental organizations, scientific researchers and private industry as a means of improving the health status of marginalized communities, in particular victims of racism, racial discrimination, xenophobia and related intolerance;

(d) To work with health professionals, scientific researchers and international and regional health organizations to study the differential impact of medical treatments and health strategies on various communities;

(e) To adopt and implement policies and programmes to improve HIV/AIDS prevention efforts in high-risk communities and work to expand availability of HIV/AIDS care, treatment and other support services;

111. Invites States to consider non-discriminatory measures to provide a safe and healthy environment for individuals and groups of individuals victims of or subject to racism, racial discrimination, xenophobia and related intolerance, and in particular:

(a) To improve access to public information on health and environment issues;

(b) To ensure that relevant concerns are taken into account in the public process of decision-making on the environment;

(c) To share technology and successful practices to improve human health and environment in all areas;

(d) To take appropriate remedial measures, as possible, to clean, re-use and redevelop contaminated sites and, where appropriate, relocate those affected on a voluntary basis after consultations;

Equal participation in political, economic, social and cultural decision-making

112. Urges States and encourages the private sector and international financial and development institutions, such as the World Bank and regional development banks, to promote participation of individuals and groups of individuals who are victims of racism, racial discrimination, xenophobia and related intolerance in economic, cultural and social decision-making at all stages, particularly in the development and implementation of poverty alleviation strategies, development projects, and trade and market assistance programmes;

113. Urges States to promote, as appropriate, effective and equal access of all members of the community, especially those who are victims of racism, racial

discrimination, xenophobia and related intolerance, to the decision-making process in society at all levels and in particular at the local level, and also urges States and encourages the private sector to facilitate their effective participation in economic life;

114. Urges all multilateral financial and development institutions, in particular the World Bank, the International Monetary Fund, the World Trade Organization and regional development banks, to promote, in accordance with their regular budgets and the procedures of their governing bodies, participation by all members of the international community in decision-making processes at all stages and levels in order to facilitate development projects and, as appropriate, trade and market access programmes;

Role of politicians and political parties

115. Underlines the key role that politicians and political parties can play in combating racism, racial discrimination, xenophobia and related intolerance and encourages political parties to take concrete steps to promote equality, solidarity and non-discrimination in society, inter alia by developing voluntary codes of conduct which include internal disciplinary measures for violations thereof, so their members refrain from public statements and actions that encourage or incite racism, racial discrimination, xenophobia and related intolerance;

116. Invites the Inter-Parliamentary Union to encourage debate in, and action by, parliaments on various measures, including laws and policies, to combat racism, racial discrimination, xenophobia and related intolerance;

3. Education and awareness-raising measures

117. Urges States, where appropriate working with other relevant bodies, to commit financial resources to anti-racism education and to media campaigns promoting the values of acceptance, tolerance, diversity and respect for the cultures of all indigenous peoples living within their national borders. In particular, States should promote an accurate understanding of the histories and cultures of indigenous peoples;

118. Urges the United Nations, other appropriate international and regional organizations and States to redress the marginalization of Africa's contribution to world history and civilization by developing and implementing a specific and comprehensive programme of research, education and mass communication to disseminate widely a balanced and objective presentation of Africa's seminal and valuable contribution to humanity;

119. Invites States and relevant international organizations and non-governmental organizations to build upon the efforts of the Slave Route Project of the United Nations Educational Scientific and Cultural Organization and its theme of "Breaking the silence" by developing texts and testimony, slavery multi-media centres and/or programmes that will collect, record, organize, exhibit and publish the existing data relevant to the history of slavery and the trans-Atlantic, Mediterranean and Indian Ocean slave trades, paying particular attention to the thoughts and actions of the victims of slavery and the slave trade, in their quest for freedom and justice;

120. Salutes the efforts of the United Nations Educational, Scientific and Cultural Organization made within the framework of the Slave Route Project and requests that the outcome be made available to the international community as soon as possible;

Access to education without discrimination

121. Urges States to commit themselves to ensuring access to education, including access to free primary education for all children, both girls and boys, and access for adults to lifelong learning and education, based on respect for human rights, diversity and tolerance, without discrimination of any kind;

122. Urges States to ensure equal access to education for all in law and in practice, and to refrain from any legal or any other measures leading to imposed racial segregation in any form in access to schooling;

123. Urges States:

(a) To adopt and implement laws that prohibit discrimination on the basis of race, colour, descent or national or ethnic origin at all levels of education, both formal and non-formal;

(b) To take all appropriate measures to eliminate obstacles limiting the access of children to education;

(c) To ensure that all children have access without discrimination to education of good quality;

(d) To establish and implement standardized methods to measure and track the educational performance of disadvantaged children and young people;

(e) To commit resources to eliminate, where they exist, inequalities in educational outcomes for children and young people;

(f) To support efforts to ensure safe school environments, free from violence and harassment motivated by racism, racial discrimination, xenophobia or related intolerance; and

(g) To consider establishing financial assistance programmes designed to enable all students, regardless of race, colour, descent or ethnic or national origin, to attend institutions of higher education;

124. Urges States to adopt, where applicable, appropriate measures to ensure that persons belonging to national or ethnic, religious and linguistic minorities have access to education without discrimination of any kind and, where possible, have an opportunity to learn their own language in order to protect them from any form of racism, racial discrimination, xenophobia and related intolerance that they may be subjected to;

Human rights education

125. Requests States to include the struggle against racism, racial discrimination, xenophobia and related intolerance among the activities undertaken within the framework of the United Nations Decade for Human Rights Education (1995-2004) and to take into account the recommendations of the mid-term evaluation report of the Decade;

126. Encourages all States, in cooperation with the United Nations, the United Nations Educational, Scientific and Cultural Organization and other relevant international organizations, to initiate and develop cultural and educational programmes aimed at countering racism, racial discrimination, xenophobia and related intolerance, in order to ensure respect for the dignity and worth of all human beings and enhance mutual understanding among all cultures and civilizations. It further urges States to support and implement public information campaigns and specific training programmes in the field of human rights, where appropriate formulated in local languages, to combat racism, racial discrimination, xenophobia and related intolerance and promote respect for the values of diversity, pluralism, tolerance, mutual respect, cultural sensitivity, integration and inclusiveness. Such programmes and campaigns should be addressed to all sectors of society, in particular children and young people;

127. Urges States to intensify their efforts in the field of education, including human rights education, in order to promote an understanding and awareness of the causes, consequences and evils of racism, racial discrimination, xenophobia and related intolerance, and also urges States, in consultation with educational authorities and the private sector, as appropriate, and encourages educational authorities and the private sector, as

appropriate, to develop educational materials, including textbooks and dictionaries, aimed at combating those phenomena and, in this context, calls upon States to give importance, if appropriate, to textbook and curriculum review and amendment, so as to eliminate any elements that might promote racism, racial discrimination, xenophobia and related intolerance or reinforce negative stereotypes, and to include material that refutes such stereotypes;

128. Urges States, if appropriate in cooperation with relevant organizations, including youth organizations, to support and implement public formal and non-formal education programmes designed to promote respect for cultural diversity;

Human rights education for children and youth

129. Urges States to introduce and, as applicable, to reinforce anti-discrimination and anti-racism components in human rights programmes in school curricula, to develop and improve relevant educational material, including history and other textbooks, and to ensure that all teachers are effectively trained and adequately motivated to shape attitudes and behavioural patterns, based on the principles of non-discrimination, mutual respect and tolerance;

130. Calls upon States to undertake and facilitate activities aimed at educating young people in human rights and democratic citizenship and instilling values of solidarity, respect and appreciation of diversity, including respect for different groups. A special effort to inform and sensitize young people to respect democratic values and human rights should be undertaken or developed to fight against ideologies based on the fallacious theory of racial superiority;

131. Urges States to encourage all schools to consider developing educational activities, including extracurricular ones, to raise awareness against racism, racial discrimination, xenophobia and related intolerance, inter alia by commemorating the International Day for the Elimination of Racial Discrimination (21 March);

132. Recommends that States introduce, or reinforce, human rights education, with a view to combating prejudices which lead to racial discrimination and to promoting understanding, tolerance and friendship between different racial or ethnic groups, in schools and in institutions of higher education, and support public formal and non-formal education programmes designed to promote respect for cultural diversity and the self-esteem of victims;

Other Instruments

Human rights education for public officials and professionals

133. Urges States to develop and strengthen anti-racist and gender-sensitive human rights training for public officials, including personnel in the administration of justice, particularly in law enforcement, correctional and security services, as well as among health-care, schools and migration authorities;

134. Urges States to pay specific attention to the negative impact of racism, racial discrimination, xenophobia and related intolerance on the administration of justice and fair trial, and to conduct nationwide campaigns, amongst other measures, to raise awareness among State organs and public officials concerning their obligations under the International Convention on the Elimination of All Forms of Racial Discrimination and other relevant instruments;

135. Requests States, wherever appropriate through cooperation with international organizations, national institutions, non-governmental organizations and the private sector, to organize and facilitate training activities, including courses or seminars, on international norms prohibiting racial discrimination and their applicability in domestic law, as well as on their international human rights obligations, for prosecutors, members of the judiciary and other public officials;

136. Calls upon States to ensure that education and training, especially teacher training, promote respect for human rights and the fight against racism, racial discrimination, xenophobia and related intolerance and that educational institutions implement policies and programmes agreed by the relevant authorities on equal opportunities, anti-racism, gender equality, and cultural, religious and other diversity, with the participation of teachers, parents and students, and follow up their implementation. It further urges all educators, including teachers at all levels of education, religious communities and the print and electronic media, to play an effective role in human rights education, including as a means to combat racism, racial discrimination, xenophobia and related intolerance;

137. Encourages States to consider taking measures to increase the recruitment, retention and promotion of women and men belonging to groups which are currently under-represented in the teaching profession as a result of racism, racial discrimination, xenophobia and related intolerance, and to guarantee them effective equality of access to the profession. Particular efforts should be made to recruit women and men who have the ability to interact effectively with all groups;

138. Urges States to strengthen the human rights training and awareness-raising activities designed for immigration officials, border police and staff of detention centres and prisons, local authorities and other civil servants in charge of enforcing laws, as well as teachers, with particular attention to the human rights of migrants, refugees and asylum-seekers, in order to prevent acts of racial discrimination and xenophobia and to avoid situations where prejudices lead to decisions based on racism, racial discrimination, xenophobia or related intolerance;

139. Urges States to provide or strengthen training for law enforcement, immigration and other relevant officials in the prevention of trafficking in persons. The training should focus on methods used in preventing such trafficking, prosecuting the traffickers and protecting the rights of victims, including protecting the victims from the traffickers. The training should also take into account the need to consider human rights and child- and gender-sensitive issues and it should encourage cooperation with non-governmental organizations, other relevant organizations and other elements of civil society;

4. Information, communication and the media, including new technologies

140. Welcomes the positive contribution made by the new information and communications technologies, including the Internet, in combating racism through rapid and wide-reaching communication;

141. Draws attention to the potential to increase the use of the new information and communications technologies, including the Internet, to create educational and awareness-raising networks against racism, racial discrimination, xenophobia and related intolerance, both in and out of school, as well as the ability of the Internet to promote universal respect for human rights and also respect for the value of cultural diversity;

142. Emphasizes the importance of recognizing the value of cultural diversity and of putting in place concrete measures to encourage the access of marginalized communities to the mainstream and alternative media through, inter alia, the presentation of programmes that reflect their cultures and languages;

143. Expresses concern at the material progression of racism, racial discrimination, xenophobia and related intolerance, including their contemporary forms and manifestations, such as the use of the new information and communications technologies, including the Internet, to disseminate ideas of racial superiority;

144. Urges States and encourages the private sector to promote the development by the media, including the print and electronic media,

including the Internet and advertising, taking into account their independence, through their relevant associations and organizations at the national, regional and international levels, of a voluntary ethical code of conduct and self-regulatory measures, and of policies and practices aimed at:

(a) Combating racism, racial discrimination, xenophobia and related intolerance;

(b) Promoting the fair, balanced and equitable representation of the diversity of their societies, as well as ensuring that this diversity is reflected among their staff;

(c) Combating the proliferation of ideas of racial superiority, justification of racial hatred and discrimination in any form;

(d) Promoting respect, tolerance and understanding among all individuals, peoples, nations and civilizations, for example through assistance in public awareness-raising campaigns;

(e) Avoiding stereotyping in all its forms, and particularly the promotion of false images of migrants, including migrant workers, and refugees, in order to prevent the spread of xenophobic sentiments among the public and to encourage the objective and balanced portrayal of people, events and history;

145. Urges States to implement legal sanctions, in accordance with relevant international human rights law, in respect of incitement to racial hatred through new information and communications technologies, including the Internet, and further urges them to apply all relevant human rights instruments to which they are parties, in particular the International Convention on the Elimination of All Forms of Racial Discrimination, to racism on the Internet;

146. Urges States to encourage the media to avoid stereotyping based on racism, racial discrimination, xenophobia and related intolerance;

147. Calls upon States to consider the following, taking fully into account existing international and regional standards on freedom of expression, while taking all necessary measures to guarantee the right to freedom of opinion and expression:

(a) Encouraging Internet service providers to establish and disseminate specific voluntary codes of conduct and self-regulatory measures against the dissemination of racist messages and those that result in racial discrimination, xenophobia or any form of intolerance and discrimination; to that end, Internet providers are encouraged to set up mediating bodies at national and international levels, involving relevant civil society institutions;

(b) Adopting and applying, to the extent possible, appropriate legislation for prosecuting those responsible for incitement to racial hatred or violence through the new information and communications technologies, including the Internet;

(c) Addressing the problem of dissemination of racist material through the new information and communications technologies, including the Internet, inter alia by imparting training to law enforcement authorities;

(d) Denouncing and actively discouraging the transmission of racist and xenophobic messages through all communications media, including new information and communications technologies, such as the Internet;

(e) Considering a prompt and coordinated international response to the rapidly evolving phenomenon of the dissemination of hate speech and racist material through the new information and communications technologies, including the Internet; and in this context strengthening international cooperation;

(f) Encouraging access and use by all people of the Internet as an international and equal forum, aware that there are disparities in use of and access to the Internet;

(g) Examining ways in which the positive contribution made by the new information and communications technologies, such as the Internet, can be enhanced through replication of good practices in combating racism, racial discrimination, xenophobia and related intolerance;

(h) Encouraging the reflection of the diversity of societies among the personnel of media organizations and the new information and communications technologies, such as the Internet, by promoting adequate representation of different segments within societies at all levels of their organizational structure;

B. International level

148. Urges all actors on the international scene to build an international order based on inclusion, justice, equality and equity, human dignity, mutual understanding and promotion of and respect for cultural diversity and universal human rights, and to reject all doctrines of exclusion based on racism, racial discrimination, xenophobia and related intolerance;

149. Believes that all conflicts and disputes should be resolved through peaceful means and political dialogue. The Conference calls on all parties involved in such conflicts to exercise restraint and to respect human rights and international humanitarian law;

150. Calls upon States, in opposing all forms of racism, to recognize the need to counter anti-Semitism, anti-Arabism and Islamophobia world-wide, and urges all States to take effective measures to prevent the emergence of movements based on racism and discriminatory ideas concerning these communities;

151. As for the situation in the Middle East, calls for the end of violence and the swift resumption of negotiations, respect for international human rights and humanitarian law, respect for the principle of self-determination and the end of all suffering, thus allowing Israel and the Palestinians to resume the peace process, and to develop and prosper in security and freedom;

152. Encourages States, regional and international organizations, including financial institutions, as well as civil society, to address within existing mechanisms, or where necessary to put in place and/or develop mechanisms, to address those aspects of globalization which may lead to racism, racial discrimination, xenophobia and related intolerance;

153. Recommends that the Department of Peacekeeping Operations of the Secretariat and other concerned United Nations agencies, bodies and programmes strengthen their coordination to discern patterns of serious violations of human rights and humanitarian law with a view to assessing the risk of further deterioration that could lead to genocide, war crimes or crimes against humanity;

154. Encourages the World Health Organization and other relevant international organizations to promote and develop activities for the recognition of the impact of racism, racial discrimination, xenophobia and related intolerance as significant social determinants of physical and mental health status, including the HIV/AIDS pandemic, and access to health care, and to prepare specific projects, including research, to ensure equitable health systems for the victims;

155. Encourages the International Labour Organization to carry out activities and programmes to combat racism, racial discrimination, xenophobia and related intolerance in the world of work, and to support actions of States, employers' organizations and trade unions in this field;

156. Urges the United Nations Educational, Scientific and Cultural Organization to provide support to States in the preparation of teaching materials and tools for promoting teaching, training and educational activities relating to human rights and the struggle against racism, racial discrimination, xenophobia and related intolerance;

IV. Provision of effective remedies, recourse, redress, and other
measures at the national, regional and international levels

157. Recognizes the efforts of developing countries, in particular the commitment and the determination of the African leaders, to seriously address the challenges of poverty, underdevelopment, marginalization, social exclusion, economic disparities, instability and insecurity, through initiatives such as the New African Initiative and other innovative mechanisms such as the World Solidarity Fund for the Eradication of Poverty, and calls upon developed countries, the United Nations and its specialized agencies, as well as international financial institutions, to provide, through their operational programmes, new and additional financial resources, as appropriate, to support these initiatives;

158. Recognizes that these historical injustices have undeniably contributed to the poverty, underdevelopment, marginalization, social exclusion, economic disparities, instability and insecurity that affect many people in different parts of the world, in particular in developing countries. The Conference recognizes the need to develop programmes for the social and economic development of these societies and the Diaspora, within the framework of a new partnership based on the spirit of solidarity and mutual respect, in the following areas:

Debt relief;

Poverty eradication;

Building or strengthening democratic institutions;

Promotion of foreign direct investment;

Market access;

Intensifying efforts to meet the internationally agreed targets for official development assistance transfers to developing countries;

New information and communication technologies bridging the digital divide;

Agriculture and food security;

Transfer of technology;

Transparent and accountable governance;

Investment in health infrastructure tackling HIV/AIDS, tuberculosis and malaria, including through the Global AIDS and Health Fund;

Infrastructure development;

Human resource development, including capacity-building;

Education, training and cultural development;

Mutual legal assistance in the repatriation of illegally obtained and illegally transferred (stashed) funds, in accordance with national and international instruments;

Illicit traffic in small arms and light weapons;

Restitution of art objects, historical artefacts and documents to their countries of origin, in accordance with bilateral agreements or international instruments;

Trafficking in persons, particularly women and children;

Facilitation of welcomed return and resettlement of the descendants of enslaved Africans;

159. Urges international financial and development institutions and the operational programmes and specialized agencies of the United Nations to give greater priority to, and allocate appropriate funding for, programmes addressing the development challenges of the affected States and societies, in particular those on the African continent and in the Diaspora;

Legal assistance

160. Urges States to take all necessary measures to address, as a matter of urgency, the pressing requirement for justice for the victims of racism, racial discrimination, xenophobia and related intolerance and to ensure that victims have full access to information, support, effective protection and national, administrative and judicial remedies, including the right to seek just and adequate reparation or satisfaction for damage, as well as legal assistance, where required;

161. Urges States to facilitate for victims of racial discrimination, including victims of torture and ill-treatment, access to all appropriate legal procedures and free legal assistance in a manner adapted to their specific needs and vulnerability, including through legal representation;

162. Urges States to ensure the protection against victimization of complainants and witnesses of acts of racism, racial discrimination, xenophobia and related intolerance, and to consider measures such as, where appropriate, making legal assistance, including legal aid, available to complainants seeking a legal remedy and, if possible, affording the possibility

for non-governmental organizations to support complainants of racism, with their consent, in legal procedures;

National legislation and programmes

163. For the purposes of effectively combating racism and racial discrimination, xenophobia and related intolerance in the civil, political, economic, social and cultural fields, the Conference recommends to all States that their national legislative framework should expressly and specifically prohibit racial discrimination and provide effective judicial and other remedies or redress, including through the designation of national, independent, specialized bodies;

164. Urges States, with regard to the procedural remedies provided for in their domestic law, to bear in mind the following considerations:

(a) Access to such remedies should be widely available, on a non-discriminatory and equal basis;

(b) Existing procedural remedies should be made known in the context of the relevant action, and victims of racial discrimination should be helped to avail themselves of them in accordance with the particular case;

(c) Inquiries into complaints of racial discrimination and the adjudication of such complaints must be carried out as rapidly as possible;

(d) Persons who are victims of racial discrimination should be accorded legal assistance and aid in complaint proceedings, where applicable free of charge, and, where necessary, should be provided with the help of competent interpreters in such complaint proceedings or in any civil or criminal cases arising therefrom or connected thereto;

(e) The creation of competent national bodies to investigate effectively allegations of racial discrimination and to give protection to complainants against intimidation or harassment is a desirable development and should be undertaken; steps should be taken towards the enactment of legislation to prohibit discriminatory practices on grounds of race, colour, descent, or national or ethnic origin, and to provide for the application of appropriate penalties against offenders and remedies, including adequate compensation, for the victims;

(f) Access to legal remedies should be facilitated for victims of discrimination and, in this regard, the innovation of conferring a capacity on national and other institutions, as well as relevant non-governmental organizations, to assist such victims should be seriously considered, and programmes should be developed to enable the most vulnerable groups to have access to the legal system;

(g) New and innovative methods and procedures of conflict resolution, mediation and conciliation between parties involved in conflicts or disputes based on racism, racial discrimination, xenophobia and related intolerance should be explored and, where possible, established;

(h) The development of restorative justice policies and programmes for the benefit of victims of relevant forms of discrimination is desirable and should be seriously considered;

(i) States which have made the declaration under article 14 of the International Convention on the Elimination of All Forms of Racial Discrimination should make increased efforts to inform their public of the existence of the complaints mechanism under article 14;

Remedies, reparations, compensation

165. Urges States to reinforce protection against racism, racial discrimination, xenophobia and related intolerance by ensuring that all persons have access to effective and adequate remedies and enjoy the right to seek from competent national tribunals and other national institutions just and adequate reparation and satisfaction for any damage as a result of such discrimination. It further underlines the importance of access to the law and to the courts for complainants of racism and racial discrimination and draws attention to the need for judicial and other remedies to be made widely known, easily accessible, expeditious and not unduly complicated;

166. Urges States to adopt the necessary measures, as provided by national law, to ensure the right of victims to seek just and adequate reparation and satisfaction to redress acts of racism, racial discrimination, xenophobia and related intolerance, and to design effective measures to prevent the repetition of such acts;

V. Strategies to achieve full and effective equality, including international cooperation and enhancement of the United Nations and other international mechanisms in combating racism, racial discrimination, xenophobia and related intolerance and follow-up

167. Calls upon States to apply diligently all commitments undertaken by them in the declarations and plans of action of the regional conferences in which they participated, and to formulate national policies and action plans to combat racism, racial discrimination, xenophobia and related intolerance

in compliance with the objectives set forth therein, and as provided for in other relevant instruments and decisions; and further requests that, in cases where such national policies and action plans to combat racism, racial discrimination, xenophobia and related intolerance already exist, States incorporate in them the commitments arising from their regional conferences;

168. Urges States that have not yet done so to consider acceding to the Geneva Conventions of 12 August 1949 and their two Additional Protocols of 1977, as well as to other treaties of international humanitarian law, and to enact, with the highest priority, appropriate legislation, taking the measures required to give full effect to their obligations under international humanitarian law, in particular in relation to the rules prohibiting discrimination;

169. Urges States to develop cooperation programmes to promote equal opportunities for the benefit of victims of racism, racial discrimination, xenophobia and related intolerance and encourages them to propose the creation of multilateral cooperation programmes with the same objective;

170. Invites States to include the subject of the struggle against racism, racial discrimination, xenophobia and related intolerance in the work programmes of the regional integration agencies and of the regional cross-boundary dialogue forums;

171. Urges States to recognize the challenges that people of different socially constructed races, colours, descent, national or ethnic origins, religions and languages experience in seeking to live together and to develop harmonious multiracial and multicultural societies; also urges States to recognize that the positive examples of relatively successful multiracial and multicultural societies, such as some of those in the Caribbean region, need to be examined and analysed, and that techniques, mechanisms, policies and programmes for reconciling conflicts based on factors related to race, colour, descent, language, religion, or national or ethnic origin and for developing harmonious multiracial and multicultural societies need to be systematically considered and developed, and therefore requests the United Nations and its relevant specialized agencies to consider establishing an international centre for multiracial and multicultural studies and policy development to undertake this critical work for the benefit of the international community;

172. Urges States to protect the national or ethnic, cultural, religious and linguistic identity of minorities within their respective territories and to develop appropriate legislative and other measures to encourage conditions for the promotion of that identity, in order to protect them from any form of

racism, racial discrimination, xenophobia and related intolerance. In this context, forms of multiple discrimination should be fully taken into account;

173. Further urges States to ensure the equal protection and promotion of the identities of the historically disadvantaged communities in those unique circumstances where this may be appropriate;

174. Urges States to take or strengthen measures, including through bilateral or multilateral cooperation, to address root causes, such as poverty, underdevelopment and lack of equal opportunity, some of which may be associated with discriminatory practices, that make persons, especially women and children, vulnerable to trafficking, which may give rise to racism, racial discrimination, xenophobia and related intolerance;

175. Encourages States, in cooperation with non-governmental organizations, to undertake campaigns aimed at clarifying opportunities, limitations and rights in the event of migration, so as to enable everyone, in particular women, to make informed decisions and to prevent them from becoming victims of trafficking;

176. Urges States to adopt and implement social development policies based on reliable statistical data and centred on the attainment, by the year 2015, of the commitments to meet the basic needs of all set forth in paragraph 36 of the Programme of Action of the World Summit for Social Development, held at Copenhagen in 1995, with a view to closing significantly the existing gaps in living conditions faced by victims of racism, racial discrimination, xenophobia and related intolerance, especially regarding the illiteracy rate, universal primary education, infant mortality, under-five child mortality, health, reproductive health care for all and access to safe drinking water. Promotion of gender equality will also be taken into account in the adoption and implementation of these policies;

International legal framework

177. Urges States to continue cooperating with the Committee on the Elimination of Racial Discrimination and other human rights treaty monitoring bodies in order to promote, including by means of a constructive and transparent dialogue, the effective implementation of the instruments concerned and proper consideration of the recommendations adopted by these bodies with regard to complaints of racism, racial discrimination, xenophobia and related intolerance;

178. Requests adequate resources for the Committee on the Elimination of Racial Discrimination in order to enable it to discharge its mandate fully and

stresses the importance of providing adequate resources for all the United Nations human rights treaty bodies;

General international instruments

179. Endorses efforts of the international community, in particular steps taken under the auspices of the United Nations Educational, Scientific and Cultural Organization, to promote respect for and preserve cultural diversity within and between communities and nations with a view to creating a harmonious multicultural world, including elaboration of a possible international instrument in this respect in a manner consistent with international human rights instruments;

180. Invites the United Nations General Assembly to consider elaborating an integral and comprehensive international convention to protect and promote the rights and dignity of disabled people, including, especially, provisions that address the discriminatory practices and treatment affecting them;

Regional/international cooperation

181. Invites the Inter-Parliamentary Union to contribute to the activities of the International Year of Mobilization against Racism, Racial Discrimination, Xenophobia and Related Intolerance by encouraging national parliaments to review progress on the objectives of the Conference;

182. Encourages States to participate in regional dialogues on problems of migration and invites them to consider negotiating bilateral and regional agreements on migrant workers and designing and implementing programmes with States of other regions to protect the rights of migrants;

183. Urges States, in consultation with civil society, to support or otherwise establish, as appropriate, regional, comprehensive dialogues on the causes and consequences of migration that focus not only on law enforcement and border control, but also on the promotion and protection of the human rights of migrants and on the relationship between migration and development;

184. Encourages international organizations having mandates dealing specifically with migration issues to exchange information and coordinate their activities on matters involving racism, racial discrimination, xenophobia and related intolerance against migrants, including migrant workers, with the support of the Office of the United Nations High Commissioner for Human Rights;

185. Expresses its deep concern over the severity of the humanitarian suffering of affected civilian populations and the burden carried by many

receiving countries, particularly developing countries and countries in transition, and requests the relevant international institutions to ensure that urgent adequate financial and humanitarian assistance is maintained for the host countries to enable them to help the victims and to address, on an equitable basis, difficulties of populations expelled from their homes, and calls for sufficient safeguards to enable refugees to exercise freely their right of return to their countries of origin voluntarily, in safety and dignity;

186. Encourages States to conclude bilateral, subregional, regional and international agreements to address the problem of trafficking in women and children, in particular girls, as well as the smuggling of migrants;

187. Calls upon States, to promote, as appropriate, exchanges at the regional and international levels among independent national institutions and, as applicable, other relevant independent bodies with a view to enhancing cooperation to combat racism, racial discrimination, xenophobia and related intolerance;

188. Urges States to support the activities of regional bodies or centres which combat racism, racial discrimination, xenophobia and related intolerance where they exist in their region, and recommends the establishment of such bodies or centres in all regions where they do not exist. These bodies or centres may undertake the following activities, amongst others: assess and follow up the situation of racism, racial discrimination, xenophobia and related intolerance, and of individuals or groups of individuals who are victims thereof or subject thereto; identify trends, issues and problems; collect, disseminate and exchange information, inter alia relevant to the outcome of the regional conferences and the World Conference, and build networks to these ends; highlight examples of good practices; organize awareness-raising campaigns; develop proposals, solutions and preventive measures, where possible and appropriate, through joint efforts by coordinating with the United Nations, regional organizations and States and national human rights institutions;

189. Urges international organizations, within their mandates, to contribute to the fight against racism, racial discrimination, xenophobia and related intolerance;

190. Encourages financial and development institutions and the operational programmes and specialized agencies of the United Nations, in accordance with their regular budgets and the procedures of their governing bodies:

(a) To assign particular priority and allocate sufficient funding, within their areas of competence and budgets, to improve the situation of victims of racism, racial discrimination, xenophobia and related intolerance in order to combat manifestations of racism, racial discrimination, xenophobia and related intolerance, and to include them in the development and implementation of projects concerning them;

(b) To integrate human rights principles and standards into their policies and programmes;

(c) To consider including in their regular reporting to their boards of governors information on their contribution to promoting the participation of victims of racism, racial discrimination, xenophobia and related intolerance within their programmes and activities, and information on the efforts taken to facilitate such participation and to ensure that these policies and practices contribute to the eradication of racism, racial discrimination, xenophobia and related intolerance;

(d) To examine how their policies and practices affect victims of racism, racial discrimination, xenophobia and related intolerance, and to ensure that these policies and practices contribute to the eradication of racism, racial discrimination, xenophobia and related intolerance;

191. (a) Calls upon States to elaborate action plans in consultation with national human rights institutions, other institutions created by law to combat racism, and civil society and to provide the United Nations High Commissioner for Human Rights with such action plans and other relevant materials on the measures undertaken in order to implement provisions of the present Declaration and the Programme of Action;

(b) Requests the United Nations High Commissioner for Human Rights, in follow-up to the Conference, to cooperate with five independent eminent experts, one from each region, appointed by the Secretary-General from among candidates proposed by the Chairperson of the Commission on Human Rights, after consultation with the regional groups, to follow the implementation of the provisions of the Declaration and Programme of Action. An annual progress report on the implementation of these provisions will be presented by the High Commissioner to the Commission on Human Rights and to the General Assembly, taking into account information and views provided by States, relevant human rights treaty bodies, special procedures and other mechanisms of the Commission on Human Rights of the United Nations, international, regional and non-governmental organizations and national human rights institutions;

(c) Welcomes the intention of the United Nations High Commissioner for Human Rights to establish, within the Office of the High Commissioner for

Human Rights, an anti-discrimination unit to combat racism, racial discrimination, xenophobia and related intolerance and to promote equality and non-discrimination, and invites her to consider the inclusion in its mandate of, inter alia, the compilation of information on racial discrimination and its development, and on legal and administrative support and advice to victims of racial discrimination and the collection of background materials provided by States, international, regional and non-governmental organizations and national human rights institutions under the follow-up mechanism of the Conference;

(d) Recommends that the Office of the High Commissioner for Human Rights, in cooperation with States, international, regional and non-governmental organizations and national human rights institutions, create a database containing information on practical means to address racism, racial discrimination, xenophobia and related intolerance, particularly international and regional instruments and national legislation, including anti-discrimination legislation, as well as legal means to combat racial discrimination; remedies available through international mechanisms to victims of racial discrimination, as well as national remedies; educational and preventive programmes implemented in various countries and regions; best practices to address racism, racial discrimination, xenophobia and related intolerance; opportunities for technical cooperation; and academic studies and specialized documents; and ensure that such a database is as accessible as possible to those in authority and the public at large, through its Web site and by other appropriate means;

192. Invites the United Nations and the United Nations Educational, Scientific and Cultural Organization to continue to organize high-level and other meetings on the Dialogue among Civilizations and, for this purpose, to mobilize funds and promote partnerships;

Office of the High Commissioner for Human Rights

193. Encourages the United Nations High Commissioner for Human Rights to continue and expand the appointment and designation of goodwill ambassadors in all countries of the world in order, inter alia, to promote respect for human rights and a culture of tolerance and to increase the level of awareness about the scourge of racism, racial discrimination, xenophobia and related intolerance;

194. Calls upon the Office of the High Commissioner for Human Rights to continue its efforts further to increase awareness of the work of the Committee on the Elimination of Racial Discrimination and the other United Nations human rights treaty bodies;

195. Invites the Office of the High Commissioner for Human Rights, in consultation with the United Nations Educational, Scientific and Cultural Organization, and non-governmental organizations active in the field of the promotion and protection of human rights, to undertake regular consultations with them and to encourage research activities aimed at collecting, maintaining and adapting the technical, scientific, educational and information materials produced by all cultures around the world to fight racism;

196. Requests the Office of the High Commissioner for Human Rights to pay special attention to violations of the human rights of victims of racism, racial discrimination, xenophobia and related intolerance, in particular migrants, including migrant workers, to promote international cooperation in combating xenophobia and, to this end, to develop programmes which can be implemented in countries on the basis of appropriate cooperation agreements;

197. Invites States to assist the Office of the High Commissioner for Human Rights in developing and funding, upon the request of States, specific technical cooperation projects aimed at combating racism, racial discrimination, xenophobia and related intolerance;

198. (a) Invites the Commission on Human Rights to include in the mandates of the special rapporteurs and working groups of the Commission, in particular the Special Rapporteur on contemporary forms of racism, racial discrimination, xenophobia and related intolerance, recommendations that they consider the relevant provisions of the Declaration and the Programme of Action while exercising their mandates, in particular reporting to the General Assembly and the Commission on Human Rights, and also to consider any other appropriate means to follow up on the outcome on the Conference;

(b) Calls upon States to cooperate with the relevant special procedures of the Commission on Human Rights and other mechanisms of the United Nations in matters pertaining to racism, racial discrimination, xenophobia and related intolerance, in particular with the special rapporteurs, independent experts and special representatives;

199. Recommends that the Commission on Human Rights prepare complementary international standards to strengthen and update international instruments against racism, racial discrimination, xenophobia and related intolerance in all their aspects;

Decades

200. Urges States and the international community to support the activities of the Third Decade to Combat Racism and Racial Discrimination;

201. Recommends that the General Assembly consider declaring a United Nations year or decade against trafficking in persons, especially in women, youth and children, in order to protect their dignity and human rights;

202. Urges States, in close cooperation with the United Nations Educational, Scientific and Cultural Organization, to promote the implementation of the Declaration and Programme of Action on a Culture of Peace and the objectives of the International Decade for a Culture of Peace and Non-Violence for the Children of the World, which started in 2001, and invites the United Nations Educational, Scientific and Cultural Organization to contribute to these activities;

Indigenous peoples

203. Recommends that the United Nations Secretary-General conduct an evaluation of the results of the International Decade of the World's Indigenous People (1995-2004) and make recommendations concerning how to mark the end of the Decade, including an appropriate follow-up;

204. Requests States to ensure adequate funding for the establishment of an operational framework and a firm basis for the future development of the Permanent Forum on Indigenous Issues within the United Nations system;

205. Urges States to cooperate with the work of the Special Rapporteur on the situation of human rights and fundamental freedoms of indigenous people and requests the Secretary-General and the United Nations High Commissioner for Human Rights to ensure that the Special Rapporteur is provided with all the necessary human, technical and financial resources to fulfil his responsibilities;

206. Calls upon States to conclude negotiations on and approve as soon as possible the text of the draft declaration on the rights of indigenous peoples, under discussion by the working group of the Commission on Human Rights to elaborate a draft declaration, in accordance with Commission resolution 1995/32 of 3 March 1995;

207. Urges States, in the light of the relationship between racism, racial discrimination, xenophobia and related intolerance and poverty, marginality and social exclusion of peoples and individuals at both the national and international levels, to enhance their policies and measures to reduce income and wealth inequalities and to take appropriate steps, individually and

through international cooperation, to promote and protect economic, social and cultural rights on a non-discriminatory basis;

208. Urges States and international financial and development institutions to mitigate any negative effects of globalization by examining, inter alia, how their policies and practices affect national populations in general and indigenous peoples in particular; by ensuring that their policies and practices contribute to the eradication of racism through the participation of national populations and, in particular, indigenous peoples in development projects; by further democratizing international financial institutions; and by consulting with indigenous peoples on any matter that may affect their physical, spiritual or cultural integrity;

209. Invites financial and development institutions and the operational programmes and specialized agencies of the United Nations, in accordance with their regular budgets and the procedures of their governing bodies:

(a) To assign particular priority to and allocate sufficient funding, within their areas of competence, to the improvement of the status of indigenous peoples, with special attention to the needs of these populations in developing countries, including the preparation of specific programmes with a view to achieving the objectives of the International Decade of the World's Indigenous People;

(b) To carry out special projects, through appropriate channels and in collaboration with indigenous peoples, to support their initiatives at the community level and to facilitate the exchange of information and technical know-how between indigenous peoples and experts in these areas;

Civil society

210. Calls upon States to strengthen cooperation, develop partnerships and consult regularly with non-governmental organizations and all other sectors of the civil society to harness their experience and expertise, thereby contributing to the development of legislation, policies and other governmental initiatives, as well as involving them more closely in the elaboration and implementation of policies and programmes designed to combat racism, racial discrimination, xenophobia and related intolerance;

211. Urges leaders of religious communities to continue to confront racism, racial discrimination, xenophobia and related intolerance through, inter alia, promotion and sponsoring of dialogue and partnerships to bring about reconciliation, healing and harmony within and among societies, invites religious communities to participate in promoting economic and social

revitalization and encourages religious leaders to foster greater cooperation and contact between diverse racial groups;

212. Urges States to establish and strengthen effective partnerships with and provide support, as appropriate, to all relevant actors of civil society, including non-governmental organizations working to promote gender equality and the advancement of women, particularly women subject to multiple discrimination, and to promote an integrated and holistic approach to the elimination of all forms of discrimination against women and girls;

Non-governmental organizations

213. Urges States to provide an open and conducive environment to enable non-governmental organizations to function freely and openly within their societies and thereby make an effective contribution to the elimination of racism, racial discrimination, xenophobia and related intolerance throughout the world, and to promote a wider role for grass-roots organizations;

214. Calls upon States to explore means to expand the role of non-governmental organizations in society through, in particular, deepening the ties of solidarity amongst citizens and promoting greater trust across racial and social class divides by promoting wider citizen involvement and more voluntary cooperation;

The private sector

215. Urges States to take measures, including, where appropriate, legislative measures, to ensure that transnational corporations and other foreign enterprises operating within their national territories conform to precepts and practices of non-racism and non-discrimination, and further encourages the business sector, including transnational corporations and foreign enterprises, to collaborate with trade unions and other relevant sectors of civil society to develop voluntary codes of conduct for all businesses, designed to prevent, address and eradicate racism, racial discrimination, xenophobia and related intolerance;

Youth

216. Urges States to encourage the full and active participation of, as well as involve more closely, youth in the elaboration, planning and implementation of activities to fight racism, racial discrimination, xenophobia and related intolerance, and calls upon States, in partnership with non-governmental organizations and other sectors of society, to facilitate both national and international youth dialogue on racism, racial discrimination, xenophobia

and related intolerance, through the World Youth Forum of the United Nations system and through the use of new technologies, exchanges and other means;

217. Urges States to encourage and facilitate the establishment and maintenance of youth mechanisms, set up by youth organizations and young women and men themselves, in the spirit of combating racism, racial discrimination, xenophobia and related intolerance, through such activities as: disseminating and exchanging information and building networks to these ends; organizing awareness-raising campaigns and participating in multicultural education programmes; developing proposals and solutions, where possible and appropriate; cooperating and consulting regularly with non-governmental organizations and other actors in civil society in developing initiatives and programmes that promote intercultural exchange and dialogue;

218. Urges States, in cooperation with intergovernmental organizations, the International Olympic Committee and international and regional sports federations, to intensify the fight against racism in sport by, among other things, educating the youth of the world through sport practised without discrimination of any kind and in the Olympic spirit, which requires human understanding, tolerance, fair play and solidarity;

219. Recognizes that the success of this Programme of Action will require political will and adequate funding at the national, regional and international levels, and international cooperation.

Declaration on Race and Racial Prejudice

Adopted and proclaimed by the General Conference of the United Nations Educational, Scientific and Cultural Organization at its 20th session 27 November 1978.

Article 1

1. All human beings belong to a single species and are descended from a common stock. They are born equal in dignity and rights and all form an integral part of humanity.

2. All individuals and groups have the right to be different, to consider themselves as different and to be regarded as such. However, the diversity of life styles and the right to be different may not, in any circumstances, serve as a pretext for racial prejudice; they may not justify either in law or in fact any discriminatory practice whatsoever, nor provide a ground for the policy of apartheid, which is the extreme form of racism.

3. Identity of origin in no way affects the fact that human beings can and may live differently, nor does it preclude the existence of differences based on cultural, environmental and historical diversity nor the right to maintain cultural identity.

4. All peoples of the world possess equal faculties for attaining the highest level in intellectual, technical, social, economic, cultural and political development.

5. The differences between the achievements of the different peoples are entirely attributable to geographical, historical, political, economic, social and cultural factors. Such differences can in no case serve as a pretext for any rank-ordered classification of nations or peoples.

Article 2

1. Any theory which involves the claim that racial or ethnic groups are inherently superior or inferior, thus implying that some would be entitled to dominate or eliminate others, presumed to be inferior, or which bases value judgments on racial differentiation, has no scientific foundation and is contrary to the moral and ethical principles of humanity.

2. Racism includes racist ideologies, prejudiced attitudes, discriminatory behaviour, structural arrangements and institutionalized practices resulting in racial inequality as well as the fallacious notion that discriminatory relations between groups are morally and scientifically justifiable; it is reflected in discriminatory provisions in legislation or regulations and discriminatory

practices as well as in anti-social beliefs and acts; it hinders the development of its victims, perverts those who practise it, divides nations internally, impedes international co-operation and gives rise to political tensions between peoples; it is contrary to the fundamental principles of international law and, consequently, seriously disturbs international peace and security.

3. Racial prejudice, historically linked with inequalities in power, reinforced by economic and social differences between individuals and groups, and still seeking today to justify such inequalities, is totally without justification.

Article 3

Any distinction, exclusion, restriction or preference based on race, colour, ethnic or national origin or religious intolerance motivated by racist considerations, which destroys or compromises the sovereign equality of States and the right of peoples to self-determination, or which limits in an arbitrary or discriminatory manner the right of every human being and group to full development is incompatible with the requirements of an international order which is just and guarantees respect for human rights; the right to full development implies equal access to the means of personal and collective advancement and fulfilment in a climate of respect for the values of civilizations and cultures, both national and world-wide.

Article 4

1. Any restriction on the complete self-fulfilment of human beings and free communication between them which is based on racial or ethnic considerations is contrary to the principle of equality in dignity and rights; it cannot be admitted.

2. One of the most serious violations of this principle is represented by apartheid , which, like genocide, is a crime against humanity, and gravely disturbs international peace and security.

3. Other policies and practices of racial segregation and discrimination constitute crimes against the conscience and dignity of mankind and may lead to political tensions and gravely endanger international peace and security.

Article 5

1. Culture, as a product of all human beings and a common heritage of mankind, and education in its broadest sense, offer men and women increasingly effective means of adaptation, enabling them not only to affirm that they are born equal in dignity and rights, but also to recognize that they

should respect the right of all groups to their own cultural identity and the development of their distinctive cultural life within the national and international contexts, it being understood that it rests with each group to decide in complete freedom on the maintenance, and, if appropriate, the adaptation or enrichment of the values which it regards as essential to its identity.

2. States, in accordance with their constitutional principles and procedures, as well as all other competent authorities and the entire teaching profession, have a responsibility to see that the educational resources of all countries are used to combat racism, more especially by ensuring that curricula and textbooks include scientific and ethical considerations concerning human unity and diversity and that no invidious distinctions are made with regard to any people; by training teachers to achieve these ends; by making the resources of the educational system available to all groups of the population without racial restriction or discrimination; and by taking appropriate steps to remedy the handicaps from which certain racial or ethnic groups suffer with regard to their level of education and standard of living and in particular to prevent such handicaps from being passed on to children.

3. The mass media and those who control or serve them, as well as all organized groups within national communities, are urged-with due regard to the principles embodied in the Universal Declaration of Human Rights, particularly the principle of freedom of expression-to promote understanding, tolerance and friendship among individuals and groups and to contribute to the eradication of racism, racial discrimination and racial prejudice, in particular by refraining from presenting a stereotyped, partial, unilateral or tendentious picture of individuals and of various human groups. Communication between racial and ethnic groups must be a reciprocal process, enabling them to express themselves and to be fully heard without let or hindrance. The mass media should therefore be freely receptive to ideas of individuals and groups which facilitate such communication.

Article 6

1. The State has prime responsibility for ensuring human rights and fundamental freedoms on an entirely equal footing in dignity and rights for all individuals and all groups.

2. So far as its competence extends and in accordance with its constitutional principles and procedures, the State should take all appropriate steps, inter alia by legislation, particularly in the spheres of education, culture and communication, to prevent, prohibit and eradicate racism, racist propaganda, racial segregation and apartheid and to encourage the dissemination of

knowledge and the findings of appropriate research in natural and social sciences on the causes and prevention of racial prejudice and racist attitudes, with due regard to the principles embodied in the Universal Declaration of Human Rights and in the International Covenant on Civil and Political Rights.

3. Since laws proscribing racial discrimination are not in themselves sufficient, it is also incumbent on States to supplement them by administrative machinery for the systematic investigation of instances of racial discrimination, by a comprehensive framework of legal remedies against acts of racial discrimination, by broadly based education and research programmes designed to combat racial prejudice and racial discrimination and by programmes of positive political, social, educational and cultural measures calculated to promote genuine mutual respect among groups. Where circumstances warrant, special programmes should be undertaken to promote the advancement of disadvantaged groups and, in the case of nationals, to ensure their effective participation in the decision-making processes of the community.

Article 7

In addition to political, economic and social measures, law is one of the principal means of ensuring equality in dignity and rights among individuals, and of curbing any propaganda, any form of organization or any practice which is based on ideas or theories referring to the alleged superiority of racial or ethnic groups or which seeks to justify or encourage racial hatred and discrimination in any form. States should adopt such legislation as is appropriate to this end and see that it is given effect and applied by all their services, with due regard to the principles embodied in the Universal Declaration of Human Rights. Such legislation should form part of a political, economic and social framework conducive to its implementation. Individuals and other legal entities, both public and private, must conform with such legislation and use all appropriate means to help the population as a whole to understand and apply it.

Article 8

1. Individuals, being entitled to an economic, social, cultural and legal order, on the national and international planes, such as to allow them to exercise all their capabilities on a basis of entire equality of rights and opportunities, have corresponding duties towards their fellows, towards the society in which they live and towards the international community. They are accordingly under an obligation to promote harmony among the peoples, to combat

racism and racial prejudice and to assist by every means available to them in eradicating racial discrimination in all its forms.

2. In the field of racial prejudice and racist attitudes and practices, specialists in natural and social sciences and cultural studies, as well as scientific organizations and associations, are called upon to undertake objective research on a wide interdisciplinary basis; all States should encourage them to this end.

3. It is, in particular, incumbent upon such specialists to ensure, by all means available to them, that their research findings are not misinterpreted, and also that they assist the public in understanding such findings.

Article 9

1. The principle of the equality in dignity and rights of all human beings and all peoples, irrespective of race, colour and origin, is a generally accepted and recognized principle of international law. Consequently any form of racial discrimination practised by a State constitutes a violation of international law giving rise to its international responsibility.

2. Special measures must be taken to ensure equality in dignity and rights for individuals and groups wherever necessary, while ensuring that they are not such as to appear racially discriminatory. In this respect, particular attention should be paid to racial or ethnic groups which are socially or economically disadvantaged, so as to afford them, on a completely equal footing and without discrimination or restriction, the protection of the laws and regulations and the advantages of the social measures in force, in particular in regard to housing, employment and health; to respect the authenticity of their culture and values; and to facilitate their social and occupational advancement, especially through education.

3. Population groups of foreign origin, particularly migrant workers and their families who contribute to the development of the host country, should benefit from appropriate measures designed to afford them security and respect for their dignity and cultural values and to facilitate their adaptation to the host environment and their professional advancement with a view to their subsequent reintegration in their country of origin and their contribution to its development; steps should be taken to make it possible for their children to be taught their mother tongue.

4. Existing disequilibria in international economic relations contribute to the exacerbation of racism and racial prejudice; all States should consequently endeavour to contribute to the restructuring of the international economy on a more equitable basis.

Article 10

International organizations, whether universal or regional, governmental or non-governmental, are called upon to co-operate and assist, so far as their respective fields of competence and means allow, in the full and complete implementation of the principles set out in this Declaration, thus contributing to the legitimate struggle of all men, born equal in dignity and rights, against the tyranny and oppression of racism, racial segregation, apartheid and genocide, so that all the peoples of the world may be forever delivered from these scourges.

Declaration on the Elimination of All Forms of Intolerance and of Discrimination Based on

Religion or Belief

UN GA Res. 36/55 (25 November 1981)

Article 1

1. Everyone shall have the right to freedom of thought, conscience and religion. This right shall include freedom to have a religion or whatever belief of his choice, and freedom, either individually or in community with others and in public or private, to manifest his religion or belief in worship, observance, practice and teaching.

2. No one shall be subject to coercion which would impair his freedom to have a religion or belief of his choice.

3. Freedom to manifest one's religion or belief may be subject only to such limitations as are prescribed by law and are necessary to protect public safety, order, health or morals or the fundamental rights and freedoms of others.

Article 2

1. No one shall be subject to discrimination by any State, institution, group of persons, or person on the grounds of religion or other belief.

2. For the purposes of the present Declaration, the expression "intolerance and discrimination based on religion or belief" means any distinction, exclusion, restriction or preference based on religion or belief and having as its purpose or as its effect nullification or impairment of the recognition, enjoyment or exercise of human rights and fundamental freedoms on an equal basis.

Article 3

Discrimination between human beings on the grounds of religion or belief constitutes an affront to human dignity and a disavowal of the principles of the Charter of the United Nations, and shall be condemned as a violation of the human rights and fundamental freedoms proclaimed in the Universal Declaration of Human Rights and enunciated in detail in the International Covenants on Human Rights, and as an obstacle to friendly and peaceful relations between nations.

Article 4

1. All States shall take effective measures to prevent and eliminate discrimination on the grounds of religion or belief in the recognition, exercise and enjoyment of human rights and fundamental freedoms in all fields of civil, economic, political, social and cultural life.

2. All States shall make all efforts to enact or rescind legislation where necessary to prohibit any such discrimination, and to take all appropriate measures to combat intolerance on the grounds of religion or other beliefs in this matter.

Article 5

1. The parents or, as the case may be, the legal guardians of the child have the right to organize the life within the family in accordance with their religion or belief and bearing in mind the moral education in which they believe the child should be brought up.

2. Every child shall enjoy the right to have access to education in the matter of religion or belief in accordance with the wishes of his parents or, as the case may be, legal guardians, and shall not be compelled to receive teaching on religion or belief against the wishes of his parents or legal guardians, the best interests of the child being the guiding principle.

3. The child shall be protected from any form of discrimination on the ground of religion or belief. He shall be brought up in a spirit of understanding, tolerance, friendship among peoples, peace and universal brotherhood, respect for freedom of religion or belief of others, and in full consciousness that his energy and talents should be devoted to the service of his fellow men.

4. In the case of a child who is not under the care either of his parents or of legal guardians, due account shall be taken of their expressed wishes or of any other proof of their wishes in the matter of religion or belief, the best interests of the child being the guiding principle.

5. Practices of a religion or belief in which a child is brought up must not be injurious to his physical or mental health or to his full development, taking into account article 1, paragraph 3, of the present Declaration.

Article 6

In accordance with article 1 of the present Declaration, and subject to the provisions of article 1, paragraph 3, the right to freedom of thought, conscience, religion or belief shall include, *inter alia* , the following freedoms:

(a) To worship or assemble in connection with a religion or belief, and to establish and maintain places for these purposes;

(b) To establish and maintain appropriate charitable or humanitarian institutions;

(c) To make, acquire and use to an adequate extent the necessary articles and materials related to the rites or customs of a religion or belief;

(d) To write, issue and disseminate relevant publications in these areas;

(e) To teach a religion or belief in places suitable for these purposes;

(f) To solicit and receive voluntary financial and other contributions from individuals and institutions;

(g) To train, appoint, elect or designate by succession appropriate leaders called for by the requirements and standards of any religion or belief;

(h) To observe days of rest and to celebrate holidays and ceremonies in accordance with the precepts of one's religion or belief;

(i) To establish and maintain communications with individuals and communities in matters of religion and belief at the national and international levels.

Article 7

The rights and freedoms set forth in the present Declaration shall be accorded in national legislation in such a manner that everyone shall be able to avail himself of such rights and freedoms in practice ...

American Declaration of the Rights and Duties of Man

OAS Res. XXX, adopted by the 9th International
Conference of American States (1948).

Article II

All persons are equal before the law and have the rights and duties established in this Declaration, without distinction as to race, sex, language, creed or any other factor.

European Union Race Directive 2000/43

Council Directive 2000/43/EC (29 June 2000)
Official Journal L 180, 19/07/2000 P. 0022 - 0026.

Directive implementing the principle of equal treatment between persons
irrespective of racial or ethnic origin

CHAPTER I
GENERAL PROVISIONS

Article 1
Purpose

The purpose of this Directive is to lay down a framework for combating
discrimination on the grounds of racial or ethnic origin, with a view to
putting into effect in the Member States the principle of equal treatment.

Article 2
Concept of discrimination

1. For the purposes of this Directive, the principle of equal treatment shall
mean that there shall be no direct or indirect discrimination based on racial
or ethnic origin.

2. For the purposes of paragraph 1:

(a) direct discrimination shall be taken to occur where one person is treated
less favourably than another is, has been or would be treated in a comparable
situation on grounds of racial or ethnic origin;

(b) indirect discrimination shall be taken to occur where an apparently
neutral provision, criterion or practice would put persons of a racial or ethnic
origin at a particular disadvantage compared with other persons, unless that
provision, criterion or practice is objectively justified by a legitimate aim and
the means of achieving that aim are appropriate and necessary.

3. Harassment shall be deemed to be discrimination within the meaning of
paragraph 1, when an unwanted conduct related to racial or ethnic origin
takes place with the purpose or effect of violating the dignity of a person and
of creating an intimidating, hostile, degrading, humiliating or offensive
environment. In this context, the concept of harassment may be defined in
accordance with the national laws and practice of the Member States.

4. An instruction to discriminate against persons on grounds of racial or ethnic origin shall be deemed to be discrimination within the meaning of paragraph 1.

Article 3
Scope

1. Within the limits of the powers conferred upon the Community, this Directive shall apply to all persons, as regards both the public and private sectors, including public bodies, in relation to:

(a) conditions for access to employment, to self-employment and to occupation, including selection criteria and recruitment conditions, whatever the branch of activity and at all levels of the professional hierarchy, including promotion;

(b) access to all types and to all levels of vocational guidance, vocational training, advanced vocational training and retraining, including practical work experience;

(c) employment and working conditions, including dismissals and pay;

(d) membership of and involvement in an organisation of workers or employers, or any organisation whose members carry on a particular profession, including the benefits provided for by such organisations;

(e) social protection, including social security and healthcare;

(f) social advantages;

(g) education;

(h) access to and supply of goods and services which are available to the public, including housing.

2. This Directive does not cover difference of treatment based on nationality and is without prejudice to provisions and conditions relating to the entry into and residence of third-country nationals and stateless persons on the territory of Member States, and to any treatment which arises from the legal status of the third-country nationals and stateless persons concerned.

Article 4
Genuine and determining occupational requirements

Notwithstanding Article 2(1) and (2), Member States may provide that a difference of treatment which is based on a characteristic related to racial or ethnic origin shall not constitute discrimination where, by reason of the nature of the particular occupational activities concerned or of the context in which they are carried out, such a characteristic constitutes a genuine and determining occupational requirement, provided that the objective is legitimate and the requirement is proportionate.

Article 5
Positive action

With a view to ensuring full equality in practice, the principle of equal treatment shall not prevent any Member State from maintaining or adopting specific measures to prevent or compensate for disadvantages linked to racial or ethnic origin.

Article 6
Minimum requirements

1. Member States may introduce or maintain provisions which are more favourable to the protection of the principle of equal treatment than those laid down in this Directive.

2. The implementation of this Directive shall under no circumstances constitute grounds for a reduction in the level of protection against discrimination already afforded by Member States in the fields covered by this Directive.

CHAPTER II
REMEDIES AND ENFORCEMENT

Article 7
Defence of rights

1. Member States shall ensure that judicial and/or administrative procedures, including where they deem it appropriate conciliation procedures, for the enforcement of obligations under this Directive are available to all persons who consider themselves wronged by failure to apply the principle of equal treatment to them, even after the relationship in which the discrimination is alleged to have occurred has ended.

2. Member States shall ensure that associations, organisations or other legal entities, which have, in accordance with the criteria laid down by their national law, a legitimate interest in ensuring that the provisions of this Directive are complied with, may engage, either on behalf or in support of the complainant, with his or her approval, in any judicial and/or administrative procedure provided for the enforcement of obligations under this Directive.

3. Paragraphs 1 and 2 are without prejudice to national rules relating to time limits for bringing actions as regards the principle of equality of treatment.

Article 8
Burden of proof

1. Member States shall take such measures as are necessary, in accordance with their national judicial systems, to ensure that, when persons who consider themselves wronged because the principle of equal treatment has not been applied to them establish, before a court or other competent authority, facts from which it may be presumed that there has been direct or indirect discrimination, it shall be for the respondent to prove that there has been no breach of the principle of equal treatment.

2. Paragraph 1 shall not prevent Member States from introducing rules of evidence which are more favourable to plaintiffs.

3. Paragraph 1 shall not apply to criminal procedures.

4. Paragraphs 1, 2 and 3 shall also apply to any proceedings brought in accordance with Article 7(2).

5. Member States need not apply paragraph 1 to proceedings in which it is for the court or competent body to investigate the facts of the case.

Article 9
Victimisation

Member States shall introduce into their national legal systems such measures as are necessary to protect individuals from any adverse treatment or adverse consequence as a reaction to a complaint or to proceedings aimed at enforcing compliance with the principle of equal treatment.

Article 10
Dissemination of information

Member States shall take care that the provisions adopted pursuant to this Directive, together with the relevant provisions already in force, are brought to the attention of the persons concerned by all appropriate means throughout their territory.

Article 11
Social dialogue

1. Member States shall, in accordance with national traditions and practice, take adequate measures to promote the social dialogue between the two sides

of industry with a view to fostering equal treatment, including through the monitoring of workplace practices, collective agreements, codes of conduct, research or exchange of experiences and good practices.

2. Where consistent with national traditions and practice, Member States shall encourage the two sides of the industry without prejudice to their autonomy to conclude, at the appropriate level, agreements laying down anti-discrimination rules in the fields referred to in Article 3 which fall within the scope of collective bargaining. These agreements shall respect the minimum requirements laid down by this Directive and the relevant national implementing measures.

Article 12
Dialogue with non-governmental organisations

Member States shall encourage dialogue with appropriate non-governmental organisations which have, in accordance with their national law and practice, a legitimate interest in contributing to the fight against discrimination on grounds of racial and ethnic origin with a view to promoting the principle of equal treatment.

CHAPTER III
BODIES FOR THE PROMOTION OF EQUAL TREATMENT

Article 13

1. Member States shall designate a body or bodies for the promotion of equal treatment of all persons without discrimination on the grounds of racial or ethnic origin. These bodies may form part of agencies charged at national level with the defence of human rights or the safeguard of individuals' rights.

2. Member States shall ensure that the competences of these bodies include:

— without prejudice to the right of victims and of associations, organisations or other legal entities referred to in Article 7(2), providing independent assistance to victims of discrimination in pursuing their complaints about discrimination,

— conducting independent surveys concerning discrimination,

— publishing independent reports and making recommendations on any issue relating to such discrimination.

CHAPTER IV
FINAL PROVISIONS

Article 14
Compliance

Member States shall take the necessary measures to ensure that:

(a) any laws, regulations and administrative provisions contrary to the principle of equal treatment are abolished;

(b) any provisions contrary to the principle of equal treatment which are included in individual or collective contracts or agreements, internal rules of undertakings, rules governing profit-making or non-profit-making associations, and rules governing the independent professions and workers' and employers' organisations, are or may be declared, null and void or are amended.

Article 15
Sanctions

Member States shall lay down the rules on sanctions applicable to infringements of the national provisions adopted pursuant to this Directive and shall take all measures necessary to ensure that they are applied. The sanctions, which may comprise the payment of compensation to the victim, must be effective, proportionate and dissuasive. The Member States shall notify those provisions to the Commission by 19 July 2003 at the latest and shall notify it without delay of any subsequent amendment affecting them.

Article 16
Implementation

Member States shall adopt the laws, regulations and administrative provisions necessary to comply with this Directive by 19 July 2003 or may entrust management and labour, at their joint request, with the implementation of this Directive as regards provisions falling within the scope of collective agreements. In such cases, Member States shall ensure that by 19 July 2003, management and labour introduce the necessary measures by agreement, Member States being required to take any necessary measures to enable them at any time to be in a position to guarantee the results imposed by this Directive. They shall forthwith inform the Commission thereof.

When Member States adopt these measures, they shall contain a reference to this Directive or be accompanied by such a reference on the occasion of their official publication. The methods of making such a reference shall be laid down by the Member States.

Article 17
Report

1. Member States shall communicate to the Commission by 19 July 2005, and every five years thereafter, all the information necessary for the Commission to draw up a report to the European Parliament and the Council on the application of this Directive.

2. The Commission's report shall take into account, as appropriate, the views of the European Monitoring Centre on Racism and Xenophobia, as well as the viewpoints of the social partners and relevant non-governmental organisations. In accordance with the principle of gender mainstreaming, this report shall, inter alia, provide an assessment of the impact of the measures taken on women and men. In the light of the information received, this report shall include, if necessary, proposals to revise and update this Directive.

European Council Framework Directive 2000/78/EC

of 27 November 2000 establishing a general framework for equal treatment
in employment and occupation

CHAPTER I
GENERAL PROVISIONS
Article 1
Purpose

The purpose of this Directive is to lay down a general framework for
combating discrimination on the grounds of religion or belief, disability, age
or sexual orientation as regards employment and occupation, with a view to
putting into effect in the Member States the principle of equal treatment.

Article 2
Concept of discrimination

1. For the purposes of this Directive, the 'principle of equal treatment' shall
mean that there shall be no direct or indirect discrimination whatsoever on
any of the grounds referred to in Article 1.

2. For the purposes of paragraph 1:

(a) direct discrimination shall be taken to occur where one person is treated
less favourably than another is, has been or would be treated in a comparable
situation, on any of the grounds referred to in Article 1;

(b) indirect discrimination shall be taken to occur where an apparently
neutral provision, criterion or practice would put persons having a particular
religion or belief, a particular disability, a particular age, or a particular sexual
orientation at a particular disadvantage compared with other persons unless:

(i) that provision, criterion or practice is objectively justified by a legitimate
aim and the means of achieving that aim are appropriate and necessary, or (ii)
as regards persons with a particular disability, the employer or any person or
organisation to whom this Directive applies, is obliged, under national
legislation, to take appropriate measures in line with the principles contained
in Article 5 in order to eliminate disadvantages entailed by such provision,
criterion or practice.

3. Harassment shall be deemed to be a form of discrimination within the
meaning of paragraph 1, when unwanted conduct related to any of the
grounds referred to in Article 1 takes place with the purpose or effect of
violating the dignity of a person and of creating an intimidating, hostile,
degrading, humiliating or offensive environment. In this context, the concept

of harassment may be defined in accordance with the national laws and practice of the Member States.

4. An instruction to discriminate against persons on any of the grounds referred to in Article 1 shall be deemed to be discrimination within the meaning of paragraph 1.

5. This Directive shall be without prejudice to measures laid down by national law which, in a democratic society, are necessary for public security, for the maintenance of public order and the prevention of criminal offences, for the protection of health and for the protection of the rights and freedoms of others.

Article 3
Scope

1. Within the limits of the areas of competence conferred on the Community, this Directive shall apply to all persons, as regards both the public and private sectors, including public bodies, in relation to:

(a) conditions for access to employment, to self-employment or to occupation, including selection criteria and recruitment conditions, whatever the branch of activity and at all levels of the professional hierarchy, including promotion;

(b) access to all types and to all levels of vocational guidance, vocational training, advanced vocational training and retraining, including practical work experience;

(c) employment and working conditions, including dismissals and pay;

(d) membership of, and involvement in, an organisation of workers or employers, or any organisation whose members carry on a particular profession, including the benefits provided for by such organisations.

2. This Directive does not cover differences of treatment based on nationality and is without prejudice to provisions and conditions relating to the entry into and residence of third country nationals and stateless persons in the territory of Member States, and to any treatment which arises from the legal status of the third-country nationals and stateless persons concerned.

3. This Directive does not apply to payments of any kind made by state schemes or similar, including state social security or social protection schemes.

4. Member States may provide that this Directive, in so far as it relates to discrimination on the grounds of disability and age, shall not apply to the armed forces.

Article 4
Occupational requirements

1. Notwithstanding Article 2(1) and (2), Member States may provide that a difference of treatment which is based on a characteristic related to any of the grounds referred to in Article 1 shall not constitute discrimination where, by reason of the nature of the particular occupational activities concerned or of the context in which they are carried out, such a characteristic constitutes a genuine and determining occupational requirement, provided that the objective is legitimate and the requirement is proportionate.

2. Member States may maintain national legislation in force at the date of adoption of this Directive or provide for future legislation incorporating national practices existing at the date of adoption of this Directive pursuant to which, in the case of occupational activities within churches and other public or private organisations the ethos of which is based on religion or belief, a difference of treatment based on a person's religion or belief shall not constitute discrimination where, by reason of the nature of these activities or of the context in which they are carried out, a person's religion or belief constitute a genuine, legitimate and justified occupational requirement, having regard to the organisation's ethos. This difference of treatment shall be implemented taking account of Member States' constitutional provisions and principles, as well as the general principles of Community law, and should not justify discrimination on another ground. Provided that its provisions are otherwise complied with, this Directive shall thus not prejudice the right of churches and other public or private organisations, the ethos of which is based on religion or belief, acting in conformity with national constitutions and laws, to require individuals working for them to act in good faith and with loyalty to the organisation's ethos.

Article 5
Reasonable accommodation for disabled persons

In order to guarantee compliance with the principle of equal treatment in relation to persons with disabilities, reasonable accommodation shall be provided. This means that employers shall take appropriate measures, where needed in a particular case, to enable a person with a disability to have access to, participate in, or advance in employment, or to undergo training, unless such measures would impose a disproportionate burden on the employer. This burden shall not be disproportionate when it is sufficiently remedied by measures existing within the framework of the disability policy of the Member State concerned.

Article 6
Justification of differences of treatment on grounds of age

1. Notwithstanding Article 2(2), Member States may provide that differences of treatment on grounds of age shall not constitute discrimination, if, within the context of national law, they are objectively and reasonably justified by a legitimate aim, including legitimate employment policy, labour market and vocational training objectives, and if the means of achieving that aim are appropriate and necessary. Such differences of treatment may include, among others:

(a) the setting of special conditions on access to employment and vocational training, employment and occupation, including dismissal and remuneration conditions, for young people, older workers and persons with caring responsibilities in order to promote their vocational integration or ensure their protection;

(b) the fixing of minimum conditions of age, professional experience or seniority in service for access to employment or to certain advantages linked to employment;

(c) the fixing of a maximum age for recruitment which is based on the training requirements of the post in question or the need for a reasonable period of employment before retirement.

2. Notwithstanding Article 2(2), Member States may provide that the fixing for occupational social security schemes of ages for admission or entitlement to retirement or invalidity benefits, including the fixing under those schemes of different ages for employees or groups or categories of employees, and the use, in the context of such schemes, of age criteria in actuarial calculations, does not constitute discrimination on the grounds of age, provided this does not result in discrimination on the grounds of sex.

Article 7
Positive action

1. With a view to ensuring full equality in practice, the principle of equal treatment shall not prevent any Member State from maintaining or adopting specific measures to prevent or compensate for disadvantages linked to any of the grounds referred to in Article 1.

2. With regard to disabled persons, the principle of equal treatment shall be without prejudice to the right of Member States to maintain or adopt

provisions on the protection of health and safety at work or to measures aimed at creating or maintaining provisions or facilities for safeguarding or promoting their integration into the working environment.

Article 8
Minimum requirements

1. Member States may introduce or maintain provisions which are more favourable to the protection of the principle of equal treatment than those laid down in this Directive.

2. The implementation of this Directive shall under no circumstances constitute grounds for a reduction in the level of protection against discrimination already afforded by Member States in the fields covered by this Directive.

CHAPTER II
REMEDIES AND ENFORCEMENT

Article 9
Defence of rights

1. Member States shall ensure that judicial and/or administrative procedures, including where they deem it appropriate conciliation procedures, for the enforcement of obligations under this Directive are available to all persons who consider themselves wronged by failure to apply the principle of equal treatment to them, even after the relationship in which the discrimination is alleged to have occurred has ended.

2. Member States shall ensure that associations, organizations or other legal entities which have, in accordance with the criteria laid down by their national law, a legitimate interest in ensuring that the provisions of this Directive are complied with, may engage, either on behalf or in support of the complainant, with his or her approval, in any judicial and/or administrative procedure provided for the enforcement of obligations under this Directive.

3. Paragraphs 1 and 2 are without prejudice to national rules relating to time limits for bringing actions as regards the principle of equality of treatment.

Article 10
Burden of proof

1. Member States shall take such measures as are necessary, in accordance with their national judicial systems, to ensure that, when persons who consider themselves wronged because the principle of equal treatment has

not been applied to them establish, before a court or other competent authority, facts from which it may be presumed that there has been direct or indirect discrimination, it shall be for the respondent to prove that there has been no breach of the principle of equal treatment.

2. Paragraph 1 shall not prevent Member States from introducing rules of evidence which are more favourable to plaintiffs.

3. Paragraph 1 shall not apply to criminal procedures.

4. Paragraphs 1, 2 and 3 shall also apply to any legal proceedings commenced in accordance with Article 9(2).

5. Member States need not apply paragraph 1 to proceedings in

which it is for the court or competent body to investigate the facts of the case.

Article 11
Victimisation

Member States shall introduce into their national legal systems such measures as are necessary to protect employees against dismissal or other adverse treatment by the employer as a reaction to a complaint within the undertaking or to any legal proceedings aimed at enforcing compliance with the principle of equal treatment.

Article 12
Dissemination of information

Member States shall take care that the provisions adopted pursuant to this Directive, together with the relevant provisions already in force in this field, are brought to the attention of the persons concerned by all appropriate means, for example at the workplace, throughout their territory.

Article 13
Social dialogue

1. Member States shall, in accordance with their national traditions and practice, take adequate measures to promote dialogue between the social partners with a view to fostering equal treatment, including through the monitoring of workplace practices, collective agreements, codes of conduct and through research or exchange of experiences and good practices.

2. Where consistent with their national traditions and practice, Member States shall encourage the social partners, without prejudice to their autonomy, to conclude at the appropriate level agreements laying down anti-discrimination rules in the fields referred to in Article 3 which fall within the scope of collective bargaining. These agreements shall respect the minimum

requirements laid down by this Directive and by the relevant national implementing measures.

Article 14
Dialogue with non-governmental organisations

Member States shall encourage dialogue with appropriate nongovernmental organisations which have, in accordance with their national law and practice, a legitimate interest in contributing to the fight against discrimination on any of the grounds referred to in Article 1 with a view to promoting the principle of equal treatment.

United Nations Human Rights Committee
General Comment 18 on Non-Discrimination

Adopted at the 37th Sess. (1989).
UN Doc. HRI/GEN/1/Rev.6 at 146 (2003).

1. Non-discrimination, together with equality before the law and equal protection of the law without any discrimination, constitute a basic and general principle relating to the protection of human rights. Thus, article 2, paragraph 1, of the International Covenant on Civil and Political Rights obligates each State party to respect and ensure to all persons within its territory and subject to its jurisdiction the rights recognized in the Covenant without distinction of any kind, such as race, colour, sex, language, religion, political or other opinion, national or social origin, property, birth or other status. Article 26 not only entitles all persons to equality before the law as well as equal protection of the law but also prohibits any discrimination under the law and guarantees to all persons equal and effective protection against discrimination on any ground such as race, colour, sex, language, religion, political or other opinion, national or social origin, property, birth or other status.

2. Indeed, the principle of non-discrimination is so basic that article 3 obligates each State party to ensure the equal right of men and women to the enjoyment of the rights set forth in the Covenant. While article 4, paragraph 1, allows States parties to take measures derogating from certain obligations under the Covenant in time of public emergency, the same article requires, inter alia, that those measures should not involve discrimination solely on the ground of race, colour, sex, language, religion or social origin. Furthermore, article 20, paragraph 2, obligates States parties to prohibit, by law, any advocacy of national, racial or religious hatred which constitutes incitement to discrimination.

3. Because of their basic and general character, the principle of non-discrimination as well as that of equality before the law and equal protection of the law are sometimes expressly referred to in articles relating to particular categories of human rights. Article 14, paragraph 1, provides that all persons shall be equal before the courts and tribunals, and paragraph 3 of the same article provides that, in the determination of any criminal charge against him, everyone shall be entitled, in full equality, to the minimum guarantees enumerated in subparagraphs (a) to (g) of paragraph 3. Similarly, article 25 provides for the equal participation in public life of all citizens, without any of the distinctions mentioned in article 2.

4. It is for the States parties to determine appropriate measures to implement the relevant provisions. However, the Committee is to be informed about the nature of such measures and their conformity with the principles of non-discrimination and equality before the law and equal protection of the law.

5. The Committee wishes to draw the attention of States parties to the fact that the Covenant sometimes expressly requires them to take measures to guarantee the equality of rights of the persons concerned. For example, article 23, paragraph 4, stipulates that States parties shall take appropriate steps to ensure equality of rights as well as responsibilities of spouses as to marriage, during marriage and at its dissolution. Such steps may take the form of legislative, administrative or other measures, but it is a positive duty of States parties to make certain that spouses have equal rights as required by the Covenant. In relation to children, article 24 provides that all children, without any discrimination as to race, colour, sex, language, religion, national or social origin, property or birth, have the right to such measures of protection as are required by their status as minors, on the part of their family, society and the State.

6. The Committee notes that the Covenant neither defines the term "discrimination" nor indicates what constitutes discrimination. However, article 1 of the International Convention on the Elimination of All Forms of Racial Discrimination provides that the term "racial discrimination" shall mean any distinction, exclusion, restriction or preference based on race, colour, descent, or national or ethnic origin which has the purpose or effect of nullifying or impairing the recognition, enjoyment or exercise, on an equal footing, of human rights and fundamental freedoms in the political, economic, social, cultural or any other field of public life. Similarly, article 1 of the Convention on the Elimination of All Forms of Discrimination against Women provides that "discrimination against women" shall mean any distinction, exclusion or restriction made on the basis of sex which has the effect or purpose of impairing or nullifying the recognition, enjoyment or exercise by women, irrespective of their marital status, on a basis of equality of men and women, of human rights and fundamental freedoms in the political, economic, social, cultural, civil or any other field.

7. While these conventions deal only with cases of discrimination on specific grounds, the Committee believes that the term "discrimination" as used in the Covenant should be understood to imply any distinction, exclusion, restriction or preference which is based on any ground such as race, colour, sex, language, religion, political or other opinion, national or social origin,

property, birth or other status, and which has the purpose or effect of nullifying or impairing the recognition, enjoyment or exercise by all persons, on an equal footing, of all rights and freedoms.

8. The enjoyment of rights and freedoms on an equal footing, however, does not mean identical treatment in every instance. In this connection, the provisions of the Covenant are explicit. For example, article 6, paragraph 5, prohibits the death sentence from being imposed on persons below 18 years of age. The same paragraph prohibits that sentence from being carried out on pregnant women. Similarly, article 10, paragraph 3, requires the segregation of juvenile offenders from adults. Furthermore, article 25 guarantees certain political rights, differentiating on grounds of citizenship.

9. Reports of many States parties contain information regarding legislative as well as administrative measures and court decisions which relate to protection against discrimination in law, but they very often lack information which would reveal discrimination in fact. When reporting on articles 2 (1), 3 and 26 of the Covenant, States parties usually cite provisions of their constitution or equal opportunity laws with respect to equality of persons. While such information is of course useful, the Committee wishes to know if there remain any problems of discrimination in fact, which may be practised either by public authorities, by the community, or by private persons or bodies. The Committee wishes to be informed about legal provisions and administrative measures directed at diminishing or eliminating such discrimination.

10. The Committee also wishes to point out that the principle of equality sometimes requires States parties to take affirmative action in order to diminish or eliminate conditions which cause or help to perpetuate discrimination prohibited by the Covenant. For example, in a State where the general conditions of a certain part of the population prevent or impair their enjoyment of human rights, the State should take specific action to correct those conditions. Such action may involve granting for a time to the part of the population concerned certain preferential treatment in specific matters as compared with the rest of the population. However, as long as such action is needed to correct discrimination in fact, it is a case of legitimate differentiation under the Covenant.

11. Both article 2, paragraph 1, and article 26 enumerate grounds of discrimination such as race, colour, sex, language, religion, political or other opinion, national or social origin, property, birth or other status. The Committee has observed that in a number of constitutions and laws not all

the grounds on which discrimination is prohibited, as cited in article 2, paragraph 1, are enumerated. The Committee would therefore like to receive information from States parties as to the significance of such omissions.

12. While article 2 limits the scope of the rights to be protected against discrimination to those provided for in the Covenant, article 26 does not specify such limitations. That is to say, article 26 provides that all persons are equal before the law and are entitled to equal protection of the law without discrimination, and that the law shall guarantee to all persons equal and effective protection against discrimination on any of the enumerated grounds. In the view of the Committee, article 26 does not merely duplicate the guarantee already provided for in article 2 but provides in itself an autonomous right. It prohibits discrimination in law or in fact in any field regulated and protected by public authorities. Article 26 is therefore concerned with the obligations imposed on States parties in regard to their legislation and the application thereof. Thus, when legislation is adopted by a State party, it must comply with the requirement of article 26 that its content should not be discriminatory. In other words, the application of the principle of non-discrimination contained in article 26 is not limited to those rights which are provided for in the Covenant.

13. Finally, the Committee observes that not every differentiation of treatment will constitute discrimination, if the criteria for such differentiation are reasonable and objective and if the aim is to achieve a purpose which is legitimate under the Covenant.

CASES

Minority Schools in Albania

PCIJ, Advisory Opinion, Ser. A/B, No. 64 (1935).

[Due to attention from the League of Nations for the position of minorities in Albania, the government of Albania signed an undertaking declaring in relevant article 5 that

> Albanian nationals who belong to racial, linguistic or religious minorities will enjoy the same treatment and security in law and in fact as other Albanian nationals. In particular, they shall have an equal right to maintain, manage and control at their own expense or to establish in the future, charitable, religious and social institutions, schools and other educational establishments, with the right to use their own language and to exercise their own religion freely therein.

A few years later the government of Albania decided to nationalize education and order all private schools closed by amending its Constitution. Relying on the complaint procedures under the Minority treaties entered into after World War I members of the Greek minority in Albania complained that they were being denied their rights.]

The contention of the Albanian government is that the abovementioned clause imposes no other obligation upon it, in educational matters, than to grant to its nationals belonging to racial, religious, or linguistic minorities a right equal to that possessed by other Albanian nationals. Once the latter have ceased to be entitled to have private schools, the former cannot claim to have them either. This conclusion, which is alleged ... it is contended, [is] in complete conformity with the meaning and the spirit of the treaties for the protection of minorities, an essential characteristic of which is the full and complete equality of all nationals of the State, whether belonging to the majority or to the minority. On the other hand, it is argued, any interpretation which would compel Albania to respect the private minority schools would create a privilege in favour of the minority and run counter to the essential idea of the law governing minorities. Moreover, as the minority régime is an extraordinary régime constituting a derogation from the ordinary law, the text in question should, in case of doubt, be construed in the manner most favourable to the sovereignty of the Albanian State.

According to the explanations furnished to the Court by the Greek Government, the fundamental idea of Article 5 of the Declaration was on the contrary to guarantee freedom of education to the minorities by granting them the right to retain their existing schools and to establish others, if they desired; equality of treatment is, in the Greek Government's opinion, merely an adjunct to that right, and cannot impede the purpose in view, which is to ensure full and effectual liberty in matters of education. Moreover, the application of the same régime to a majority as to a minority, whose needs are quite different, would only create an apparent equality, whereas the Albanian Declaration, consistently with ordinary minority law, was designed to ensure a genuine and effective equality, not merely a formal equality....

The idea underlying the treaties for the protection of minorities is to secure for certain elements incorporated in a State, the population of which differs from them in race, language or religion, the possibility of living peaceably alongside that population and co-operating amicably with it, while at the same time preserving the characteristics which distinguish them from the majority, and satisfying the ensuing special needs.

In order to attain this object, two things were regarded as particularly necessary, and have formed the subject of provisions in these treaties. The first is to ensure that nationals belonging to racial, religious or linguistic minorities shall be placed in every respect on a footing of perfect equality with the other nationals of the State. The second is to ensure for the minority elements suitable means for the preservation of their racial peculiarities, their traditions and their national characteristics.

These two requirements are indeed closely interlocked, for there would be no true equality between a majority and a minority if the latter were deprived of its own institutions, and were consequently compelled to renounce that which constitutes the very essence of its being as a minority.

In common with the other treaties for the protection of minorities ... the Declaration of October 2nd, 1921, begins by laying down that no person shall be placed, in his relations with the Albanian authorities, in a position of inferiority by reason of his language, race or religion ....

In all these cases, the Declaration provides for a régime of legal equality for all persons mentioned in the clause; in fact no standard of comparison was indicated, and none was necessary, for at the same time that it provides for equality of treatment the Declaration specifies the rights which are to be enjoyed equally by all....

It has already been remarked that paragraph I of Article 5 consists of two sentences, the second of which is linked to the first by the words in particular: for a right apprehension of the second part, it is therefore first necessary to determine the meaning and the scope of the first sentence.

This sentence is worded as follows:

Albanian nationals who belong to racial, linguistic or religious minorities, will enjoy the same treatment and security in law and in fact as other Albanian nationals.

The question that arises is what is meant by the same treatment and security in law and in fact.

It must be noted to begin with that the equality of all Albanian nationals before the law has already been stipulated in the widest terms in Article 4. As it is difficult to admit that Article 5 set out to repeat in different words what had already been said in Article 4, one is led to the conclusion that 'the same treatment and security in law and in fact' which is provided for in Article 5 is not the same notion as the equality before the law which is provided for in Article 4....

This special conception finds expression in the idea of an equality in fact which in Article 5 supplements equality in law. All Albanian nationals enjoy the equality in law stipulated in Article 4; on the other hand, the equality between members of the majority and of the minority must, according to the terms of Article 5 [of the declaration], be an equality in law and in fact.

It is perhaps not easy to define the distinction between the notions of equality in fact and equality in law; nevertheless, it may be said that the former notion excludes the idea of a merely formal equality; that is indeed what the Court laid down in its Advisory Opinion of September 10th, 1923, concerning the case of the *German settlers in Poland* ([Advisory] Opinion No. 6), in which it said that:

There must be equality in fact as well as ostensible legal equality in the sense of the absence of discrimination in the words of the law.

Equality in law precludes discrimination of any kind; whereas equality in fact may involve the necessity of different treatment in order to attain a result which establishes an equilibrium between different situations.

It is easy to imagine cases in which equality of treatment of the majority and of the minority, whose situation and requirements are different, would result in inequality in fact; treatment of this description would counter to the first sentence of paragraph I of Article 5. The equality between members of the majority and of the minority must be an effective, genuine equality; that is the meaning of this provision.

The second sentence of this paragraph provides as follows:

[i]n particular they shall have an equal right to maintain, manage and control at their own expense or to establish in the future, charitable, religious and social institutions, schools and other educational establishments, with the right to use their own language and to exercise their religion freely therein.

This sentence of the paragraph being linked to the first by the words 'in particular', it is natural to conclude that it envisages a particularly important illustration of the application of the principle of identical treatment in law and in fact that is stipulated in the first sentence of the paragraph. For the institutions mentioned in the second sentence are indispensable to enable the minority to enjoy the same treatment as the majority, not only in law but also in fact. The abolition of these institutions, which alone can satisfy the special requirements of the minority groups, and their replacement by government institutions, would destroy this equality of treatment, for its effect would be to deprive the minority of the institutions appropriate to its needs, whereas the majority would continue to have them supplied in the institutions created by the State.

Far from creating a privilege in favour of the minority, as the Albanian Government avers, this stipulation ensures that the majority shall not be given a privileged situation as compared with the minority.

It may further be observed that, even disregarding the link between the two parts of paragraph I of Article 5, it seems difficult to maintain that the adjective 'equal', which qualifies the word 'right', has the effect of empowering the State to abolish the right, and thus to render the clause in question illusory; for, if so, the stipulation which confers so important a right on the members of the minority would not only add nothing to what has already been provided in Article 4, but it would become a weapon by which the State could deprive the minority régime of a great part of its practical value. It should be observed that in its Advisory Opinion ... concerning the question of the acquisition of Polish nationality ... the Court referred to the opinion which it had already expressed ... to the effect that 'an interpretation which would deprive the Minorities Treaty of a great part of its value is inadmissible'....

The idea embodied in the expression 'equal right' is that the right thus conferred on the members of the minority cannot in any case be inferior to the corresponding right of other Albanian nationals. In other words, the members of the minority must always enjoy the right stipulated in the Declaration, and, in addition, any more extensive rights which the State may accord to other nationals. The construction which the Court places on paragraph I of Article 5 is confirmed by the history of this provision.

The Court, having thus established that paragraph I of Article 5 of the Declaration, both according to its letter and its spirit, confers on Albanian nationals of racial, religious or linguistic minorities the right that is stipulated in the second sentence of that paragraph, finds it unnecessary to examine the subsidiary argument adduced by the Albanian Government to the effect that the text in question should in case of doubt be interpreted in the sense that is most favourable to the sovereignty of the State....

For these reasons,

The Court is of opinion, by eight votes to three,

that the plea of the Albanian Government that, as the abolition of private schools in Albania constitutes a general measure applicable to the majority as well as to the minority, it is in conformity with the letter and spirit of the stipulations laid down in Article 5, first paragraph, of the Declaration of October 2nd,1921, is not well founded.

Cases

R. D. Stalla Costa v. Uruguay

UN HRC Comm. No. 198/1985,
U.N. Doc. Supp. No. 40 (A/42/40) at 170 (1987)

1. The author of the communication ... claims to be a victim of violations of articles 2, 25(c) and 26 of the International Covenant on Civil and Political Rights.

2.1 The author states that he has submitted job applications to various governmental agencies in order to have access to and obtain a job in the public service in his country. He has allegedly been told that only former public employees who were dismissed as a result of the application of Institutional Act No. 7 of June 1977 are currently admitted to the public service. He refers in this connection to article 25 of Law 15,737 of 22 March 1985, which provides that all public employees who were dismissed as a result of the application of Institutional Act No. 7 have the right to be reinstated in their respective posts.

2.2 The author claims that article 25 of Law 15,737 gives more rights to former public employees than to other individuals, such as the author himself, and that it is therefore discriminatory and in violation of articles 2, 25(c) and 26 of the International Covenant on Civil and Political Rights.

2.3 The author claims to have exhausted all internal remedies. He submitted an action for *amparo* on grounds of violation of his constitutional rights, in particular his right not to be discriminated against, before the Supreme Court of Justice in June 1985. The Supreme Court dismissed the case.

3. By its decision of 26 March 1986, the Human Rights Committee transmitted the communication under rule 91 of the provisional rules of procedure to the State party, requesting information and observations relevant to the question of admissibility of the communication.

4. In its submission under rule 91, dated 24 July 1986, the State party requested that the communication be declared inadmissible, explaining, inter alia, that Act No. 15,737 of 22 March 1985, which the author claimed was discriminatory, had been passed with the unanimous support of all Uruguayan political parties as an instrument of national reconstruction:

> This Act ... seeks to restore the rights of those citizens who were wrongfully treated by the de facto Government. In addition to proclaiming a broad-ranging and generous amnesty, it provides under article 25, that all public officials dismissed on ideological, political or trade-union grounds or for purely arbitrary reasons shall

have the right to be reinstated in their jobs, to resume their career in the public service and to receive a pension.

The right of any citizen to have access, on an equal footing, to public employment cannot be deemed to be impaired by virtue of this Act, the purpose of which is to provide redress.

Lastly, so far as exhaustion of remedies is concerned, there is an irrefutable presumption that a right has been violated or claimed beforehand. This is not the case here, as the complainant does not have any such right but only the legitimate expectation, common to all Uruguayan citizens, of being recruited to the public service.

5. In his comments on the State party's submission, the author argues, inter alia, that "the enactment of Act No. 15,737 did not have the support of all the political parties ... It is also asserted that article 25 seeks to provide redress and does not infringe the right to access on an equal footing to posts in the public service. I join in this spirit of reconciliation, like all people in my country, but redress will have to take the form of money.'

6.1 In further observations, dated 10 February 1987, the State party elucidates Uruguayan legislation and practice regarding access to public service:

Mr. Stalla regards himself as having a subjective right to demand that a given course of action be followed, namely, his admission to the public service. The Government of Uruguay reiterates that Mr. Stalla, like any other citizen of the Republic, may legitimately aspire to enter the public service, but by no means has a subjective right to do so.

For a subjective right to exist, it must be founded on an objective legal norm. Accordingly, any subjective right presumes the existence of a possession [bien] or legal asset [valor jurídico] attached to the subject by a bond of ownership established in objective law, so that the person in question may demand that right or asset as his own. In the case in question, Mr. Stalla has no such subjective right, since the filling of public posts is the prerogative of the executive organs of the State, of State enterprises or of municipal authorities. Any inhabitant of the Republic meeting the requirements laid down in the legal norms (age requirement, physical and moral suitability, technical qualifications for the post in question) may be appointed to a public post and may have a legitimate aspiration to be vested with the status of public servant, should the competent bodies so decide."

6.2 With regard to article 8 of the Uruguayan Constitution, which provides that "all persons are equal before the law, no other distinctions being recognized among them save those of talent and virtue," the State party comments:

> This provision of the Constitution embodies the principle of the equality of all persons before the law. The Government of Uruguay wishes to state in this respect that to uphold Mr. Stalla's petition would unquestionably violate this principle by according him preference over other university graduates who, like Mr. Stalla, have a legitimate aspiration to secure such posts, without any distinction being made between them, other than on the basis of talent and virtue."

6.3 With regard to article 55 of the Uruguayan Constitution, which provides that "the law shall regulate the impartial and equitable distribution of labour," the State party comments:

> This provision is one of the 'framework rules', under which legal measures will be enacted developing the established right to work (art. 53) and combining the existence of this right with good administration.

> It will not have escaped the Committee that it is obviously impossible for the Government of Uruguay, or of any other State with a similar system, to absorb all university graduates into the public service.

6.4 The State party further emphasizes the necessity of "provision for redress made in the legislation enacted by the first elected Parliament after more than 12 years of military authoritarianism, legislation" which has made it possible to restore the rights of those public and private officials who were removed from their posts as a result of ideological persecution.

7.1 Before considering any claim contained in a communication, the Human Rights Committee must ... decide whether the communication is admissible ....

7.2 The Human Rights Committee therefore ascertained, as required under article 5, paragraph 2(a), of the Optional Protocol, that the same matter was not being examined under another procedure of international investigation or settlement. Regarding the requirement of prior exhaustion of domestic remedies, the Committee concluded, based on the information before it, that there were no further domestic remedies which the author could resort to in the particular circumstances of his case. The Committee noted in that connection the author's statement that his action for *amparo* had been dismissed by the Supreme Court ... as well as the State party's observation to the effect that there could be no remedy in the case as there had been no breach of a right under domestic law ....

7.3 With regard to the State party's submission that the communication should have been declared inadmissible on the ground that the author had no subjective right in law to be appointed to a public post, but only the legitimate aspiration to be so employed ... the Committee observed that the author had made a reasonable effort to substantiate his claim and that he had invoked specific provisions of the Covenant in that respect. The question whether the author's claim was well-founded should, therefore, be examined on the merits.

7.4 The Committee noted that the facts of the case, as set out by the author and the State party, were already sufficiently clear to permit an examination on the merits. However, the Committee deemed it appropriate at that juncture to limit itself to the procedural requirement of deciding on the admissibility of the communication. It noted that, if the State party should wish to add to its earlier submissions within six months of the transmittal to it of the decision on admissibility, the author of the communication would be given an opportunity to comment thereon. If no further explanations or statements were received from the State party under article 4, paragraph 2, of the Optional Protocol, the Committee would then proceed to adopt its final views in the light of the written information already submitted by the parties.

7.5 On 8 April 1987 the Human Rights Committee therefore decided that the communication was admissible ....

8. By note dated 26 May 1987, the State party informed the Committee that, in the light of its prior submission, it would not make a further submission in the case.

9. The Human Rights Committee has considered the merits of the present communication in the light of all information made available to it by the parties, as provided in article 5, paragraph 1, of the Optional Protocol. The facts of the case are not in dispute.

10. The main question before the Committee is whether the author of the communication is a victim of a violation of article 25(c) of the Covenant because, as he alleges, he has not been permitted to have access to public

service on general terms of equality. Taking into account the social and political situation in Uruguay during the years of military rule, in particular the dismissal of many public servants pursuant to Institutional Act No. 7, the Committee understands the enactment of Act No. 15.737 of 22 March 1985 by the new democratic Government of Uruguay as a measure of redress. Indeed, the Committee observes that Uruguayan public officials dismissed on ideological, political or trade-union grounds were victims of violations of article 25 of the Covenant and as such are entitled to have an effective remedy under article 2, paragraph 3 (a), of the Covenant. The Act should be looked upon as such a remedy. The implementation of the Act, therefore, cannot be regarded as incompatible with the reference to 'general terms of equality' in article 25(c) of the Covenant. Neither can the implementation of the Act be regarded as an invidious distinction under article 2, paragraph 1, or as prohibited discrimination within the terms of article 26 of the Covenant.

11. The Human Rights Committee, acting under article 5, paragraph 4, of the Optional Protocol to the International Covenant on Civil and Political Rights, is of the view that the facts as submitted do not sustain the author's claim that he has been denied access to public service in violation of article 25(c) or that he is a victim of an invidious distinction, that is, of discrimination within the meaning of articles 2 and 26 of the Covenant.

S. W. M. Broeks v. The Netherlands

UN HRC Comm. No. 172/1984
UN Doc. Supp. No. 40 (A/42/40) at 139 (1987).

1. The author of the communication ... is Mrs. S. W. M. Broeks, a Netherlands citizen born on 14 March 1951 and living in the Netherlands. She is represented by legal counsel.

2.1 Mrs. Broeks, who was married at the time when the dispute in question arose (she has since divorced and not remarried), was employed as a nurse from 7 August 1972 to 1 February 1979, when she was dismissed for reasons of disability. She had become ill in 1975, and from that time she benefited from the Netherlands social security system until 1 June 1980 (as regards disability and as regards unemployment), when unemployment payments were terminated in accordance with Netherlands law.

2.2 Mrs. Broeks contested the decision of the relevant Netherlands authorities to discontinue unemployment payments to her and in the course of exhausting domestic remedies invoked article 26 of the International Covenant on Civil and Political Rights, claiming that the relevant Netherlands legal provisions were contrary 'to the right to equality before the law and equal protection of the law without discrimination guaranteed by article 26 of the International Covenant on Civil and Political Rights. Legal counsel submits that domestic remedies were exhausted on 26 November 1983, when the appropriate administrative authority, the Central Board of Appeal, confirmed a decision of a lower municipal authority not to continue unemployment payments to Mrs. Broeks.

2.3 Mrs. Brooks claims that, under existing law (Unemployment Benefits Act (WWV), sect. 13, subsect. 1 (1), and Decree No. 61 452/IIIa of 5 April 1976, to give effect to sect. 13, subsect. 1 (1), of the Unemployment Benefits Act) an unacceptable distinction has been made on the grounds of sex and status. She bases her claim on the following: if she were a man, married or unmarried, the law in question would not deprive her of unemployment benefits. Because she is a woman, and was married at the time in question, the law excludes her from continued unemployment benefits. This, she claims, makes her a victim of a violation of article 26 of the Covenant on the grounds of sex and status. She claims that article 26 of the International Covenant on Civil and Political Rights was meant to give protection to individuals beyond the specific civil and political rights enumerated in the Covenant.

2.4 The author states that she has not submitted the matter to other international procedures.

3. By its decision of 26 October 1984, the Human Rights Committee transmitted the communication, under rule 91 of the provisional rules of procedure, to the State party concerned, requesting information and observations relevant to the question 'of admissibility of the communication.

4.1 In its submission dated 29 May 1985 the State party underlined, *inter alia*, that:

(a) "The principle that elements of discrimination in the realization of the right to social security are to be eliminated is embodied in article 9 in conjunction with articles 2 and 3 of the International Covenant on Economic, Social and Cultural Rights;

(b) "The Government of the Kingdom of the Netherlands has accepted to implement this principle under the terms of the International Covenant on Economic, Social and Cultural Rights. Under these terms, States parties have undertaken to take steps to the maximum of their available resources with a view to achieving progressively the full realization of the rights recognized in that Covenant (art. 2, para. 1);

(c) "The process of gradual realization to the maximum of available resources is well on its way in the Netherlands. Remaining elements of discrimination in the realization of the rights are being and will be gradually eliminated;

(d) "The International Covenant on Economic, Social and Cultural Rights has established its own system for international control of the way in which States parties are fulfilling their obligations. To this end States parties have undertaken to submit to the Economic and Social Council reports on the measures they have adopted and the progress they are making. The Government of the Kingdom of the Netherlands to this end submitted its first report in 1983."

4.2 The State party then posed the question whether the way in which the Netherlands was fulfilling its obligations Under article 9 in conjunction with articles 2 and 3 of the International Covenant on Economic, Social and Cultural Rights could become, by way of article 26 of the International Covenant on Civil and Political Rights, the object of an examination by the Human Rights Committee. The State party submitted that the question was relevant for the decision whether the communication was admissible.

4.3 The State party stressed that it would greatly benefit from receiving an answer from the Human Rights Committee to the question mentioned in paragraph 4.2 above. "Since such an answer could hardly be given without going into one aspect of the merits of the case—i.e. the question of the scope of article 26 of the International Covenant on Civil and Political Rights—the Government would respectfully request the Committee to join the question of admissibility to an examination of the merits of the case."

4.4 In case the Committee did not grant that request and declared the communication admissible, the State party reserved the right to submit, in the course of the proceedings, observations which might have an effect on the question of admissibility.

4.5 The State party also indicated that a change of legislation had been adopted recently in the Netherlands, eliminating article 13, paragraph 1, of WWV, which was the subject of the author's claim. This is the Act of 29 April 1985, S 230, having a retroactive effect to 23 December 1984.

4.6 The State party confirmed that the author had exhausted domestic remedies.

5.1 In a memorandum dated 5 July 1985, the author commented on the State party's submission under rule 91. The main issues dealt with in the comments are set out in paragraphs 5.2 to 5.10 below.

5.2 Firstly, the author stated that in the preambles to the International Covenant on Economic, Social and Cultural Rights and the International Covenant on Civil and Political Rights an explicit connection was made between an individual's exercise of his civil and political rights and his economic, social and cultural rights. The fact that those different kinds of rights had been incorporated into two different covenants did not detract from their interdependence. It was striking, the author submitted, that in the International Covenant on Civil and Political Rights, apart from in article 26, there were specific references on numerous occasions to the principle of equality or non-discrimination. She listed them as follows:

article 2, paragraph 1: non-discrimination with reference to the rights recognized in the Covenant;

article 3: non-discrimination on the grounds of sex with reference to the rights recognized in the Covenant;

article 14: equality before the courts;

article 23, paragraph 4: article 24, paragraph 1: equal rights of spouses;

article 24, paragraph 1: equal rights of children to protective measures;

article 25 and under (c): equal right to vote and equal access to government service.

5.3 Further, the author stated that article 26 of the Covenant was explicitly not confined to equal treatment with reference to certain rights, but stipulated a general principle of equality. It was even regarded as of such importance that under article 4, paragraph 1, of the Covenant, in a time of public emergency, the prohibition of discrimination on the grounds of race, colour, sex, religion or social origin must be observed. In other words, even in time of public emergency, the equal treatment of men and women should remain intact. In the procedure to approve the Covenant it had been assumed by the Netherlands legislative authority, as the Netherlands Government wrote in the explanatory memorandum to the Bill of Approval, that "the provision of article 26 is also applicable to areas otherwise not covered by the Covenant." That (undisputed) conclusion was based on the difference in formulation between article 2, paragraph 1, of the Covenant and of article 14 of the European Convention on Human Rights on the one hand and article 26 of the Covenant on the other.

5.4 The author recalled that during the discussion by the Human Rights Committee, at its fourteenth session, of the Netherlands report submitted in compliance with article 40 of the Covenant ... it had been assumed by the Netherlands Government that article 26 of the Covenant also applied in the field of economic, social and cultural rights. Mr. Olde Kalter had stated, on behalf of the Netherlands Government, that by virtue of national, constitutional law "direct application of article 26 in the area of social, economic and cultural rights depended on the character of the regulations or policy for which that direct application was requested".... In other words, in his opinion, article 26 of the Covenant was applicable to those rights and the only relevant question in terms of internal, constitutional law in the Netherlands (sects. 93 and 94 of the Constitution) was whether in such instances article 26 was self-executing and could be applied by the courts. He had regarded it as self-evident that the Netherlands in its legislation, among other things, was bound by article 26 of the Covenant. "In that connection he [Mr. Olde Kalter] noted that the Government of the Netherlands was currently analysing national legislation concerning discrimination on grounds of sex or race." In the observations of the State party in the present case, the author adds, this last point is confirmed.

5.5 The author further stated that in various national constitutional systems of countries which have acceded to the Covenant, generally formulated principles of equality could be found which were also regarded as being applicable in the field of economic, social and cultural rights. Thus, in the

Netherlands Constitution, partly inspired, the author submitted, by article 26 of the Covenant, a generally formulated prohibition of discrimination (sect. 1) was laid down which was irrefutably regarded in the Netherlands as being applicable to economic, social and cultural rights as well. The only reason, she submitted, why the present issue had not been settled at a national level by virtue of section 1 of the Constitution was because the courts were forbidden to test legislation, such as that being dealt with currently, against the Constitution (sect. 120 of the Constitution). The courts, she stated, were allowed to test legislation against self-executing provisions of international conventions.

5.6 The author submitted that judicial practice in the Netherlands had been consistent in applying article 26 of the Covenant also in cases where economic, social and cultural rights had been at stake ...

5.7 The author further submitted that the question of equal treatment in the field of economic, social and cultural rights was not fundamentally different from the problem of equality with regard to freedom to express one's opinion or the freedom of association, in other words with regard to civil and political rights. The fact was, she argued, that in both cases it was not a question of the level at which social security had been set or the degree to which freedom of opinion was guaranteed, but purely and simply whether equal treatment or the prohibition of discrimination was respected. The level of social security did not come within the scope of the International Covenant on Civil and Political Rights nor was it relevant in a case of unequal treatment. The only relevant question, she submitted, was whether unequal treatment was compatible with article 26 of the Covenant. A contrary interpretation of article 26, the author argued, would turn that article into a completely superfluous provision, for then it would not differ from article 2, paragraph 1, of the Covenant. Consequently, she submitted, such an interpretation would be incompatible with the text of article 26 of the Covenant and with the object and purpose of the Covenant as laid down in article 26 of the preamble.

5.8 The author recalled that in its observations the State party had put forward the question whether the way in which the Netherlands was meeting its commitments under the International Covenant on Economic, Social and Cultural Rights (via article 26 of the International Covenant on Civil and Political Rights), might be judged by the Human Rights Committee. The question, she submitted, was based on a wrong point of departure, and therefore required no answer. The fact was, the author argued, that the only question that the Human Rights Committee was required to answer in that case was whether, *ratione materiae*, the alleged violation came under article 26 of the International Covenant on Civil and Political Rights. The author submitted that that question must be answered in the affirmative.

5.9 The author further recalled that the State party was of the opinion that the alleged violation could also fall under article 9 of the International Covenant on Economic, Social and Cultural Rights in conjunction with articles 2 and 3 of the same Covenant. Although that question was not relevant in the case in point, the author submitted, it was obvious that certain issues were related to provisions in both Covenants. Although civil and political rights on the one hand and economic and social and cultural rights on the other had been incorporated for technical reasons into two different Covenants, it was a fact, the author submitted, that those rights were highly interdependent. That interdependence, she argued, had not only emerged in the preamble to both Covenants, but was also once again underlined in General Assembly resolution 543 (VI), in which it had been decided to draw up two covenants: "the enjoyment of civic and political freedoms and of economic, social and cultural rights are interconnected and interdependent." The State party, too, she submitted, had explicitly recognized that interdependence earlier in the Explanatory Memorandum to the Act of Approval ...: 'the drafters of the two Covenants wanted to underline the parallel nature of the present international conventions by formulating the preambles in almost entirely identical words. The point is that they have expressed in the preambles that, although civil rights and political rights on the one hand and economic, social and cultural rights on the other, have been incorporated into two separate documents, the enjoyment of all these rights is essential'. If the State party was intending to imply that the subject-matter covered by the one covenant did not come under the other, that was demonstrably incorrect: even a summary comparison of the opening articles of the two covenants bore witness to the contrary, the author argued.

5.10 In her opinion, the author added, the State party seemed to wish to say that the Human Rights Committee was not competent to take note of the present complaint because the matter could also be brought up as part of the supervisory procedure under the International Covenant on Economic, Social and Cultural Rights .... That assertion, the author contended, was not valid because the reporting procedure under the International Covenant on Economic, Social and Cultural Rights could not be regarded as 'another procedure of international investigation or settlement' in the sense of article 5, paragraph 2 (a) of the Optional Protocol ...

10. The Human Rights Committee has considered the present communication in the light of all information made available to it by the parties, as provided in article 5, paragraph 1, of the Optional Protocol. The facts of the case are not in dispute ...

12.1 The State party contends that there is considerable overlapping of the provisions of article 26 with the provisions of article 2 of the International Covenant on Economic, Social and Cultural Rights. The Committee is of the view that the International Covenant on Civil and Political Rights would still apply even if a particular subject-matter is referred to or covered in other international instruments, for example, the International Convention on the Elimination of All Forms of Racial Discrimination, the Convention on the Elimination of All Forms of Discrimination against Women, or, as in the present case, the International Covenant on Economic, Social and Cultural Rights. Notwithstanding the interrelated drafting history of the two Covenants, it remains necessary for the Committee to apply fully the terms of the International Covenant on Civil and Political Rights. The Committee observes in this connection that the provisions of article 2 of the International Covenant on Economic, Social and Cultural Rights do not detract from the full application of article 26 of the International Covenant on Civil and Political Rights.

12.2 The Committee has also examined the contention of the State party that article 26 of the International Covenant on Civil and Political Rights cannot be invoked in respect of a right which is specifically provided for under article 9 of the International Covenant on Economic, Social and Cultural Rights (social security, including social insurance). In so doing, the Committee has perused the relevant *travaux préparatoires* of the International Covenant on Civil and Political Rights, namely, the summary records of the discussions that took place in the Commission on Human Rights in 1948, 1949, 1950 and 1952 and in the Third Committee of the General Assembly in 1961, which provide a 'supplementary means of interpretation' (art. 32 of the Vienna Convention on the Law of Treaties). The discussions, at the time of drafting, concerning the question whether the scope of article 26 extended to rights not otherwise guaranteed by the Covenant, were inconclusive and cannot alter the conclusion arrived at by the ordinary means of interpretation referred to in paragraph 12.3 below.

12.3 For the purpose of determining the scope of article 26, the Committee has taken into account the 'ordinary meaning' of each element of the article in its context and in the light of its object and purpose (art. 31 of the Vienna Convention on the Law of Treaties). The Committee begins by noting that article 26 does not merely duplicate the guarantees already provided for in article 2. It derives from the principle of equal protection of the law without discrimination, as contained in article 7 of the Universal Declaration of Human Rights, which prohibits discrimination in law or in practice in any field regulated and protected by public authorities. Article 26 is thus concerned with the obligations imposed on States in regard to their legislation and the application thereof.

12.4 Although article 26 requires that legislation should prohibit discrimination, it does not of itself contain any obligation with respect to the matters that may be provided for by legislation. Thus it does not, for example, require any State to enact legislation to provide for social security. However, when such legislation is adopted in the exercise of a State's sovereign power, then such legislation must comply with article 26 of the Covenant.

12.5 The Committee observes in this connection that what is at issue is not whether or not social security should be progressively established in the Netherlands but whether the legislation providing for social security violates the prohibition against discrimination contained in article 26 of the International Covenant on Civil and Political Rights and the guarantee given therein to all persons regarding equal and effective protection against discrimination.

13. The right to equality before the law and to equal protection of the law without any discrimination does not make all differences of treatment discriminatory. A differentiation based on reasonable and objective criteria does not amount to prohibited discrimination within the meaning of article 26.

14. It therefore remains for the Committee to determine whether the differentiation in Netherlands law at the time in question and as applied to Mrs. Brooks constituted discrimination within the meaning of article 26. The Committee notes that in Netherlands law the provisions of articles 84 and 85 of the Netherlands Civil Code impose equal rights and obligations on both spouses with regard to their joint income. Under section 13, subsection 1 (1), of the Unemployment Benefits Act (WWV), a married woman, in order to receive WWV benefits, had to prove that she was a 'breadwinner' — a condition that did not apply to married men. Thus a differentiation which appears on one level to be one of status is in fact one of sex, placing married women at a disadvantage compared with married men. Such a differentiation is not reasonable; and this seems to have been effectively acknowledged even

by the State party by the enactment of a change in the law on 29 April 1985,' with retroactive effect to 23 December 1984 ...

15. The circumstances in which Mrs. Brooks found herself at the material time and the application of the then valid Netherlands law made her a victim of a violation, based on sex, of article 26 of the International Covenant on Civil and Political Rights, because she was denied a social security benefit on an equal footing with men.

16. The Committee notes that the State party had not intended to discriminate against women and further notes with appreciation that the discriminatory provisions in the law applied to Mrs. Brooks have, subsequently, been eliminated. Although the State party has thus taken the necessary measures to put an end to the kind of discrimination suffered by Mrs. Brooks at the time complained of, the Committee is of the view that the State party should offer Mrs. Brooks an appropriate remedy.

Josef Frank Adam v. Czech Republic

UN Human Rights Committee Communication No. 586/1994,
UN Doc. CCPR/C/57/D/586/1994 (1996).

...2.1 The author's father, Vlatislav Adam, was a Czech citizen, whose property and business were confiscated by the Czechoslovak Government in 1949. Mr. Adam fled the country and eventually moved to Australia, where his three sons, including the author of the communication, were born. In 1985, Vlatislav Adam died and, in his last will and testament, left his Czech property to his sons. Since then, the sons have been trying in vain to have their property returned to them.

2.2 In 1991, the Czech and Slovak Republic enacted a law, rehabilitating Czech citizens who had left the country under communist pressure and providing for restitution of their property or compensation for the loss thereof. On 6 December 1991, the author and his brothers, through Czech solicitors, submitted a claim for restitution of their property. Their claim was rejected on the grounds that they did not fulfil the then applicable dual requirement of Act 87/91 that applicants have Czech citizenship and be permanent residents in the Czech Republic.

2.3 Since the rejection of their claim, the author has on several occasions petitioned the Czech authorities, explaining his situation and seeking a solution, all to no avail. The authorities in their replies refer to the legislation in force and argue that the provisions of the law, limiting restitution and compensation to Czech citizens are necessary and apply uniformly to all potential claimants.

The complaint:

3. The author claims that the application of the provision of the law, that property be returned or its loss be compensated only when claimants are Czech citizens, makes him and his brothers victims of discrimination under article 26 of the Covenant ...

Examination of the merits

... 12.2 This communication was declared admissible only insofar as it may raise issues under article 26 of the Covenant. As the Committee has already explained in its decision on admissibility ... the right to property, as such, is not protected under the Covenant. However, a confiscation of private property or the failure by a State party to pay compensation for such confiscation could still entail a breach of the Covenant if the relevant act or omission was based on discriminatory grounds in violation of article 26 of the Covenant.

12.3 The issue before the Committee is whether the application of Act 87/1991 to the author and his brothers entailed a violation of their right to equality before the law and to the equal protection of the law. The Committee observes that the confiscations themselves are not here at issue, but rather the denial of a restitution to the author and his brothers, whereas other claimants under the Act have recovered their properties or received compensation therefor.

12.4 In the instant case, the author has been affected by the exclusionary effect of the requirement in Act 87/1991 that claimants be Czech citizens. The question before the Committee, therefore, is whether the precondition to restitution or compensation is compatible with the non-discrimination requirement of article 26 of the Covenant. In this context the Committee reiterates its jurisprudence that not all differentiation in treatment can be deemed to be discriminatory under article 26 of the Covenant 2. A differentiation which is compatible with the provisions of the Covenant and is based on reasonable grounds does not amount to prohibited discrimination within the meaning of article 26.

12.5 In examining whether the conditions for restitution or compensation are compatible with the Covenant, the Committee must consider all relevant factors, including the original entitlement of the author's father to the property in question and the nature of the confiscation. The State party itself has acknowledged that the confiscations under the Communist governments were injurious and this is the reason why specific legislation was enacted to provide for a form of restitution. The Committee observes that such legislation must not discriminate among the victims of the prior confiscations, since all victims are entitled to redress without arbitrary distinctions. Bearing in mind that the author's original entitlement to his property by virtue of inheritance was not predicated on citizenship, the Committee finds that the condition of citizenship in Act 87/1991 is unreasonable.

12.6 ... Taking into account that the State party itself is responsible for the departure of the author's parents in 1949, it would be incompatible with the Covenant to require him and his brothers to obtain Czech citizenship as a prerequisite for the restitution of their property or, in the alternative, for the payment of appropriate compensation.

12.7 The State party contends that there is no violation of the Covenant because the Czech and Slovak legislators had no discriminatory intent at the time of the adoption of Act 87/1991. The Committee is of the view, however, that the intent of the legislature is not dispositive in determining a breach of article 26 of the Covenant, but rather the consequences of the enacted legislation. Whatever the motivation or intent of the legislature, a law may still contravene article 26 of the Covenant if its effects are discriminatory.

12.8 In the light of the above considerations, the Committee concludes that Act 87/1991 and the continued practice of non-restitution to non-citizens of the Czech Republic have had effects upon the author and his brothers that violate their rights under article 26 of the Covenant.

13.1 The Human Rights Committee, acting under article 5, paragraph 4, of the Optional Protocol, is of the view that the denial of restitution or compensation to the author and his brothers constitutes a violation of article 26 of the International Covenant on Civil and Political Rights.

13.2 In accordance with article 2, paragraph 3 (a), of the Covenant, the State party is under an obligation to provide the author and his brothers with an effective remedy, which may be compensation if the property in question cannot be returned. The Committee further encourages the State party to review its relevant legislation to ensure that neither the law itself nor its application is discriminatory.

13.3 ... the Committee wishes to receive from the State party, within ninety days, information about the measures taken to give effect to the Committee's Views.

Toonen v. Australia

UN HRC, Comm. No. 488/1992
UN Doc CCPR/C/50/D/488/1992 (1994).

1. The author of the communication is Nicholas Toonen, an Australian citizen born in 1964, currently residing in Hobart in the state of Tasmania, Australia. He is a leading member of the Tasmanian Gay Law Reform Group (TGLRG) and claims to be a victim of violations by Australia of articles 2, paragraphs 1, 17 and 26 of the International Covenant on Civil and Political Rights.

The facts as submitted by the author:

2.1 The author is an activist for the promotion of the rights of homosexuals in Tasmania, one of Australia's six constitutive states. He challenges two provisions of the Tasmanian Criminal Code, namely Sections 122(a) and (c) and 123, which criminalize various forms of sexual contacts between men, including all forms of sexual contacts between consenting adult homosexual men in private.

2.2 The author observes that the above sections of the Tasmanian Criminal Code empower Tasmanian police officers to investigate intimate aspects of his private life and to detain him, if they have reason to believe that he is involved in sexual activities which contravene the above sections. He adds that the Director of Public Prosecutions announced, in August 1988, that proceedings pursuant to Sections 122(a), (c) and 123 would be initiated if there was sufficient evidence of the commission of a crime.

2.3 Although in practice the Tasmanian police has not charged anyone either with "unnatural sexual intercourse" or "intercourse against nature" (Section 122) nor with "indecent practice between male persons" (Section 123) for several years, the author argues that because of his long-term relationship with another man, his active lobbying of Tasmanian politicians and the reports about his activities in the local media, and because of his activities as a gay rights activist and gay HIV/AIDS worker, his private life and his liberty are threatened by the continued existence of Sections 122(a), (c) and 123 of the Criminal Code.

2.4 Mr. Toonen further argues that the criminalization of homosexuality in private has not permitted him to expose openly his sexuality and to publicize his views on reform of the relevant laws on sexual matters, as he felt that this would have been extremely prejudicial to his employment. In this context, he contends that Sections 122(a), (c) and 123 have created the conditions for discrimination in employment, constant stigmatization, vilification, threats of physical violence and the violation of basic democratic rights.

2.5 The author observes that numerous "figures of authority" in Tasmania have made either derogatory or downright insulting remarks about homosexual men and women over the past few years. These include statements made by members of the Lower House of Parliament, municipal councillors (such as "representatives of the gay community are no better than Saddam Hussein"; "the act of homosexuality is unacceptable in any society, let alone a civilized society"), of the church and of members of the general public, whose statements have been directed against the integrity and welfare of homosexual men and women in Tasmania (such as "[g]ays want to lower society to their level"; "You are 15 times more likely to be murdered by a homosexual than a heterosexual..."). In some public meetings, it has been suggested that all Tasmanian homosexuals should be rounded up and "dumped" on an uninhabited island, or be subjected to compulsory sterilization. Remarks such as these, the author affirms, have had the effect of creating constant stress and suspicion in what ought to be routine contacts with the authorities in Tasmania.

2.6 The author further argues that Tasmania has witnessed, and continues to witness, a "campaign of official and unofficial hatred" against homosexuals and lesbians. This campaign has made it difficult for the Tasmanian Gay Law Reform Group to disseminate information about its activities and advocate the decriminalization of homosexuality. Thus, in September 1988, for example, the TGLRG was refused permission to put up a stand in a public square in the city of Hobart, and the author claims that he, as a leading protester against the ban, was subjected to police intimidation.

2.7 Finally, the author argues that the continued existence of Sections 122(a), (c) and 123 of the Criminal Code of Tasmania continue to have profound and harmful impacts on many people in Tasmania, including himself, in that it fuels discrimination and harassment of, and violence against, the homosexual community of Tasmania.

The complaint:

3.1 The author affirms that Sections 122 and 123 of the Tasmanian Criminal Code violate articles 2, paragraphs 1, 17 and 26 of the Covenant because:

(a) they do not distinguish between sexual activity in private and sexual activity in public and bring private activity into the public domain. In their enforcement, these provisions result in a violation of the right to privacy, since they enable the police to enter a household on the mere suspicion that two consenting adult homosexual men may be committing a criminal offence. Given the stigma attached to homosexuality in Australian society (and especially in Tasmania), the violation of the right to privacy may lead to unlawful attacks on the honour and the reputation of the individuals concerned.

(b) they distinguish between individuals in the exercise of their right to privacy on the basis of sexual activity, sexual orientation and sexual identity, and

(c) the Tasmanian Criminal Code does not outlaw any form of homosexual activity between consenting homosexual women in private and only some forms of consenting heterosexual activity between adult men and women in private. That the laws in question are not currently enforced by the judicial authorities of Tasmania should not be taken to mean that homosexual men in Tasmania enjoy effective equality under the law.

3.2 For the author, the only remedy for the rights infringed by Sections 122(a), (c) and 123 of the Criminal Code through the criminalization of all forms of sexual activity between consenting adult homosexual men in private would be the repeal of these provisions.

3.3 The author submits that no effective remedies are available against Sections 122(a), (c) and 123. At the legislative level, state jurisdictions have primary responsibility for the enactment and enforcement of criminal law. As the Upper and Lower Houses of the Tasmanian Parliament have been deeply divided over the decriminalization of homosexual activities and reform of the Criminal Code, this potential avenue of redress is said to be ineffective. The author further observes that effective administrative remedies are not available, as they would depend on the support of a majority of members of both Houses of Parliament, support which is lacking. Finally, the author contends that no judicial remedies for a violation of the Covenant are available, as the Covenant has not been incorporated into Australian law, and Australian courts have been unwilling to apply treaties not incorporated into domestic law.

The State party's information and observations:

4.1 The State party did not challenge the admissibility of the communication on any grounds, while reserving its position on the substance of the author's claims.

4.2 The State party notes that the laws challenged by Mr. Toonen are those of the state of Tasmania and only apply within the jurisdiction of that state.

Laws similar to those challenged by the author once applied in other Australian jurisdictions but have since been repealed.

The Committee's admissibility decision:

5.1 During its forty-sixth session, the Committee considered the admissibility of the communication. As to whether the author could be deemed a "victim" within the meaning of article 1 of the Optional Protocol, it noted that the legislative provisions challenged by the author had not been enforced by the judicial authorities of Tasmania for a number of years. It considered, however, that the author had made reasonable efforts to demonstrate that the threat of enforcement and the pervasive impact of the continued existence of these provisions on administrative practices and public opinion had affected him and continued to affect him personally, and that they could raise issues under articles 17 and 26 of the Covenant. Accordingly, the Committee was satisfied that the author could be deemed a victim within the meaning of article 1 of the Optional Protocol, and that his claims were admissible ratione temporis.

5.2 On 5 November 1992, therefore, the Committee declared the communication admissible inasmuch as it appeared to raise issues under articles 17 and 26 of the Covenant.

The State party's observations on the merits and author's comments thereon:

6.1 In its submission under article 4, paragraph 2, of the Optional Protocol, dated 15 September 1993, the State party concedes that the author has been a victim of arbitrary interference with his privacy, and that the legislative provisions challenged by him cannot be justified on public health or moral grounds. It incorporates into its submission the observations of the government of Tasmania, which denies that the author has been the victim of a violation of the Covenant.

6.2 With regard to article 17, the Federal Government notes that the Tasmanian government submits that article 17 does not create a "right to privacy" but only a right to freedom from arbitrary or unlawful interference with privacy, and that as the challenged laws were enacted by democratic process, they cannot be an unlawful interference with privacy. The Federal Government, after reviewing the travaux préparatoires of article 17, subscribes to the following definition of "private": matters which are individual, personal, or confidential, or which are kept or removed from public observation." The State party acknowledges that based on this definition, consensual sexual activity in private is encompassed by the concept of "privacy" in article 17.

6.3 As to whether Sections 122 and 123 of the Tasmanian Criminal Code "interfere" with the author's privacy, the State party notes that the Tasmanian authorities advised that there is no policy to treat investigations or the prosecution of offences under the disputed provisions any differently from the investigation or prosecution of offences under the Tasmanian Criminal Code in general, and that the most recent prosecution under the challenged provisions dates back to 1984. The State party acknowledges, however, that in the absence of any specific policy on the part of the Tasmanian authorities not to enforce the laws, the risk of the provisions being applied to Mr. Toonen remains, and that this risk is relevant to the assessment of whether the provisions "interfere" with his privacy. On balance, the State party concedes that Mr. Toonen is personally and actually affected by the Tasmanian laws.

6.4 As to whether the interference with the author's privacy was arbitrary or unlawful, the State party refers to the travaux préparatoires of article 17 and observes that the drafting history of the provision in the Commission on Human Rights appears to indicate that the term "arbitrary" was meant to cover interferences which, under Australian law, would be covered by the concept of "unreasonableness." Furthermore, the Human Rights Committee, in its General Comment on article 17, states that the "concept of arbitrariness is intended to guarantee that even interference provided for by law should be in accordance with the provisions, aims and objectives of the [Covenant] and should be ... reasonable in the particular circumstances." On the basis of this and the Committee's jurisprudence on the concept of "reasonableness", the State party interprets "reasonable" interferences with privacy as measures which are based on reasonable and objective criteria and which are proportional to the purpose for which they are adopted.

6.5 The State party does not accept the argument of the Tasmanian authorities that the retention of the challenged provisions is partly motivated by a concern to protect Tasmania from the spread of HIV/AIDS, and that the laws are justified on public health and moral grounds. This assessment in fact goes against the Australian Government's National HIV/AIDS Strategy, which emphasizes that laws criminalizing homosexual activity obstruct public health programmes promoting safer sex. The State party further disagrees with the Tasmanian authorities' contention that the laws are justified on moral grounds, noting that moral issues were not at issue when article 17 of the Covenant was drafted.

Cases

6.6 None the less, the State party cautions that the formulation of article 17 allows for <u>some</u> infringement of the right to privacy if there are reasonable grounds, and that domestic social mores may be relevant to the reasonableness of an interference with privacy. The State party observes that while laws penalizing homosexual activity existed in the past in other Australian states, they have since been repealed with the exception of Tasmania. Furthermore, discrimination on the basis of homosexuality or sexuality is unlawful in three of six Australian states and the two self-governing internal Australian territories. The Federal Government has declared sexual preference to be a ground of discrimination that may be invoked under ILO Convention No. 111 (Discrimination in Employment or Occupation Convention), and created a mechanism through which complaints about discrimination in employment on the basis of sexual preference may be considered by the Australian Human Rights and Equal Opportunity Commission.

6.7 On the basis of the above, the State party contends that there is now a general Australian acceptance that no individual should be disadvantaged on the basis of his or her sexual orientation. Given the legal and social situation in all of Australia except Tasmania, the State party acknowledges that a complete prohibition on sexual activity between men is unnecessary to sustain the moral fabric of Australian society. On balance, the State party "does not seek to claim that the challenged laws are based on reasonable and objective criteria."

6.8 Finally, the State party examines, in the context of article 17, whether the challenged laws are a proportional response to the aim sought. It does not accept the argument of the Tasmanian authorities that the extent of interference with personal privacy occasioned by Sections 122 and 123 of the Tasmanian Criminal Code is a proportional response to the perceived threat to the moral standards of Tasmanian society. In this context, it notes that the very fact that the laws are not enforced against individuals engaging in private, consensual sexual activity indicates that the laws are not essential to the protection of that society's moral standards. In the light of all the above, the State party concludes that the challenged laws are not reasonable in the circumstances, and that their interference with privacy is arbitrary. It notes that the repeal of the laws has been proposed at various times in the recent past by Tasmanian governments.

6.9 In respect of the alleged violation of article 26, the State party seeks the Committee's guidance as to whether sexual orientation may be subsumed under the term "... or other status" in article 26. In this context, the Tasmanian authorities concede that sexual orientation is an "other status" for the purposes of the Covenant. The State party itself, after review of the travaux préparatoires, the Committee's General Comment on articles 2 and 26 and its jurisprudence under these provisions, contends that there "appears to be a strong argument that the words of the two articles should not be read restrictively." The formulation of these provisions—"without distinction of any kind, such as" and "on any ground such as" support an inclusive rather than exhaustive interpretation. While the travaux préparatoires do not provide specific guidance on this question, they also appear to support this interpretation.

6.10 The State party continues that if the Committee considers sexual orientation as "other status" for purposes of the Covenant, the following issues must be examined:

-whether Tasmanian laws draw a distinction on the basis of sex or sexual orientation;

-whether Mr. Toonen is a victim of discrimination;

-whether there are reasonable and objective criteria for the distinction; and

-whether Tasmanian laws are a proportional means to achieve a legitimate aim under the Covenant.

6.11 The State party concedes that Section 123 of the Tasmanian Criminal Code clearly draws a distinction on the basis of sex, as it prohibits sexual acts only between males. If the Committee were to find that sexual orientation is an "other status" within the meaning of article 26, the State party would concede that this section draws a distinction on the basis of sexual orientation. As to the author's argument that it is necessary to consider the impact of Sections 122 and 123 together, the State party seeks the Committee's guidance on "whether it is appropriate to consider Section 122 in isolation or whether it is necessary to consider the combined impact of Sections 122 and 123 on Mr. Toonen."

6.12 As to whether the author is a victim of discrimination the State party concedes, as referred to in paragraph 6.3 above, that the author is actually and personally affected by the challenged provisions, and accepts the general proposition that legislation does affect public opinion. However, the State party contends that it has been unable to ascertain whether all instances of anti-homosexual prejudice and discrimination referred to by the author are traceable to the effect of Sections 122 and 123.

6.13 Concerning the issue of whether the differentiation in treatment in Sections 122 and 123 is based on reasonable and objective criteria, the State party refers, mutatis mutandis, to its observations made in respect of article 17 (paragraphs 6.4 to 6.8 above). In a similar context, the State party takes issue with the argument of the Tasmanian authority that the challenged laws do not discriminate between classes of citizens but merely identify acts which are unacceptable to the Tasmanian community. This, according to the State party, inaccurately reflects the domestic perception of the purpose or the effect of the challenged provisions. While they specifically target acts, their impact is to distinguish an identifiable class of individuals and to prohibit certain of their acts. Such laws thus are clearly understood by the community as being directed at male homosexuals as a group. Accordingly, if the Committee were to find the Tasmanian laws discriminatory which interfere with privacy, the State party concedes that they constitute a discriminatory interference with privacy.

6.14 Finally, the State party examines a number of issues of potential relevance in the context of article 26. As to the concept of "equality before the law" within the meaning of article 26, the State party argues that the complaint does not raise an issue of procedural inequality. As regards the issue of whether Sections 122 and 123 discriminate in "equal protection of the law", the State party acknowledges that if the Committee were to find the laws to be discriminatory, they would discriminate in the right to equal protection of the law. Concerning whether the author is a victim of prohibited discrimination, the State party concedes that Sections 122 and 123 do have an actual effect on the author and his complaint does not, as affirmed by the Tasmanian authorities, constitute a challenge in abstracto to domestic laws.

7.1 In his comments, the author welcomes the State party's concession that Sections 122 and 123 violate article 17 of the Covenant but expresses concern that the Australian Government's argumentation is entirely based on the fact that he is threatened with prosecution under the aforementioned provisions and does not take into account the general adverse effect of the laws on himself. He further expresses concern, in the context of the "arbitrariness" of the interference with his privacy, that the State party has found it difficult to ascertain with certainty whether the prohibition on private homosexual activity represents the moral position of a significant portion of the Tasmanian populace. He contends that, in fact, there is significant popular and institutional support for the repeal of Tasmania's anti-gay criminal laws, and provides a detailed list of associations and groups from a broad spectrum of Australian and Tasmanian society, as well as a detailed survey of national and international concern about gay and lesbian rights in general and Tasmania's anti-gay statutes in particular.

7.2 In response to the Tasmanian authorities' argument that moral considerations must be taken into account when dealing with the right to privacy, the author notes that Australia is a pluralistic and multi-cultural society whose citizens have different and at times conflicting moral codes. In these circumstances it must be the proper role of criminal laws to entrench these different codes as little as possible; in so far as some values must be entrenched in criminal codes, these values should relate to human dignity and diversity.

7.3 As to the alleged violations of article 2, paragraph 1, and article 26, the author welcomes the State party's willingness to follow the Committee's guidance on the interpretation of these provisions but regrets that the State party has failed to give its own interpretation of these provisions. This, he submits, is inconsistent with the Australian Government's domestic views on these provisions, as it has made clear domestically that it interprets them to guarantee freedom from discrimination and equal protection of the law on grounds of sexual orientation. He proceeds to review recent developments in Australia on the status of sexual orientation in international human rights law and notes that before the Main Committee of the World Conference on Human Rights, Australia made a statement which "remains the strongest advocacy of ... gay rights by any Government in an international forum." The author submits that Australia's call for the proscription, at the international level, of discrimination on the grounds of sexual preference is pertinent to his case.

7.4 Mr. Toonen further notes that in 1994, Australia will raise the issue of sexual orientation discrimination in a variety of forums: "It is understood that the National Action Plan on Human Rights which will be tabled by Australia in the Commission on Human Rights early next year will include as one of its objectives the elimination of discrimination on the grounds of sexual orientation at an international level".

7.5 In the light of the above, the author urges the Committee to take account of the fact that the State party has consistently found that sexual orientation is a protected status in international human rights law and, in particular, constitutes an "other status" for purposes of articles 2, paragraphs 1 and 26. The author notes that a precedent for such a finding can be found in several judgements of the European Court of Human Rights.

7.6 As to the discriminatory effect of Sections 122 and 123 of the Tasmanian Criminal Code, the author reaffirms that the combined effect of the provisions is discriminatory because together they outlaw all forms of intimacy between men. Despite its apparent neutrality, Section 122 is said to be by itself discriminatory. In spite of the gender neutrality of Tasmanian laws against "unnatural sexual intercourse", this provision, like similar and now repealed laws in different Australian states, has been enforced far more often against men engaged in homosexual activity than against men or women who are heterosexually active. At the same time, the provision criminalizes an activity practised more often by men sexually active with other men than by men or women who are heterosexually active. The author contends that in its General Comment on article 26 and in some of its views, the Human Rights Committee itself has accepted the notion of "indirect discrimination."

7.7 Concerning the absence of "reasonable and objective criteria" for the differentiation operated by Sections 122 and 123, Mr. Toonen welcomes the State party's conclusion that the provisions are not reasonably justified on public health or moral grounds. At the same time, he questions the State party's ambivalence about the moral perceptions held among the inhabitants of Tasmania.

7.8 Finally, the author develops his initial argument related to the link between the existence of anti-gay criminal legislation and what he refers to as "wider discrimination", i.e. harassment and violence against homosexuals and anti-gay prejudice. He argues that the existence of the law has adverse social and psychological impacts on himself and on others in his situation and cites numerous recent examples of harassment of and discrimination against homosexuals and lesbians in Tasmania.

7.9 Mr. Toonen explains that since lodging his complaint with the Committee, he has continued to be the subject of personal vilification and harassment. This occurred in the context of the debate on gay law reform in Tasmania and his role as a leading voluntary worker in the Tasmanian community welfare sector. He adds that more importantly, since filing his complaint, he lost his employment partly as a result of his communication before the Committee.

7.10 In this context, he explains that when he submitted the communication to the Committee, he had been employed for three years as General Manager of the Tasmanian AIDS Council (Inc.). His employment was terminated on 2 July 1993 following an external review of the Council's work which had been imposed by the Tasmanian government, through the Department of Community and Health Services. When the Council expressed reluctance to dismiss the author, the Department threatened to withdraw the Council's funding unless Mr. Toonen was given immediate notice. Mr. Toonen submits that the action of the Department was motivated by its concerns over his high profile complaint to the Committee and his gay activism in general. He notes that his complaint has become a source of embarrassment to the Tasmanian government, and emphasizes that at no time had there been any question of his work performance being unsatisfactory.

7.11 The author concludes that Sections 122 and 123 continue to have an adverse impact on his private and his public life by creating the conditions for discrimination, continuous harassment and personal disadvantage.

Examination of the merits:

8.1 The Committee is called upon to determine whether Mr. Toonen has been the victim of an unlawful or arbitrary interference with his privacy, contrary to article 17, paragraph 1, and whether he has been discriminated against in his right to equal protection of the law, contrary to article 26.

8.2 Inasmuch as article 17 is concerned, it is undisputed that adult consensual sexual activity in private is covered by the concept of "privacy", and that Mr. Toonen is actually and currently affected by the continued existence of the Tasmanian laws. The Committee considers that Sections 122(a), (c) and 123 of the Tasmanian Criminal Code "interfere" with the author's privacy, even if these provisions have not been enforced for a decade. In this context, it notes that the policy of the Department of Public Prosecutions not to initiate criminal proceedings in respect of private homosexual conduct does not amount to a guarantee that no actions will be brought against homosexuals in the future, particularly in the light of undisputed statements of the Director of Public Prosecutions of Tasmania in 1988 and those of members of the Tasmanian Parliament. The continued existence of the challenged provisions therefore continuously and directly "interferes" with the author's privacy.

8.3 The prohibition against private homosexual behaviour is provided for by law, namely, Sections 122 and 123 of the Tasmanian Criminal Code. As to whether it may be deemed arbitrary, the Committee recalls that pursuant to its General Comment 16[32] on article 17, the "introduction of the concept of arbitrariness is intended to guarantee that even interference provided for by the law should be in accordance with the provisions, aims and objectives of the Covenant and should be, in any event, reasonable in the circumstances." The Committee interprets the requirement of reasonableness to imply that any interference with privacy must be proportional to the end sought and be necessary in the circumstances of any given case.

8.4 While the State party acknowledges that the impugned provisions constitute an arbitrary interference with Mr. Toonen's privacy, the

Tasmanian authorities submit that the challenged laws are justified on public health and moral grounds, as they are intended in part to prevent the spread of HIV/AIDS in Tasmania, and because, in the absence of specific limitation clauses in article 17, moral issues must be deemed a matter for domestic decision.

8.5 As far as the public health argument of the Tasmanian authorities is concerned, the Committee notes that the criminalization of homosexual practices cannot be considered a reasonable means or proportionate measure to achieve the aim of preventing the spread of AIDS/HIV. The Australian Government observes that statutes criminalizing homosexual activity tend to impede public health programmes "by driving underground many of the people at the risk of infection." Criminalization of homosexual activity thus would appear to run counter to the implementation of effective education programmes in respect of the HIV/AIDS prevention. Secondly, the Committee notes that no link has been shown between the continued criminalization of homosexual activity and the effective control of the spread of the HIV/AIDS virus.

8.6 The Committee cannot accept either that for the purposes of article 17 of the Covenant, moral issues are exclusively a matter of domestic concern, as this would open the door to withdrawing from the Committee's scrutiny a potentially large number of statutes interfering with privacy. It further notes that with the exception of Tasmania, all laws criminalizing homosexuality have been repealed throughout Australia and that, even in Tasmania, it is apparent that there is no consensus as to whether Sections 122 and 123 should not also be repealed. Considering further that these provisions are not currently enforced, which implies that they are not deemed essential to the protection of morals in Tasmania, the Committee concludes that the provisions do not meet the "reasonableness" test in the circumstances of the case, and that they arbitrarily interfere with Mr. Toonen's right under article 17, paragraph 1.

8.7 The State party has sought the Committee's guidance as to whether sexual orientation may be considered an "other status" for the purposes of article 26. The same issue could arise under article 2, paragraph 1, of the Covenant. The Committee confines itself to noting, however, that in its view the reference to "sex" in articles 2, paragraph 1, and 26 is to be taken as including sexual orientation.

9. The Human Rights Committee, acting under article 5, paragraph 4, of the Optional Protocol to the International Covenant on Civil and Political

Rights, is of the view that the facts before it reveal a violation of articles 17, paragraph 1, juncto 2, paragraph 1, of the Covenant.

10. Under article 2(3)(a) of the Covenant, the author, victim of a violation of articles 17, paragraph 1, juncto 2, paragraph 1, of the Covenant, is entitled to a remedy. In the opinion of the Committee, an effective remedy would be the repeal of Sections 122(a), (c) and 123 of the Tasmanian Criminal Code.

11. Since the Committee has found a violation of Mr. Toonen's rights under articles 17(1) and 2(1) of the Covenant requiring the repeal of the offending law, the Committee does not consider it necessary to consider whether there has also been a violation of article 26 of the Covenant.

Cases

Hajrizi Dzemajl, *et al.*, v. Serbia and Montenegro

UN CAT, Complaint No. 161/2000 (21 November 2002).

<u>The Committee against Torture</u>, established under article 17 of the Convention against Torture and Other Cruel, Inhuman or Degrading Treatment or Punishment,

<u>Meeting</u> on 21 November 2002,

<u>Having concluded</u> its consideration of complaint No. 161/2000, submitted to the Committee against Torture by Mr. Hajrizi Dzemajl et al. under article 22 of the Convention against Torture and Other Cruel, Inhuman or Degrading Treatment or Punishment,

<u>Having taken into account</u> all information made available to it by the complainants, their counsel and the State party,

<u>Adopts the following</u> decision under article 22, paragraph 7, of the Convention.

1.1 The complainants are 65 persons, all of Romani origin and nationals of Serbia and Montenegro. They claim that Serbia and Montenegro has violated articles 1, paragraph 1, 2, paragraph 1, 12, 13, 14 and 16, paragraph 1, of the Convention. They are represented by Mr. Dragan Prelevic, attorney at law, the Humanitarian Law Center, a non-governmental organization based in Serbia and Montenegro, and the European Roma Rights Center, an NGO based in Hungary.

1.2 In accordance with article 22, paragraph 3 of the Convention, the Committee transmitted the complaint to the State party on 13 April 2000.

The facts as presented by the complainants

2.1 On 14 April 1995 at around 10 p.m., the Danilovgrad Police Department received a report indicating that two Romani minors had raped S.B., a minor ethnic Montenegrin girl. In response to this report, at around midnight, the police entered and searched a number of houses in the Bozova Glavica Roma settlement and took into custody all of the young male Romani men present in the settlement (all of them among the complainants to the Committee).

2.2 The same day, also at around midnight, 200 ethnic Montenegrins, led by relatives and neighbours of the raped girl, assembled in front of the police station and publicly demanded that the Municipal Assembly adopt a decision expelling all Roma from Danilovgrad. The crowd shouted slogans against the Roma, threatening to "exterminate" them and "burn down" their houses.

2.3 Later, two Romani minors confessed under duress. On 15 April, at between 4 and 5 a.m., all of the detainees except those who had confessed were released from police custody. Before their release, they were warned by the police to leave Danilovgrad immediately with their families because they were at risk of being lynched by their non-Roma neighbours.

2.4 At the same time, police officer Ljubo Radovic went to the Bozova Glavica Roma settlement and told the Romani residents of the settlement that they must evacuate the settlement immediately. The officer's announcement caused panic. Most residents fled towards a nearby highway, where they could take buses for Podgorica. Only a few men and women remained in the settlement to safeguard their homes and livestock. At approximately 5 a.m., officer Radovic returned to the settlement, accompanied by police inspector Branko Micanovic. The officers told the remaining Roma still in their homes (including some of the complainants) to leave Danilovgrad immediately, as no one could guarantee their safety or provide them with protection.

2.5 At around 8 a.m. the same day, a group of non-Roma residents of Danilovgrad entered the Bozova Glavica Roma settlement, hurling stones and breaking windows of houses owned by the complainants. Those Roma who had still not left the settlement (all of them among the complainants) hid in the cellar of one of the houses from which they eventually managed to flee through the fields and woods towards Podgorica.

2.6 In the course of the morning of 15 April, a police car repeatedly patrolled the deserted Bozova Glavica settlement. Groups of non-Roma residents of Danilovgrad gathered in different locations in the town and in the surrounding villages. Around 2 p.m. the non-Roma crowd arrived in the Bozova Glavica settlement - in cars and on foot. Soon a crowd of at least several hundred non-Roma (according to different sources, between 400 and 3,000 persons were present) assembled in the then deserted Roma settlement.

2.7 Between 2 and 3 p.m., the crowd continued to grow and some began to shout: "We shall evict them!" "We shall burn down the settlement!" "We shall raze the settlement!" Shortly after 3 p.m., the demolition of the settlement began. The mob, with stones and other objects, first broke windows of cars and houses belonging to Roma and then set them on fire. The crowd also destroyed and set fire to the haystacks, farming and other machines, animal feed sheds, stables, as well as all other objects belonging to the Roma. They hurled explosive devices and "Molotov" cocktails that they had prepared beforehand, and threw burning cloth and foam rubber into houses through the broken windows. Shots and explosions could be heard amid the sounds of destruction. At the same time, valuables were looted and cattle slaughtered. The devastation endured unhindered for hours.

2.8 Throughout the course of the destruction, the police officers present failed to act in accordance with their legal obligations. Shortly after the attack began, rather than intervening to halt the violence, the officers simply moved their police car to a safe distance and reported to their superior officer. As the violence unfolded, police officers did no more than feebly seek to persuade some of the attackers to calm down pending a final decision of the Municipal Assembly with respect to a popular request to evict Roma from the Bozova Glavica settlement.

2.9 The outcome of the anti-Roma rage was the levelling of the entire settlement and the burning or complete destruction of all properties belonging to its Roma residents. Although the police did nothing to halt the destruction of the Roma settlement, they did ensure that the fire did not spread to any of the surrounding buildings, which belonged to the non-Roma.

2.10 The police and the investigating magistrate of the Basic Court in Danilovgrad subsequently drew up an on-site investigation report regarding the damage caused by those who took part in the attack.

2.11 Official police documents, as well as statements given by a number of police officers and other witnesses, both before the court and in the initial stage of the investigation, indicate that the following non-Roma residents of Danilovgrad were among those who took part in the destruction of the Bozova Glavica Roma settlement: Veselin Popovic, Dragisa Makocevic, Gojko Popovic, Bosko Mitrovic, Joksim Bobicic, Darko Janjusevic, Vlatko Cacic, Radojica Makocevic.

2.12 Moreover, there is evidence that police officers Miladin Dragas, Rajko Radulovic, Dragan Buric, Djordjije Stankovic and Vuk Radovic were all present as the violence unfolded and did nothing or not enough to protect the Roma residents of Bozova Glavica or their property.

2.13 Several days following the incident, the debris of the Roma settlement was completely cleared away by heavy construction machines of the Public Utility Company. All traces of the existence of the Roma in Danilovgrad were obliterated.

2.14 Following the attack, and pursuant to the relevant domestic legislation, on 17 April 1995, the Podgorica Police Department filed a criminal complaint with the Basic Public Prosecutor's Office in Podgorica. The complaint alleged that a number of unknown perpetrators had committed the criminal offence of causing public danger under article 164 of the Montenegrin Criminal Code and, inter alia, explicitly stated that there are "reasonable grounds to believe that, in an organized manner and by using open flames ... they caused a fire to break out ... on 15 April 1995 ... which completely consumed dwellings ... and other propert[ies] belonging to persons who used to reside in ... [the Bozova Glavica] settlement".

2.15 On 17 April 1995 the police brought in 20 individuals for questioning. On 18 April 1995, a memorandum was drawn up by the Podgorica Police Department which quoted the statement of Veselin Popovic as follows: "... I noticed flames in a hut which led me to conclude that the crowd had started setting fire to huts so I found several pieces of foam rubber which I lit with a lighter I had on me and threw them, alight, into two huts, one of which caught fire."

2.16 On the basis of this testimony and the official police memorandum, the Podgorica Police Department, on 18 April 1995, ordered that Veselin Popovic be remanded into custody, on the grounds that there were reasons to believe that he had committed the criminal offence of causing public danger in the sense of article 164 of the Montenegrin Criminal Code.

2.17 On 25 April 1995, and with respect to the incident at the origin of the present complaint, the Public Prosecutor instituted proceedings against one person only - Veselin Popovic.

2.18 Veselin Popovic was charged under article 164 of the Montenegrin Criminal Code. The same indictment charged Dragisa Makocevic with illegally obtaining firearms in 1993 - an offence unrelated to the incident at issue notwithstanding the evidence implicating him in the destruction of the Roma Bozova Glavica settlement.

2.19 Throughout the investigation, the investigating magistrate of the Basic Court of Danilovgrad heard a number of witnesses all of whom stated that they had been present as the violence unfolded but were not able to identify a single perpetrator. On 22 June 1995, the investigating magistrate of the Basic Court of Danilovgrad heard officer Miladin Dragas. Contrary to the official memorandum he had personally drawn up on 16 April 1995, officer Dragas now stated that he had not seen anyone throwing an inflammable device, nor could he identify any of the individuals involved.

2.20 On 25 October 1995, the Basic Public Prosecutor in Podgorica requested that the investigating magistrate of the Basic Court of Danilovgrad undertake additional investigations into the facts of the case. Specifically, the prosecutor proposed that new witnesses be heard, including officers from the Danilovgrad Police Department who had been entrusted with protecting the Bozova Glavica Roma settlement. The investigating magistrate of the Basic Court of Danilovgrad then heard the additional witnesses, all of whom stated that they had seen none of the individuals who had caused the fire. The investigating magistrate took no further action.

2.21 Due to the "lack of evidence", the Basic Public Prosecutor in Podgorica dropped all charges against Veselin Popovic on 23 January 1996. On 8 February 1996, the investigating magistrate of the Basic Court of Danilovgrad issued a decision to discontinue the investigation. From February 1996 up to and including the date of filing of the present complaint, the authorities took no further steps to identify and/or punish those individuals responsible for the incident at issue - "civilians" and police officers alike.

2.22 In violation of domestic legislation, the complainants were not served with the court decision of 8 February 1996 to discontinue the investigation. They were thus prevented from assuming the prosecution of the case themselves, as was their legal right.

2.23 Even prior to the closing of the proceedings, on 18 and 21 September 1995, the investigating magistrate, while hearing witnesses (among them a number of the complainants), failed to advise them of their right to assume the prosecution of the case in the event that the Public Prosecutor should decide to drop the charges. This contravened domestic legislation which explicitly provides that the court is under an obligation to advise ignorant parties of avenues of legal redress available for the protection of their interests.

2.24 On 6 September 1996, all 71 complainants filed a civil claim for damages, pecuniary and non-pecuniary, with the first instance court in Podgorica - each plaintiff claiming approximately US$ 100,000. The pecuniary damages claim was based on the complete destruction of all properties belonging to the plaintiffs, while the non-pecuniary damages claim was based on the pain and suffering of the plaintiffs associated with the fear they were subjected to, and the violation of their honour, reputation, freedom of movement and the right to choose their own place of residence. The plaintiffs addressed these claims against the Republic of Montenegro and cited articles 154, 180 (1), 200, and 203 of the Federal Law on Obligations. More than five years after the submission of their claim, the civil proceedings for damages are still pending.

2.25 On 15 August 1996, eight of the Danilovgrad Roma, all of them among the complainants, who were dismissed by their employers for failing to report to work, filed a lawsuit requesting that the court order their return to work. Throughout the proceedings, the plaintiffs argued that their failure to appear at work during the relevant time period was justified by their reasonable fear that their lives would have been endangered had they come to work so soon after the incident. On 26 February 1997, the Podgorica first instance court rendered its decision dismissing the claims of the plaintiffs on the grounds that they had been absent from work for five consecutive days without justification. In doing so the court cited article 75, paragraph 2 of the Federal Labour Code which, inter alia, provides that "if a person fails to report to work for five consecutive days without proper justification his employment will be terminated." On 11 June 1997, the plaintiffs appealed this decision and almost five months later, on 29 October 1997, the second instance court in Podgorica quashed the first instance ruling and ordered a retrial. The reasoning underlying the second instance decision was based on the fact that the plaintiffs had apparently not been properly served with their employer's decision to terminate their employment.

2.26 In the meantime, the case went again up to the Montenegrin Supreme Court which ordered another retrial before the first instance court in Podgorica. The case is still pending.

2.27 The complainants, having been driven out of their homes and their property having been completely destroyed, fled to the outskirts of Podgorica, the Montenegrin capital, where during the first few weeks following the incident they hid in parks and abandoned houses. Local Roma from Podgorica supplied them with basic food and told them that groups of angry non-Roma men had been looking for them in the Roma suburbs in Podgorica. From then on, the banished Danilovgrad Roma have continued to live in Podgorica in abject poverty, makeshift shelters or abandoned houses, and have been forced to work at the Podgorica city dump or to beg for a living.

The complaint

3.1 The complainants submit that the State party has violated articles 2, paragraph 1, read in conjunction with articles 1, 16, paragraph 1, and 12, 13, 14, taken alone or together with article 16, paragraph 1, of the Convention.

3.2 With regard to the admissibility of the complaint, and more particularly the exhaustion of local remedies, the complainants submit that, given the level of wrongs suffered, and alongside the jurisprudence of the European Court of Human Rights, only a criminal remedy would be effective in the instant case. Civil and/or administrative remedies do not provide sufficient redress in this case.

3.3 The complainants note further that the authorities had the obligation to investigate, or at least to continue their investigation if they considered the available evidence insufficient. Moreover, even though they acknowledge that they have never filed a criminal complaint against individuals responsible for the attack, they contend that both the police and the prosecuting authorities were sufficiently aware of the facts to initiate and conduct the investigation ex officio. The complainants therefore conclude that there is no effective remedy.

3.4 The complainants also note that since there is no effective remedy in respect of the alleged breach of the Convention, the issue of exhaustion of domestic remedies should be dealt with together with the merits of the case since there is a claim of violation of articles 13 and 14 of the Convention.

3.5 Referring to a number of excerpts from NGO and governmental sources, the complainants first request that the complaint be considered taking into account the situation of the Roma in Serbia and Montenegro as victims of systematic police brutality and dire human rights situation in general.

3.6 The complainants allege that Yugoslav authorities have violated the Convention under either article 2, paragraph 1, read in conjunction with article 1, because, during the events described previously, the police stood by and watched as the events unfolded, or article 16, paragraph 1, for the same reasons. In this regard, the complainants consider that the particularly vulnerable character of the Roma minority has to be taken into account in assessing the level of ill-treatment that has been committed. They suggest that "a given level of physical abuse is more likely to constitute 'degrading or inhuman treatment or punishment' when motivated by racial animus."

3.7 With regard to the fact that the acts have mostly been committed by non-State actors, the complainants rely on a review of international jurisprudence on the principle of "due diligence" and recall the current state of international law with regard to "positive" obligations that are incumbent on States. They submit that the purpose of the provisions of the Convention is not limited to negative obligations for States parties but includes positive steps that have to be taken in order to avoid torture and other related acts being committed by private persons.

3.8 The complainants further contend that the acts of violence occurred with the "consent or acquiescence" of the police whose duty under the law was to assure their safety and provide them protection.

3.9 The complainants then allege a violation of article 12 read alone or, if the acts committed do not amount to torture, taken together with article 16, paragraph 1, because the authorities failed to conduct a prompt, impartial and comprehensive investigation capable of leading to the identification and punishment of those responsible. Considering the jurisprudence of the Committee against Torture, it is submitted that the State party had the obligation to conduct "not just any investigation" but a proper investigation, even in the absence of the formal submission of a complaint, since they were in possession of abundant evidence. The complainants further suggest that the impartiality of the same investigation depends on the level of independence of the body conducting it. In this case, it is alleged that the level of independence of the investigating magistrate was not sufficient.

3.10 The complainants finally allege a violation of article 13 read alone and/or taken together with article 16, paragraph 1, because "their right to complain and to have [their] case promptly and impartially examined by [the] competent authorities" was violated. They also allege a violation of article 14 read alone and/or taken together with article 16, paragraph 1, because of the absence of redress and of fair and adequate compensation.

State party's observations on admissibility

4. In a submission dated 9 November 1998, the State party contended that the complaint was inadmissible because the case had been conducted according to the national legislation in force and because all available legal remedies had not been exhausted.

Comments by the complainants

5. In a submission dated 20 September 2000, the complainants reiterated their main arguments with regard to the admissibility of the complaint and underlined that the State party had not explained what domestic remedies would still be available to the complainants. In addition, they consider that since the State party has failed to put forward any other objections in that respect, it has in effect waived its right to contest other admissibility criteria.

Decision on admissibility

6. At its twenty-fifth session (November 2000), the Committee considered the admissibility of the complaint. The Committee ascertained, as it is required to do under article 22, paragraph 5 (a), of the Convention, that the same matter had not been and was not being examined under another procedure of international investigation or settlement. Regarding the exhaustion of domestic remedies, the Committee took note of the arguments made by the complainants and noted that it had not received any argumentation or information from the State party on this issue. Referring to rule 108,

paragraph 7, of its rules of procedure, the Committee declared the complaint admissible on 23 November 2000.

State party's observations on the merits

7. Notwithstanding the Committee's call for observations on the merits, transmitted by a note of 5 December 2000, and two reminders of 9 October 2001 and 11 February 2002, the State party has not made any further submission.

Complainants' additional comments on the merits

8.1 By a letter of 6 December 2001, the complainants transmitted to the Committee additional information and comments on the merits of the case. In the same submission, the complainants have transmitted detailed information on different questions that were asked by the Committee, namely, on the presence and behaviour of the police during the events, the actions that have been taken vis-à-vis the local population, the relations between the different ethnic groups, and their respective titles of property.

8.2 With regard to the presence and behaviour of the police during the events and the actions that have been taken vis-à-vis the local population, the complainants give a detailed description of the facts referred to in paragraphs 2.1 to 2.29 above.

8.3 With regard to the general situation of the Roma minority in Serbia and Montenegro, the complainants contend that the situation has remained largely unchanged after the departure of President Milosevic. Referring to a report that was earlier submitted by the Humanitarian Law Center to the Committee against Torture and to the 2001 Annual Report of Human Rights Watch, the complainants submit that the situation of Roma in the State party is very preoccupying and emphasize that there have been a number of serious incidents against Roma over the last few years while no significant measures to find or prosecute the perpetrators or to compensate the victims have been taken by the authorities.

8.4 With regard to the property titles, the complainants explain that most were lost or destroyed during the events of 14 and 15 April 1995 and that this was not challenged by the State party's authorities during the civil proceedings.

8.5 The complainants then make a thorough analysis of the scope of application of articles 1, paragraph 1, and 16, paragraph 1, of the Convention. They first submit that the European Court of Human Rights has ascertained in *Ireland v. United Kingdom* and in the *Greek* case, that article 3 of the European Convention on Human Rights also covered "the infliction of mental suffering by creating a state of anguish and stress by means other than bodily assault."

8.6 Moreover, the complainants reiterate that the assessment of the level of ill-treatment also depends on the vulnerability of the victim and should thus also take into account the sex, age, state of health or ethnicity of the victim. As a result, the Committee should consider the Romani ethnicity of the victims in their appreciation of the violations committed, particularly in Serbia and Montenegro. In the same line, they reiterate that a given level of physical abuse is more likely to constitute a treatment prohibited by article 16 of the Convention if it is motivated by racial considerations.

8.7 Concerning the devastation of human settlements, the complainants refer to two cases that were decided by the European Court of Human Rights and whose factual circumstances were similar to the one at issue. The European Court considered in both cases that the burning and destruction of homes as well as the eviction of their inhabitants from the village constituted acts that were contrary to article 3 of the European Convention.

8.8 Concerning the perpetrators of the alleged violations of articles 1 and 16 of the Convention, the complainants submit that although only a public official or a person acting in an official capacity could be the perpetrator of an act in the sense of either of the above provisions, both provisions state that the act of torture or of other ill-treatment may also be inflicted with the consent or acquiescence of a public official. Therefore, while they do not dispute that the acts have not been committed by the police officers or that the latter have not instigated them, the complainants consider that they have been committed with their consent and acquiescence. The police were informed of what was going to happen on 15 April 1995 and were present on the scene at the time the attack took place but did not prevent the perpetrators from committing their wrongdoing.

8.9 With regard to the positive obligations of States to prevent and suppress acts of violence committed by private individuals, the complainants refer to general comment 20 of the Human Rights Committee on article 7 of the International Covenant on Civil and Political Rights according to which this provision covers acts that are committed by private individuals, which implies a duty for States to take appropriate measures to protect everyone against such acts. The complainants also refer to the United Nations Code of Conduct for Law Enforcement Officials, the Basic Principles on the Use of Force and Firearms by Law Enforcement Officials and the Council of Europe

Framework Convention for the Protection of National Minorities, which have provisions with a similar purpose.

8.10 On the same issue, the complainants cite a decision of the Inter-American Court of Human Rights in *Velásquez Rodríguez v. Honduras* according to which:

> [a]n illegal act which violates human rights and which is initially not directly imputable to a State (for example, because it is the act of a private person or because the person responsible has not been identified) can lead to international responsibility of the State, not because of the act itself but because of the lack of due diligence to prevent the violation or to respond to it as required by the Convention.

Similarly, the European Court of Human Rights has addressed the issue in *Osman v. United Kingdom* and stated that:

> article 2 of the Convention may also imply in certain well-defined circumstances a positive obligation on the authorities to take preventive operational measures to protect an individual whose life is at risk from the criminal acts of another individual. ... [W]here there is an allegation that the authorities have violated their positive obligation to protect the right to life in the context of their above-mentioned duty to prevent and suppress offences against the person ... it must be established to its satisfaction that the authorities knew or ought to have known at the time of the existence of a real and immediate risk to the life of an identified individual or individuals from the criminal acts of a third party and that they failed to take measures within the scope of their powers which, judged reasonably, might have been expected to avoid that risk ... [H]aving regard to the nature of the right protected by article 2, a right fundamental in the scheme of the Convention, it is sufficient for an applicant to show that the authorities did not do all that could be reasonably expected of them to avoid a real and immediate risk to life of which they have or ought to have knowledge.

8.11 The complainants further contend that the extent of the obligation to take preventive measures may increase with the immediacy of the risk to life. In support of this argument, they extensively rely on the judgement of the European Court of Human Rights in *Mahmut Kaya v. Turkey* where the Court laid down the obligations of States as follows: first, States have an

- 328 -

obligation to take every reasonable step in order to prevent a real and immediate threat to the life and integrity of a person when the actions could be perpetrated by a person or group of persons with the consent or acquiescence of public authorities; second, States have an obligation to provide an effective remedy, including a proper and effective investigation, with regard to actions committed by non-State actors undertaken with the consent or acquiescence of public authorities.

8.12 The complainants also underline that the obligation of the States under the European Convention on Human Rights goes well beyond mere criminal sanctions for private individuals who have committed acts contrary to article 3 of the said Convention. In *Z. et al. v. United Kingdom*, the European Commission on Human Rights held that:

> the authorities had been aware of the serious ill-treatment and neglect suffered by the children over a period of years at the hands of their parents and failed, despite the means reasonably available to them, to take any effective steps to bring it to an end. ... [The State had therefore] failed in its positive obligation under article 3 of the Convention to provide the applicants with adequate protection against inhuman and degrading treatment.

8.13 In conclusion, the complainants submit that "they were indeed subjected to acts of community violence inflicting on them great physical and mental suffering amounting to torture and/or cruel, inhuman and degrading treatment or punishment." They further state that "this happened for the purpose of punishing them for an act committed by a third person (the rape of S.B.), and that the community violence (or rather the racist attack) at issue took place in the presence of, and thus with the 'consent or acquiescence' of, the police whose duty under law was precisely the opposite - to assume their safety and provide them protection".

8.14 Finally, concerning the absence of observations by the State party on the merits, the complainants refer to rule 108 (6) of the Committee's rules of procedure and consider that such principle should be equally applicable during the phase of the merits. Relying on the jurisprudence of the European Court of Human Rights and of the Human Rights Committee, the complainants further argue that, by not contesting the facts or the legal arguments developed in the complaint and further submissions, the State party has tacitly accepted the claims at issue.

Cases

Issues and proceedings before the Committee

9.1 The Committee has considered the complaint in the light of all information made available to it by the parties concerned, in accordance with article 22, paragraph 4, of the Convention. Moreover, in the absence of any submission from the State party following the Committee's decision on admissibility, the Committee relies on the detailed submissions made by the complainants. The Committee recalls in this respect that a State party has an obligation under article 22, paragraph 3, of the Convention to cooperate with the Committee and to submit written explanations or statements clarifying the matter and the remedy, if any, that may have been granted.

9.2 As to the legal qualification of the facts that have occurred on 15 April 1995, as they were described by the complainants, the Committee first considers that the burning and destruction of houses constitute, in the circumstances, acts of cruel, inhuman or degrading treatment or punishment. The nature of these acts is further aggravated by the fact that some of the complainants were still hidden in the settlement when the houses were burnt and destroyed, the particular vulnerability of the alleged victims and the fact that the acts were committed with a significant level of racial motivation. Moreover, the Committee considers that the complainants have sufficiently demonstrated that the police (public officials), although they had been informed of the immediate risk that the complainants were facing and had been present at the scene of the events, did not take any appropriate steps in order to protect the complainants, thus implying "acquiescence" in the sense of article 16 of the Convention. In this respect, the Committee has reiterated on many instances its concerns about "inaction by police and law enforcement officials who fail to provide adequate protection against racially motivated attacks when such groups have been threatened." Although the acts referred to by the complainants were not committed by public officials themselves, the Committee considers that they were committed with their acquiescence and therefore constitute a violation of article 16, paragraph 1, of the Convention by the State party.

9.3 Having considered that the facts described by the complainants constitute acts within the meaning of article 16, paragraph 1, of the Convention, the Committee will analyse other alleged violations in the light of that finding.

9.4 Concerning the alleged violation of article 12 of the Convention, the Committee, as it has underlined in previous cases (see, inter alia, *Encarnación Blanco Abad v. Spain*, case No. 59/1996, decided on 14 May 1998), is of the opinion that a criminal investigation must seek both to determine the nature and circumstances of the alleged acts and to establish the identity of any person who might have been involved therein. In the present case, the Committee notes that, despite the participation of at least several hundred non-Roma in the events of 15 April 1995 and the presence of a number of police officers both at the time and at the scene of those events, no person nor any member of the police forces has been tried by the courts of the State party. In these circumstances, the Committee is of the view that the investigation conducted by the authorities of the State party did not satisfy the requirements of article 12 of the Convention.

9.5 Concerning the alleged violation of article 13 of the Convention, the Committee considers that the absence of an investigation as described in the previous paragraph also constitutes a violation of article 13 of the Convention. Moreover, the Committee is of the view that the State party's failure to inform the complainants of the results of the investigation by, inter alia, not serving on them the decision to discontinue the investigation effectively prevented them from assuming "private prosecution" of their case. In the circumstances, the Committee finds that this constitutes a further violation of article 13 of the Convention.

9.6 Concerning the alleged violation of article 14 of the Convention, the Committee notes that the scope of application of the said provision only refers to torture in the sense of article 1 of the Convention and does not cover other forms of ill-treatment. Moreover, article 16, paragraph 1, of the Convention, while specifically referring to articles 10, 11, 12 and 13, does not mention article 14 of the Convention. Nevertheless, article 14 of the Convention does not mean that the State party is not obliged to grant redress and fair and adequate compensation to the victim of an act in breach of article 16 of the Convention. The positive obligations that flow from the first sentence of article 16 of the Convention include an obligation to grant redress and compensate the victims of an act in breach of that provision. The Committee is therefore of the view that the State party has failed to observe its obligations under article 16 of the Convention by failing to enable the complainants to obtain redress and to provide them with fair and adequate compensation.

10. The Committee, acting under article 22, paragraph 7, of the Convention, is of the view that the facts before it disclose a violation of articles 16, paragraph 1, 12 and 13 of the Convention against Torture and Other Cruel, Inhuman or Degrading Treatment or Punishment.

11. ... the Committee urges the State party to conduct a proper investigation into the facts that occurred on 15 April 1995, prosecute and punish the persons responsible for those acts and provide the complainants with redress,

including fair and adequate compensation, and to inform it, within 90 days from the date of the transmittal of this decision, of the steps it has taken in response to the views expressed above.

Ahmad Najaati Sadic v. Denmark

CERD Comm. No. 25 (2002),
UN Doc. CERD/C/62/D/25/2002 (2003).

... 2.1 On 25 July 2000, the petitioner was working on a construction site in a public housing area in Randers, Denmark, for the company "Assentoft Painters and Decorators" owned by Jesper Christensen. When the petitioner approached Mr. Christensen to claim overdue payments, their conversation developed into an argument during which Mr. Christensen reportedly made the following comments to the petitioner: "Push off home, you Arab pig", "Immigrant pig", "Both you and all Arabs smell", "Disappear from here, God damned idiots and psychopaths." The argument between the complainant and Mr. Christensen was overheard by at least two other workers, Mr. Carsten Thomassen and Mr. Frank Lasse Hendriksen.

2.2 On 1 March 2001, the DRC, on behalf of the petitioner, informed the police in Åarhus of the incident, arguing that section 266 b of the Danish Criminal Code had been violated by the petitioner's by then former employer.

2.3 On 9 July 2001, Frank Lasse Henriksen was interviewed by telephone by the police of Randers. The interview report states:

> The witness stated that he was working when his boss, Mr. Christensen, came and presented a new apprentice; also present was the victim, Ahmad. A discussion/quarrel arose between Mr. Christensen and the victim, and the discussion concerned holiday pay, wages and missing wage slips [...]. [T]he witness went to Mr. Christensen, who at this point was angry about the quarrel with the victim, and felt - at least he said so - that, if the witness felt like the victim, he could consider himself sacked. The witness was so infuriated with the treatment that he took his boss at his word. Mr. Christensen now shouted that it was all just about an Arab bastard - which, in the witness' opinion, was far too rude. According to the witness, Mr. Christensen went far beyond the line. The witness was read the racist statements mentioned in the complaint and stated that they corresponded to what Mr. Christensen had called the victim. After this, the witness immediately left the workplace and has not worked for Mr. Christensen since [...].

2.4 On 12 July 2001, Carsten Thomassen was interviewed by telephone by the police of Åarhus. The interview report states:

On the relevant day, at about 10.30 a.m., Mr. Sadic and his boss were standing on the external gallery on the first floor - below the witness. The witness could hear that they were quarrelling about both work and money. However, the witness had only heard fragments of the quarrel, in which both parties had obviously become 'over-excited'. At some stage, the witness heard Mr. Christensen say something like: 'You can just go home' - 'black bastard'. The witness could not hear what Mr. Sadic said as he did not speak Danish very well and was difficult to understand - particularly when he was upset, as in that moment. However, to a large extent, the witness took the quarrel to be one that may arise once in a while at the workplace [...].

2.5 Mr. Christensen was interviewed by the police of Randers on 23 July 2001, without any charges being brought against him and without prejudice to his right to refuse testimony. The interview report states:

Mr. Christensen stated that, on the relevant day, he had a quarrel with the victim about payment for overtime [...]. Mr. Christensen and the victim [...] used abusive language [...]. Mr. Christensen never used [...] words like 'Arab bastard', 'Paki bastard', 'Arabs smell', etc., towards the victim. Mr. Christensen was confronted with the witness statement of Mr. Henriksen. To this, Mr. Christensen stated that he had previously sacked Mr. Henriksen due to disagreements. [...] After Mr. Henriksen had been sacked, he left the workplace and, consequently, cannot have overheard the conversation with the victim. [...] On the basis of the information presented, Mr. Christensen cannot admit [a] violation of section 266 b of the Criminal Code. [...].

2.6 By letter of 24 August 2001, the Chief Constable of the Århus police informed the DRC that the investigation of the case had been discontinued, stating that it could not reasonably be presumed that a criminal offence subject to ex officio prosecution had been committed. The discontinuation of the investigation was mainly based on the fact that the argument between the petitioner and Mr. Christensen had taken place at work, "where only two other persons were present." Apart from the question whether or not Mr. Christensen had made the statements in question, the Chief Constable found that, in any event, these statements had not been made publicly or with the intention of wider dissemination. As to a claim for damages, the petitioner was advised to pursue civil proceedings.

2.7 On 28 September 2001, the petitioner appealed the decision to discontinue investigations before the Regional Public Prosecutor in Viborg, arguing that the petitioner's former employer had made his statements on a construction site in a public housing area and, therefore, had at least accepted the possibility that other people would hear his comments. Moreover, the petitioner referred to several judgements of Danish courts which construed the requirement, in section 266 b of the Criminal Code, of statements being made publicly quite broadly. He challenged the Chief Constable's finding that only two other persons were present at the incident. The petitioner quoted from a written statement in which Mr. Thomassen asserted that "[o]n Tuesday, 25 July 2000, at about 10.30 a.m., I, Carsten Thomassen, was standing together with three other colleagues [...] on the external gallery for a short break, when, to our great surprise, we overheard a conversation/quarrel between the master [...] and Ahmad."

2.8 By letter of 27 November 2001, the Regional Public Prosecutor of Viborg dismissed the appeal, arguing that, although it could not be established with certainty that only two other persons were present at the incident, the statements by Mr. Christensen were made in connection with a dispute between the petitioner and his employer at a stage where both parties had become over-excited and that the witnesses were some distance away from the exact place of the quarrel and only heard fragments of the dispute. Given that "this was only a loud-voiced quarrel which others happened to overhear - at a distance [...]", the Regional Public Prosecutor concluded that the employer's statements could not be considered public. Since the argument was not likely to disturb the public peace or cause a nuisance to other people present, the police regulations had not been violated either. The petitioner was thus advised to pursue any claim for damages through civil proceedings. The decision of the Regional Public Prosecutor was final and could not be appealed.

The complaint

3.1 The petitioner claims that he has exhausted domestic remedies, as there is no possibility to appeal the decision of the Regional Public Prosecutor and he cannot bring the case before the Danish courts. He submits that, under section 275 of the Danish Criminal Code, violations of section 266 b are subject only to prosecution ex officio and that direct legal action against his former employer would have been without prospect, given that the police and the Regional Public Prosecutor had rejected his complaint. In support of the latter claim, the petitioner submits that, pursuant to a decision of the Eastern High Court dated 5 February 1999, an incident of racial discrimination does not in itself constitute a violation of the honour and reputation of a person within the meaning of section 26 of the Liability for Damages Act.

3.2 The petitioner claims that the State party has violated its obligations under articles 2, paragraph 1 (d), and 6 of the Convention by not investigating effectively to what extent the construction site was accessible to the public, how many people were present at the incident and to what extent it would have been possible for others to overhear the employer's statements. The petitioner argues that, following the decision of the Committee in L.K. v. The Netherlands (case No. 4/1991, Opinion adopted on 16 March 1993), States parties have a positive obligation under the above provisions to take effective action against reported incidents of racial discrimination.

3.3 By reference to another case decided by the Committee (*Kashif Ahmad v. Denmark*) (case No. 16/1999, Opinion adopted on 13 March 2000) [in which racist comments were made in a hallway outside a classroom], the petitioner submits that the State party did not claim in that case that the statements had not been made publicly and that a violation was found by the Committee. He furthermore refers to two cases in which Danish courts found violations of section 266 b of the Criminal Code in what he considers similar circumstances.

3.4 The petitioner asks the Committee to request the State party to carry out a full investigation into the incident reported by him and to award him financial compensation, in accordance with article 6 of the Convention.

The State party's submission on the admissibility and the merits of the communication

4.1 By note verbale of 20 November 2002, the State party made its submissions on the admissibility and, subsidiarily, on the merits of the communication.

4.2 On admissibility, the State party submits that the petitioner failed to exhaust domestic remedies. Contrary to violations of section 266 b, which are subject to prosecution ex officio, violations of section 267 of the Criminal Code - the general provision on defamatory statements which supplements section 266 b - are prosecuted only at the request of the individual concerned, pursuant to section 275 of the Criminal Code. The petitioner could have requested the institution of criminal proceedings under section 267 against his employer and, by doing so, could have obtained a decision on whether his former employer had made the reported statements and, subject to fulfilling the conditions of section 267, a conviction of Mr. Christensen.

4.3 The State party contends that the institution of criminal proceedings under section 267 of the Criminal Code is an effective remedy. Moreover, the decision of the Danish authorities to discontinue investigations under section 266 b was without prejudice to the effectiveness of that remedy, since neither the Chief Constable nor the Regional Public Prosecutor had taken any position on the question whether Mr. Christensen had made the statements complained of. The State party argues that, for the same reason, the discontinuation of investigations under section 266 b did not preclude a legal action for non-pecuniary damages against his former employer, under section 26 of the Liability for Damages Act.

4.4 The State party argues that the communication is incompatible with the Convention ratione materiae, since the central claim is that the Danish authorities did not interpret and apply section 266 b of the Criminal Code correctly. The concrete elements which, according to the petitioner, should have been investigated all relate to the conditions for punishment under section 266 b, i.e. the place where the statements were made, the number of persons who heard or might have heard Mr. Christensen's statements, etc. in the State party's opinion, the legal assessment by the Chief Constable and the Regional Public Prosecutor of Viborg that the requirements of section 266 b were not met in the present case is primarily a matter which relates to interpretation and application of domestic legislation and which the Committee has no competence to review.

4.5 On the basis of the above arguments, the State party concludes that the communication should be declared inadmissible under article 14, paragraphs 1 and 7 (a), of the Convention.

4.6 Subsidiarily and on the merits, the State party submits that the Danish authorities took the petitioner's complaint seriously, as they initiated investigations and interviewed witnesses, as well as the petitioner's former employer, as a result of the complaint. It concludes that the processing and assessment of the complaint by the Chief Constable and the Regional Public Prosecutor therefore fully complies with the State party's obligations under article 2, paragraph 1, and article 6 of the Convention.

4.7 With regard to the requirement that a statement should be made "publicly or with the intention of wider dissemination", the State party admits that grey zones in the delimitation between public and private are unavoidable and argues that it should therefore be for the national authorities to assess whether these requirements have been met in a specific case.

4.8 The State party submits that the two judgements adduced in support of his arguments by the petitioner could not be relied upon because, in one case, the judgement contained no specific information on the number of persons present in the news store and, in the other case, the court observed that "many persons must have overheard [...] the incident."

4.9 The State party argues, moreover, that section 266 b of the Criminal Code is not the only provision designed to ensure compliance with the State party's obligations under the Convention, since it is supplemented by other provisions, including section 267 of the same Code.

4.10 The State party concludes that, even if the Committee were to declare the communication admissible, it does in any event not disclose a violation of the Convention.

Comments by the petitioner

5.1 The petitioner submits that section 267 of the Criminal Code, as well as section 26 of the Liability for Damages Act, do not address the issue of racial discrimination and therefore do not provide an effective remedy against acts of racial discrimination, as required by article 2, paragraph 1 (d), and article 6 of the Convention. He claims that the only relevant remedy is section 266 b of the Criminal Code, indicating that, in previous cases, it was not held by the Committee that, in order to exhaust domestic remedies, a petitioner should have initiated criminal proceedings under section 267 of the Criminal Code or civil proceedings under section 26 of the Liability for Damages Act.

5.2 As to the requirements of section 266 b of the Criminal Code, the petitioner reiterates that Danish courts found violations of that provision in the past even where only one other person apart from the victim(s) had been present during an incident of racial discrimination....

5.3 Based on the written statement of Mr. Thomassen, the petitioner claims that at least five persons overheard his argument with his employer and that the police failed to contact the other three colleagues mentioned in that statement.

5.4 The petitioner rejects the State party's argument that the core of his communication is related to the interpretation of domestic legislation and the evaluation of facts and evidence. He argues that the lack of an effective investigation is closely connected to the fact that the Danish authorities concluded that his complaint fell outside the scope of section 266 b of the Criminal Code.

Issues and proceedings before the Committee

6.1 Before considering the substance of a communication, the Committee on the Elimination of Racial Discrimination must, in accordance with rule 91 of its rules of procedure, examine whether or not the communication is admissible.

6.2 The Committee notes that the petitioner brought a complaint under section 266 b of the Criminal Code before the police and the Regional Public Prosecutor; and that these authorities, after having interviewed two witnesses and the petitioner's former employer, decided to discontinue criminal proceedings under section 266 b, as they considered that the requirements of this provision were not satisfied. It has taken note of the State party's argument that, despite the discontinuation of proceedings under section 266 b of the Criminal Code, the petitioner could have requested the institution of criminal proceedings against his former employer under the general provision on defamatory statements .... The petitioner does not deny the availability of this remedy, but questions its effectiveness in relation to incidents of racial discrimination.

6.3 The Committee observes that the notion of "effective remedy", within the meaning of article 6 of the Convention, is not limited to criminal proceedings based on provisions which specifically, expressly and exclusively penalize acts of racial discrimination. In particular, the Committee does not consider it contrary to articles 2, paragraph 1 (d), and 6 of the Convention if, as in the State party's case, the provisions of criminal law specifically adopted to outlaw acts of racial discrimination are supplemented by a general provision criminalizing defamatory statements which is applicable to racist statements even if they are not covered by specific legislation.

6.4 As to the petitioner's argument that criminal proceedings against his former employer under section 267 would have been without prospect because the authorities had already rejected his complaint under section 266 b of the Criminal Code, the Committee notes, on the basis of the material before it, that the requirements for prosecution under section 266 b are not identical to those for prosecution under section 267 of the Criminal Code. It therefore does not appear that the Danish authorities' decision to discontinue proceedings under section 266 b on the ground of lack of evidence as to whether the employer's statements were made publicly or with the intention of wider dissemination have prejudiced a request by the petitioner to institute criminal proceedings under section 267 (together with section 275) of the Criminal Code. The Committee therefore considers that the institution of such proceedings can be regarded as an effective remedy which the petitioner failed to exhaust.

6.5 As to the question of damages, the Committee recalls the State party's argument that the petitioner did not institute civil proceedings against his former employer under section 26 of the Liability for Damages Act and therefore did not exhaust domestic remedies. With regard to the petitioner's arguments that a previous decision of the Eastern High Court held that an incident of racial discrimination does not in itself constitute a violation of the honour and reputation of a person, the Committee considers that mere doubts about the effectiveness of available civil remedies do not absolve a petitioner from pursuing them ...

6.6. Accordingly, the Committee considers that, by not exhausting the available domestic remedies, the petitioner has failed to meet the requirements of article 14, paragraph 7 (a), of the Convention.

6.7 The ... [CERD] ... therefore decides:

(a) That the communication is inadmissible;

(b) That this decision shall be communicated to the State party and to the petitioner.

6.8 However, the Committee invites the State party to reconsider its legislation, since the restrictive condition of "broad publicity" or "wider dissemination" required by article 266 b of the Danish Criminal Code for the criminalization of racial insults does not appear to be fully in conformity with the requirements of articles 4 and 6 of the Convention.

Case Relating to Certain Aspects of the Laws on the Use of Languages in Education in Belgium (Belgian Linguistics Case)

ECtHR, Appls. No. 1474/62; 1677/62; 1691/62; 1769/63; 1994/63; 2126/64 (23 July 1968).

THE FACTS

1. The [Court is asked to] decide whether or not certain provisions of the Belgian linguistic legislation relating to education are in conformity with the requirements of Articles 8 and 14 of the Convention and Article 2 of the Protocol of 20th March 1952 (hereinafter referred to as "the Protocol").

2. The Applicants, who are parents of families of Belgian nationality, applied to the Commission both on their own behalf and on behalf of their children under age, of whom there are more than 800. Pointing out that they are French-speaking or that they express themselves most frequently in French, they want their children to be educated in that language ...

3. Though the six applications differ on a number of points, they are similar in many respects. For the time being it is sufficient to note that in substance they complain that the Belgian State:

—does not provide any French-language education in the municipalities where the Applicants live or, in the case of Kraainem, that the provision made for such education is, in their opinion, inadequate;

—withholds grants from any institutions in the said municipalities which may fail to comply with the linguistic provisions of the legislation for schools;

—refuses to homologate leaving certificates issued by such institutions;

—does not allow the Applicants' children to attend the French classes which exist in certain places;

—thereby obliges the Applicants either to enrol their children in local schools, a solution which they consider contrary to their aspirations, or to send them to school in the "Greater Brussels district", where the language of instruction is Dutch or French according to the child's mother-tongue or usual language or in the "French-speaking region" (Walloon area). Such "scholastic emigration" is said to entail serious risks and hardships.

4. The Applications in so far as they have been declared admissible by the Commission, allege that Articles 8 and 14 of the Convention and Article 2 of the Protocol have been violated. The violation is said to be a result of the

Applicants and their children being subjected to various provisions of the Act of 14th July 1932 "on language regulations in primary and intermediate education", the Act of 15th July 1932 "on the conferring of academic degrees", the Acts of 27th July 1955 and 29th May 1959, the Act of 30th July 1963 "relating to the use of languages in education" and the Act of 2nd August 1963 "on the use of languages in administrative matters" ....

THE LAW ...

I. THE MEANING AND SCOPE OF ARTICLE 2 OF THE PROTOCOL AND OF ARTICLES 8 AND 14 OF THE CONVENTION

1. The Court, in examining the complaints which have been referred to it, is at the outset confronted with the general question as to the extent to which any of the Articles of the Convention or Protocol may contain provisions touching the rights or freedoms of a child with respect to his education or of a parent with respect to the education of his child, and more especially in the matter of the language of instruction.

The Court notes that although certain further Articles (Articles 9 and 10 of the Convention) were invoked by the Applicants before the Commission, it is Article 2 of the Protocol and Articles 8 and 14 of the Convention alone which are dealt with in the arguments and submissions both of the Commission and the Belgian Government. While the provisions of the Convention and Protocol must be read as a whole, the Court considers that it is essentially upon the content and scope of these three Articles that the decision which it has to take turns.

2. The Court will address itself first to Article 2 of the Protocol because the Contracting States made express provision with reference to the right to education in this Article.

3. By the terms of the first sentence of this Article, "no person shall be denied the right to education."

In spite of its negative formulation, this provision uses the term "right" and speaks of a "right to education." Likewise the preamble to the Protocol specifies that the object of the Protocol lies in the collective enforcement of "rights and freedoms." There is therefore no doubt that Article 2 does enshrine a right.

It remains however to determine the content of this right and the scope of the obligation which is thereby placed upon States.

The negative formulation indicates, as is confirmed by the "preparatory work" ... that the Contracting Parties do not recognise such a right to education as would require them to establish at their own expense, or to subsidise, education of any particular type or at any particular level. However, it cannot be concluded from this that the State has no positive obligation to ensure respect for such a right as is protected by Article 2 of the Protocol. As a "right" does exist, it is secured, by virtue of Article 1 of the Convention, to everyone within the jurisdiction of a Contracting State.

To determine the scope of the "right to education", within the meaning of the first sentence of Article 2 of the Protocol, the Court must bear in mind the aim of this provision. It notes in this context that all member States of the Council of Europe possessed, at the time of the opening of the Protocol to their signature, and still do possess, a general and official educational system. There neither was, nor is now, therefore, any question of requiring each State to establish such a system, but merely of guaranteeing to persons subject to the jurisdiction of the Contracting Parties the right, in principle, to avail themselves of the means of instruction existing at a given time.

The Convention lays down no specific obligations concerning the extent of these means and the manner of their organisation or subsidisation. In particular the first sentence of Article 2 does not specify the language in which education must be conducted in order that the right to education should be respected. It does not contain precise provisions similar to those which appear in Articles 5(2) and 6(3)(a) and (e). However the right to education would be meaningless if it did not imply in favour of its beneficiaries, the right to be educated in the national language or in one of the national languages, as the case may be.

4. The first sentence of Article 2 of the Protocol consequently guarantees, in the first place, a right of access to educational institutions existing at a given time, but such access constitutes only a part of the right to education. For the "right to education" to be effective, it is further necessary that, inter alia, the individual who is the beneficiary should have the possibility of drawing profit from the education received, that is to say, the right to obtain, in conformity with the rules in force in each State, and in one form or another, official recognition of the studies which he has completed. The Court will deal with this matter in greater detail when it examines the last of the six specific questions listed in the submissions of those who appeared before it.

5. The right to education guaranteed by the first sentence of Article 2 of the Protocol by its very nature calls for regulation by the State, regulation which may vary in time and place according to the needs and resources of the community and of individuals. It goes without saying that such regulation

must never injure the substance of the right to education nor conflict with other rights enshrined in the Convention ...

8. According to Article 14 of the Convention, the enjoyment of the rights and freedoms set forth therein shall be secured without discrimination ("*sans distinction aucune*") on the ground, *inter alia*, of language; and by the terms of Article 5 of the Protocol, this same guarantee applies equally to the rights and freedoms set forth in this instrument. It follows that both Article 2 of the Protocol and Article 8 of the Convention must be interpreted and applied by the Court not only in isolation but also having regard to the guarantee laid down in Article 14.

9. While it is true that this guarantee has no independent existence in the sense that under the terms of Article 14 it relates solely to "rights and freedoms set forth in the Convention," a measure which in itself is in conformity with the requirements of the Article enshrining the right or freedom in question may however infringe this Article when read in conjunction with Article 14 for the reason that it is of a discriminatory nature.

Thus, persons subject to the jurisdiction of a Contracting State cannot draw from Article 2 of the Protocol the right to obtain from the public authorities the creation of a particular kind of educational establishment; nevertheless, a State which had set up such an establishment could not, in laying down entrance requirements, take discriminatory measures within the meaning of Article 14.

To recall a further example, cited in the course of the proceedings, Article 6 of the Convention does not compel States to institute a system of appeal courts. A State which does set up such courts consequently goes beyond its obligations under Article 6. However it would violate that Article, read in conjunction with Article 14, were it to debar certain persons from these remedies without a legitimate reason while making them available to others in respect of the same type of actions.

In such cases there would be a violation of a guaranteed right or freedom as it is proclaimed by the relevant Article read in conjunction with Article 14. It is as though the latter formed an integral part of each of the Articles laying down rights and freedoms. No distinctions should be made in this respect according to the nature of these rights and freedoms and of their correlative obligations, and for instance as to whether the respect due to the right concerned implies positive action or mere abstention. This is, moreover,

clearly shown by the very general nature of the terms employed in Article 14
...

10. In spite of the very general wording of the French version ("*sans distinction aucune*"), Article 14 does not forbid every difference in treatment in the exercise of the rights and freedoms recognised. This version must be read in the light of the more restrictive text of the English version ("without discrimination"). In addition, and in particular, one would reach absurd results were one to give Article 14 an interpretation as wide as that which the French version seems to imply. One would, in effect, be led to judge as contrary to the Convention every one of the many legal or administrative provisions which do not secure to everyone complete equality of treatment in the enjoyment of the rights and freedoms recognised. The competent national authorities are frequently confronted with situations and problems which, on account of differences inherent therein, call for different legal solutions; moreover, certain legal inequalities tend only to correct factual inequalities. The extensive interpretation mentioned above cannot consequently be accepted.

It is important, then, to look for the criteria which enable a determination to be made as to whether or not a given difference in treatment, concerning of course the exercise of one of the rights and freedoms set forth, contravenes Article 14. On this question the Court, following the principles which may be extracted from the legal practice of a large number of democratic States, holds that the principle of equality of treatment is violated if the distinction has no objective and reasonable justification. The existence of such a justification must be assessed in relation to the aim and effects of the measure under consideration, regard being had to the principles which normally prevail in democratic societies. A difference of treatment in the exercise of a right laid down in the Convention must not only pursue a legitimate aim: Article 14 is likewise violated when it is clearly established that there is no reasonable relationship of proportionality between the means employed and the aim sought to be realised.

In attempting to find out in a given case, whether or not there has been an arbitrary distinction, the Court cannot disregard those legal and factual features which characterise the life of the society in the State which, as a Contracting Party, has to answer for the measure in dispute. In so doing it cannot assume the rôle of the competent national authorities, for it would thereby lose sight of the subsidiary nature of the international machinery of collective enforcement established by the Convention. The national authorities remain free to choose the measures which they consider appropriate in those matters which are governed by the Convention. Review by the Court concerns only the conformity of these measures with the requirements of the Convention.

11. In the present case the Court notes that Article 14, even when read in conjunction with Article 2 of the Protocol, does not have the effect of guaranteeing to a child or to his parent the right to obtain instruction in a language of his choice. The object of these two Articles, read in conjunction, is more limited: it is to ensure that the right to education shall be secured by each Contracting Party to everyone within its jurisdiction without discrimination on the ground, for instance, of language. This is the natural and ordinary meaning of Article 14 read in conjunction with Article 2. Furthermore, to interpret the two provisions as conferring on everyone within the jurisdiction of a State a right to obtain education in the language of his own choice would lead to absurd results, for it would be open to anyone to claim any language of instruction in any of the territories of the Contracting Parties.

The Court notes that, where the Contracting Parties intended to confer upon everyone within their jurisdiction specific rights with respect to the use or understanding of a language, as in Article 5(2) and Article 6(3)(a) and (e) of the Convention, they did so in clear terms. It must be concluded that if they had intended to create for everyone within their jurisdiction a specific right with respect to the language of instruction, they would have done so in express terms in Article 2 of the Protocol. For this reason also, the Court cannot attribute to Article 14, when read in conjunction with Article 2 of the Protocol, a meaning which would secure to everyone within the jurisdiction of a Contracting Party a right to education conducted in the language of his own choice.

It remains true that, by virtue of Article 14, the enjoyment of the right to education and the right to respect of family life, guaranteed respectively by Article 2 of the Protocol and Article 8 of the Convention, are to be secured to everyone without discrimination on the ground, inter alia, of language.

12. In order to determine the questions referred to it, the Court will therefore examine whether or not there exist in the present case unjustified distinctions, that is to say discriminations, which affect the exercise of the rights enshrined in Article 2 of the Protocol and Article 8 of the Convention, read in conjunction with Article 14. In this examination, the Court will take into account the factual and legal features that characterise the situation in Belgium, which is a plurilingual State comprising several linguistic areas.

II. THE SIX QUESTIONS REFERRED TO THE COURT

A. As to the first question

2. The first question concerns the laws on the use of languages in education in the regions considered by the law as being unilingual, except for two aspects which are dealt with under the second and sixth questions. It relates, more precisely, to whether or not in the case of the Applicants, there is a violation of Article 2 of the Protocol and Articles 8 and 14 of the Convention, or of any of those Articles: "in so far as the Acts of 1932 prevented, and those of 1963 prevent, the establishment or the subsidisation by the State, of schools not in conformity with the general linguistic requirements."

3. On this point the facts of the case appear sufficiently from the general outline of the Acts in issue ... given above ...

4. Decision of the Court

13. The situation with which the second question is concerned is bound up with that dealt with in the first. The legal provisions mentioned in the first render impossible, in the Dutch unilingual region, the establishment or subsidising by the State of schools which conduct education in French. The legal and administrative measures to which the second question relates, merely supplement them: they tend to prevent the operating of "mixed language" schools which, in a unilingual region—in this case, the Dutch unilingual region—provide, in the form of non-subsidised classes and in addition to instruction given in the language of the region, full or partial instruction in another language. What is in issue, therefore, is a whole series of provisions with a common aim, namely, the protection of the linguistic homogeneity of the region.

The Court's reply to the second question is the same as that already given to the first. Neither Article 2 of the Protocol, nor Article 8 of the Convention are violated by the provisions in dispute.

As the first sentence of Article 2 of the Protocol taken by itself leaves intact the freedom of States to subsidise private schools or to refrain from so doing, the withdrawal of subsidies from schools which do not satisfy the requirements to which the State subjects the grant of such subsidies—in this case the condition that teaching should be conducted exclusively in accordance with the linguistic legislation - does not come within the scope of this Article.

There is likewise no breach of Article 8 of the Convention for the same reasons as were explained above in the reply to the first question.

Nor does the Court find any violation of Article 2 of the Protocol and of Article 8 ... read in conjunction with Article 14.

The Court has already stated, with respect to the first question, that measures which tend to ensure that, in the unilingual regions, the teaching language of official or subsidised schools should be exclusively that of the region, are not arbitrary and therefore not discriminatory. These measures do not prevent French-speaking parents who wish to provide a French education for their children from doing so, either in non-subsidised private schools, or in schools in the French unilingual region or in the Greater Brussels District.

The legislation to which the first question has reference does not permit the establishment or functioning, in the Dutch unilingual region, of official or subsidised schools providing education in French. The legislation with which the second question is concerned goes further; by the total withdrawal of subsidies, it makes it impossible, in the same region, for teaching in French to be conducted as a secondary activity by a subsidised Dutch-language school.

The Commission has emphasised that such a withdrawal "bears hard on the French-speaking children" in Flanders, particularly since the majority of the schools in Flanders which provided education in French were "mixed-language" schools.

However, while recognising that this is a harsh measure, the Court cannot share the Commission's opinion that such a hardship is forbidden by a joint reading of the first sentence of Article 2 of the Protocol and Article 14 of the Convention. This opinion could be accepted only if the "hardship" were to amount to a distinction in treatment of an arbitrary and therefore discriminatory nature. The Court has, however, found that, whatever their severity, the legal or administrative provisions touched on by the first question are based on objective criteria. The same is true of the measure here in question. Its purpose is to avoid the possibility of education which the State does not wish to subsidise—for reasons which are completely compatible with Article 2 of the Protocol and Articles 8 and 14 of the Convention—benefiting, in some way or another, from subsidies destined for education which is in conformity with the linguistic legislation. This purpose is plausible in itself and it is not for the Court to determine whether it is possible to realise it in another way.

For their part, the effects of this measure are solely of such a kind as to prevent subsidised and unsubsidised education being conducted in the same school. They in no way affect the freedom to organise, independently of subsidised education, private French-language education.

Hence the legal and administrative measures in question create no impediment to the exercise of the individual rights enshrined in the Convention with the result that the necessary balance between the collective interest of society and the individual rights guaranteed is respected. Consequently, they are not incompatible with the provisions of Article 2 of the Protocol and of Article 8 of the Convention, read in conjunction with Article 14.

C. As to the third question

14. The third question concerns the issue of whether or not in the case of the Applicants there is a violation of Article 2 of the Protocol and of Articles 8 and 14 of the Convention or of any of those Articles, "with regard to the special status conferred by Section 7, third paragraph, of the Act of 2nd August 1963, on six communes, of which Kraainem is one, on the periphery of Brussels," this being without prejudice to the conditions of residence referred to in the fifth question.

1. The Facts

15. Situated some kilometres to the east of Brussels, the commune of Kraainem belonged, under the system created by the 1932 Acts, to the unilingual Flemish region. Following "a considerable migration of French-speaking persons from Brussels" to the "more airy periphery" and as a result of a "spontaneous phenomenon (...) of francisation," Kraainem gradually lost its character of a purely Flemish locality. The last linguistic census which took place in 1947, showed that 47% of the population were French-speaking. According to the signatories of Application No. 1677/62, an "indirect linguistic census" was taken in Kraainem on 31 December 1961 despite the Act of 24th July 1961: the commune administration, having distributed bilingual forms to the population, ascertained that 61.18% of the population was French-speaking, and today it is 65%. On the other hand, the Belgian Government is of the opinion that these "so called statistics", "compiled in circumstances far removed from objective scientific research," should be treated "with the greatest reserve."

Be this as it may, Kraainem at present forms part neither of "the Dutch-language region," nor "the French-language region," nor yet again of "the Greater Brussels area," the respective composition of which is fixed by Sections 3, 4 and 6 of the Act of 2nd August 1963. Under Section 7(1) of the same Act, it forms, together with five other communes in the immediate neighbourhood of the capital of the Kingdom ... "a separate administrative district" with its own "special status." This status is essentially defined in paragraphs 2 and 3 of Section 7. Paragraph 2 in substance provides that the six communes concerned shall enjoy a bilingual system "in administrative matters," at least in relations between the local services and the public. As regards paragraph 3, which is applicable to "the question of schools," it is worded as follows:

A. Teaching shall be in Dutch.

The second language may be taught at the primary level to the extent of four hours a week in the second form and eight hours a week in the third and fourth forms.

B. Nursery and primary schooling may be given to children in French if that is their maternal or usual language and if the head of the family resides in one of these communes.

Such schooling may be provided only on the request of 16 heads of families residing within the commune.

The commune to which such an application is made must organise such schooling.

The teaching of the second national language shall be compulsory in primary schools to the extent of four hours a week in the second form and eight hours a week in the third and fourth forms.

C. The teaching of the second language may include exercises of revising the other subjects of the programme.

For the six communes in question, the linguistic control set up by ... the Act of 30th July 1963 is supplemented by that exercised by the Government commissioner, Vice-Governor of the province of Brabant (Section 7 (1) and (5) of the Act of 2nd August 1963) ...

4. Decision of the Court

19. The residence conditions to which the fifth question relates being reserved until later, the special status conferred by Section 7 (3) of the Act of 2nd August 1963 on six communes on the periphery of Brussels, including

Kraainem, does not violate, in the case of the signatories of Application No. 1677/62, any of the three Articles invoked by them before the Commission.

As is the case with the legal and administrative provisions with which the first and second questions are concerned, the status of the six communes involves neither a denial of the right to education, guaranteed by the first sentence of Article 2 of the Protocol, nor any derogation from the right to respect for private and family life enshrined in Article 8 of the Convention.

On this point, the Court first emphasises that the French-language nursery and primary schools existing in the six communes are open to the children of the signatories of Application No. 1677/62. The right to education of these children, within the meaning of the first sentence of Article 2 of the Protocol, is thus respected.

Moreover, no interference with the exercise of the right to respect for private and family life protected by Article 8 of the Convention can be found in this case. In alleging before the Commission that this provision had been violated, the Applicants have misunderstood its scope. To require a child to study in depth that national language which is not his own, cannot be characterised as an act of "depersonalisation." As regards the decision of certain Applicants to send their children to a French-language school in Greater Brussels, rather than to a school governed by Section 7 (3) (B) of the Act of 2nd August 1963, this is the result of their own choice and not of an interference by the authorities in their private and family life.

It remains to be decided whether the measures in issue violate the first sentence of Article 2 of the Protocol or Article 8 of the Convention, read in conjunction with Article 14.

Here again the reply must be negative.

The six communes in question belong to an area which is by tradition Dutch-speaking. In consideration of the large number of French-speaking persons who are resident there, the legislature has established a system which departs from the principle of territoriality. It makes the organisation of official or subsidised education in French subject to the deposit of a request by 16 heads of family living in the commune in question; moreover, this education is compulsorily accompanied by a study in depth of Dutch. In so doing, the Act does not go outside limits drawn according to objective criteria and is based on a public interest. Furthermore, the establishment and maintenance of education conducted in French is possible in the communes concerned. Finally, the fact that this education is tied to a study in depth of Dutch, whereas the study of French remains optional in Dutch schools in the same communes, does not constitute a discrimination as the latter belong to a region which is, by tradition, Dutch-speaking.

As regards the argument based on the absence, at Kraainem, of official or subsidised secondary education in French, the Court recalls that Article 2 of the Protocol does not require the Contracting States to establish educational establishments: the question is thus one which is left to the evaluation of the competent national authorities. The Court also notes once again that in Belgium compulsory schooling extends essentially to primary education. It points out, incidentally, that Kraainem does not even possess, at present, education in Dutch at the secondary level.

D. As to the fourth question

20. The fourth question concerns the issue of whether or not in the case of the Applicants, there is a violation of Article 2 of the Protocol and Articles 8 and 14 of the Convention, or of any of those Articles, "with regard to the conditions on which children whose parents reside outside the Greater Brussels district may be enrolled in the schools of that district ...."

1. The Facts

21. The second, third, fourth and fifth paragraphs of Section 17 of the Act of 30th July 1963 provide that:

> In all cases in which the child's language of instruction is determined by his maternal or usual language, the head of the school may register the child for a particular system only on production of one of the following:
>
> (a) a certificate issued by the head of the school which the pupil has just left, certifying that his previous schooling has been through that language;
>
> (b) a language declaration by the head of the child's family, and approved by the language inspectorate in all cases where the inspectorate has no doubts as to the correctness of such declaration;
>
> (c) a decision by the Commission or Board referred to in Section 18.
>
> Where a child is registered at a nursery school for the first time, the head of the school may, however, admit him on production of a language declaration. The latter must within one month be forwarded to the language inspectorate for verification.

In the case of pupils who enrol in a school in the Greater Brussels district and whose parents reside outside that district, the language of instruction shall, in the absence of any declaration to the contrary made by the head of the family and approved by the language inspectorate, be the language of the region in which the parents are resident.

The King shall lay down standard forms for the certificate and declaration which shall comprise any information likely to facilitate the verification of their correctness.

A Royal Decree was issued on 30 November 1966 which implemented this last paragraph; two other Royal Decrees of the same date stipulated the status and rules governing the functioning of the language inspectorate as provided for by Section 18 of the Act of 30th July 1963 ...

4. Decision of the Court

25. The conditions which regulate the enrolment in the schools of the Greater Brussels District of children whose parents are resident outside this district, are laid down in Section 17 of the Act of 30th July 1963. The application of this provision does not, in the case of the Applicants, violate any of the three Articles of the Convention and Protocol invoked by them before the Commission.

The Court recalls that the first sentence of Article 2 of the Protocol does not, by itself, imply any requirement of a linguistic nature and that Article 8 of the Convention does not lay down any personal right of parents in relation to the education of their children. It further finds that the legal provision in issue has not caused unjustifiable disturbance to the private and family life of the Applicants.

Nor does the Court find, on the point under consideration, any discrimination contrary to Article 14 of the Convention, read in conjunction with the first sentence of Article 2 of the Protocol or with Article 8 of the Convention; such discrimination has not, in any case, been shown by the Applicants.

In its memorial of 16th December 1965, the Commission drew the attention of the Court to the fact that where there exists a dual system of official or subsidised education, as for instance at Brussels, parents are not free to choose between French and Dutch as the language of education for their children. In the present case, this question assumes a theoretical character since the Applicants declare themselves to be French-speaking and wish their children to be educated in French; indeed the Commission has not failed to point out this fact. The Court cannot settle a problem which does not arise in the present case.

E. As to the fifth question

26. The fifth question concerns the issue as to whether or not, in the case of the Applicants, there is a violation of Article 2 of the Protocol or of Articles 8 and 14 of the Convention, or of any of those Articles ...

4. Decision of the Court

32. The Court will examine in turn the legal and administrative measures governing access to French-language education at, on the one hand, Louvain and Heverlee, and, on the other, the six communes with special facilities.

Louvain and Heverlee belong to the Dutch-unilingual region. Although the legislature has authorised the maintenance of French-language education there, it has done so, above all, in consideration of the needs arising from the bilingual nature of the University of Louvain. The principles which govern the functioning of education in French in the two communes likewise determine the entrance requirements to this education. The benefits conferred by the provisions in dispute ... therefore depend upon their purpose. Essentially, they are accorded to the French-speaking teaching staff, employees and students of the University of Louvain in whose absence the establishment could no longer retain its bilingual character. Likewise, if the French classes at Louvain and Heverlee are still open to children of French-speaking families living outside the Dutch-unilingual region, it is because they serve as teacher training classes for the bilingual University of Louvain. As for the privilege granted to certain children of foreign nationality, this is justified by the customs of international courtesy. Consequently, the exclusion of French-speaking children living in the Dutch unilingual region whose parents are not members of the teaching staff, students or employees of the University, does not amount to a discriminatory measure in view of the legitimacy of the specific objective of the legislature.

The situation is completely different in the case of the six communes "with special facilities," which belong to the agglomeration surrounding Brussels, the capital of a bilingual State and an international centre. According to the information supplied to the Court, the number of French-speaking families in these communes is high; they constitute, up to a certain point, a zone of a "mixed" character.

It is in recognition of this fact that Section 7 of the Act of 2nd August 1963 departed from the territorial principle, as the Court noted when dealing with the third question. It appears, indeed, from its first paragraph that the six communes no longer form part of the Dutch unilingual region, but constitute a "distinct administrative district" invested with its own "special status." From this the second paragraph draws a first set of consequences: it provides in substance that the six communes concerned enjoy a bilingual system "in administrative matters." As to the third paragraph, the compatibility of which with Articles 8 and 14 of the Convention and with Article 2 of the Protocol is contested by the Applicants, it applies to "educational matter." It provides that the language of instruction is Dutch in the six communes; it requires nevertheless, the organisation, for the benefit of children whose maternal or usual language is French, of official or subsidised education in French at the nursery and primary levels, on condition that it is asked for by sixteen heads of family. However, this education is not available to children whose parents live outside the communes under consideration. The Dutch classes in the same communes, on the other hand, in principle accept all children, whatever their maternal or usual language and place of residence of their parents. The residence condition affecting therefore only one of the two linguistic groups, the Court is called upon to examine whether there results therefrom a discrimination contrary to Article 14 of the Convention, read in conjunction with the first sentence of Article 2 of the Protocol or with Article 8 of the Convention.

Such a measure is not justified in the light of the requirements of the Convention in that it involves elements of discriminatory treatment of certain individuals, founded even more on language than on residence.

First, this measure is not applied uniformly to families speaking one or the other national language. The Dutch-speaking children resident in the French unilingual region, which incidentally is very near, have access to Dutch-language schools in the six communes, whereas French-speaking children living in the Dutch unilingual region are refused access to French-language schools in those same communes. Likewise, the Dutch classes in the six communes are open to Dutch-speaking children of the Dutch unilingual region whereas the French classes in those communes are closed to the French-speaking children of that region.

Such a situation, moreover, contrasts with that which arises from the possibility of access to French-language schools in the Greater Brussels District, which are open to French-speaking children irrespective of their parents' place of residence ....

It consequently appears that the residence condition is not imposed in the interest of schools, for administrative or financial reasons: it proceeds solely, in the case of the Applicants, from considerations relating to language.

Cases

Furthermore the measure in issue does not fully respect, in the case of the majority of the Applicants and their children, the relationship of proportionality between the means employed and the aim sought. In this regard the Court, in particular, points out that the impossibility of entering official or subsidised French-language schools in the six communes "with special facilities" affects the children of the Applicants in the exercise of their right to education, all the more in that there exist no such schools in the communes in which they live.

The enjoyment of the right to education as the Court conceives it, and more precisely that of the right of access to existing schools, is not therefore on the point under consideration secured to everyone without discrimination on the ground, in particular, of language. In other words, the measure in question is, in this respect, incompatible with the first sentence of Article 2 of the Protocol, read in conjunction with Article 14 of the Convention. In these circumstances, the Court does not consider it necessary to examine whether the said measure respects Article 8 of the Convention, read in conjunction with Article 14 or in isolation.

F. As to the sixth question

33. The sixth question concerns the issue of whether or not, in the case of the Applicants, there is a violation of Article 2 of the Protocol and Articles 8 and 14 of the Convention, or of any of these Articles "[i]n so far as the Acts of 1932 resulted, and those of 1963 result, in absolute refusal to homologate certificates relating to secondary schooling not in conformity with the language requirements in education" ....

4. Decision of the Court

42. The provisions of the Acts of 1932 and 1963 which provided for or still provide for the refusal of homologation of certificates relating to secondary schooling not in conformity with the language requirements in education, infringe neither the first sentence of Article 2 of the Protocol nor Article 8 of the Convention considered by themselves.

The right to education, which is enshrined in the first sentence of Article 2 of the Protocol is not frustrated by the Acts criticised. In particular the right to obtain, in conformity with the rules in force in each State and in one form or another, the official recognition of studies completed has not been disregarded by these legal provisions. Leaving this right intact, they merely subject its exercise to the express condition of an examination before a central board. This examination does not constitute a test of excessive difficulty. It appears from the documents produced and the statements made

- 356 -

before the Court that the candidate may take it in two stages and in the national language of his choice and that any candidate who fails may present himself before the Central Board as many times as he wishes. Moreover, the percentage of failures recorded before the Central Board at the higher level of secondary education is in no way abnormal. Moreover, the entrance fees for the examination are very small.

As regards Article 8 of the Convention, invoked by the Applicants before the Commission, it is impossible to see how the system of the Central Board for secondary education could entail a violation of the right to respect for private and family life. Here again, the Court finds that there is no violation.

It remains to be decided whether the legal provisions referred to in the sixth question are compatible with the first sentence of Article 2 of the Protocol, read in conjunction with Article 14 of the Convention.

This question must be examined in connection with the criteria which the Court has set out above for determining whether a given measure is of a discriminatory character within the meaning of Article 14.

On this matter, the Court first notes that the legislature, in adopting the system in issue, has pursued an objective concerned with the public interest: to favour linguistic unity within the unilingual regions and, in particular, to promote among pupils knowledge in depth of the usual language of the region. This objective concerned with the public interest does not, in itself, involve any element of discrimination.

As regards the relationship of proportionality between the means employed and the objective aimed at, greater difficulties are encountered in finding the answer.

One of them lies in the fact that the children who, as holders of a certificate that is not admissible for homologation for purely linguistic reasons, must take an examination before the Central Board, are in a less advantageous position than those pupils who have obtained a school leaving certificate which is admissible for homologation. However, this inequality in treatment in general results from a difference relating to the administrative system of the school attended: in the first of the two cases mentioned above, the position usually is that the establishment is one which, by virtue of the legislation in force, is not subject to school inspection; in the second, on the other hand, the certificate is necessarily issued by a school which is subjected to such inspection. Thus the State treats unequally situations which are themselves unequal. It does not deprive the pupil of the profit to be drawn from his studies. The holder of a certificate not admissible for homologation may, indeed, obtain official recognition of his studies by presenting himself before the Central Board. The exercise of the right to education is not therefore fettered in a discriminatory manner within the meaning of Article 14.

It is not, however, impossible that the application of the legal provisions in issue might lead, in individual cases, to results which put in question the existence of a reasonable relationship of proportionality between the means employed and the objective aimed at, to such an extent as to constitute discrimination.

During the oral hearing before the Court, the Commission put forward the case of a refusal of homologation in respect of a pupil who, from the beginning of his secondary studies, had received an education not in conformity with the linguistic legislation, even if only for a few months, and whose later studies took place in accordance with the provisions of this legislation and this in an establishment subject to school inspection. Even in a case of this kind, where it is not reasonably possible to speak of an evasion of the law, the legal provisions complained of would prevent the award of a certificate admissible for homologation.

Such a result, to the extent to which it may follow from the application of the law, must cause serious doubts as to its compatibility with the right to education—the enjoyment of which the Convention and the Protocol secure to everyone without any discrimination.

In the present case, however, it has been neither established nor even alleged that there is such a result with respect to any one of the children of the Applicants.

The examination of the case thus envisaged does not prevent the Court from concluding that the legal provisions referred to in the sixth question are not, in themselves, in contradiction with the requirements of the Convention ...

Nachova v. Bulgaria

ECtHR (Grand Chamber), Appls. Nos. 43577/98 & 43579/98,
(6 July 2005).

[This leading case involved the murder of two Roma, Mr. Angelov and Mr. Petkov by Bulgarian policemen. The Bulgarian government was found to be responsible for a violation of the right to life because the police had used excessive force. The parts of the judgment that are excerpted below consider whether the Bulgarian government has also violated article 14 ECHR in conjunction with article 2 by its failure to adequately investigate the discriminatory motives behind the killings.]

IV. ALLEGED VIOLATION OF ARTICLE 14 IN CONJUNCTION WITH ARTICLE 2 OF THE CONVENTION

124. The applicants alleged a violation of Article 14 of the Convention in that prejudice and hostile attitudes towards persons of Roma origin had played a role in the events leading up to the deaths of Mr. Angelov and Mr. Petkov. They also argued that the authorities had failed in their duty to investigate possible racist motives in their killing. The Government disputed the applicants' allegations ....

A. The Chamber judgment

126. The Chamber noted that in cases of deprivation of life Articles 2 and 14 of the Convention combined imposed a duty on State authorities to conduct an effective investigation irrespective of the victim's racial or ethnic origin. It also considered that the authorities had the additional duty to take all reasonable steps to unmask any racist motive in an incident involving the use of force by law-enforcement agents.

127. In the present case, despite Mr. M.M.'s statement about racist verbal abuse and other evidence which should have alerted the authorities to the need to investigate possible racist motives, no such investigation had been undertaken. The authorities had on that account failed in their duty under Article 14 of the Convention taken together with Article 2.

128. Considering that the particular evidentiary difficulties involved in proving discrimination called for a specific approach to the issue of proof, the Chamber held that in cases where the authorities had not pursued lines of inquiry that had been clearly warranted in their investigation into acts of violence by State agents and had disregarded evidence of possible discrimination, the Court might, when examining complaints under Article

14 of the Convention, draw negative inferences or shift the burden of proof to the respondent Government.

129. On the facts of the case, the Chamber considered that the conduct of the investigating authorities – which had omitted to refer to a number of disquieting facts such as the excessive nature of the force used by Major G. and the evidence that he had uttered a racist slur – warranted a shift of the burden of proof. It thus fell to the respondent Government to satisfy the Court, on the basis of additional evidence or a convincing explanation of the facts, that the events complained of had not been shaped by discrimination on the part of State agents.

130. As the Government had not offered a convincing explanation, and noting that there had been previous cases in which the Court had found that law enforcement officers in Bulgaria had subjected Roma to violence resulting in death, the Chamber concluded that there had also been a violation of the substantive aspect of Article 14 taken together with Article 2 of the Convention.

B. The parties' submissions

1. The Government

131. The Government took issue with the Chamber's finding of a violation of Article 14, stating that the Chamber had relied solely on general material about events outside the scope of the case and on two fortuitous facts – the testimony of Mr M.M. about an offensive remark that Major G. had allegedly made against him, not against the victims, and the fact that the events had taken place in a Roma neighbourhood. In the Government's view, these considerations could not justify, by any acceptable standard of proof, a conclusion that the use of firearms had been motivated by racial prejudice.

132. The Government emphasised that the Court had always required "proof beyond reasonable doubt." The burden of proof could shift where the events in issue were wholly, or in large part, within the exclusive knowledge of the authorities, as in the case of death occurring during detention. However, no such circumstances had obtained in the present case.

133. As there had been no racial element in the incident at issue, any further investigation by the domestic authorities would have been to no avail. The Government accepted that racially motivated violence had to be punished more severely than violent acts without a racial overtone. However, States could not be required to investigate for possible racist attitudes in the absence of sufficient evidence supporting the allegations of racism. The Government considered that the Chamber's approach would lead to the

responsibility of Contracting States being engaged in each and every case where an allegation of discrimination, however unfounded, had been made.

134. Moreover, the Chamber's approach lacked clarity and foreseeability. In particular, it was contradictory to state – as the Chamber did – that the Court could not examine intent and state of mind in the context of Article 2 of the Convention and then to reach the conclusion that there had been a substantive violation of Article 14 in conjunction with Article 2 because the death of Mr. Angelov and Mr. Petkov had been the result of a racially motivated act.

135. The Government, in both their written and oral submissions, gave a detailed overview of legislation, social programmes and other measures that had been adopted in recent years in Bulgaria with the aim of combating discrimination and intolerance and promoting the integration of Roma in society.

2. The applicants

136. ... the applicants argued that the Convention had so far failed to provide effective protection against racial discrimination and invited the Grand Chamber to adopt an innovative interpretation of Article 14. The applicants welcomed the Chamber's views that Contracting States were under a duty to investigate possible racist motives for an act of violence and that the burden of proof might shift to the respondent Government. In their written submissions they considered, however, that the standard of proof in discrimination cases should not be "proof beyond reasonable doubt" and that in cases such as the instant case the burden of proof should always shift to the Government once a prima facie case of discrimination had been established...

137. As to the facts of the case, the applicants stated that there had been a substantive violation of Article 14 as they had established a prima facie case of discrimination and the Government had failed to present evidence to the contrary. In particular, the ethnicity of Mr. Angelov and Mr. Petkov had been known to the officers who had sought to arrest them. Major G. had addressed racially offensive remarks to a bystander on the basis of his Roma origin. Also, strong inferences were to be drawn from the fact that Major G. had used grossly disproportionate firepower in a populated area, the Roma neighbourhood of the village. Those facts should be assessed against the background of persistent discrimination against Roma on the part of law-enforcement agents in Bulgaria. Furthermore, the authorities should have investigated whether the deaths of Mr. Angelov and Mr. Petkov had been motivated by racial prejudice but had failed to do so.

3. The interveners

(a) The European Roma Rights Centre

138. The Centre pointed out that over the last few years various international bodies and non-governmental organisations had reported numerous incidents of ill-treatment and killing of Roma by law enforcement agents and private individuals of Bulgarian ethnic origin. It was widely acknowledged that racially-motivated violence against Roma was a serious problem in Bulgaria. The Roma community was furthermore largely excluded from social life as it laboured under high levels of poverty, illiteracy and unemployment.

139. Despite high levels of racially-motivated violence and repeated calls on the part of international bodies, such as the UN Committee Against Torture, for the establishment of "an effective, reliable and independent complaint system" and for adequate investigation of police abuse, the authorities had failed to act. Bulgarian penal legislation did not treat racist animus as an aggravating circumstance in cases of violent offences. In 1999 the Bulgarian authorities had acknowledged the need for an amendment but had never taken any action. Also, Article 162 of the Criminal Code, which made racist attacks punishable, provided for lighter sentences than the provisions dealing with common bodily harm. As a result, Article 162 was never applied, charges were brought – if at all – under the general provisions on bodily harm or murder and the racist nature of the attacks remained hidden. There was a climate of impunity, as noted by the Court in its Velikova and Anguelova judgments.

(b) Interights

140. Interights criticised the Court's "beyond reasonable doubt" standard as erecting insurmountable obstacles to establishing discrimination. In Interights' submission, those national jurisdictions in which judicial protection against discrimination was strongest tended to be common-law jurisdictions, which applied a "balance of probabilities" standard of proof for discrimination cases. While in civil-law jurisdictions judges enjoyed a fact-finding role and were therefore, theoretically at least, able to satisfy themselves to a higher standard of proof, a review of judicial responses to discrimination suggested that the common-law approach lent itself to stronger judicial protection against discrimination. In Interights' submission, the Court had in practice adopted an intermediate standard, as it did not require the same high level of proof as in criminal trials, but its approach lacked clarity and foreseeability.

141. Interights further stated that international practice supported the view that in discrimination cases the burden of proof should shift to the respondent upon the claimant establishing a prima facie case. That was the approach adopted by several EU directives, by the Court of Justice of the European Communities, the United Nations Human Rights Committee and the national courts in a number of European countries and also in the United States, Canada and other countries.

142. Interights also cited examples of the types of evidence that national jurisdictions had accepted as capable of establishing a prima facie case of discrimination: evidence of a "general picture" of disadvantage, "common knowledge" of discrimination, facts from "general life", facts that were generally known, background facts and circumstantial evidence. Relying on inferences was also a common approach.

(c) Open Society Justice Initiative (OSJI)

143. The OSJI commented on the obligation of States, in international and comparative law, to investigate racial discrimination and violence. In their view, the widely accepted principle that no effective protection of substantive rights was possible without adequate procedural guarantees was also applicable to discrimination cases. Therefore, a procedural duty was inherent in Article 14 of the Convention. Furthermore, in accordance with the prevailing European and international practice racial motivation was an aggravating circumstance in criminal law and, hence, subject to investigation. States had, therefore, a duty to investigate acts of racial violence. That was an ex officio obligation and arose whenever there was a reasonable suspicion that a racially motivated act had been committed.

C. The Court's assessment

1. Whether the respondent State is liable for deprivation of life on the basis of the victims' race or ethnic origin

144. The Court has established above that agents of the respondent State unlawfully killed Mr. Angelov and Mr. Petkov in violation of Article 2 of the Convention. The applicants have further alleged that there has been a separate violation of Article 14 of the Convention in that racial prejudice played a role in their deaths.

145. Discrimination is treating differently, without an objective and reasonable justification, persons in relevantly similar situations .... Racial violence is a particular affront to human dignity and, in view of its perilous consequences, requires from the authorities special vigilance and a vigorous reaction. It is for this reason that the authorities must use all available means

to combat racism and racist violence, thereby reinforcing democracy's vision of a society in which diversity is not perceived as a threat but as a source of its enrichment. The Court will revert to that issue below.

146. Faced with the applicants' complaint of a violation of Article 14, as formulated, the Court's task is to establish whether or not racism was a causal factor in the shooting that led to the deaths of Mr. Angelov and Mr. Petkov so as to give rise to a breach of Article 14 of the Convention taken in conjunction with Article 2.

147. It notes in this connection that in assessing evidence, the Court has adopted the standard of proof "beyond reasonable doubt". However, it has never been its purpose to borrow the approach of the national legal systems that use that standard. Its role is not to rule on criminal guilt or civil liability but on Contracting States' responsibility under the Convention. The specificity of its task under Article 19 of the Convention – to ensure the observance by the Contracting States of their engagement to secure the fundamental rights enshrined in the Convention – conditions its approach to the issues of evidence and proof. In the proceedings before the Court, there are no procedural barriers to the admissibility of evidence or pre-determined formulae for its assessment. It adopts the conclusions that are, in its view, supported by the free evaluation of all evidence, including such inferences as may flow from the facts and the parties' submissions. According to its established case-law, proof may follow from the coexistence of sufficiently strong, clear and concordant inferences or of similar unrebutted presumptions of fact. Moreover, the level of persuasion necessary for reaching a particular conclusion and, in this connection, the distribution of the burden of proof are intrinsically linked to the specificity of the facts, the nature of the allegation made and the Convention right at stake. The Court is also attentive to the seriousness that attaches to a ruling that a Contracting State has violated fundamental rights ....

148. The applicants have referred to several separate facts and they maintain that sufficient inferences of a racist act can be drawn from them.

149. First, the applicants considered revealing the fact that Major G. had discharged bursts of automatic fire in a populated area, in disregard of the public's safety. Considering that there was no rational explanation for such behaviour, the applicants were of the view that racist hatred on the part of Major G. was the only plausible explanation and that he would not have acted in that manner in a non-Roma neighbourhood.

150. The Court notes, however, that the use of firearms in the circumstances at issue was regrettably not prohibited under the relevant domestic regulations, a flagrant deficiency which it has earlier condemned .... The military police officers carried their automatic rifles "in accordance with the rules" and were instructed to use all necessary means to effect the arrest .... The possibility that Major G. was simply adhering strictly to the regulations and would have acted as he did in any similar context, regardless of the ethnicity of the fugitives, cannot therefore be excluded. While the relevant regulations were fundamentally flawed and fell well short of the Convention requirements on the protection of the right to life, there is nothing to suggest that Major G. would not have used his weapon in a non-Roma neighbourhood.

151. It is true, as the Court has found above, that Major G.'s conduct during the arrest operation calls for serious criticism in that he used grossly excessive force .... Nonetheless, it cannot be excluded either that his reaction was shaped by the inadequacy of the legal framework governing the use of firearms and by the fact that he was trained to operate within that framework ....

152. The applicants also stated that the military police officers' attitude had been strongly influenced by their knowledge of the victims' Roma origin. However, it is not possible to speculate on whether or not Mr. Angelov's and Mr. Petkov's Roma origin had any bearing on the officers' perception of them. Furthermore, there is evidence that some of the officers knew one or both of the victims personally....

153. The applicants referred to the statement given by Mr M. M., a neighbour of one of the victims, who reported that Major G. had shouted at him "you damn Gypsies" immediately after the shooting. While such evidence of a racial slur being uttered in connection with a violent act should have led the authorities in this case to verify Mr M.M.'s statement, that statement is of itself an insufficient basis for concluding that the respondent State is liable for a racist killing.

154. Lastly, the applicants relied on information about numerous incidents involving the use of force against Roma by Bulgarian law enforcement officers that had not resulted in the conviction of those responsible.

155. It is true that a number of organisations, including intergovernmental bodies, have expressed concern about the occurrence of such incidents .... However, the Court cannot lose sight of the fact that its sole concern is to ascertain whether in the case at hand the killing of Mr Angelov and Mr Petkov was motivated by racism.

156. In its judgment the Chamber decided to shift the burden of proof to the respondent Government on account of the authorities' failure to carry out an effective investigation into the alleged racist motive for the killing. The inability of the Government to satisfy the Chamber that the events complained of were not shaped by racism resulted in its finding a substantive violation of Article 14 of the Convention, taken together with Article 2.

157. The Grand Chamber reiterates that in certain circumstances, where the events lie wholly, or in large part, within the exclusive knowledge of the authorities, as in the case of death of a person within their control in custody, the burden of proof may be regarded as resting on the authorities to provide a satisfactory and convincing explanation of, in particular, the causes of the detained person's death ..... The Grand Chamber cannot exclude the possibility that in certain cases of alleged discrimination it may require the respondent Government to disprove an arguable allegation of discrimination and – if they fail to do so – find a violation of Article 14 of the Convention on that basis. However, where it is alleged – as here – that a violent act was motivated by racial prejudice, such an approach would amount to requiring the respondent Government to prove the absence of a particular subjective attitude on the part of the person concerned. While in the legal systems of many countries proof of the discriminatory effect of a policy or decision will dispense with the need to prove intent in respect of alleged discrimination in employment or the provision of services, that approach is difficult to transpose to a case where it is alleged that an act of violence was racially motivated. The Grand Chamber, departing from the Chamber's approach, does not consider that the alleged failure of the authorities to carry out an effective investigation into the alleged racist motive for the killing should shift the burden of proof to the respondent Government with regard to the alleged violation of Article 14 in conjunction with the substantive aspect of Article 2 of the Convention. The question of the authorities' compliance with their procedural obligation is a separate issue, to which the Court will revert below.

158. In sum, having assessed all relevant elements, the Court does not consider that it has been established that racist attitudes played a role in Mr. Angelov's and Mr. Petkov's deaths.

159. It thus finds that there has been no violation of Article 14 of the Convention taken together with Article 2 in its substantive aspect.

2. Procedural aspect: whether the respondent State complied with its obligation to investigate possible racist motives

(a) General principles

160. The Grand Chamber endorses the Chamber's analysis in the present case of the Contracting States' procedural obligation to investigate possible racist motives for acts of violence. The Chamber stated ... :

> ... States have a general obligation under Article 2 of the Convention to conduct an effective investigation in cases of deprivation of life.

> ... That obligation must be discharged without discrimination, as required by Article 14 of the Convention... [W]here there is suspicion that racial attitudes induced a violent act it is particularly important that the official investigation is pursued with vigour and impartiality, having regard to the need to reassert continuously society's condemnation of racism and ethnic hatred and to maintain the confidence of minorities in the ability of the authorities to protect them from the threat of racist violence. Compliance with the State's positive obligations under Article 2 of the Convention requires that the domestic legal system must demonstrate its capacity to enforce criminal law against those who unlawfully took the life of another, irrespective of the victim's racial or ethnic origin
> ...

> ... [W]hen investigating violent incidents and, in particular, deaths at the hands of State agents, State authorities have the additional duty to take all reasonable steps to unmask any racist motive and to establish whether or not ethnic hatred or prejudice may have played a role in the events. Failing to do so and treating racially induced violence and brutality on an equal footing with cases that have no racist overtones would be to turn a blind eye to the specific nature of acts that are particularly destructive of fundamental rights. A failure to make a distinction in the way in which situations that are essentially different are handled may constitute unjustified treatment irreconcilable with Article 14 of the Convention .... In order to maintain public confidence in their law enforcement machinery, Contracting States must ensure that in the investigation of incidents involving the use of force a distinction is made both in

- 367 -

their legal systems and in practice between cases of excessive use of force and of racist killing.

Admittedly, proving racial motivation will often be extremely difficult in practice. The respondent State's obligation to investigate possible racist overtones to a violent act is an obligation to use best endeavours and not absolute .... The authorities must do what is reasonable in the circumstances to collect and secure the evidence, explore all practical means of discovering the truth and deliver fully reasoned, impartial and objective decisions, without omitting suspicious facts that may be indicative of a racially induced violence.

161. The Grand Chamber would add that the authorities' duty to investigate the existence of a possible link between racist attitudes and an act of violence is an aspect of their procedural obligations arising under Article 2 of the Convention, but may also be seen as implicit in their responsibilities under Article 14 of the Convention taken in conjunction with Article 2 to secure the enjoyment of the right to life without discrimination. Owing to the interplay of the two provisions, issues such as those in the present case may fall to be examined under one of the two provisions only, with no separate issue arising under the other, or may require examination under both Articles. This is a question to be decided in each case on its facts and depending on the nature of the allegations made.

(b) Application of these principles in the present case

162. The Court has already found that the Bulgarian authorities violated Article 2 of the Convention in that they failed to conduct a meaningful investigation into the deaths of Mr. Angelov and Mr. Petkov .... It considers that in the present case it must examine separately the complaint that there was also a failure to investigate a possible causal link between alleged racist attitudes and the killing of the two men.

163. The authorities investigating the deaths of Mr. Angelov and Mr. Petkov had before them the statement of Mr. M.M., a neighbour of the victims, who stated that Major G. had shouted: "You damn Gypsies" while pointing a gun at him immediately after the shooting .... That statement, seen against the background of the many published accounts of the existence in Bulgaria of prejudice and hostility against Roma, called for verification.

164. The Grand Chamber considers – as the Chamber did – that any evidence of racist verbal abuse being uttered by law enforcement agents in connection with an operation involving the use of force against persons from an ethnic or other minority is highly relevant to the question whether or not

unlawful, hatred-induced violence has taken place. Where such evidence comes to light in the investigation, it must be verified and – if confirmed – a thorough examination of all the facts should be undertaken in order to uncover any possible racist motives.

165. Furthermore, the fact that Major G. used grossly excessive force against two unarmed and non-violent men also called for a careful investigation.

166. In sum, the investigator and the prosecutors involved in the present case had before them plausible information which was sufficient to alert them to the need to carry out an initial verification and, depending on the outcome, an investigation into possible racist overtones in the events that led to the death of the two men.

167. However, the authorities did nothing to verify Mr. M.M.'s statement. They omitted to question witnesses about it. Major G. was not asked to explain why he had considered it necessary to use such a degree of force. No attempt was made to verify Major G.'s record and to ascertain, for example, whether he had previously been involved in similar incidents or whether he had ever been accused in the past of displaying anti-Roma sentiment. Those failings were compounded by the behaviour of the investigator and the prosecutors, who, as the Court has found above, disregarded relevant facts and terminated the investigation, thereby shielding Major G. from prosecution...

168. The Court thus finds that the authorities failed in their duty under Article 14 of the Convention taken together with Article 2 to take all possible steps to investigate whether or not discrimination may have played a role in the events. It follows that there has been a violation of Article 14 of the Convention taken together with Article 2 in its procedural aspect.

Abdulaziz, Cabales and Balkandali v. United Kingdom

ECtHR, Ser. A, No. 94 (28 May 1985).

AS TO THE FACTS

10. The applicants are lawfully and permanently settled in the United Kingdom. In accordance with the immigration rules in force at the material time, Mr. Abdulaziz, Mr. Cabales and Mr. Balkandali were refused permission to remain with or join them in that country as their husbands. The applicants maintained that, on this account, they had been victims of a practice of discrimination on the grounds of sex, race and also, in the case of Mrs. Balkandali, birth, and that there had been violations of Article 3 of the Convention and of Article 8, taken alone or in conjunction with Article 14 ....

AS TO THE LAW

II. ALLEGED VIOLATION OF ARTICLE 14 TAKEN TOGETHER WITH ARTICLE 8

A. Introduction

70. The applicants claimed that, as a result of unjustified differences of treatment in securing the right to respect for their family life, based on sex, race and also—in the case of Mrs. Balkandali—birth, they had been victims of a violation of Article 14 of the Convention, taken together with Article 8 ... In the event that the Court should find Article 8 to be applicable in the present case, the Government denied that there was any difference of treatment on the ground of race and submitted that since the differences of treatment on the ground of sex and of birth had objective and reasonable justifications and were proportionate to the aims pursued, they were compatible with Article 14.

71. According to the Court's established case-law, Article 14 complements the other substantive provisions of the Convention and the Protocols. It has no independent existence since it has effect solely in relation to "the enjoyment of the rights and freedoms" safeguarded by those provisions. Although the application of Article 14 does not necessarily presuppose a breach of those provisions-and to this extent it is autonomous-there can be no room for its application unless the facts at issue fall within the ambit of one or more of the latter ... The Court has found Article 8 to be applicable...Although the United Kingdom was not obliged to accept Mr. Abdulaziz, Mr. Cabales and Mr. Balkandali for settlement and the Court therefore did not find a violation of Article 8

taken alone..., the facts at issue nevertheless fall within the ambit of that Article. In this respect, a parallel may be drawn, mutatis mutandis, with the *National Union of Belgian Police Case*. Article 14 also is therefore applicable.

72. For the purposes of Article 14, a difference of treatment is discriminatory if it "has no objective and reasonable justification", that is, if it does not pursue a "legitimate aim" or if there is not a "reasonable relationship of proportionality between the means employed and the aim sought to be realised" .... The Contracting States enjoy a certain margin of appreciation in assessing whether and to what extent differences in otherwise similar situations justify a different treatment in law ... but it is for the Court to give the final ruling in this respect.

73. In the particular circumstances of the case, the Court considers that it must examine in turn the three grounds on which it was alleged that a discriminatory difference of treatment was based.

B. Alleged discrimination on the ground of sex

74. As regards the alleged discrimination on the ground of sex, it was not disputed that under the 1980 Rules it was easier for a man settled in the United Kingdom than for a woman so settled to obtain permission for his or her non-national spouse to enter or remain in the country for settlement .... [The a]rgument centred on the question whether this difference had an objective and reasonable justification.

75. According to the Government, the difference of treatment complained of had the aim of limiting "primary immigration" ... and was justified by the need to protect the domestic labour market at a time of high unemployment. They placed strong reliance on the margin of appreciation enjoyed by the Contracting States in this area and laid particular stress on what they described as a statistical fact: men were more likely to seek work than women, with the result that male immigrants would have a greater impact than female immigrants on the said market. Furthermore, the reduction, attributed by the Government to the 1980 Rules, of approximately 5,700 per annum in the number of husbands accepted for settlement in the United Kingdom ... was claimed to be significant. This was said to be so especially when the reduction was viewed in relation to its cumulative effect over the years and to the total number of acceptances for settlement. This view was contested by the applicants. For them, the Government's plea ignored the modern role of women and the fact that men may be self-employed and also, as

was exemplified by the case of Mr. Balkandali ..., create rather than seek jobs. Furthermore, the Government's figure of 5,700 was said to be insignificant and, for a number of reasons, in any event unreliable....

76. The Government further contended that the measures in question were justified by the need to maintain effective immigration control, which benefited settled immigrants as well as the indigenous population. Immigration caused strains on society; the Government's aim was to advance public tranquillity, and a firm and fair control secured good relations between the different communities living in the United Kingdom. To this, the applicants replied that the racial prejudice of the United Kingdom population could not be advanced as a justification for the measures.

77. In its report, the Commission considered that, when seen in the context of the immigration of other groups, annual emigration and unemployment and economic activity rates, the impact on the domestic labour market of an annual reduction of 2,000 ... in the number of husbands accepted for settlement in the United Kingdom ... was not of a size or importance to justify a difference of treatment on the ground of sex and the detrimental consequences thereof on the family life of the women concerned ... the long-standing commitment to the reunification of the families of male immigrants, to which the Government had referred as a reason for accepting wives whilst excluding husbands, no longer corresponded to modern requirements as to the equal treatment of the sexes. Neither was it established that race relations or immigration controls were enhanced by the rules: they might create resentment in part of the immigrant population and it had not been shown that it was more difficult to limit abuses by non-national husbands than by other immigrant groups. The Commission unanimously concluded that there had been discrimination on the ground of sex, contrary to Article 14, in securing the applicants' right to respect for family life, the application of the relevant rules being disproportionate to the purported aims. At the hearings before the Court, the Commission's Delegate stated that this conclusion was not affected by the Government's revised figure (about 5,700) for the annual reduction in the number of husbands accepted for settlement.

78. The Court accepts that the 1980 Rules had the aim of protecting the domestic labour market. The fact that, as was suggested by the applicants, this aim might have been further advanced by the abolition of the "United Kingdom ancestry" and the "working holiday" rules ... in no way alters this finding. Neither does the Court perceive any

conclusive evidence to contradict it in the Parliamentary debates, on which the applicants also relied. It is true, as they pointed out, that unemployment in the United Kingdom in 1980 was lower than in subsequent years, but it had nevertheless already attained a significant level and there was a considerable increase as compared with previous years ... Whilst the aforesaid aim was without doubt legitimate, this does not in itself establish the legitimacy of the difference made in the 1980 Rules as to the possibility for male and female immigrants settled in the United Kingdom to obtain permission for, on the one hand, their non-national wives or fiancées and, on the other hand, their non-national husbands or fiancés to enter or remain in the country. Although the Contracting States enjoy a certain "margin of appreciation" in assessing whether and to what extent differences in otherwise similar situations justify a different treatment, the scope of this margin will vary according to the circumstances, the subject-matter and its background....

As to the present matter, it can be said that the advancement of the equality of the sexes is today a major goal in the member States of the Council of Europe. This means that very weighty reasons would have to be advanced before a difference of treatment on the ground of sex could be regarded as compatible with the Convention.

79. In the Court's opinion, the Government's arguments summarized in paragraph 75 above are not convincing. It may be correct that on average there is a greater percentage of men of working age than of women of working age who are "economically active" (for Great Britain 90 per cent of the men and 63 per cent of the women) and that comparable figures hold good for immigrants (according to the statistics, 86 per cent for men and 41 per cent for women for immigrants from the Indian sub-continent and 90 per cent for men and 70 per cent for women for immigrants from the West Indies and Guyana) .... Nevertheless, this does not show that similar differences in fact exist—or would but for the effect of the 1980 Rules have existed—as regards the respective impact on the United Kingdom labour market of immigrant wives and of immigrant husbands. In this connection, other factors must also be taken into account. Being "economically active" does not always mean that one is seeking to be employed by someone else. Moreover, although a greater number of men than of women may be inclined to seek employment, immigrant husbands were already by far outnumbered, before the introduction of the 1980 Rules, by immigrant wives ... many of whom were also "economically active." Whilst a considerable proportion of those wives, in so far as they were "economically active",

were engaged in part-time work, the impact on the domestic labour market of women immigrants as compared with men ought not to be underestimated. In any event, the Court is not convinced that the difference that may nevertheless exist between the respective impact of men and of women on the domestic labour market is sufficiently important to justify the difference of treatment, complained of by the applicants, as to the possibility for a person settled in the United Kingdom to be joined by, as the case may be, his wife or her husband.

80. In this context the Government stressed the importance of the effect on the immigration of husbands of the restrictions contained in the 1980 Rules, which had led, according to their estimate, to an annual reduction of 5,700 (rather than 2,000, as mentioned in the Commission's report) in the number of husbands accepted for settlement. Without expressing a conclusion on the correctness of the figure of 5,700, the Court notes that in point of time the claimed reduction coincided with a significant increase in unemployment in the United Kingdom and that the Government accepted that some part of the reduction was due to economic conditions rather than to the 1980 Rules themselves .... In any event, for the reasons stated in paragraph 79 above, the reduction achieved does not justify the difference in treatment between men and women.

81. The Court accepts that the 1980 Rules also had, as the Government stated, the aim of advancing public tranquillity. However, it is not persuaded that this aim was served by the distinction drawn in those rules between husbands and wives.

82. There remains a more general argument advanced by the Government, namely that the United Kingdom was not in violation of Article 14 by reason of the fact that it acted more generously in some respects—that is, as regards the admission of non-national wives and fiancées of men settled in the country—than the Convention required. The Court cannot accept this argument. It would point out that Article 14 is concerned with the avoidance of discrimination in the enjoyment of the Convention rights in so far as the requirements of the Convention as to those rights can be complied with in different ways. The notion of discrimination within the meaning of Article 14 includes in general cases where a person or group is treated, without proper justification, less favourably than another, even though the more favourable treatment is not called for by the Convention.

83. The Court thus concludes that the applicants have been victims of discrimination on the ground of sex, in violation of Article 14 taken together with Article 8.

C. Alleged discrimination on the ground of race

84. As regards the alleged discrimination on the ground of race, the applicants relied on the opinion of a minority of the Commission. They referred, inter alia, to the whole history of and background to the United Kingdom immigration legislation ... and to the Parliamentary debates on the immigration rules. In contesting this claim, the Government submitted that the 1980 Rules were not racially motivated, their aim being to limit "primary immigration".... A majority of the Commission concluded that there had been no violation of Article 14 under this head. Most immigration policies—restricting, as they do, free entry—differentiated on the basis of people's nationality, and indirectly their race, ethnic origin and possibly their colour. Whilst a Contracting State could not implement "policies of a purely racist nature," to give preferential treatment to its nationals or to persons from countries with which it had the closest links did not constitute "racial discrimination." The effect in practice of the United Kingdom rules did not mean that they were abhorrent on the grounds of racial discrimination, there being no evidence of an actual difference of treatment on grounds of race. A minority of the Commission, on the other hand, noted that the main effect of the rules was to prevent immigration from the New Commonwealth and Pakistan. This was not coincidental: the legislative history showed that the intention was to "lower the number of coloured immigrants." By their effect and purpose, the rules were indirectly racist and there had thus been a violation of Article 14 under this head in the cases of Mrs. Abdulaziz and Mrs. Cabales.

85. The Court agrees in this respect with the majority of the Commission. The 1980 Rules, which were applicable in general to all "non-patrials" wanting to enter and settle in the United Kingdom, did not contain regulations differentiating between persons or groups on the ground of their race or ethnic origin. The rules included in paragraph 2 a specific instruction to immigration officers to carry out their duties without regard to the race, colour or religion of the intending entrant ... and they were applicable across the board to intending immigrants from all parts of the world, irrespective of their race or origin. As the Court has already accepted, the main and essential purpose of the 1980 Rules was to curtail "primary immigration" in order to protect the labour market at a time of high unemployment. This means that their

reinforcement of the restrictions on immigration was grounded not on objections regarding the origin of the non-nationals wanting to enter the country but on the need to stem the flow of immigrants at the relevant time. That the mass immigration against which the rules were directed consisted mainly of would-be immigrants from the New Commonwealth and Pakistan, and that as a result they affected at the material time fewer white people than others, is not a sufficient reason to consider them as racist in character: it is an effect which derives not from the content of the 1980 Rules but from the fact that, among those wishing to immigrate, some ethnic groups outnumbered others. The Court concludes from the foregoing that the 1980 Rules made no distinction on the ground of race and were therefore not discriminatory on that account. This conclusion is not altered by the following two arguments on which the applicants relied.

(a) The requirement that the wife or fiancée of the intending entrant be born or have a parent born in the United Kingdom and also the "United Kingdom ancestry rule" ... were said to favour persons of a particular ethnic origin. However, the Court regards these provisions as being exceptions designed for the benefit of persons having close links with the United Kingdom, which do not affect the general tenor of the rules.

(b) The requirement that the parties to the marriage or intended marriage must have met ... was said to operate to the disadvantage of individuals from the Indian sub-continent, where the practice of arranged marriages is customary. In the Court's view, however, such a requirement cannot be taken as an indication of racial discrimination: its main purpose was to prevent evasion of the rules by means of bogus marriages or engagements. It is, besides, a requirement that has nothing to do with the present cases.

86. The Court accordingly holds that the applicants have not been victims of discrimination on the ground of race.

D. Alleged discrimination on the ground of birth

87. Mrs. Balkandali claimed that she had also been the victim of discrimination on the ground of birth, in that, as between women citizens of the United Kingdom and Colonies settled in the United Kingdom, only those born or having a parent born in that country could, under the 1980 Rules, have their nonnational husband accepted for settlement there. It was not disputed that the 1980 Rules established a difference of treatment on the ground of birth, argument being

centred on the question whether it had an objective and reasonable justification. In addition to relying on the Commission's report, Mrs. Balkandali submitted that the elimination of this distinction from subsequent immigration rules ... demonstrated that it was not previously justified. The Government maintained that the difference in question was justified by the concern to avoid the hardship which women having close ties to the United Kingdom would encounter if, on marriage, they were obliged to move abroad in order to remain with their husbands. The Commission considered that, notwithstanding the subsequent elimination of this difference, the general interest and the possibly temporary nature of immigration rules required it to express an opinion. It took the view that a difference of treatment based on the mere accident of birth, without regard to the individual's personal circumstances or merits, constituted discrimination in violation of Article 14.

88. The Court is unable to share the Commission's opinion. The aim cited by the Government is unquestionably legitimate, for the purposes of Article 14. It is true that a person who, like Mrs. Balkandali, has been settled in a country for several years may also have formed close ties with it, even if he or she was not born there. Nevertheless, there are in general persuasive social reasons for giving special treatment to those whose link with a country stems from birth within it. The difference of treatment must therefore be regarded as having had an objective and reasonable justification and, in particular, its results have not been shown to transgress the principle of proportionality. This conclusion is not altered by the fact that the immigration rules were subsequently amended on this point.

89. The Court thus holds that Mrs. Balkandali was not the victim of discrimination on the ground of birth.

Legal Status and Rights of Undocumented Migrants

IACtHR Advisory Opinion No. OC-18/03 (17 September 2003).
(footnotes omitted)

Obligation to respect and guarantee human rights and the fundamental
nature of the principle of equality and non-discrimination

...The principle of equality and non-discrimination

82. Having established the State obligation to respect and guarantee human
rights, the Court will now refer to the elements of the principle of equality
and non-discrimination.

83. Non-discrimination, together with equality before the law and equal
protection of the law, are elements of a general basic principle related to the
protection of human rights. The element of equality is difficult to separate
from non-discrimination. Indeed, when referring to equality before the law,
the instruments cited above ... indicate that this principle must be guaranteed
with no discrimination. This Court has indicated that "[r]ecognizing equality
before the law, [...] prohibits all discriminatory treatment."

84. This Advisory Opinion will differentiate by using the terms distinction
and discrimination. The term distinction will be used to indicate what is
admissible, because it is reasonable, proportionate and objective.
Discrimination will be used to refer to what is inadmissible, because it
violates human rights. Therefore, the term "discrimination" will be used to
refer to any exclusion, restriction or privilege that is not objective and
reasonable, and which adversely affects human rights.

85. There is an inseparable connection between the obligation to respect and
guarantee human rights and the principle of equality and non-
discrimination. States are obliged to respect and guarantee the full and free
exercise of rights and freedoms without any discrimination. Non-compliance
by the State with the general obligation to respect and guarantee human
rights, owing to any discriminatory treatment, gives rise to its international
responsibility.

86. The principle of the equal and effective protection of the law and of non-
discrimination is embodied in many international instruments. The fact that
the principle of equality and non-discrimination is regulated in so many
international instruments is evidence that there is a universal obligation to
respect and guarantee the human rights arising from that general basic
principle.

87. The principle of equality before the law and non-discrimination has been developed in international case law and legal writings. The Inter-American Court has understood that:

> [t]he notion of equality springs directly from the oneness of the human family and is linked to the essential dignity of the individual. That principle cannot be reconciled with the notion that a given group has the right to privileged treatment because of its perceived superiority. It is equally irreconcilable with that notion to characterize a group as inferior and treat it with hostility or otherwise subject it to discrimination in the enjoyment of rights that are accorded to others not so classified. It is impermissible to subject human beings to differences in treatment that are inconsistent with their unique and congenerous character...

88. The principle of equality and non-discrimination is fundamental for the safeguard of human rights in both international and domestic law. Consequently, States have the obligation to combat discriminatory practices and not to introduce discriminatory regulations into their laws.

89. Nevertheless, when examining the implications of the differentiated treatment that some norms may give to the persons they affect, it is important to refer to the words of this Court declaring that "not all differences in treatment are in themselves offensive to human dignity." In the same way, the European Court of Human Rights, following "the principles which may be extracted from the legal practice of a large number of democratic States," has held that a difference in treatment is only discriminatory when "it has no objective and reasonable justification." Distinctions based on *de facto* inequalities may be established; such distinctions constitute an instrument for the protection of those who should be protected, considering their situation of greater or lesser weakness or helplessness. For example, the fact that minors who are detained in a prison may not be imprisoned together with adults who are also detained is an inequality permitted by law. Another example of these inequalities is the limitation to the exercise of specific political rights owing to nationality or citizenship...

91. Likewise, the Inter-American Court has established that:

> [n]o discrimination exists if the difference in treatment has a legitimate purpose and if it does not lead to situations which are contrary to justice, to reason or to the nature of things. It follows that there would be no discrimination in differences in treatment of

individuals by a state when the classifications selected are based on substantial factual differences and there exists a reasonable relationship of proportionality between these differences and the aims of the legal rule under review. These aims may not be unjust or unreasonable, that is, they may not be arbitrary, capricious, despotic or in conflict with the essential oneness and dignity of humankind.

92. The United Nations Committee on Human Rights has defined discrimination as:

[...] any distinction, exclusion, restriction or preference which is based on any ground such as race, colour, sex, language, religion, political or other opinion, national or social origin, property, birth or other status, and which has the purpose or effect of nullifying or impairing the recognition, enjoyment or exercise by all persons, on an equal footing, of all rights and freedoms.

93. Likewise, this Committee has indicated that:

[...] the enjoyment of rights and freedoms on an equal footing, however, does not mean identical treatment in every instance.

94. The Human Rights Committee has also stated that:

[...] each State party must ensure the rights in the Covenant to "all individuals within its territory and subject to its jurisdiction" [...]. In general, the rights set forth in the Covenant apply to everyone, irrespective of reciprocity, and irrespective of his or her nationality or statelessness ...

Thus, the general rule is that each one of the rights of the Covenant must be guaranteed without discrimination between citizens and aliens ...

95. With regard to the principle of equality and non-discrimination, the African Commission of Human and Peoples' Rights has established that this:

[m]eans that citizens should expect to be treated fairly and justly within the legal system and be assured of equal treatment before the law and equal enjoyment of the rights available to all other citizens. The right to equality is important for a second reason. Equality or lack of it affects the capacity of one to enjoy many other rights.

96. In accordance with the foregoing, States must respect and ensure human rights in light of the general basic principle of equality and non-discrimination. Any discriminatory treatment with regard to the protection

and exercise of human rights entails the international responsibility of the State ...

The fundamental nature of the principle of equality and non-discrimination

97. The Court now proceeds to consider whether this is a *jus cogens* principle.

98. Originally, the concept of *jus cogens* was linked specifically to the law of treaties. As *jus cogens* is formulated in Article 53 of the Vienna Convention on the Law of Treaties, "[a] treaty is void if, at the time of its conclusion, it conflicts with a peremptory norm of general international law." Likewise, Article 64 of the Convention refers to *jus cogens superviniente*, when it indicates that "[i]f a new peremptory norm of general international law emerges, any existing treaty which is in conflict with that norm becomes void and terminates." *Jus cogens* has been developed by international case law and legal writings.

99. In its development and by its definition, *jus cogens* is not limited to treaty law. The sphere of *jus cogens* has expanded to encompass general international law, including all legal acts. *Jus cogens* has also emerged in the law of the international responsibility of States and, finally, has had an influence on the basic principles of the international legal order.

100. In particular, when referring to the obligation to respect and ensure human rights, regardless of which of those rights are recognized by each State in domestic or international norms, the Court considers it clear that all States, as members of the international community, must comply with these obligations without any discrimination; this is intrinsically related to the right to equal protection before the law, which, in turn, derives "directly from the oneness of the human family and is linked to the essential dignity of the individual." The principle of equality before the law and non-discrimination permeates every act of the powers of the State, in all their manifestations, related to respecting and ensuring human rights. Indeed, this principle may be considered peremptory under general international law, inasmuch as it applies to all States, whether or not they are party to a specific international treaty, and gives rise to effects with regard to third parties, including individuals. This implies that the State, both internationally and in its domestic legal system, and by means of the acts of any of its powers or of third parties who act under its tolerance, acquiescence or negligence, cannot behave in a way that is contrary to the principle of equality and non-discrimination, to the detriment of a determined group of persons.

101. Accordingly, this Court considers that the principle of equality before the law, equal protection before the law and non-discrimination belongs to

jus cogens, because the whole legal structure of national and international public order rests on it and it is a fundamental principle that permeates all laws ...

Effects of the principle of equality and non-discrimination

102. This general obligation to respect and guarantee human rights, without any discrimination and on an equal footing, has various consequences and effects that are defined in specific obligations. The Court will now refer to the effects derived from this obligation.

103. In compliance with this obligation, States must abstain from carrying out any action that, in any way, directly or indirectly, is aimed at creating situations of de jure or de facto discrimination. This translates, for example, into the prohibition to enact laws, in the broadest sense, formulate civil, administrative or any other measures, or encourage acts or practices of their officials, in implementation or interpretation of the law that discriminate against a specific group of persons because of their race, gender, color or other reasons.

104. In addition, States are obliged to take affirmative action to reverse or change discriminatory situations that exist in their societies to the detriment of a specific group of persons. This implies the special obligation to protect that the State must exercise with regard to acts and practices of third parties who, with its tolerance or acquiescence, create, maintain or promote discriminatory situations.

105. Because of the effects derived from this general obligation, States may only establish objective and reasonable distinctions when these are made with due respect for human rights and in accordance with the principle of applying the norm that grants protection to the individual.

106. Non-compliance with these obligations gives rise to the international responsibility of the State, and this is exacerbated insofar as non-compliance violates peremptory norms of international human rights law. Hence, the general obligation to respect and ensure human rights binds States, regardless of any circumstance or consideration, including a person's migratory status.

107. One of the results of the foregoing is that, in their domestic laws, States must ensure that all persons have access, without any restriction, to a simple and effective recourse that protects them in determining their rights, irrespective of their migratory status.

108. In this respect, the Inter-American Court has indicated that:

> [...] the absence of an effective remedy to violations of the rights recognized by the Convention is itself a violation of the Convention by the State Party in which the remedy is lacking. In that sense, it should be emphasized that, for such a remedy to exist, it is not sufficient that it be provided for by the Constitution or by law or that it be formally recognized, but rather it must be truly effective in establishing whether there has been a violation of human rights and in providing redress. A remedy which proves illusory because of the general conditions prevailing in the country, or even in the particular circumstances of a given case, cannot be considered effective. That could be the case, for example, when practice has shown its ineffectiveness: when the Judicial Power lacks the necessary independence to render impartial decisions or the means to carry out its judgments; or in any other situation that constitutes a denial of justice, as when there is an unjustified delay in the decision; or when, for any reason, the alleged victim is denied access to a judicial remedy.

109. This general obligation to respect and ensure the exercise of rights has an *erga omnes* character. The obligation is imposed on States to benefit the persons under their respective jurisdictions, irrespective of the migratory status of the protected persons. This obligation encompasses all the rights included in the American Convention and the International Covenant on Civil and Political Rights, including the right to judicial guarantees. In this way, the right of access to justice for all persons is preserved, understood as the right to effective jurisdictional protection.

110. ... The effects of the fundamental principle of equality and non-discrimination encompass all States, precisely because this principle, which belongs to the realm of *jus cogens* and is of a peremptory character, entails obligations *erga omnes* of protection that bind all States and give rise to effects with regard to third parties, including individuals...

And is of the opinion, unanimously,

1. That States have the general obligation to respect and ensure the fundamental rights. To this end, they must take affirmative action, avoid taking measures that limit or infringe a fundamental right, and eliminate measures and practices that restrict or violate a fundamental right.

2. That non-compliance by the State with the general obligation to respect and ensure human rights, owing to any discriminatory treatment, gives rise to international responsibility.

3. That the principle of equality and non-discrimination is fundamental for the safeguard of human rights in both international law and domestic law.

4. That the fundamental principle of equality and non-discrimination forms part of general international law, because it is applicable to all States, regardless of whether or not they are a party to a specific international treaty. At the current stage of the development of international law, the fundamental principle of equality and non-discrimination has entered the domain of jus cogens.

5. That the fundamental principle of equality and non-discrimination, which is of a peremptory nature, entails obligations erga omnes of protection that bind all States and generate effects with regard to third parties, including individuals ...

Proposed Amendments to the Naturalization Provision of the Constitution of Costa Rica

IACtHR Advisory Opinion No. OC-4/84 (19 January 1984).

IV
ISSUES RELATING TO DISCRIMINATION

52. The provisions of the proposed amendments that have been brought before the Court for interpretation as well as the text of the Constitution that is now in force establish different classifications as far as the conditions for the acquisition of Costa Rican nationality through naturalization are concerned. Thus, under ... the proposed amendment, the periods of official residence in the country required as a condition for the acquisition of nationality differ, depending on whether the applicants qualify as native-born nationals of "other countries of Central America, Spaniards and Ibero-Americans" or whether they acquired the nationality of those countries by naturalization. [Another paragraph] of that same Article in turn lays down special conditions applicable to the naturalization of "a foreign woman" who marries a Costa Rican. Article 14 of the Constitution now in force makes similar distinctions which, even though they may not have the same purpose and meaning, suggest the question whether they do not constitute discriminatory classifications incompatible with the relevant texts of the Convention.

53. Article 1(1) of the Convention, a rule general in scope which applies to all the provisions of the treaty, imposes on the States Parties the obligation to respect and guarantee the free and full exercise of the rights and freedoms recognized therein "without any discrimination." In other words, regardless of its origin or the form it may assume, any treatment that can be considered to be discriminatory with regard to the exercise of any of the rights guaranteed under the Convention is per se incompatible with that instrument ...

54. Article 24 of the Convention, in turn, reads as follows:

Article 24. Right to Equal Protection

All persons are equal before the law. Consequently, they are entitled, without discrimination, to equal protection of the law.

Although Articles 24 and 1(1) are conceptually not identical—the Court may perhaps have occasion at some future date to articulate the differences—Article 24 restates to a certain degree the principle established in Article 1(1). In recognizing equality before the law, it prohibits all discriminatory treatment originating in a legal prescription. The prohibition against discrimination so broadly proclaimed in Article 1(1) with regard to the rights and guarantees enumerated in the Convention thus extends to the domestic law of the States Parties, permitting the conclusion that in these provisions the States Parties, by acceding to the Convention, have undertaken to maintain their laws free of discriminatory regulations.

55. The notion of equality springs directly from the oneness of the human family and is linked to the essential dignity of the individual. That principle cannot be reconciled with the notion that a given group has the right to privileged treatment because of its perceived superiority. It is equally irreconcilable with that notion to characterize a group as inferior and treat it with hostility or otherwise subject it to discrimination in the enjoyment of rights which are accorded to others not so classified. It is impermissible to subject human beings to differences in treatment that are inconsistent with their unique and congenerous character.

56. Precisely because equality and nondiscrimination are inherent in the idea of the oneness in dignity and worth of all human beings, it follows that not all differences in legal treatment are discriminatory as such, for not all differences in treatment are in themselves offensive to human dignity. The European Court of Human Rights, "following the principles which may be extracted from the legal practice of a large number of democratic States," has held that a difference in treatment is only discriminatory when it "has no objective and reasonable justification." ... There may well exist certain factual inequalities that might legitimately give rise to inequalities in legal treatment that do not violate principles of justice. They may in fact be instrumental in achieving justice or in protecting those who find themselves in a weak legal position. For example, it cannot be deemed discrimination on the grounds of age or social status for the law to impose limits on the legal capacity of minors or mentally incompetent persons who lack the capacity to protect their interests.

57. Accordingly, no discrimination exists if the difference in treatment has a legitimate purpose and if it does not lead to situations which are contrary to justice, to reason or to the nature of things. It follows that there would be no discrimination in differences in treatment of individuals by a state when the classifications selected are based on substantial factual differences and there exists a reasonable relationship of proportionality between these differences and the aims of the legal rule under review. These aims may not be unjust or unreasonable, that is, they may not be arbitrary, capricious, despotic or in conflict with the essential oneness and dignity of humankind.

58. Although it cannot be denied that a given factual context may make it more or less difficult to determine whether or not one has encountered the situation described in the foregoing paragraph, it is equally true that, starting with the notion of the essential oneness and dignity of the human family, it is possible to identify circumstances in which considerations of public welfare may justify departures to a greater or lesser degree from the standards articulated above. One is here dealing with values which take on concrete dimensions in the face of those real situations in which they have to be applied and which permit in each case a certain margin of appreciation in giving expression to them.

59. With this approach in mind, the Court repeats its prior observation that as far as the granting of naturalization is concerned, it is for the granting state to determine whether and to what extent applicants for naturalization have complied with the conditions deemed to ensure an effective link between them and the value system and interests of the society to which they wish to belong. To this extent there exists no doubt that it is within the sovereign power of Costa Rica to decide what standards should determine the granting or denial of nationality to aliens who seek it, and to establish certain reasonable differentiations based on factual differences which, viewed objectively, recognize that some applicants have a closer affinity than others to Costa Rica's value system and interests.

60. Given the above considerations, one example of a non-discriminatory differentiation would be the establishment of less stringent residency requirements for Central Americans, Ibero-Americans and Spaniards than for other foreigners seeking to acquire Costa Rican nationality. It would not appear to be inconsistent with the nature and purpose of the grant of nationality to expedite the naturalization procedures for those who, viewed objectively, share much closer historical, cultural and spiritual bonds with the people of Costa Rica. The existence of these bonds permits the assumption that these individuals will be more easily and more rapidly assimilated within the national community and identify more readily with the traditional beliefs, values and institutions of Costa Rica, which the state has the right and duty to preserve.

61. Less obvious is the basis for the distinction, made in ... the proposed amendment, between those Central Americans, Ibero-Americans and Spaniards who acquired their nationality by birth and those who obtained it by naturalization. Since nationality is a bond that exists equally for the one group as for the other, the proposed classification appears to be based on the place of birth and not on the culture of the applicant for naturalization. The

provisions in question may, however, have been prompted by certain doubts about the strictness of the conditions that were applied by those states which conferred their nationality on the individuals now seeking to obtain that of Costa Rica, the assumption being that the previously acquired nationality—be it Spanish, Ibero-American or that of some other Central American country—does not constitute an adequate guarantee of affinity with the value system and interests of the Costa Rican society. Although the distinctions being made are debatable on various grounds, the Court will not consider those issues now. Notwithstanding the fact that the classification resorted to is more difficult to understand given the additional requirements that an applicant would have to meet under Article 15 of the proposed amendment, the Court cannot conclude that the proposed amendment is clearly discriminatory in character.

62. In reaching this conclusion, the Court is fully mindful of the margin of appreciation which is reserved to states when it comes to the establishment of requirements for the acquisition of nationality and the determination whether they have been complied with. But the Court's conclusion should not be viewed as approval of the practice which prevails in some areas to limit to an exaggerated and unjustified degree the political rights of naturalized individuals. Most of these situations involve cases not now before the Court that do, however, constitute clear instances of discrimination on the basis of origin or place of birth, unjustly creating two distinct hierarchies of nationals in one single country.

63. Consistent with its clearly restrictive approach, the proposed amendment also provides for new conditions which must be complied with by those applying for naturalization. [One of the proposed articles] requires, among other things, proof of the ability to "speak, write and read" the Spanish language; it also prescribes a "comprehensive examination on the history of the country and its values." These conditions can be deemed, prima facie, to fall within the margin of appreciation reserved to the state as far as concerns the enactment and assessment of the requirements designed to ensure the existence of real and effective links upon which to base the acquisition of the new nationality. So viewed, it cannot be said to be unreasonable and unjustified to require proof of the ability to communicate in the language of the country or, although this is less clear, to require the applicant to "speak, write and read" the language. The same can be said of the requirement of a "comprehensive examination on the history of the country and its values." The Court feels compelled to emphasize, however, that in practice, and given the broad discretion with which tests such as those mandated by the draft

amendment tend to be administered, there exists the risk that these requirements will become the vehicle for subjective and arbitrary judgments as well as instruments for the effectuation of discriminatory policies which, although not directly apparent on the face of the law, could well be the consequence of its application.

64. [Another paragraph of the proposed amendments] accords "a foreign woman who [marries] a Costa Rican" special consideration for obtaining Costa Rican nationality. In doing so, it follows the formula adopted in the current Constitution, which gives women but not men who marry Costa Ricans a special status for purposes of naturalization. This approach or system was based on the so-called principle of family unity and is traceable to two assumptions. One has to do with the proposition that all members of a family should have the same nationality. The other derives from notions about paternal authority and the fact that authority over minor children was as a rule vested in the father and that it was the husband on whom the law conferred a privileged status of power, giving him authority, for example, to fix the marital domicile and to administer the marital property. Viewed in this light, the right accorded to women to acquire the nationality of their husbands was an outgrowth of conjugal inequality.

65. In the early 1930's, there developed a movement opposing these traditional notions. It had its roots in the acquisition of legal capacity by women and the more widespread acceptance of equality among the sexes based on the principle of nondiscrimination. These developments, which can be documented by means of a comparative law analysis, received a decisive impulse on the international plane. In the Americas, the Contracting Parties to the Montevideo Convention on the Nationality of Women of December 26, 1933 declared in Article 1 of that treaty that "There shall be no distinction based on sex as regards nationality, in their legislation or in their practice." ... And the Convention on Nationality, signed also in Montevideo on that same date, provided in Article 6 that "Neither matrimony nor its dissolution affects the nationality of the husband or wife or of their children." ... The American Declaration, in turn, declares in Article II that "All persons are equal before the law and have the rights and duties established in this declaration, without distinction as to race, sex, language, creed or any other factor." These same principles have been embodied in Article 1(3) of the United Nations Charter and in Article 3(j) of the OAS Charter.

66. The same idea is reflected in Article 17(4) of the [ACHR] ...

67. The Court consequently concludes that the different treatment envisaged for spouses [in] ... the proposed amendment, which applies to the acquisition of Costa Rican nationality in cases involving special circumstances brought about by marriage, cannot be justified and must be considered to be discriminatory ...

Kalliope Schöning-Kougebetopoulou and Freie und Hansestadt Hamburg

ECJ Judgment No. C-15/96 (15 January 1998).

[Footnotes removed]

JUDGMENT OF THE COURT

REFERENCE to the Court under Article 177 of the EC Treaty by the Arbeitsgericht (Labour Court) Hamburg, Germany, for a preliminary ruling in the proceedings pending before that court ...

1. By order of 1 December 1995, received at the Court on 19 January 1996, the Arbeitsgericht (Labour Court) Hamburg referred to the Court for a preliminary ruling under Article 177 of the EC Treaty two questions on the interpretation of Article 48 of that Treaty and Article 7(1) and (4) of Regulation (EEC) No 1612/68 of the Council of 15 October 1968 on freedom of movement for workers within the Community ...

2. Those questions have been raised in proceedings between Mrs Schöning-Kougebetopoulou, of Greek nationality, and the Freie und Hansestadt Hamburg (Free Hanseatic City of Hamburg) concerning her classification in a higher salary group under the Bundes-Angestelltentarifvertrag (Federal Collective Wage Agreement for Contractual Employees, hereinafter 'the BAT') ...

4. Since 1 August 1993 Mrs Schöning-Kougebetopoulou has been employed under a contract of employment as a specialist doctor in the public service of the Freie und Hansestadt Hamburg in Germany. In her contract of employment, drawn up on the basis of the BAT, she is classified in Salary Group Ib, sub-group 7, as a 'specialist doctor employed as such'.

5. From 1 October 1986 until 31 August 1992 Mrs Schöning-Kougebetopoulou worked in the Greek public service as a specialist doctor under the staff regulations applicable to civil servants of that State.

6. Since that period was not taken into account for the purposes of calculating her seniority, she brought an action on 22 June 1995 before the Arbeitsgericht Hamburg seeking classification in a higher salary group under the BAT. In support of that claim she submits that she has suffered indirect discrimination contrary to Article 48 of the Treaty and to Article 7(1) and (4) of Regulation No 1612/68.

7. Article 7(1) and (4) of Regulation No 1612/68 provides:

'1. A worker who is a national of a Member State may not, in the territory of another Member State, be treated differently from national workers by reason of his nationality in respect of any conditions of employment and work, in particular as regards remuneration, dismissal, and should he become unemployed, reinstatement or re-employment ...

4. Any clause of a collective or individual agreement or of any other collective regulation concerning eligibility for employment, employment, remuneration and other conditions of work or dismissal shall be null and void in so far as it lays down or authorizes discriminatory conditions in respect of workers who are nationals of the other Member States.

8. The Arbeitsgericht Hamburg decided to stay proceedings and to refer the following questions to the Court for a preliminary ruling:

'1. Is there an infringement of Article 48 of the EC Treaty and Article 7(1) and (4) of Regulation (EEC) No 1612/68 of the Council, on freedom of movement for workers within the Community, where a collective agreement for the public service provides for promotion on grounds of seniority after eight years' service only in a particular salary bracket provided for by the collective wage agreement in force for all employees in the public service of the Federal Republic of Germany ("the BAT") and therefore does not take account of comparable activities carried out in the public service of another Member State of the EC?

2. If the reply to Question 1 is in the affirmative:

Does Article 48 together with Regulation (EEC) No 1612/68 of the Council on freedom of movement for workers within the Community require that, where doctors have worked as such in the public service of another Member State of the EC, the time spent in such employment should likewise be taken into account for the purposes of promotion on grounds of seniority as provided for in the BAT or should the court take no such decision and leave this matter instead to the parties to the collective agreement, having regard to their freedom to agree terms?'

The first question

9. The Court has consistently held that, in the context of the application of Article 177 of the Treaty, it has no jurisdiction to decide whether a national provision is compatible with Community law. The Court may, however, extract from the wording of the questions formulated by the national court, having regard to the facts stated by it, those elements which concern the interpretation of Community law for the purpose of enabling that court to resolve the legal problem before it ...

10. In the present case, the person concerned claims only that periods during which she worked as a specialist doctor in the public service of another Member State should be taken into account.

11. Second, it is clear from the first question that her activity as a specialist doctor in the public service of her Member State of origin and her activity as a specialized doctor in the public service of the host Member State must be regarded as comparable. The profession concerned is, moreover, one which is regulated at Community level.

12. Third, Article 48 of the Treaty lays down the fundamental principle of freedom of movement for workers. Article 7(4) of Regulation No 1612/68, which merely clarifies and gives effect to rights already conferred by Article 48 of the Treaty ... guarantees equal treatment of workers who are nationals of other Member States in regard to any clause of a collective or individual agreement or any other collective regulation concerning, in particular, pay.

13. Fourth, the derogation in Article 48(4) of the Treaty, according to which the provisions on freedom of movement for workers are not to apply to 'employment in the public service', concerns only access for nationals of other Member States to certain posts in the civil service ... It does not concern the activities of a specialist doctor, which do not involve direct or indirect participation in the exercise of powers conferred by public law and duties designed to safeguard the general interests of the State or of public authorities ...

14. In those circumstances, the first question asked by the Arbeitsgericht must be read as seeking to ascertain whether Article 48 of the Treaty and Article 7(1) and (4) of Regulation No 1612/68 prohibit a clause of a collective agreement applicable to the public service of a Member State, such as the clause in question, which provides for promotion on grounds of seniority of employees of that public service after eight years' employment in a salary group determined by that agreement, without regard to previous

periods of comparable employment completed in the public service of another Member State.

15. The German Government argues that the BAT clause at issue has neither the object nor the effect of treating only, or mainly, nationals of other Member States less favourably than German nationals. It points out that the clause at issue not only takes no account of periods of employment completed abroad but also takes no account of periods completed in Germany that are not covered by the BAT or of periods completed in a Salary Group other than Group Ib.

16. According to the Spanish Government, the clause at issue cannot be characterized as discriminatory. Years of seniority acquired in the German and Greek public administrations are based on different rules and are not comparable. Clauses which treat such situations differently cannot be regarded as contrary to the principle of equal treatment.

17. The German, Spanish and French Governments consider in any event that the clause at issue is based on objectively justified factors unconnected with any discrimination. In that regard, they put forward two arguments.

18. First, the French and Spanish Governments submit that the conditions for promotion on grounds of seniority laid down by the BAT may be justified by characteristics specific to employment in the public service. In the absence of harmonization or even coordination of national organizational and operating rules applicable to the public service, the recognition of service completed in the public service of another Member State would disrupt the application of the various schemes applicable to public service posts in the different Member States, in particular as regards the rules for taking seniority into account for the purposes of internal promotion and career progression.

19. Second, although the national court's questions are based on the premiss that the BAT is a public sector agreement which aims to engender loyalty amongst qualified staff throughout the sector, the German Government submits that the aim of promotion on grounds of seniority provided for by that agreement is, like that of collective agreements in the private sector, to reward an employee's loyalty to the whole of a given group of employers and to motivate him by the prospect of improvement in his financial situation. Community law does not preclude an employee's loyalty to a private-sector employer from being rewarded in that way.

20. The French and Spanish Governments also point out the difficulties in comparing the rules on promotion on grounds of seniority in the public sector with those in the private sector.

21. The questions for consideration are therefore whether a clause of a collective agreement applicable to the public service of a Member State, such as the clause in question, is such as to infringe the principle of non-discrimination laid down in Article 48 of the Treaty and Article 7(1) and (4) of Regulation No 1612/68 and, if so, whether such rules are justified by objective considerations independent of the nationality of the employees concerned and whether they are proportionate to the legitimate aim of the national provisions ...

The principle of non-discrimination

22. It is common ground that the BAT does not allow periods of employment completed in the public service of another Member State to be taken into account.

23. As is explained in paragraphs 12 to 14 of the Advocate General's Opinion, the conditions for promotion on grounds of seniority laid down in the BAT thus manifestly work to the detriment of migrant workers who have spent part of their careers in the public service of another Member State. For that reason they are such as to contravene the principle of non-discrimination laid down by Article 48 of the Treaty and Article 7(1) and (4) of Regulation No 1612/68.

24. That finding is not called into question in the circumstances of the present case either by the fact that some employees of the German public service might encounter the same situation as migrant workers or by the fact that the public service is governed by different organizational and operational rules in the Member States.

Justification

25. As regards the argument based on the particular characteristics of employment in public service, it is sufficient to point out, as is explained in paragraph 13 of this judgment, that the dispute before the national court concerns only the occupation of specialist doctor which does not fall within the scope of Article 48(4) of the Treaty.

26. As regards the argument claiming, as a ground of justification, that one purpose of the BAT is to reward an employee's loyalty to his employer and to motivate him by the prospect of improvement in his financial situation, the German Government explained at the hearing that the BAT covers not only the majority of German public institutions but also undertakings performing public interest tasks.

27. However, if that is the case, to take into account periods of employment completed with one of those institutions or undertakings in determining seniority for the purposes of promotion cannot, given the multiplicity of employers, be justified by the desire to reward employee loyalty. On the contrary, the system affords employees covered by the BAT considerable mobility within a group of legally separate employers.

28. Consequently, the answer to be given to the first question must be that Article 48 of the Treaty and Article 7(1) and (4) of Regulation No 1612/68 preclude a clause in a collective agreement applicable to the public service of a Member State which provides for promotion on grounds of seniority for employees of that service after eight years' employment in a salary group determined by that agreement without taking any account of previous periods of comparable employment completed in the public service of another Member State.

The second question

29. The second question concerns the consequences which, given the freedom of contract of the parties to a collective agreement, would arise from the national court's finding that a clause in a collective agreement, such as that at issue in the main proceedings, is incompatible with Article 48 of the Treaty and Article 7(1) and (4) of Regulation No 1612/68.

30. A clause in a collective agreement applicable to the public service of a Member State which provides for promotion on grounds of seniority after eight years' employment in a salary group determined by that agreement but which takes no account of periods of comparable employment previously completed in the public service of another Member State is null and void under Article 7(4) of Regulation No 1612/68 in so far as it lays down or authorizes discriminatory conditions in relation to workers who are nationals of other Member States.

31. Therefore, having regard to the answer given to the first question, it is necessary to determine the consequences which ensue from Article 7(4) of Regulation No 1612/68 pending the adoption by the parties to the collective agreement of the amendments necessary to eliminate the discrimination.

32. As Mrs Schöning-Kougebetopoulou and the Commission have submitted, it is appropriate to apply here the Court's case-law on the principle of equal pay for men and women.

33. According to that case-law, where a provision discriminates against women, the members of the disadvantaged group are to be treated in the same way and to have applied to them the same rules as the other workers

- 396 -

and, failing correct implementation of Article 119 of the Treaty in national law, those rules remain the only valid point of reference ...

34. As was found in paragraph 11 of this judgment, the activities of specialist doctor pursued by Mrs Schöning-Kougebetopoulou in this case, in the public service of the Member State of origin and in that of the host Member State, must be regarded as comparable.

35. In reply to the second question, it is therefore sufficient to state that a clause in a collective agreement entailing discrimination contrary to Article 48 of the Treaty and to Article 7(1) of Regulation No 1612/68 is null and void by virtue of Article 7(4) of that regulation. Without requiring or waiting for that clause to be abolished by collective negotiation or by some other procedure, the national court must therefore apply the same rules to the members of the group disadvantaged by that discrimination as those applicable to the other workers.

Cases

European Commission and Italy

ECJ (6th Chamber) Opinion No. C-388/01 (16 January 2003).

1. By application lodged at the Court Registry on 8 October 2001, the Commission of the European Communities brought an action under Article 226 EC for a declaration that, by allowing discriminatory, advantageous rates for admission to museums, monuments, galleries, archaeological digs, parks and gardens classified as public monuments, granted by local or decentralised State authorities only in favour of Italian nationals and persons resident within the territory of those authorities running the cultural sites in question, who are aged over 60 or 65 years, and by excluding from such advantages tourists who are nationals of other Member States and non-residents who fulfil the same objective age requirements, the Italian Republic has failed to fulfil its obligations under Articles 12 EC and 49 EC.

12. The Court has already held that national legislation on admission to the museums of one Member State which entails discrimination affecting only foreign tourists is, for nationals of other Member States, prohibited by Articles ... Articles 12 EC and 49 EC)

...13. It is also clear from the Court's case-law ... that the principle of equal treatment, of which Article 49 EC embodies a specific instance, prohibits not only overt discrimination by reason of nationality but also all covert forms of discrimination which, by the application of other criteria of differentiation, lead in fact to the same result.

14. That is true, in particular, of a measure under which a distinction is drawn on the basis of residence, in that that requirement is liable to operate mainly to the detriment of nationals of other Member States, since non-residents are in the majority of cases foreigners ... In that context, it is immaterial whether the contested measure affects, in some circumstances, nationals of the State in question resident in other parts of the national territory as well as nationals of other Member States. In order for a measure to be treated as being discriminatory, it is not necessary for it to have the effect of putting at an advantage all the nationals of the State in question or of putting at a disadvantage only nationals of other Member States, but not nationals of the State in question ...

15. In the present case, it is common ground that the free admission to museums, monuments, galleries, archaeological digs, parks and gardens classified as public monuments, granted by local or decentralised authorities, is only in favour of Italian nationals and persons resident within the territory of the authorities running the museum or public monument in question, in

particular where they are aged over 60 or 65 years, so that the benefit of free admission is denied to tourists who are nationals of other Member States and non-residents who fulfil the same objective age requirements.

16. The Italian Government does not deny that the amendments made ... in order to extend to the nationals of all Member States the benefit of the advantageous rates at issue, do not apply to the museums or other monuments run by local or decentralised State authorities ...

18. The Italian Republic none the less puts forward various reasons in the general interest in order to justify the advantageous rates at issue. First, in the light of the cost of managing cultural assets, free admission to the sites cannot be granted in disregard of economic considerations. Second, the favourable treatment afforded only to Italian nationals and certain residents is justified by reasons of cohesion of the tax system, in that those advantages constitute consideration for the payment of the taxes by which those nationals and residents contribute to the running of the sites concerned.

19. First of all, to the extent that the advantageous rates at issue provide for a distinction on the basis of nationality, it should be recalled that such advantages are compatible with Community law only if they can be covered by an express derogating provision, such as Article 46 EC, to which Article 55 EC refers, namely public policy, public security or public health. Economic aims cannot constitute grounds of public policy within the meaning of Article 46 EC ...

20. Consequently, since neither the necessity to preserve the cohesion of the tax system nor the economic considerations put forward by the Italian Government come within the exceptions allowed by Article 46 EC, the advantageous rates at issue, in so far as they are allowed only for Italian nationals, are incompatible with Community law.

21. Next, in so far as those advantageous rates provide for a distinction on the basis of residence, it is appropriate to examine whether the justifications on which the Italian Government relies constitute overriding reasons in the general interest which may justify such advantages.

22. As regards, first, the economic grounds put forward by the Italian Government, suffice it to note that they cannot be accepted, since aims of a purely economic nature cannot constitute overriding reasons in the general interest justifying a restriction of a fundamental freedom guaranteed by the Treaty ...

23. As regards, second, the necessity to preserve the cohesion of the tax system ...

24. In the present case, there is no direct link of that kind between any taxation and the application of preferential rates for admission to the museums and public monuments referred to in the action for failure to comply with obligations under the Treaty. That is all the more true given that the benefit of the advantageous rates at issue depends on the beneficiary's residence within the territory of the authority running the museum or public monument concerned, to the exclusion of other persons resident in Italy who, as such, are also subject to tax in that Member State.

25. Accordingly, the advantageous rates at issue, in so far as they are allowed only for persons resident within the territory of the authorities running the museum or public monument concerned, are also incompatible with Community law.

26. Finally, the Italian Government contends that the regulations which introduced the advantageous rates at issue are not within its competence. They concern museums or other exhibition spaces run by local authorities, whereas, in accordance with Article 47 of Presidential Decree No 616 of 24 July 1977 (GURI No 234 of 29 August 1977, Ordinary Supplement, III, p. 3), all services and activities relating to the existence, conservation, functioning, public enjoyment and development of museums, collections of artistic, historic or bibliographic interest ... belonging to the region or to other local authorities including non-territorial authorities subject to its control or, in any event, of local interest come within the exclusive competence of the regions.

27. In that regard, suffice it to recall that a Member State cannot plead conditions existing within its own legal system in order to justify its failure to comply with obligations arising under Community law. While each Member State may be free to allocate areas of internal legal competence as it sees fit, the fact still remains that it alone is responsible towards the Community under Article 226 EC for compliance with its obligations ...

28. In the light of the foregoing considerations, it must be declared that, by allowing discriminatory, advantageous rates for admission to museums, monuments, galleries, archaeological digs, parks and gardens classified as public monuments, granted by local or decentralised State authorities only in favour of Italian nationals and persons resident within the territory of those authorities running the cultural sites in question, who are aged over 60 or 65 years, and by excluding from such advantages tourists who are nationals of other Member States and non-residents who fulfil the same objective age requirements, the Italian Republic has failed to fulfil its obligations under Articles 12 EC and 49 EC.

Margaret Boyle and Others and Equal Opportunities Commission

ECJ, Opinion No. C-411/96 (27 October 1998).

By order of 15 October 1996, received at the Court on 23 December 1996, the Industrial Tribunal, Manchester, referred to the Court for a preliminary ruling under Article 177 of the EC Treaty five questions on the interpretation of Article 119 of the EC Treaty, Council Directive 75/117/EEC of 10 February 1975 on the approximation of the laws of the Member States relating to the application of the principle of equal pay for men and women ...

2. Those questions were raised in proceedings between Mrs Boyle and Others and their employer, the Equal Opportunities Commission (hereinafter 'the EOC'), concerning the Maternity Scheme applied by the latter to its staff. The national court states that the EOC is agreed to be an emanation of the State for the purposes, as far as it is concerned, of the direct effect of the directive at issue ...

9. The six applicants in the main proceedings are all employees of the EOC of childbearing age. They have completed at least one year's service with their employer and are not employed on a casual, standby or short-notice appointment, nor are they employed on a fixed-term appointment of less than two years. At least three of them have taken maternity leave in the recent past.

10. The employment contract entered between EOC and its employees comprises, first, the Staff Handbook, which applies to all workers and, second, the Maternity Scheme, which applies to female workers.

11. According to the Staff Handbook, staff who are unfit to work because of illness are entitled to their full salary for a maximum of six months in any 12 month period. Thereafter, they receive half pay up to a maximum of 12 months in any four-year period. Another clause provides that any leave taken without pay reduces the annual leave entitlement by a proportion of the amount of unpaid leave taken.

12. The dispute in the main proceedings centres on the Maternity Scheme. The persons concerned applied to the Industrial Tribunal, Manchester, for a declaration that certain conditions of the scheme are void or unenforceable in so far as they discriminate against female employees and are thus contrary to Article 119 of the Treaty or Directives 75/117, 76/207 or 92/85.

13. According to one of those clauses, any member of staff who has rendered at least one year's paid service with the EOC and is not employed on a casual, standby or short-notice appointment, or employed on a fixed-term appointment of less than two years is entitled to three months and one week's maternity leave on full pay for the period of continuous absence before and after childbirth. However, in order to benefit from that right, the employee must state that she intends to return to work in the EOC after childbirth and agree to be liable to repay any payment made during that period (excluding SMP to which she is entitled in any event), should she fail to return.

14. According to another contested clause of the Maternity Scheme, a member of staff who is entitled to paid maternity leave may also qualify for supplementary unpaid maternity leave provided, *inter alia*, that the total of those two periods of leave do not exceed 52 weeks.

15. Furthermore, the Maternity Scheme provides that if a member of staff specifies that she wishes to begin her maternity leave during the six weeks before the expected week of childbirth, and is absent on account of a pregnancy-related sickness immediately before the date on which she asked to begin her maternity leave and childbirth occurs during that period of absence, the date on which paid maternity leave commences can be brought forward to whichever is the later of the sixth week before the expected week of childbirth and the beginning of the period of absence on account of sickness.

16. Furthermore, according to the Maternity Scheme, paid sick leave is not granted once paid maternity leave has begun or during a period of supplementary unpaid maternity leave. There may, however, be an entitlement to SSP during unpaid maternity leave. Where a member of staff provides at least three weeks notification of her intention to return to work on a specified date, she is entitled to paid sick leave from that date. Paid sick leave following childbirth terminates the maternity leave and the supplementary unpaid maternity leave arrangements.

17. Finally, the Maternity Scheme states that members of staff who are not entitled to paid leave of absence retain their contractual rights and benefits, except remuneration, during the first 14 weeks of leave. In particular, annual leave continues to accrue. The period of absence only accrues for pension purposes if the employee is in receipt of SMP.

18. The national court points out that, pursuant to the foregoing provisions, employees on any form of paid leave, apart from paid maternity leave,

including sick leave and paid special leave, are not required to agree to repay any part of their salary if they do not return to work after the period of leave. Furthermore, it is agreed that substantially more women employees than men employees take periods of unpaid leave in the course of their careers, largely because they take supplementary maternity leave.

19. The Industrial Tribunal, Manchester, had doubts as to the compatibility of such provisions with Community law and decided to stay proceedings in order to refer the following questions to the Court for a preliminary ruling:

> In circumstances such as those of the present case, do any of the following matters infringe the prohibition of unfair and/or unfavourable treatment of women because of pregnancy, childbirth, maternity and/or sickness in relation thereto under EC law (in particular Article 119 of the Treaty of Rome and/or Council Directive 75/117/EEC and/or Council Directive 76/207/EEC and/or Council Directive 92/85/EEC):
>
> (1) A condition that maternity pay, beyond the Statutory Maternity Pay, is paid only if the woman states that she intends to return to work and agrees to be liable to repay such maternity pay if she does not return to work for one month on the conclusion of maternity leave.
>
> (2) A condition that where a woman, who is absent on paid sick leave with a pregnancy related illness, gives birth during such absence, her maternity leave may be backdated to the later date of either six weeks before the expected week of childbirth or when the sickness leave began.
>
> (3) A prohibition on a woman, who is unfit for work for any reason whilst on maternity leave, from taking paid sick leave, unless she elects to return to work and terminate her maternity leave.
>
> (4) A condition limiting the time during which annual leave accrues to the statutory minimum period of 14 weeks' maternity leave and accordingly excluding any other period of maternity leave.
>
> (5) A condition limiting the time in which pensionable service accrues during maternity leave to when the woman is in receipt of contractual or statutory maternity pay and accordingly excluding any period of unpaid maternity leave?

Cases

The Community legislation

20. Article 119 of the Treaty provides that Member States are required to ensure and to maintain 'the application of the principle that men and women should receive equal pay for equal work'.

21. According to Article 1 of Directive 75/117, the principle of equal pay laid down in Article 119 of the Treaty is intended to eliminate, for the same work or for work to which equal value is attributed, all discrimination on grounds of sex with regard to all aspects and conditions of remuneration.

22. According to Article 1(1) thereof, Directive 76/207 is intended 'to put into effect in the Member States the principle of equal treatment for men and women as regards access to employment, including promotion, and to vocational training and as regards working conditions'.

23. Article 2(1) of that directive provides:

> For the purposes of the following provisions, the principle of equal treatment shall mean that there shall be no discrimination whatsoever on grounds of sex either directly or indirectly by reference in particular to marital or family status.

24. However, according to Article 2(3), Directive 76/207 is 'without prejudice to provisions concerning the protection of women, particularly as regards pregnancy and maternity'.

25. Article 5(1) of that directive provides:

> Application of the principle of equal treatment with regard to working conditions, including the conditions governing dismissal, means that men and women shall be guaranteed the same conditions without discrimination on grounds of sex.

26. As regards Directive 92/85, Article 8 of that directive, concerning maternity leave, provides:

> 1. Member States shall take the necessary measures to ensure that workers within the meaning of Article 2 are entitled to a continuous period of maternity leave of at least 14 weeks allocated before and/or after confinement in accordance with national legislation and/or practice.
>
> 2. The maternity leave stipulated in paragraph 1 must include compulsory maternity leave of at least two weeks allocated before and/or after confinement in accordance with national legislation and/or practice.

27. As regards employment rights, Article 11 of Directive 92/85 states:

> In order to guarantee workers within the meaning of Article 2 the exercise of their health and safety protection rights as recognised in this Article, it shall be provided that: ...
>
> (2) in the case referred to in Article 8, the following must be ensured:
>
> (a) the rights connected with the employment contract of workers within the meaning of Article 2, other than those referred to in point (b) below;
>
> (b) maintenance of a payment to, and/or entitlement to an adequate allowance for, workers within the meaning of Article 2;
>
> (3) the allowance referred to in point 2(b) shall be deemed adequate if it guarantees income at least equivalent to that which the worker concerned would receive in the event of a break in her activities on grounds connected with her state of health, subject to any ceiling laid down under national legislation;
>
> (4) Member States may make entitlement to pay or the allowance referred to in points 1 and 2(b) conditional upon the worker concerned fulfilling the conditions of eligibility for such benefits laid down under national legislation.
>
> These conditions may under no circumstances provide for periods of previous employment in excess of 12 months immediately prior to the presumed date of confinement.

The first question

28. By its first question, the national court essentially asks whether Article 119 of the Treaty, as given specific expression by Directive 75/117 and Directives 76/207 or 92/85, precludes a clause in an employment contract which makes the payment, during the period of maternity leave referred to by Article 8 of Directive 92/85, of pay higher than the statutory payments in respect of maternity leave conditional on the woman's undertaking to return to work after the birth of the child for at least one month, failing which she is required to repay the difference between the amount of the pay she will have received during the period of maternity leave, on the one hand, and the amount of those payments, on the other.

29. As regards, first, Directive 92/85, the Commission submits that Article 11(2)(b) and (3) requires the payment to a worker on maternity leave of an

amount at least equivalent to that which that woman would receive under her employment contract if she were on sick leave. Where, as in this case, the employer has undertaken to pay workers on sick leave their full salary, women on maternity leave should, in accordance with the aforementioned provisions of the directive, receive an equivalent income. In those circumstances, it would be inconsistent with Article 11 of Directive 92/85 if female workers were required to repay the difference between the full salary they received from their employer during their maternity leave and the payments to which they are entitled during maternity leave under national legislation, in the event that they did not return to work after childbirth.

30. In that respect, it should be noted that it was in view of the risk that the provisions relating to maternity leave would be ineffective if rights connected with the employment contract were not maintained, that the Community legislature provided, in Article 11(2)(b) of Directive 92/85, that 'maintenance of a payment to, and/or entitlement to an adequate allowance' for workers to whom the directive applies must be ensured in the case of the maternity leave referred to in Article 8.

31. The concept of pay used in Article 11 of that directive, like the definition in the second paragraph of Article 119 of the Treaty, encompasses the consideration paid directly or indirectly by the employer during the worker's maternity leave in respect of her employment (see Case C-342/93 Gillespie and Others [1996] ECR I-475, paragraph 12). By contrast, the concept of allowance to which that provision also refers includes all income received by the worker during her maternity leave which is not paid to her by her employer pursuant to the employment relationship.

32. According to Article 11(3) of Directive 92/85, the allowance 'shall be deemed adequate if it guarantees income at least equivalent to that which the worker concerned would receive in the event of a break in her activities on grounds connected with her state of health, subject to any ceiling laid down under national legislation'. This is intended to ensure that, during her maternity leave, the worker receives an income at least equivalent to the sickness allowance provided for by national social security legislation in the event of a break in her activities on health grounds.

33. Female workers must be guaranteed an income of that level during their maternity leave, irrespective of whether, in accordance with Article 11(2)(b) of Directive 92/85, it is paid in the form of an allowance, pay or a combination of the two.

34. Although the wording of Article 11 refers only to the adequate nature of the allowance, the income guaranteed to female workers during maternity

leave must none the less also be adequate within the meaning of Article 11(3) of Directive 92/85 if it is paid in the form of pay or in conjunction with an allowance, as the case may be.

35. However, although Article 11(2)(b) and (3) requires the female worker to receive, during the period of maternity leave referred to in Article 8, income at least equivalent to the sickness allowance provided for under national social security legislation in the event of a break in her activities on health grounds, it is not intended to guarantee her any higher income which the employer may have undertaken to pay her, under the employment contract, should she be on sick leave.

36. It follows that a clause in an employment contract according to which a worker who does not return to work after childbirth is required to repay the difference between the pay received by her during her maternity leave and the statutory payments to which she was entitled in respect of maternity leave is compatible with Article 11(2)(b) and (3) of Directive 92/85 in so far as the level of those payments is not lower than the income which the worker concerned would receive, under the relevant national social security legislation, in the event of a break in her activities on grounds connected with her state of health.

37. Next, as regards Article 119 of the Treaty, as given specific expression by Directive 75/117 and Directive 76/207, the applicants in the main proceedings submit that the requirement that a woman must repay the contractual pay received by her during maternity leave, in so far as it exceeds SMP, if she does not return to work after childbirth constitutes discrimination against a woman for reasons of pregnancy, and is therefore contrary to the principle of equal pay. For other forms of paid leave, such as sick leave, workers in general are entitled to the agreed salary without having to undertake to return to work at the end of their leave.

38. Since the consideration paid by an employer under legislation or an employment contract to a woman on maternity leave is based on the employment relationship, it constitutes pay within the meaning of Article 119 of the Treaty and Article 1 of Directive 75/117 ... It therefore cannot also fall within the scope of Directive 76/207.

39. Furthermore, it is settled case-law that discrimination involves the application of different rules to comparable situations or the application of the same rule to different situations ...

40. As the Community legislature acknowledged when adopting Directive 92/85, pregnant workers and workers who have recently given birth or who

are breastfeeding are in an especially vulnerable situation which makes it necessary for the right to maternity leave to be granted to them but which, particularly during that leave, cannot be compared to that of a man or a woman on sick leave.

41. The maternity leave granted to a worker is intended, first, to protect a woman's biological condition during and after pregnancy and, second, to protect the special relationship between a woman and her child over the period which follows pregnancy and childbirth ...

42. A clause in an employment contract which makes the application of a more favourable set of rules than that prescribed by national legislation conditional on the pregnant woman, unlike any worker on sick leave, returning to work after childbirth, failing which she must repay the contractual maternity pay in so far as it exceeds the level of the statutory payments in respect of that leave, therefore does not constitute discrimination on grounds of sex for the purposes of Article 119 of the Treaty and Article 1 of Directive 75/117.

43. However, the level of those payments must satisfy the requirements laid down in Article 11(2)(b) and (3) of Directive 92/85.

44. In view of the foregoing, the answer to the first question must be that Article 119 of the Treaty, Article 1 of Directive 75/117 and Article 11 of Directive 92/85 do not preclude a clause in an employment contract which makes the payment, during the period of maternity leave referred to by Article 8 of Directive 92/85, of pay higher than the statutory payments in respect of maternity leave conditional on the worker's undertaking to return to work after the birth of the child for at least one month, failing which she is required to repay the difference between the amount of the pay she will have received during the period of maternity leave, on the one hand, and the amount of those payments, on the other.

The second question

45. By its second question, the national court essentially asks whether Article 119 of the Treaty, as given specific expression by Directive 75/117 and Directives 76/207 or 92/85, precludes a clause in an employment contract from requiring an employee who has expressed her intention to commence her maternity leave during the six weeks preceding the expected week of childbirth, and is on sick leave with a pregnancy-related illness immediately before that date and gives birth during the period of sick leave, to bring forward the date on which her paid maternity leave commences either to the

beginning of the sixth week preceding the expected week of childbirth or to the beginning of the period of sick leave, whichever is the later.

46. The applicants in the main proceedings submit that such a clause constitutes discrimination against women in so far as, unlike any other worker who is sick, a female worker who is unfit for work is not able to exercise her contractual right to unconditional paid sick leave if her illness is pregnancy-related and she gives birth while on sick leave. The female worker is thus required to take paid maternity leave on less favourable terms and, in particular, to repay a part of the salary received during that period if she does not return to work after the birth of the child.

47. It should be noted at the outset that, in so far as it concerns the determination of the beginning of the period of maternity leave, the question falls within the scope of Directive 76/207, in particular Article 5(1) thereof on working conditions, and not Article 119 of the Treaty or Directive 75/117.

48. Next, the contested clause applies to the case of a pregnant employee who has expressed her wish to commence her maternity leave during the six weeks preceding the expected week of childbirth.

49. In that respect, although Article 8 of Directive 92/85 provides for a continuous period of maternity leave of at least 14 weeks, including compulsory maternity leave of at least two weeks, it none the less leaves it open to the Member States to determine the date on which maternity leave is to commence.

50. Furthermore, pursuant to Article 2(3) of Directive 76/207, it is for every Member State, within the limits laid down in Article 8 of Directive 92/85, to fix periods of maternity leave so as to enable female workers to be absent during the period in which the disorders inherent in pregnancy and confinement occur ...

51. National legislation may therefore, as here, provide that the period of maternity leave commences with the date notified by the person concerned to her employer as the date on which she intends to commence her period of absence, or the first day after the beginning of the sixth week preceding the expected week of childbirth during which the employee is wholly or partly absent because of pregnancy, should that day fall on an earlier date.

52. The clause to which the second question relates merely reflects the choice made in such national legislation.

53. Furthermore, for the reasons described at paragraphs 42 and 43 above, the requirement that a female worker on maternity leave undertake to repay the pay received under her contract during her maternity leave, in so far as it exceeds the level of the payments provided for by national legislation during that leave, if she fails to return to work after childbirth cannot constitute unfavourable treatment of that worker.

54. The answer to the second question must therefore be that Article 8 of Directive 92/85 and Article 5(1) of Directive 76/207 do not preclude a clause in an employment contract from requiring an employee who has expressed her intention to commence her maternity leave during the six weeks preceding the expected week of childbirth, and is on sick leave with a pregnancy-related illness immediately before that date and gives birth during the period of sick leave, to bring forward the date on which her paid maternity leave commences either to the beginning of the sixth week preceding the expected week of childbirth or to the beginning of the period of sick leave, whichever is the later.

The third question

55. By its third question, the national court asks whether Article 119 of the Treaty, as given specific expression by Directive 75/117 and Directives 76/207 and 92/85, precludes a clause in an employment contract from prohibiting a woman from taking sick leave during the minimum period of 14 weeks' maternity leave to which a female worker is entitled pursuant to Article 8 of Directive 92/85 or any supplementary period of maternity leave granted to her by the employer, unless she elects to return to work and thus terminate her maternity leave.

56. First, as regards Directive 92/85, a distinction must be drawn between, on the one hand, the period of maternity leave of at least 14 weeks referred to by Article 8 of that directive and, on the other, any supplementary leave which, as in the present case, the employer is prepared to offer pregnant workers, and workers who have recently given birth or are breastfeeding.

57. In so far as the clause at issue prohibits a woman from taking sick leave during the period of maternity leave referred to by Article 8 of Directive 92/85 – which, in the United Kingdom is, in principle, 14 weeks – unless she terminates that leave, it must be examined in the light of that provision.

58. In that respect, although the Member States are required, pursuant to Article 8 of the aforesaid directive, to take the necessary measures to ensure that workers are entitled to a period of maternity leave of at least 14 weeks, those workers may waive that right, with the exception of the two weeks

compulsory maternity leave provided for in paragraph 2, which, in the United Kingdom, commence on the day on which the child is born.

59. Furthermore, Article 8 of Directive 92/85 provides that the period of maternity leave provided for therein must be at least 14 continuous weeks, allocated before and/or after confinement. It follows from the purpose of that provision that the woman cannot interrupt or be required to interrupt her maternity leave and return to work, and complete the remaining period of maternity leave later.

60. In contrast, if a woman becomes ill during the period of maternity leave referred to by Article 8 of Directive 92/85 and places herself under the sick leave arrangements, and that sick leave ends before the expiry of the period of maternity leave, she cannot be deprived of the right to continued enjoyment, after that date, of the maternity leave provided for by the aforementioned provision until the expiry of the minimum period of 14 weeks, that period being calculated from the date on which the maternity leave commenced.

61. Any other interpretation would compromise the purpose of maternity leave, in so far as that leave is intended to protect not only the woman's biological condition but also the special relationship between a woman and her child over the period which follows pregnancy and childbirth. The continuous period of maternity leave of at least 14 weeks, allocated before and/or after confinement, is intended in particular to provide the woman with the guarantee that she can look after her new-born baby in the weeks following childbirth. Except in exceptional circumstances, she cannot therefore be deprived of that guarantee for reasons of health.

62. In so far as it prohibits a woman from taking sick leave during any leave granted by the employer in addition to the period of maternity leave provided for by Article 8 of Directive 92/85, unless she terminates that leave, such a clause does not fall within the scope of that provision.

63. The third question also seeks to ascertain whether the clause at issue constitutes discrimination as regards the right to sick leave and, therefore, falls within the scope of Directive 76/207, in particular Article 5(1) thereof, concerning conditions of employment. Article 119 of the Treaty and Directive 75/117 are therefore not in point. In view of the foregoing, the third question need be examined only in so far as the clause of the employment contract referred to therein applies to the supplementary period of maternity leave granted by the employer to female workers.

64. In that respect, the principle of non-discrimination laid down in Article 5 of Directive 76/207 does not require a woman to be able to exercise simultaneously both the right to supplementary maternity leave granted to her by the employer and the right to sick leave.

65. Consequently, in order for a woman on maternity leave to qualify for sick leave, she may be required to terminate the period of supplementary maternity leave granted to her by the employer.

66. The answer must therefore be that a clause in an employment contract which prohibits a woman from taking sick leave during the minimum period of 14 weeks' maternity leave to which a female worker is entitled pursuant to Article 8(1) of Directive 92/85, unless she elects to return to work and thus terminate her maternity leave, is not compatible with Directive 92/85. By contrast, a clause in an employment contract which prohibits a woman from taking sick leave during a period of supplementary maternity leave granted to her by the employer, unless she elects to return to work and thus terminate her maternity leave, is compatible with Directives 76/207 and 92/85.

The fourth question

67. By its fourth question, the national court essentially seeks to ascertain whether Article 119 of the Treaty, as given specific expression by Directive 75/117 and Directives 76/207 or 92/85, precludes a clause in an employment contract from limiting the period during which annual leave accrues to the minimum period of 14 weeks' maternity leave to which female workers are entitled under Article 8 of

Directive 92/85 and from providing that annual leave ceases to accrue during any period of supplementary maternity leave granted to them by their employer.

68. First, the accrual of annual leave constitutes a right connected with the employment contract of workers for the purposes of Article 11(2)(a) of Directive 92/85.

69. It follows from that provision that such a right need only be ensured during the period of maternity leave of at least 14 weeks to which workers are entitled under Article 8 of Directive 92/85.

70. Here, the duration of that period of leave is, in principle, fixed at 14 weeks in the United Kingdom.

71. Consequently, the directive does not preclude a clause, such as that to which the question referred to the Court relates, according to which annual leave ceases to accrue during any period of supplementary maternity leave

granted by employers to pregnant workers or workers who have recently given birth or who are breastfeeding.

72. Second, the particular rules concerning the accrual of annual leave constitute an integral part of working conditions within the meaning of Article 5(1) of Directive 76/207 and cannot therefore also fall within the scope of Article 119 of the Treaty or Directive 75/117.

73. In that respect, the applicants point out that, according to the EOC's Staff Handbook, if unpaid leave is taken (sick leave, special leave or supplementary maternity leave), the annual leave entitlement is reduced by a proportion of the amount of unpaid leave taken. However, since a substantially greater proportion of women than men take periods of unpaid leave because they take supplementary maternity leave, that rule – which is ostensibly gender-neutral – constitutes indirect discrimination against women, contrary to Article 5(1) of Directive 76/207.

74. First, as is clear from the documents before the Court, all employees of EOC who take unpaid leave cease to accrue annual leave during that period. According to the EOC Staff Handbook, unpaid leave includes both sick leave and special leave, which are available to any worker, as well as supplementary maternity leave granted by EOC in addition to the 14 weeks' maternity leave provided for by the Employment Rights Act 1996.

75. Such a clause therefore does not constitute direct discrimination since the accrual of annual leave during the period of unpaid leave is interrupted for both men and for women who take unpaid leave. It is therefore necessary to consider whether such a clause can constitute indirect discrimination.

76. The Court has consistently held that indirect discrimination arises where a national measure, albeit formulated in neutral terms, works to the disadvantage of far more women than men...

77. In that respect, it should be noted that, as the national court points out, substantially more women than men take periods of unpaid leave during their career because they take supplementary maternity leave, so that, in practice, the clause at issue applies to a greater percentage of women than men.

78. However, the fact that such a clause applies more frequently to women results from the exercise of the right to unpaid maternity leave granted to them by their employers in addition to the period of protection guaranteed by Article 8 of Directive 92/85.

79. Female workers who exercise that right subject to the condition that annual leave ceases to accrue during the period of unpaid leave cannot be regarded as at a disadvantage compared to male workers. The supplementary unpaid maternity leave constitutes a special advantage, over and above the protection provided for by Directive 92/85 and is available only to women, so that the fact that annual leave ceases to accrue during that period of leave cannot amount to less favourable treatment of women.

80. The answer must therefore be that Directives 92/85 and 76/207 do not preclude a clause in an employment contract from limiting the period during which annual leave accrues to the minimum period of 14 weeks' maternity leave to which female workers are entitled under Article 8 of Directive 92/85 and from providing that annual leave ceases to accrue during any period of supplementary maternity leave granted to them by their employer.

The fifth question

81. It appears from the documents before the Court that, by its fifth question, the national court essentially seeks to ascertain whether Article 119 of the Treaty, as given specific expression by Directive 75/117 and Directives 92/85 or 76/207, precludes a clause in an employment contract from limiting, in the context of an occupational scheme wholly financed by the employer, the accrual of pension rights during maternity leave to the period during which the woman receives the pay provided for by that employment contract or national legislation.

82. The accrual of pension rights in the context of an occupational scheme wholly financed by the employer constitutes one of the rights connected with the employment contracts of the workers for the purposes of Article 11(2)(a) of Directive 92/85.

83. As stated at paragraph 69 above, in accordance with that provision, such rights must be ensured during the period of maternity leave of at least 14 weeks to which female workers are entitled under Article 8 of Directive 92/85.

84. Although, in accordance with Article 11(4) of Directive 92/85, it is open to Member States to make entitlement to pay or the adequate allowance referred to in Article 11(2)(b) conditional upon the worker concerned fulfilling the conditions of eligibility for such benefits laid down under national legislation, no such possibility exists in respect of rights connected with the employment contract within the meaning of Article 11(2)(a).

85. The accrual of pension rights under an occupational scheme during the period of maternity leave referred to by Article 8 of Directive 92/85 cannot

therefore be made conditional upon the woman's receiving the pay provided for by her employment contract or SMP during that period.

86. Since the clause to which the fifth question relates is contrary to Directive 92/85, it is not necessary to interpret Article 119 of the Treaty, as given specific expression by Directive 75/117 and Directive 76/207.

87. The answer to the fifth question must therefore be that Directive 92/85 precludes a clause in an employment contract from limiting, in the context of an occupational scheme wholly financed by the employer, the accrual of pension rights during the period of maternity leave referred to by Article 8 of that directive to the period during which the woman receives the pay provided for by that contract or national legislation.

Legal Resources Foundation v. Zambia

ACHPR, Comm. No. 211/98 (2001).

[footnotes omitted]

1. The Complainant, an NGO that has Observer Status with the African Commission and is based in Zambia, is bringing this complaint against a State Party to the Charter, Zambia.

2. The Complainant alleges that the Zambian Government has enacted into law, a constitution which is discriminatory, divisive and violates the human rights of 35 percent of the entire population. The Constitution (Amendment) Act of 1996, it is alleged, has not only violated the rights of its citizens, but has also taken away the accrued rights of other citizens, including the first President, Dr. Kenneth Kaunda.

3. The Complainant alleges that the said Constitution of Zambia Amendment Act of 1996 provides *inter- alia*, that anyone who wants to contest the office of the president has to prove that both parents are/were Zambians by birth or descent.

4. [The] ... Constitution Amendment Act further provides that nobody who has served two five-year terms as President shall be eligible for re-election to that office.

5. Complainant alleges that the amended constitutional provisions are in contravention of international human rights instruments in general and the African Charter on Human and Peoples' Rights in particular.

6. Complainant has taken the case to the Supreme Court of Zambia between May and August 1996 ... The Complainant's case was ... thrown out of court. ...

9. The Supreme Court of Zambia is the highest Court of jurisdiction in the land ... all local remedies have been exhausted ...

[Representations by the Government of Zambia]

36. The matter concerns the Republican Constitution of Zambia and is therefore an open matter for discussion. The background to the Constitution of Zambia (Amendment) Act of 1996 is attributable to the desire of the Zambian people to save and preserve the Office of the President for Zambians with traceable descent.

37. The position was arrived at in the Mwanakatwe Commission of Inquiry Report commissioned to gather views on the content of the Republican

Constitution. The amendment to the Constitution was not targeted at any person in the country.

38. Zambia welcomes views expressed on its Republican Constitution as a way of building a strong democracy. It is open to expert opinions on the issue, and will continue to listen to views expressed on it.

39. Zambia views the complaint filed by the Legal Resources Foundation as an opinion on the Constitution. The variance of opinion of the Complainant from that of the majority therefore is in accordance with democratic principle of freedom of opinion. Despite this difference, democracy entails the rule of the majority. Hence the amendment to the Republican Constitution incorporating the views expressed in the Mwanakatwe Commission of inquiry Report for an indigenous Zambian to hold Office of President.

40. Zambia is prepared to co-operate with the Commission and to elaborate further on the issues, if necessary ...

41. The Government avers that although the communication is vague as to the details of the judicial process that was exhausted, Zambia would however assume that the issues raised by the Complainant were finally settled by the Supreme Court ...

42. the Zambian Parliament has the power to adopt an alteration to the Constitution and the President may assent to a Constitution that has been altered. However, if Parliament had amended the entire Constitution, there would have been a mandatory need for a national referendum in respect of Article 79 and Part III of the Constitution, which contains the Bill of Rights.

43. The Government contends that the powers, jurisdiction and competence of Parliament to alter the Constitution of Zambia are extensive provided that Parliament adheres to the provisions of ... of the Constitution. The constitutional history of Zambia has shown that the alteration of the Constitution has depended on who controls the majority in Parliament. The ruling Party dominated Parliament could therefore adopt the altered Constitution.

44. All individuals in Zambia are equal before the law and everyone enjoys the protection of his/her human rights and fundamental freedoms as provided for by the law.

45. Zambia abhors any type of discrimination ...

46. The Government points out that it is in this context that Zambian people were of the view that it was reasonable for the Office of the President to be

subject to other qualifications i.e. an indigenous Zambian candidate of traceable descent. Therefore there was no contravention of Article 2 of the Charter.

47. The limitations [in the Constitution] being reasonable within the law, the Government avers further that there has therefore been no violation of Article 2 of the Charter as the limitations provided for by Article 34 of the Republican Constitution are within the law. Zambia also submits that there is no violation of Article 13 of the Charter, which guarantees every citizen the right to participate in government. If anything, there is a proviso that such should be "in accordance with the provisions of the law."

48. It underscores the fact that Articles 34 and 35 of the Constitution are within Zambia's laws and therefore there is no violation of Article 13 of the Charter.

49. It stated that Zambia considers the inclusion of a violation of Article 19 of the Charter by the Complainant as not being within the purview of the present communication. It is of the opinion that Article 19 of the Charter relates to the principle of "self-determination" by the mere mention of the term "peoples." This position notwithstanding, the peoples of Zambia are equal. It urges the Commission not to entertain this ground, as it is inappropriate to the issues raised in the communication.

50. It argues that the discrimination alleged in Articles 34 and 35 of the Constitution is not unlawful and it reflects the popular desire of the majority of the Zambian people to save and preserve the "Office of the President" for Zambians. The Constitution of Zambia (Amendment) Act, 1996, therefore, seeks to give effect to the will of the people.

THE LAW
Merits

52. The allegation before the Commission is that Respondent State has violated Articles 2, 3 and 19 of the Charter in that the Constitution of Zambia Amendment Act of 1996 is discriminatory. Article 34 provides that anyone who wishes to contest the office of President of Zambia had to prove that both parents were Zambian citizens by birth or descent. The effect of this amendment was to prohibit a Zambian citizen, former President Dr. Kenneth David Kaunda from contesting the elections having been duly nominated by a legitimate political party. It is alleged that the effect of the amendment was to disenfranchise some 35% of the electorate of Zambia from standing as candidate Presidents in any future elections for the highest office in the land.

53. The enactment of the amendment to the Constitution is not in dispute. Neither is it denied that Dr. Kenneth Kaunda was thus denied the right to contest the elections for the office of President. Respondent State, however, denies that some 35% of Zambian citizens would be constitutionally denied the right to stand as President and alleges that in any event such facts have no relevance to the matter at hand. It nevertheless argues that the said amendment was constitutional, justifiable and not in violation of the Charter.

54. ... the Zambia Supreme Court was petitioned to declare the then proposed amendments to the Constitution unconstitutional in that the amendments contained in Articles 34(3)(b) and 35(2) of the Constitution (Amendment) Act bar persons qualified to stand for election as President of the Republic under the 1991 Constitution and deny them the right to participate fully without hindrance in the affairs of government and shaping the destiny of the country and undermine democracy and free and fair elections which are the basic features of the Constitution of 1991.

55. It is alleged that the matter was rushed through parliament by the ruling party and enacted into law while the legal and constitutional principles were before the courts for adjudication. In the event, the court dismissed the appeal for the reason that the petition was "attacking an Act of Parliament on the ground that it violated Part III of the Constitution relating to Fundamental Rights. We are satisfied that the application was commenced by a wrong procedure and that in our jurisdiction the application was untenable" (per Sakala JS at 292) ...

58. In the task of interpretation and application of the Charter, the Commission is enjoined by Articles 60 and 61 to "draw inspiration from international law on human and peoples' rights" as reflected in the instruments of the OAU and the UN as well as other international standard setting principles (Article 60). The Commission is also required to take into consideration other international conventions and African practices consistent with international norms etc.

59. Although international agreements are not self-executing in Zambia, the government of Zambia does not seek to avoid its international responsibilities in terms of the treaties it is party to (*vide Communication 212/98 Amnesty International / Zambia*). This is just as well because international treaty law prohibits states from relying on their national law as justification for their non-compliance with international obligations (Article 27, Vienna Convention on the Law of Treaties). Likewise an international treaty body like the Commission has no jurisdiction in interpreting and applying

domestic law. Instead a body like the Commission may examine a State's compliance with the treaty in this case the African Charter. In other words the point of the exercise is to interpret and apply the African Charter rather than to test the validity of domestic law for its own sake ...

60. What this does mean, however, is that international treaties which are not part of domestic law and which may not be directly enforceable in the national courts, nonetheless impose obligations on State Parties. It is noticeable that the application of the Charter was not part of the argument before the national courts.

61. Conscious of the ramifications of any decision on this matter, the Commission had invited the parties to address the question of the extent of the jurisdiction of the Commission when it comes to domestic law including as is the case in this instance the Constitution. Counsel for the Respondent State argued that the Commission had no *locus standi* to adjudicate on the validity of domestic law. That position is correct. What must be asserted, however, is that the Commission has the duty to "give its views or make recommendations to Governments ... to formulate and lay down principles and rules aimed at solving legal problems relating to human and peoples' rights and fundamental freedoms upon which African Governments may base their legislation and interpret all the provisions of the present Charter..." (Article 45).

62. In addition, the Commission is mindful of the positive obligations incumbent on State Parties to the Charter in terms of Article 1 not only to "recognise" the rights under the Charter but to go on to "undertake to adopt legislative or other measures to give effect to them." The obligation is peremptory, States *"shall* undertake ...." Indeed, it is only if the States take their obligations seriously that the rights of citizens can be protected. In addition, it is only to the extent that the Commission is prepared to interpret and apply the Charter that Governments would appreciate the extent of its obligations and citizens understand the scope of the rights they have under the Charter.

63. Article 2 of the Charter abjures discrimination on the basis of any of the grounds set out, among them "language... national or social origin ... birth or other status ...." The right to equality is very important. It means that citizens should expect to be treated fairly and justly within the legal system and be assured of equal treatment before the law and equal enjoyment of the rights available to all other citizens. The right to equality is important for a second reason. Equality or lack of it affects the capacity of one to enjoy many other rights. For example, one who bears the burden of disadvantage because of

one's place of birth or social origin suffers indignity as a human being and equal and proud citizen. He may vote for others but has limitations when it comes to standing for office. In other words the country may be deprived of the leadership and resourcefulness such a person may bring to national life. Finally, the Commission should take note of the fact that in a growing number of African States, these forms of discrimination have caused violence and social and economic instability which has benefited no one. It has cast doubt on the legitimacy of national elections and the democratic credentials of States.

64. All parties are agreed that any measure which seeks to exclude a section of the citizenry from participating in the democratic processes as the amendment in question has managed to do, is discriminatory and falls foul of the Charter. Article 11 of the Constitution of Zambia provides that there shall be no discrimination on the grounds of "race, place of origin, political opinions, colour, creed, sex or marital status ...." The African Charter has "national or social origin ...." which could be encompassed within the expression "place of origin" in the Zambian Constitution. Article 23(1) of the Zambian Constitution says that parliament shall not make any law that "is discriminatory of itself or in its effect ...."

65. The Respondent State, however, seeks to rely on some exceptions as justification in Zambian law for the exception. It is held that the right to equality has limitations which are justifiable and that the justifications are based on Zambian law and the Charter.

66. Article 11 of the Zambian Constitution states clearly that the right to non-discrimination is "subject to limitations ...." Among the limitations reference is made to Article 23(5) which provides that:

> ... nothing contained in any law shall be held to be inconsistent with or in contravention of clause (1) to the extent that it is shown that it makes reasonable provision with respect to qualifications for service as a public officer..." It is argued that following a consultative process, the Zambian people were of the view that the Office of President be subject to the additional qualification that the President be "an indigenous Zambian candidate of traceable descent.

67. There has been some persistent confusion in arguments before us between "limitations" and "justification." Limitations refer to what may be referred to as the statute of limitations which gives a lower threshold of enjoyment of the right. Such limitations are allowed by law or provided for in the Constitution itself. In the African Charter these would typically be

referred to as the 'claw-back' clauses. "Justification" however applies in those cases where justification is sought setting perimeters on the enjoyment of a right. In other words, there has to be a two-stage process. First, the recognition of the right and the fact that such a right has been violated but that, secondly, such a violation is justifiable in law. The Vienna Declaration and Programme of Action (1993) has affirmed that "all human rights are universal, interrelated, interdependent..." and as such they must be interpreted and applied as mutually reinforcing. It is interesting to note for example, that Article 2 does not have a 'claw-back' clause while Article 13 limits the right to "every citizen" but goes on to state that "in accordance with the law."

68. In the matter before us therefore the Government of Zambia concedes that the measures were discriminatory but then goes on to argue (1) a limitation of the right, and (2) justification of the violation. It is argued that the measure was within the law and Constitution of Zambia. It was stated before the Commission that Zambia has a constitutional system of parliamentary sovereignty hence even the Supreme Court could not "attack" an Act of Parliament .... The task of the Commission, however, is not to seek to do that which even the Zambian courts could not do. The responsibility of the Commission is to examine the compatibility of domestic law and practice with the Charter. Consistent with decisions in the European and Inter-American jurisdictions, the Commission's jurisdiction does not extend to adjudicating on the legality or constitutionality or otherwise of national laws. Where the Commission finds a legislative measure to be incompatible with the Charter, this obliges the State to restore conformity ....

69. It is stated further that the limitation of the right is provided for in the Zambian Constitution and that it is justifiable by popular will in that, following the work of the Mwanakatwe Commission on the Constitution, it was recommended that the Zambian people desired "to save and preserve the Office of the President for Zambians with traceable descent ...." Regarding the claim that the measure deprived some 35% of Zambians of their rights under the previous Constitution, counsel for Respondent State dismisses this as mere speculation.

70. The Commission has argued forcefully that no State Party to the Charter should avoid its responsibilities by recourse to the limitations and "claw-back" clauses in the Charter. It was stated following developments in other jurisdictions, that the Charter cannot be used to justify violations of sections of it. The Charter must be interpreted holistically and all clauses must reinforce each other. The purpose or effect of any limitation must also be examined, as the limitation of the right cannot be used to subvert rights

already enjoyed. Justification, therefore, cannot be derived solely from popular will, as such cannot be used to limit the responsibilities of State Parties in terms of the Charter. Having arrived at this conclusion, it does not matter whether one or 35% of Zambians are disenfranchised by the measure, that anyone is, is not disputed and it constitutes a violation of the right.

71. The Commission has arrived at a decision regarding allegations of violation of Article 13 by examining closely the nature and content of the right to equality (Article 2). It cannot be denied that there are Zambian citizens born in Zambia but whose parents were not born in what has become known as the Republic of Zambia following independence in 1964. This is a particularly vexing matter as the movement of people in what had been the Central African Federation (now the States of Malawi, Zambia and Zimbabwe) was free and that by Zambia's own admission, all such residents were, upon application, granted the citizenship of Zambia at independence. Rights which have been enjoyed for over 30 years cannot be lightly taken away. To suggest that an indigenous Zambian is one who was born and whose parents were born in what came (later) to be known as the sovereign territory of the State of Zambia may be arbitrary and its application of [retroactivity] cannot be justifiable according to the Charter.

72. The Charter makes it clear that citizens should have the right to participate in the government of their country "directly or through freely chosen representatives..." The pain in such an instance is caused not just to the citizen who suffers discrimination by reason of place of origin but that the rights of the citizens of Zambia to "freely choose" political representatives of their choice, is violated. The purpose of the expression "in accordance with the provisions of the law" is surely intended to regulate how the right is to be exercised rather than that the law should be used to take away the right.

73. The Commission believes that recourse to Article 19 of the Charter was mistaken. The section dealing with "peoples" cannot apply in this instance. To do so would require evidence that the effect of the measure was to affect adversely an identifiable group of Zambian citizens by reason of their common ancestry, ethnic origin, language or cultural habits. The allegedly offensive provisions in the Zambia Constitution (Amendment) Act ... do not seek to do that.

For the above reasons, the Commission,

Finds that the Republic of Zambia is in violation of Articles 2, 3(1) and 13 of the African Charter;

Strongly urges the Republic of Zambia to take the necessary steps to bring its laws and Constitution into conformity with the African charter; and

Requests the Republic of Zambia to report back to the Commission when it submits its next country report in terms of Article 62 on measures taken to comply with this recommendation.

Ms A. T. v. Hungary

UN CEDAW Comm. No. 2/2003 (26 January 2005).
Views under article 7, paragraph 3, of the Optional Protocol

2.1 The author states that for the past four years she has been subjected to regular severe domes tic violence and serious threats by her common law husband, L. F., father of her two children, one of whom is severely brain - damaged. Although L. F. allegedly possesses a firearm and has threatened to kill the author and rape the children, the author has not gone to a shelter, reportedly because no shelter in the country is equipped to take in a fully disabled child together with his mother and sister. The author also states that there are currently no protection orders or restraining orders available under Hungarian law.

2.2 In March 1999, L. F. moved out of the family apartment. His subsequent visits allegedly typically included battering and/or loud shouting, aggravated by his being in a drunken state. In March 2000, L. F. reportedly moved in with a new female partner and left the family home, taking most of the furniture and household items with him. The author claims that he did not pay child support for three years, which forced her to claim the support by going to the court and to the police, and that he has used this form of financial abuse as a violent tactic in addition to continuing to threaten her physically. Hoping to protect herself and the children, the author states that she changed the lock on the door of the family's apartment on 11 March 2000. On 14 and 26 March 2000, L. F. filled the lock with glue and on 28 March 2000, he kicked in a part of the door when the author refused to allow him to enter the apartment. The author further states that, on 27 July 2001, L. F. broke into the apartment using violence.

2.3 L. F. is said to have battered the author severely on several occasions, beginning in March 1998. Since then, 10 medical certificates have been issued in connection with separate incidents of severe physical violence, even after L. F. left the family residence, which, the author submits, constitute a continuum of violence. The most recent incident took place on 27 July 2001 when L. F. broke into the apartment and subjected the author to a severe beating, which necessitated her hospitalization.

2.4 The author states that there have been civil proceedings regarding L. F.'s access to the family's residence, a 2 and a half room apartment (of 54 by 56 square metres) jointly owned by L. F. and the author. Decisions by the court of the first instance, the Pest Central District Court (Pesti Központi Kerületi Bíróság), were rendered on 9 March 2001 and 13 September 2002 (supplementary decision). On 4 September 2003, the Budapest Regional

- 425-

Court (Forvarosi Bíróság) issued a final decision authorizing L. F. to return and use the apartment. The judges reportedly based their decision on the following grounds: (a) lack of substantiation of the claim that L. F. regularly battered the author; and (b) that L. F.'s right to the property, including possession, could not be restricted. Since that date, and on the basis of the earlier attacks and verbal threats by her former partner, the author claims that her physical integrity, physical and mental health and life have been at serious risk and that she lives in constant fear. The author reportedly submitted to the Supreme Court a petition for review of the 4 September 2003 decision, which was pending at the time of her submission of supplementary information to the Committee on 2 January 2004.

2.5 The author states that she also initiated civil proceedings regarding division of the property, which have been suspended. She claims that L. F. refused her offer to be compensated for half of the value of the apartment and turn over ownership to her. In these proceedings the author reportedly submitted a motion for injunctive relief (for her exclusive right to use the apartment), which was rejected on 25 July 2000.

2.6 The author states that there have been two ongoing criminal procedures against L. F., one that began in 1999 at the Pest Central District Court (Pesti Központi Kerületi Bíróság) concerning two incidents of battery and assault causing her bodily harm and the second that began in July 2001 concerning an incident of battery and assault that resulted in her being hospitalized for a week with a serious kidney injury. In her submission of 2 January 2004, the author states that there would be a trial on 9 January 2004. Reportedly, the latter procedure was initiated by the hospital ex officio. The author further states that L. F. has not been detained at any time in this connection and that no action has been taken by the Hungarian authorities to protect the author from him. The author claims that, as a victim, she has not been privy to the court documents and, that, therefore, she cannot submit them to the Committee.

2.7 The author also submits that she has requested assistance in writing, in person and by phone, from the local child protection authorities, but that her requests have been to no avail since the authorities allegedly feel unable to do anything in such situations.

The Claim

3.1 The author alleges that she is a victim of violations by Hungary of articles 2 (a), (b) and (e), 5 (a) and 16 of the Convention on the Elimination of All Forms of Discrimination against Women for its failure to provide effective protection from her former common law husband. She claims that the State party passively neglected its "positive" obligations under the Convention and supported the continuation of a situation of domestic violence against her.

3.2 She claims that the irrationally lengthy criminal procedures against L. F., the lack of protection orders or restraining orders under current Hungarian law and the fact that L. F. has not spent any time in custody constitute violations of her rights under the Convention as well as violations of general recommendation 19 of the Committee. She maintains that these criminal procedures can hardly be considered effective and/or immediate protection.

3.3 The author is seeking justice for herself and her children, including fair compensation, for suffering and for the violation of the letter and spirit of the Convention by the State party.

3.4 The author is also seeking the Committee's intervention into the intolerable situation, which affects many women from all segments of Hungarian society. In particular, she calls for the (a) introduction of effective and immediate protection for victims of domestic violence into the legal system, (b) provision of training programmes on gender-sensitivity, the Convention on the Elimination of All Forms of Discrimination against Women and the Optional Protocol, including for judges, prosecutors, police and practising lawyers, and (c) provision of free legal aid to victims of gender-based violence, including domestic violence.

3.5 As to the admissibility of the communication, the author maintains that she has exhausted all available domestic remedies. She refers, however, to a pending petition for review that she submitted to the Supreme Court in respect of the decision of 4 September 2003. The author describes this remedy as an extraordinary remedy and one which is only available in cases of a violation of the law by lower courts. Such cases reportedly take some six months to be resolved. The author believes that it is very unlikely that the Supreme Court will find a violation of the law because Hungarian courts allegedly do not consider the Convention to be a law that is to be applied by them. She submits that this should not mean that she has failed to exhaust domestic remedies for the purposes of the Optional Protocol.

3.6 The author contends that, although most of the incidents complained of took place prior to March 2001 when the Optional Protocol entered into force in Hungary, they constitute elements of a clear continuum of regular domestic violence and that her life continues to be in danger. She alleges that one serious violent act took place in July 2001, that is after the Optional Protocol came into force in the country ....

Cases

4.1 On 10 October 2003, with her initial submission, the author also urgently requested effective interim measures, as may be necessary, in accordance with article 5, paragraph 1, of the Optional Protocol in order to avoid possible irreparable damage to her person, that is to save her life, which she feels is threatened by her violent former partner ....

5.1 By its submission of 20 April 2004, the State party gave an explanation of the civil proceedings to which reference is made by the author ....

5.6 The State party maintains that although the author did not make effective use of the domestic remedies available to her, and although some domestic proceedings are still pending, the State party does not wish to raise any preliminary objections as to the admissibility of the communication. At the same time, the State party admits that these remedies were not capable of providing immediate protection to the author from ill-treatment by her former partner.

5.7 Having realized that the system of remedies against domestic violence is incomplete in Hungarian law and that the effectiveness of the existing procedures is not sufficient, the State party states that it has instituted a comprehensive action programme against domestic violence in 2003. On 16 April 2003, the Hungarian Parliament adopted a resolution on the national strategy for the prevention and effective treatment of violence within the family, setting forth a number of legislative and other actions to be taken in the field by the State party. These actions include: introducing a restraining order into legislation; ensuring that proceedings before the Courts or other authorities in domestic violence cases are given priority; reinforcing existing witness protection rules and introducing new rules aimed at ensuring adequate legal protection for the personal security of victims of violence within the family; elaborating clear protocols for the police, childcare organs and social and medical institutions; extending and modernizing the network of shelters and setting up victim protection crisis centres; providing free legal aid in certain circumstances; working out a complex nationwide action programme to eliminate violence within the family that applies sanctions and protective measures; training of professionals; ensuring data collection on violence within the family; requesting the judiciary to organize training for judges and to find a way to ensure that cases relating to violence within the family are given priority; and launching a nationwide campaign to address indifference to violence within the family and the perception of domestic violence as a private matter and to raise awareness of State, municipal and social organs and journalists. In a resolution of 16 April 2003 by the Hungarian Parliament, a request with due regard to the separation of powers has been also put forward to the National Council of the Judiciary to organize training for judges and to find a way to ensure that cases relating to violence within the family are given priority. In the resolution, reference is made, inter alia, to the Convention on the Elimination of All Forms of Discrimination against Women, the concluding comments of the Committee on the combined fourth and fifth periodic report of Hungary adopted at its exceptional session in August 2002 and the Declaration on the Elimination of Violence against Women.

5.8 In a second resolution, the Parliament has also stated that prevention of violence within the family is a high priority in the national strategy of crime prevention and describes the tasks of various actors of the State and of the society. These include: prompt and effective intervention by the police and other investigating authorities; medical treatment of pathologically aggressive persons and application of protective measures for those who live in their environment; operation of 24-hour "SOS" lines; organization of rehabilitation programmes; organization of sport and leisure time activities for youth and children of violence - prone families; integration of non -violent conflict resolution techniques and family - life education into the public educational system; establishment and operation of crisis intervention houses as well as mother and child care centres and support for the accreditation of civil organizations by municipalities; and launching of a media campaign against violence within the family.

5.9 The State party further states that it has implemented various measures to eliminate domestic violence. These measures include registration of criminal proceedings (Robotzsaru) in a manner that will facilitate the identification of trends in offences related to violence within the family, as well as the collection of data, the expanded operation of family protection services by 1 July 2005, including units for ill-treated women without children in Budapest, which is to be followed by the establishment of seven regional centres. The first shelter is planned to be set up in 2004. The Government has prepared a draft law, which will enter into force on 1 July 2005, that provides for a new protective remedy for victims of domestic violence, namely the issuance of a temporary restraining order by the police and a restraining order by the Courts, accompanied by fines if intentionally disregarded, and has decided to improve the support services available to such victims.

5.10 Additionally, the State party states that special emphasis has been put on the handling of cases of domestic violence by the police. The State party observes that the efforts made in this field have already brought about significant results which were summed up by the National Headquarters of the Police in a press communication in December 2003. Non -governmental organizations have also been involved in the elaboration of the governmental policy to combat domestic violence.

6.1 By her submission of 23 June 2004, the author states that, in spite of promises, the only step that has been taken under the Decree/Decision of Parliament on the Prevention of, and Response to Domestic Violence is the entry into force of the new protocol of the police, who now respond to domestic violence cases. She states that the new protocol is still not in line with the Convention and that batterers are not taken into custody, as this would be considered a violation of their human rights. Instead, according to the media, the police mostly mediate on the spot.

6.2 The author further states that the parliamentary debate on the draft law on restraining orders has been postponed until the autumn. Resistance to change is said to be strong and decision -makers allegedly still do not fully understand why they should interfere in what they consider to be the private affairs of families. The author suggests that a timely decision in her case may help decision–makers understand that the effective prevention of, and response to domestic violence are not only demands of victims and "radical" non -governmental organizations but also of the international human rights community.

6.3 The author reports that her situation has not changed and she still lives in constant fear as regards her former partner. From time to time L. F. has harassed her and threatened to move back into the apartment.

6.4 The author submits that in the minutes of the official case conference of 9 May 2004 of the lo cal child protection authority regarding her case, it is stated that it cannot put an end to her threatening situation using official measures. It recommends that she continue to ask for help from the police, medical documentation of injuries and help from her extended family as well as to keep the local authority informed. The child protection authority also reportedly states that it would summon L. F. and give him a warning in the event that the battering continues.

6.5 As at 23 June 2004, according to the author, the criminal proceedings against L. F. were still ongoing. A hearing scheduled for 21 April was postponed to 7 May and, as the judge was reportedly too busy to hear the case, the criminal proceedings were again postponed until 25 June 2004. The author believes that, whatever the outcome, the criminal proceedings have been so lengthy and her safety so severely neglected that she has not received the timely and effective protection and the remedy to which she in entitled under the Convention and general recommendation 19 of the Committee.

6.6 The author refers to the civil proceedings, in particular to the petition for review by the Supreme Court, which she considers to be an extraordinary remedy but submitted nonetheless. She states that, in response to the Committee's intervention, the State party covered the legal costs of supplementing her petition with additional arguments.

6.7 On 23 March 2004, the Supreme Court dismissed the petition, arguing, inter alia, that the jurisprudence is established with regard to the legal issue raised in the petition.

6.8 The author refutes the State party's argument that she did not submit a request for the exclusive use of the apartment. The court of the second instance, the Budapest Regional Court, ordered the court of the first instance, the Pest Central District Court, to retry the case, namely because it had failed to decide on the merits of the request. She believes that it is clear from the context and from her court documents, including the decisions, that she had requested sole possession of the apartment to avoid a continuation of the violence. However, she states that under the established law and jurisprudence in the State party, battered individuals have no right to the exclusive use of the jointly owned/leased apartments on grounds of domestic violence.

6.9 The author requests that the Committee declare her communication admissible without delay and decide on the merits that the rights under the Convention have been violated by the State party. She re quests that the Committee recommend to the State party to urgently introduce effective laws and measures towards the prevention of and effective response to domestic violence, both in her specific case and in general. The author furthermore seeks compensation for long years of suffering that have been directly related to the severe and serious violations of the Convention. The author believes that the most effective way would be to provide her with a safe home, where she could live in safety and peace with her children, without constant fear of her batterer's "lawful" return and/or substantial financial compensation.

6.10 By her submission of 30 June 2004, the author informs the Committee that the criminal proceedings against L. F have been postponed until 1 October 2004 in order to hear the testimony of a policeman because the judge thinks that there is a slight discrepancy between two police reports.

6.11 By her submission of 19 October 2004, the author informs the Committee that the Pest Central District Court convicted L. F. of two counts of causing grievous bodily harm to her and fined him for the equivalent of approximately $365 United States dollars.

Supplementary observations of the State party

7.1 By note dated 27 August 2004, the State party argues that, although all tasks that the Decree/Decision of Parliament on the Prevention of and Response to Domestic Violence prescribe have not yet been completely implemented, some positive steps, including new norms in the field of crime prevention and Act LXXX (2003) on the conditions under which legal assistance is given to those in need, have been taken. These documents are said to provide an opportunity to establish a national network of comprehensive legal and social support for future victims of domestic violence.

7.2 The State party confirms that consideration of the Draft Act on Restraining Orders that applies to cases of violence within the family has been postponed to the autumn session of Parliament.

7.3 The State party admits that the experience o f the Office and the information it has shows that domestic violence cases as such do not enjoy high priority in court proceedings.

7.4 Based on the experience of the Office both in the present case and in general, it is conceded that the legal and institutional system in Hungary is not ready yet to ensure the internationally expected, coordinated, comprehensive and effective protection and support for the victims of domestic violence.

Issues and proceedings before the Committee

Consideration of admissibility

8.1 In accordance with rule 64 of its rules of procedure, the Committee shall decide whether the communication is admissible or inadmissible under the Optional Protocol to the Convention. Pursuant to rule 72, paragraph 4, of its rules of procedure, it shall do so before considering the merits of the communication.

8.2 The Committee has ascertained that the matter has not already been or is being examined under another procedure of international investigation or settlement.

8.3 With regard to article 4, paragraph 1, of the Optional Protocol, the Committee observes that the State party does not wish to raise any preliminary objections as to the admissibility of the communication and furthermore concedes that the currently existing remedies in Hungary have not been capable of providing immediate protection to the author from ill-treatment from L. F. The Committee agrees with this assessment and considers that it is not precluded by article 4, paragraph 1, from considering the communication.

8.4 The Committee, nevertheless, wishes to make some observations as to the State party's comment in its submission of 20 April 2004 that some domestic proceedings are still pending. In the civil matter of L. F.'s access to the family's apartment, according to the author's submission of 23 June 2004, the petition for review by the Supreme Court was dismissed on 23 March 2004. The civil matter on the distribution of the common property, on the other hand, has been suspended over the issue of registration for an undisclosed period of time. The Committee considers, however, that the eventual outcome of this proceeding is not likely to bring effective relief vis-à-vis the current life-threatening violation of the Convention of which the author has complained. In addition, the Committee notes that two sets of criminal proceedings against L. F. on charges of assault and battery allegedly committed on 19 January 2000 and 21 July 2001 were joined and, according to the author, were decided on 1 October 2004 by convicting L. F. and imposing a fine equivalent to approximately $365. The Committee has not been informed as to whether the conviction and/or sentence may or will be appealed. Nonetheless, the Committee is of the view that such a delay of over three years from the dates of the incidents in question would amount to an unreasonably prolonged delay within the meaning of article 4, paragraph 1, of the Optional Protocol, particularly considering that the author has been at risk of irreparable harm and threats to her life during that period. Additionally, the Committee takes account of the fact that she had no possibility of obtaining temporary protection while criminal proceedings were in progress and that the defendant had at no time been detained.

8.5 As to the facts that are the subject of the communication, the Committee observes that the author points out that most of the incidents complained of took place prior to March 2001 when the Optional Protocol entered into force in Hungary. She argues, however, that the 10 incidents of severe physical violence that are medically documented and which are part of an allegedly larger number constitute elements of a clear continuum of regular domestic violence and that her life was still in danger, as documented by the battering which took place 27 July 2001, that is after the Optional Protocol came into force in Hungary. The Committee is persuaded that it is competent ratione temporis to consider the communication in its entirety, because the facts that are the subject of the communication cover the alleged lack of protection/alleged culpable inaction on the part of the State party for the series of severe incidents of battering and threats of further violence that has uninterruptedly characterized the period beginning in 1998 to the present.

8.6 The Committee has no reason to find the communication inadmissible on any other grounds and thus finds the communication admissible.

Consideration of the merits

9.1 The Committee has considered the present communication in the light of all the information made available to it by the author and by the State party, as provided in article 7, paragraph 1, of the Optional Protocol.

9.2 The Committee recalls its general recommendation No. 19 on violence against women, which states that "... [T]he definition of discrimination includes gender - based violence" and that "[G]ender-based violence may breach specific provisions of the Convention, regardless of whether those provisions expressly mention violence". Furthermore, the general recommendation addresses the question of whether States parties can be held accountable for the conduct of non -State actors in stating that "... discrimination under the Convention is not restricted to action by or on behalf of Governments ..." and "[U]nder general international law and specific human rights covenants, States may also be responsible for private acts if they fail to act with due diligence to prevent violations of rights or to investigate and punish acts of violence, and for providing compensation". Against this backdrop, the immediate issue facing the Committee is whether the author of the communication is the victim of a violation of articles 2 (a), (b) and (e), 5 (a) and 16 of the Convention because, as she alleges, for the past four years the State party has failed in its duty to provide her with effective protection from the serious risk to her physical integrity, physical and mental health and her life from her former common law husband.

9.3 With regard to article 2 (a), (b), and (e), the Committee notes that the State party has admitted that the remedies pursued by the author were not capable of providing immediate protection to her against ill -treatment by her former partner and, furthermore, that legal and institutional arrangements in the State part y are not yet ready to ensure the internationally expected, coordinated, comprehensive and effective protection and support for the victims of domestic violence. While appreciating the State party's efforts at instituting a comprehensive action programme against domestic violence and the legal and other measures envisioned, the Committee believes that these have yet to benefit the author and address her persistent situation of insecurity. The Committee further notes the State party's general assessment that domestic violence cases as such do not enjoy high priority in court proceedings. The Committee is of the opinion that the description provided of the proceedings resorted to in the present case, both the civil and criminal proceedings, coincides with this general assessment. Women's human rights to life and to physical and mental integrity cannot be superseded by other rights, including the right to property and the right to privacy. The Committee also takes note that the State party does not offer information as to the existence of alternative avenues that the author might have pursued that would have provided sufficient protection or security from the danger of continued violence. In this connection, the Committee recalls its concluding comments from August 2002 on the State party's combined fourth and fifth periodic report, which state "... [T]he Committee is concerned about the prevalence of violence against women and girls, including domestic violence. It is particularly concerned that no specific legislation has been enacted to combat domestic violence and sexual harassment and that no protection or exclusion orders or shelters exist for the immediate protection of women victims of domestic violence". Bearing this in mind, the Committee concludes that the obligations of the State party set out in article 2 (a), (b) and (e) of the Convention extend to the prevention of and protection from violence against women, which obligations in the present case, remain unfulfilled and constitute a violation of the author's human rights and fundamental freedoms, particularly her right to security of person.

9.4 The Committee addressed articles 5 and 16 together in its general recommendation No. 19 in dealing with family violence. In its general recommendation No. 21, the Committee stressed that "the provisions of general recommendation 19 ... concerning violence against women have great significance for women's abilities to enjoy rights and freedoms on an equal basis with men". It has stated on many occasions that traditional attitudes by which women are regarded as subordinate to men contribute to violence against them. The Committee recognized those very attitudes when it considered the combined fourth and fifth periodic report of Hungary in 2002. At that time it was concerned about the "persistence of entrenched traditional stereotypes regarding the role and responsibilities of women and men in the family ...". In respect of the case now before the Committee, the facts of the communication reveal aspects of the relationships between the sexes and attitudes towards women that the Committee recognized vis-à-vis the country as a whole. For four years and continuing to the present day, the author has felt threatened by her former common law husband, the father of her two children. The author has been battered by this same man, her former common law husband. She has been unsuccessful, either through civil or criminal proceedings, to temporarily or permanently bar L. F. from the apartment where she and her children have continued to reside. The author could not have asked for a restraining or protection order since neither option currently exists in the State party. She has been unable to flee to a shelter because none are equipped to accept her together with her children, one of whom is fully disabled. None of these facts have been disputed by the State party and, considered together, they indicate that the rights of the author under articles 5 (a) and 16 of the Convention have been violated.

9.5 The Committee also notes that the lack of effective legal and other measures prevented the State party from dealing in a satisfactory manner with the Committee's request for interim measures.

9.6 Acting under article 7, paragraph 3, of the Optional Protocol to the Convention on the Elimination of All Forms of Discrimination against Women, the Committee is of the view that the State party has failed to fulfil its obligations and has thereby violated the rights of the author under article 2 (a), (b) and (e) and article 5 (a) in conjunction with article 16 of the Convention on the Elimination of All Forms of Discrimination against Women, and makes the following recommendations to the State party:

I. Concerning the author of the communication

(a) Take immediate and effective measures to guarantee the physical and mental integrity of A. T. and her family;

(b) Ensure that A. T. is given a safe home in which to live with her children, receives appropriate child support and legal assistance as well as reparation proportionate to the physical and mental harm undergone and to the gravity of the violations of her rights;

II. General

(a) Respect, protect, promote and fulfil women's human rights, including their right to be free from all forms of domestic violence, including intimidation and threats of violence;

(b) Assure victims of domestic violence the maximum protection of the law by acting with due diligence to prevent and respond to such violence against women;

(c) Take all necessary measures to ensure that the national strategy for the prevention and effective treatment of violence within the family is promptly implemented and evaluated;

(d) Take all necessary measures to provide regular training on the Convention on the Elimination of All Forms of Discrimination against

Women and the Optional Protocol thereto to judges, lawyers and law enforcement officials;

(e) Implement expeditiously and without delay the Committee's concluding comments of August 2002 on the combined fourth and fifth periodic report of Hungary in respect of violence against women and girls, in particular the Committee's recommendation that a specific law be introduced prohibiting domestic violence against women, which would provide for protection and exclusion orders as well as support services, including shelters;

(f) Investigate promptly, thoroughly, impartially and seriously all allegations of domestic violence and bring the offenders to justice in accordance with international standards;

(g) Provide victims of domestic violence with safe and prompt access to justice, including free legal aid where necessary, in order to ensure them available, effective and sufficient remedies and rehabilitation;

(h) Provide offenders with rehabilitation programmes and programmes on non-violent conflict resolution methods.

9.7 In accordance with article 7, paragraph 4, the State party shall give due consideration to the views of the Committee, together with its recommendations, and shall submit to the Committee, within six months, a written response, including any information on any action taken in the light of the views and recommendations of the Committee. The State party is also requested to publish the Committee's views and recommendations and to have them translated into the Hungarian language and widely distributed in order to reach all relevant sectors of society.

Selected Further Reading

Bayefsky, A., "The Principle of Equality or Non-discrimination in International Law," 11(1-2) *Human Rights Law Journal* 1-34 (1990).

Bossuyt, M., "Comprehensive Examination of Thematic Issues relating to Racial Discrimination: The Concept and Practice of Affirmative Action," UN Report, UN Doc. No. E/CN.4/Sub.2/2000/11 (19 June 2000).

Bossuyt, M., "Prevention of Discrimination and Protection of Indigenous People and Minorities: The Concept and Practice of Affirmative Action," UN Report, UN Doc No. E/CN.4/Sub.2/2001/15 (26 June 2001).

Bossuyt, M., "Prevention of Discrimination: The Concept and Practice of Affirmative Action," UN Report, UN Doc. No. A/CN.4/Sub.2/2002/21 (17 June 2002).

Burrows, N., "The 1979 Convention on the Elimination of All Forms of Discrimination Against Women," 4 *Netherlands International Law Review* 419-460 (1985).

Byrnes, A., "The Convention on the Elimination of All Forms of Discrimination against Women" at 119-172 in Benedek, W., *et al.*, (eds.), *The Human Rights of Women: International Instruments and African Experiences* (Zed Books: London, UK, 2002).

Choudhury, T., "Interpreting the Rights to Equality Under Article 26 of the International Covenant on Civil and Political Rights" 1 *European Human Rights Law Reports* 24-52 (2003).

Dinstein, Y., "Discrimination and International Human Rights," 15 *Israel Yearbook on Human Rights* 11-27 (1985).

Fredman, S., (ed.), *Discrimination and Human Rights: The Case of Racism* (Oxford University Press: Oxford, UK, 2001).

Fredman, S., "Beyond the Dichotomy of Formal and Substantive Equality: Towards a New Defintion of Equal Rights" at 111-118 in Boerefijn, I., *et al.*, *Temporary Special Measures: Accelerating de facto Equality of Women under Article 4(1) UN Convention on the Elimination of All Forms of Discrimination Against Women* (Intersentia: Antwerp, Belgium, 2003).

Fredman, S., "Combating Racism with Human Rights: The Right to Equality" at 9-44 in Fredman, S., (ed.), *Discrimination and Human Rights: The Case of Racism* (Oxford University Press: Oxford, UK, 2001).

Frostell, K., "Gender Difference and the Non-discrimination Principle in the CCPR and the CEDAW" at 29-57 in Hannikainen L., and Nykänen E., (eds.), *New Trends in Discrimination law, International Perspectives* (Turku Law School Law Journal, Turku, Finland,1999).

Loenen T., and Rodrigues P., (eds.), *Non-discrimination Law: Comparative Perspectives* (Kluwer Law International: Den Haag, NL, and Boston, USA, 1999).

Selected Further Readings

Hendriks, A., "The Significance of Equality and Non-discrimination for the Protection of the Rights and Dignity of Disabled Persons" at 40-62 in Degener, T., and Koster-Dreese, Y., (eds.), *Human Rights and Disabled Persons, Essays and Relevant Human Rights Instruments* (Martinus Nijhoff: Dordrecht, 1995).

Hevener-Kaufman, N. and Lindquist, S., "Critiquing Gender-Neutral Treaty Language: The Convention on the Elimination of All Forms of Discrimination Against Women" at 114-125 in Peters, J. and Wolper, A., (eds.), *Women's Rights, Human Rights: International Feminist Perspectives* (Routlegde: New York, USA, 1995).

Interights, *Non-Discrimination in International Law: A Handbook for Practitioners* (Interights: London, UK, 2006).

Lerner, N., *The UN Convention on the Elimination of all Forms of Racial Discrimination* (Sijthoff & Noordhoof: Den Haag, NL, 1980).

Lerner, N., *Group Rights and Discrimination in International Law* (Martinus Nijhoff:Den Haag, NL, 2003).

Loenen, T., "Indirect Discrimination: Oscillating Between Containment and Revolution," at 195-211 in Loenen, T., and Rodrigues, P., (eds.), *Non-discrimination Law: Comparative Perspectives* (Kluwer Law International: Den Haag, NL, 1999).

Lord Lester of Herne Hill and Joseph, S., "Obligations of Non-Discrimination" at 563-595 in Harris, D., and Joseph, S., (eds.), *The International Covenant on Civil and Political Rights and the United Kingdom Law* (Clarendon Press: Oxford, UK, 1995).

McKean, W., *Equality and Discrimination under International Law* (Clarendon Press: Oxford, 1983).

Meron, T., "The Meaning and Reach of the International Convention on the Elimination of All Forms of Racial Discrimination," 79 *American Journal of International Law* 283-318 (1985).

Opsahl, T., "Equality in Human Rights Law. With Particular Reference to Article 26 of the International Covenant on Civil and Political Rights" at 51-64 in Nowak, M., *et al.*, *Progress in the Spirit of Human Rights. Festschrift for Felix Ermacora* (N.P. Engel Verlag: Kehl, Germany, 51-64 (1988).

Pentikäinen, M., "The Prohibition of Discrimination and the 1979 UN Convention on the Elimination of All Forms of Discrimination against Women," at 59-83 in Hannikainen, L. and Nykänen, E., (eds.), *New Trends in Discrimination Law. International Perspectives*, 3(1) *Turku Law School Law Journal* 59 – 83 (1999).

Pitt, G., "Can Reverse Discrimination Be Justified?" at 281-299 in Hepple, B., and Szyszczak, E., (eds.), *Discrimination: The Limits of the Law* (Mansell Publishing: London, UK, 1992).

Polyviou, P.G., *The Equal Protection of the Laws* (Duckworth: London, UK, 1980).

Ramcharan, B.G., "Equality and Nondiscrimination," at 246-270 in Henkin. L., (ed.), *The International Bill of Rights* (Columbia University Press: New York, USA, 1981).

Rehof, L., *Guide to the Travaux Préparatoires of the United Nations Convention on the Elimination of All Forms of Discrimination against Women* (Martinus Nijhoff Publishers: Dordrecht, NL and Cambridge, UK, 1993).

Schöpp-Schilling, H.B, "Reflections on a General Recommendation on Article 4(1) of the Convention on the Elimination of All Forms of Discrimination Against Women in Boerefijn, I., et al., *Temporary Special Measures: Accelerating de facto Equality of Women under Article 4(1) UN Convention on the Elimination of All Forms of Discrimination Against Women* (Intersentia: Antwerp, Belgium, 2003).

United Nations, Division for the Advancement of Women, *Assessing the Status of Women: A Guide to Reporting Under the Convention on the Elimination of All Forms of Discrimination Against Women* (United Nations: New York, USA, 1999).

United Nations, *Manual on Human Rights Reporting. Under Six Major International Human Rights Instruments* (United Nations: Geneva, Switzerland, 1997).

Vandenhole, W., *Non-Discrimination and Equality in the View of the UN Human Rights Treaty Bodies* (Intersentia: Antwerp, Belgium, 2005).

Vierdag, E.W., *The Concept of Non-Discrimination in International Law* (Martinus Nijhoff: Den Haag, NL, 1973).

Wadstein, M., "Implementation of the UN Convention on the Elimination of All Forms of Discrimination against Women," 4 *Netherlands Quarterly of Human Rights* 5-21 (1988).

Waldorf, L., *Pathway to Gender Equality: CEDAW, Beijing and the MDGs* (UNIFEM: New York, USA, 2004).

Winteremute, R., *Sexual Orientation and Human Rights: The United States Constitution, the European Constitution, and the Canadian Charter* (Claredon Press:: Oxford, UK, 1997).

Index

human rights mechanisms, 19–22
specific human rights
mechanisms, 19
United States, 13, 37, 46

V

victimization, 7
victims, 8-9
advising, 31-32
urden of proof, 8
compensation, 6, 12-15

right to make claims,
art. 14 CERD, 81
Optional Protocol to the
Disability Convention, 128-132
Optional Protocol to CEDAW,
21, 427-428, 432-434-436
WHO, 52
women. *See* gender *and* sex
social security benefits, 20
Women, 41–43
World Health Organization. *See*
WHO

Other Publications by
Curtis F.J. Doebbler

Doebbler, C.F.J., *Introduction to International Criminal Law* (pp. xxx/249) (2007). Paperback: US$24.95, ISBN 978-0-9743570-6-5.

Doebbler, C.F.J., and Clark, R., *A Travesty of Justice: The Iraqi Special Tribunal* [a draft report] (pp.130) (February 2007). Paperback: US$10.00.

Doebbler, C.F.J., *Introduction to International Human Rights Law* (pp. x/253) (2006). Paperback: US$24.99, ISBN 978-0-9743570-2-7.

Doebbler, C.F.J., *Introduction to International Humanitarian Law* (pp. x/212) (2005). Paperback: US$16.99, ISBN 978-0-9743570-6-5.

Doebbler, C.F.J., *International Human Rights Law: Cases and Materials* (two volumes totaling 1015 pages) (2004). Paperback: US$21.99 each volume & single volume US$49.95, ISBN 978-0-97435570-0-3.

Doebbler, C.F.J., (Добблер, К.Ф.Д.), *Изучение Международного Права Прав Человека* (Russian) (2004). Paperback: US$12.99, ISBN 978-0-9743570-1-0.

International Study Team, (containing contributions by C.F.J. Doebbler), *Our Common Responsibility: The Impact of a New War on Iraqi Children* (2003). Paperback: US$15.00 and electronic book format: US$6.50.

Doebbler, C.F.J., (compiled by), *Selected Human Rights Treaties in Arabic and English* (2002). Paperback: US$12.50 and electronic book format: US$5.

Doebbler, C.F.J., (with the collaboration of Ahmed, J., and Dabhoiwala, M.), *Handbook for Using the Internet for Teaching and Research in Political Science* (2002). Paperback (spiral bound): US$10.00 and electronic book format: US$4.

Doebbler, C.F.J., *Handbook on the Human Rights Approach to Health* (2002). Paperback: US$10.00 and electronic book format: US$4.50.

[Postage charges are additional.]
All of these publications can be purchased from:
CD Publishing
website: CDPublishing.org
email: Sales@cdpublishing.org

www.ingramcontent.com/pod-product-compliance
Lightning Source LLC
Chambersburg PA
CBHW020652270326
41928CB00005B/84

* 9 780974 357041 *